AT WAR WITH OURSELVES

# At War with Ourselves

### Why America Is Squandering
### Its Chance to Build a Better World

MICHAEL HIRSH

OXFORD
UNIVERSITY PRESS

## OXFORD
### UNIVERSITY PRESS

Oxford   New York

Auckland  Bangkok  Buenos Aires  Cape Town  Chennai
Dar es Salaam  Delhi  Hong Kong  Istanbul  Karachi  Kolkata
Kuala Lumpur  Madrid  Melbourne  Mexico City  Mumbai  Nairobi
São Paulo  Shanghai  Taipei  Tokyo  Toronto

First published by Oxford University Press, Inc., 2003
198 Madison Avenue, New York, New York 10016

www.oup.com

First issued as an Oxford University Press paperback, 2004
ISBN 0-19-517602-2 (PBK)

Oxford is a registered trademark of Oxford University Press

Library of Congress Cataloging-in-Publication Data
Hirsh, Michael, 1957–
At war with ourselves : why America is squandering its chance
to build a better world / Michael Hirsh.
p. cm.
Includes bibliographical references and index.
ISBN 0-19-515269-7
1. United States—Foreign relations—2001–2.
2. United States—Foreign relations—Philosophy.
3. National characteristics, American.
4. Globalization—Political aspects. I. Title.

*Book design and composition by Mark McGarry, Texas Type & Book Works*
*Set in Minion*

1  3  5  7  9  8  6  4  2
Printed in the United States of America

*To my sons, Evan and Calder, for whom this book was written*
*To my parents, Charles and Barbara, who made everything possible*
*And to Denise, who saw it all unfold with me*

# Contents

*Preface to the Paperback Edition*                          IX

*Preface*                                                  XVII

*Introduction: The Age of the Überpower*                      1

1   Navigating the Permanent Quagmire                        26

2   The American Temptation                                  69

3   What Is the "International Community"?                    93

4   The Argument from Hard Power                             133

5   When Ideas Bite Back                                     159

6   Rethinking Multilateralism                              187

7   The Dirty Work                                           216

*Conclusion: Toward a New Consensus*                        237

*Notes*                                                     259

*Acknowledgments*                                           275

*Index*                                                     279

Sometimes people call me an idealist. Well, that is the way I know I am an American. America is the only idealistic nation in the world.

WOODROW WILSON

We are attached by a thousand cords to the world at large, to its teeming cities, to its remotest regions, to its oldest civilizations, to its newest cries for freedom.

COLIN L. POWELL

The deadliest enemies of nations are not their foreign foes; they always dwell within their borders.

WILLIAM JAMES

## Preface to the Paperback Edition

I WRITE THIS from Baghdad, where George W. Bush's grand vision for American foreign policy is dying. The life is draining from it day by day, in the tally of thousands of young Americans killed and wounded, in the vast sums of money that American taxpayers are spending with little appreciation from the Iraqis, in the arbitrary detentions of thousands of Iraqis as U.S. forces fight an insurgency they don't understand.

Americans are spending hundreds of billions of dollars on Iraq. Yet we cannot show our faces here. When we Americans, we liberators of Iraq, go out in the streets, we must cower in the back of cars to avoid detection. We pretend to be some other nationality to avoid being kidnapped or bombed or shot at by the people we have liberated. The Iraqis who work for us do not tell even their wives and children that they are employed by Americans, so great is the stigma of the botched U.S. occupation. The occupation has lasted, at this writing, less than a year, but it seems as if a generation has come and gone since Iraqis cheered the arrival of American tanks. The Bush administration consciously invited this state of affairs; the president sought to put an all-American stamp on the occupation, disdaining the need for UN or multilateral cover and international help. He hoped to inspire an I-love-Uncle-Sam gratitude in the hearts of Iraqis. Now that misguided policy has blown up in all our faces, like another giant suicide bomb.

Sometimes called unilateralist, sometimes neoconservative, Bush's vision of America's role in the world has deep roots in the American experience. But it did not have to unfold this way. This book, which first came out in mid-2003, describes a workable alternative to this simplistic, hard-edged vision. The Bush vision was infused with the hubris of its authors, men who had never heard a shot fired in anger and who were very brave with other people's courage, that of the young men and women they sent to war. It was an arrogant vision based on a profound misunderstanding of the world we live in—the idea that America, in its righteous rage after 9/11, could bypass international consensus in a global struggle against terror that required international consensus. It was a foolish vision that supposed we could "pre-emptively" make facile war on whomever we deemed a threat, and that we Americans could transform, on our own, a recalcitrant region of the world that had fueled the Islamist rage of 9/11. It was a muddled vision in which the policy never lived up to the rhetoric. Bush declared that freedom in Iraq was in America's highest national interest, that it was going to set off a virtuous chain reaction of reform, curing the terror-generating pathologies of the Arab world. The transformation of Iraq—a frank policy of nation building—would also allow us to remove our troops from Saudi Arabia, thus robbing bin Laden of his main casus belli against America. But if that was the strategy, the president apparently failed to inform Defense Secretary Donald Rumsfeld, the man he put in charge of implementing it. Rumsfeld's decision to cut *by half* the invasion and occupation force his military brass had wanted was the single most disastrous decision of the conflict. It doomed Iraq to chaos, the occupation to bloodshed and incompetence; it showed conclusively that Rumsfeld was prepared only for war, not nation building.

Some of America's goals may be achieved here in the end. The world has seen a demonstration of American will and power, a willingness to absorb casualties, that has undercut the "paper-tiger" image promulgated by Osama bin Laden and Saddam Hussein. New generations around the world now understand what can happen when America gets angry, just as earlier generations did after Pearl Harbor. The U.S. invasion sent a frisson of fear through the icy veins of dictators like Libya's Moammar Qaddafi. A few days after Saddam was captured on December 13, 2003, Qaddafi became an eager stool pigeon, revealing the extent of the nuclear-weapons "black market" created by Pakistan's rogue lead scientist, Abdul Qadir Khan. And thanks to the tireless if sometimes fumbling efforts of brave diplomats like L. Paul Bremer III, America's postwar administrator, Iraq may yet become the stable and compliant ally that the Bush administration longed to create in the heart of the Arab world. Iraq's future, at this writing, is very much unclear.

What *is* clear is that the cost of achieving this vision has been so terrible and damaging that no U.S. president, for years to come, will attempt to emulate what George W. Bush did in Iraq. We are through, for the time being, threatening regime change around the world.

President Bush once said the 2004 presidential campaign would be fought over the issue of "who can properly use American power." That is also what this book is about. It offers a "peace plan"—as one of my readers called it—for ending a war that has long roiled America's soul, a war we have fought with ourselves over how engaged we need to be in the world. Some presidents such as Bush have emphasized power; others such as Bill Clinton have emphasized cooperation. This book is about how America must make use of the lessons of both power and cooperation. It is about how we Americans must acknowledge, at long last, that the "international community" we ourselves built is our only real ally against terror.

To the extent I have serious differences with the Bush administration, it tends to be from the vantage point of a disappointed hawk. I regret the invasion of Iraq in part because it distracted us far too long from al Qaeda, the culprit responsible for the horrors of 9/11. Al Qaeda was always a unique phenomenon, the only terrorist group of global reach that had declared war on America globally; Hamas, Hezbollah, and al Qaeda "franchises" like Jemahh Islamiyah in Indonesia were all local or regional. We had only one task after 9/11: to destroy al Qaeda completely, to cauterize it from the planet and replace its influence and that of its chief political ally, the Taliban, with something more civilized in the region they called home,

Afghanistan and Pakistan. That would have really sent a message of American power. Yet we allowed our attention, money, and military and intelligence resources to be diverted; worse, we permitted the "war" on terror to grow into a strategic monstrosity, a lashing-out in all directions with no end to it in sight. We permitted al Qaeda—and the Taliban—to linger on in the world far past what should have been their meager shelf life, thus inspiring other groups to follow in bin Laden's footsteps.

More, we missed a golden opportunity. The international system was adrift after the Cold War. Some pundits were questioning whether the West would long survive the extinction of its main enemy, Soviet communism. Especially as globalization came under attack, there was a waning sense of "community" in the international community. Even so, polls still showed a remarkable degree of global consensus in favor of a one-superpower (read: American-dominated) world, at least until Bush came along. The silver lining of 9/11 was a chance to reaffirm this international system and the legitimacy of America's role in overseeing it. Terrorism of the al Qaeda type provided, as the Yale scholar Charles Hill said, a "natural bonding agent" for melding the major powers ever closer, an abiding common interest. That is why Washington had so much support when it ousted the Taliban in Afghanistan, who were clearly harboring bin Laden, and so little support when it shifted attention to Saddam, whose connection to bin Laden was tenuous at best. The post–9/11 period was a time for alliance- and institution-building every bit as much as the world wars of the last century. All that was required was American leadership.

For three critical years George W. Bush squandered that chance. Indeed, it is possible now to identify the moment in the global "war on terror" when things went really wrong, when Bush finally lost the good will and support of most of the community of nations, and turned smoldering anti-Americanism into a roaring conflagration. The moment when instead of isolating and destroying the terrorists, Bush managed to isolate America. It was not when he decided to confront Saddam, although the job against al Qaeda was unfinished. While the world grumbled, Bush made a compelling case that the United Nations could not permit its resolutions against Saddam to be defied, and he won a 15-to-nothing UN Security Council vote in November 2002.

No, it was when in the face of Saddam's cave-in—when the Iraqi dictator abruptly gave UN inspectors free run of his palaces and they found little indication of WMD (and their assessments proved far more accurate than the CIA's)—Bush decided to invade anyway. This was the moment when Bush violated a half century of American tradition, wherein Washington earned its reputation as a mostly benign and wise overseer of the international system by using its vast power judiciously. It was the moment when American power went from being an accepted enforcer of last resort to an unrestrained force acting arbitrarily. When, in the eyes of the world, American power went from being legitimate to illegitimate.

The president only exacerbated the problem of legitimacy during the occupation. Both Bush and Rumsfeld scorned UN peacekeeping efforts of the 1990s, especially in Bosnia, Kosovo and East Timor, as nightmares of disorganization. Instead they tried to emulate America's rebuilding of post-Hitler Germany, to take their time and do democracy "right," and to leave a firm friend behind. After all, we were liberators. Bremer even carried around a timeline that compared the painstaking seven-year occupation of post-Hitler Germany with that of post-Saddam Iraq. Contractors like Bechtel laboriously sought to rebuild Iraq's power grid from the ground up, never realizing that the key to legitimacy was speed, and that winning hearts and minds is not accomplished with a year of blackouts. It was only months into the occupation that the Americans realized how badly they had misread the Iraqis. A key driver of the insurgency had become hatred of the occupation, not sympathy for Saddam.

Bit by bit, the Bush administration began to edge back from its unworkable, unilateralist vision. When Bremer, America's viceroy in Iraq, went begging at the door of United Nations Secretary-General Kofi Annan in January 2004, it was a remarkable admission of inadequacy. For the first time the Bush administration recognized that a UN role in Iraq was a necessity, not merely an irksome concession to public opinion. Bremer needed the UN because quarreling Iraqis, before they could agree to a compromise plan for transferring sovereignty, needed the stamp of legitimacy that the world body could provide. Having once snubbed NATO, the administration also came begging at its door, imploring the once-great alliance to take up peacekeeping in Iraq as well as Afghanistan.

And three years into the war on terror, Bush finally asked for European help on a Greater Middle East aid initiative that would begin the generation-long task of bringing the Arab world into the modern world.

Yet this giant pendulum swing in policy—this three-year lurch from hubris to "help us!"—cost us enormously. To go into Iraq when and how we did, we seriously compromised the credibility of our foremost national-security tool: intelligence. Policymakers and leaders in other countries, when called into action by Washington over the next threat, can now point to the Potemkin case for Iraq as an excuse not to act. We also exposed the vulnerability of America's armed forces: the whole world can now see how strapped our all-volunteer military is in Iraq. All to pursue what must now be viewed as a trumped-up threat at a time when the real threats, al Qaeda and its Taliban hosts, were regrouping.

Bush's laggard interest in international cooperation—and his seeming unconcern over whether American power was seen as legitimate or not—damaged us on other fronts as well. The number-one nightmare we will bequeath to our heirs is the prospect of a nuclear terrorist attack on a major U.S. city. Bush often invoked this scenario in citing the danger from Saddam. But U.S. intelligence had known for years before the invasion of Iraq in March 2003 that Pakistan, not Iraq, was the world's most dangerous disseminator of nuclear know-how. The horse of proliferation was out of the barn: technology, bomb designs, and fissionable material are all readily available. The most delicate diplomacy is needed to wean countries away from the pursuit of nuclear weapons. Mere threats and intimidation won't work, in part because it is now possible to secretly build a nuclear weapon even while technically observing the Nuclear Non-Proliferation Treaty. That means American presidents must create an international environment wherein states feel secure enough—and see the exercise of power by America as legitimate enough—to give up their WMD hopes. Bush did little to make this happen; on the contrary, his administration continued to insist on *its* right to develop its own new nuclear weapons.

Bush always saw himself as a "war president." After 9/11, especially, he seemed to view the world as a Hobbesian jungle in which force is mainly what matters. He never fully realized that he was standing on the shoulders of giants, the Americans and allies who had built the postwar international system. Before Bush ever took power, the treaties and common value system of the international community, combined with the usually wise application of American power over the postwar and Cold War period, had worked quite well, it turned out, to contain and shrivel the ambitions of men like Saddam and Qaddafi. Saddam's "republic of fear" was crumbling from within, while Qaddafi was desperate to end his isolation. The same pressures from the international community had forced al Qaeda to operate out of dark corners of the earth—corners that became even darker for bin Laden after the fall of the Taliban.

The Bush team spent most of their time and attention warring on "state sponsors" to terror rather than on terror itself. For Bush, the war on terror was mainly about good states and rogue states, states that were "with us" versus those that were not. Seen through this simplistic, dark prism, Saddam was somehow worse than bin Laden. But it turned out Saddam was largely contained, while al Qaeda was not. The key proliferator of the dread "Islamic bomb" was not an enemy state; it was Islamist sympathizers operating within the borders of our key ally, the Pakistani government.

The "war" on terror was, in other words, less a war than a roundup of such international offenders and misfits, a policing action led by the international community's principal enforcer, America. The international community was like the missing element in one of those grand theories of the cosmos; without it, very little in our recent history makes sense. With it, everything comes into focus. I hope this book will show you why.

# Preface

GEORGE W. BUSH seemed surprised to get any applause at all. Gazing out at his audience at the United Nations, the president gave what an aide described as his "trademark smirk" as the delegates clapped coolly. There was a definite chill in the air. Only a year before, America had been bathed in sympathy from around the world after the terrorist attacks on the World Trade Center and the Pentagon. Hundreds of thousands of Germans had gathered at the Brandenburg Gate, the site of JFK's "Ich bin ein Berliner" speech, to say that they now stood with America. France's *Le Monde* newspaper, normally no friend of Washington's, declared, "We are all Americans today." But this was September 12, 2002, a year and a day after the attacks, and the mood was very different. Other nations were angry at what they perceived to be American arrogance, the Bush administration's insistence on carrying a big stick—U.S. might—and talking loudly at the same time. This same week Bush would issue a new national security strategy, one that would mark the most historic shift in American thinking since the early days of the Cold War. While couched in diplomatic language, it was an unprecedentedly frank assertion that American dominance was here to stay, and that it was American values that would define the world.

Bush, a straightshooter from Texas by way of Andover, Yale, and Harvard, was a fervent believer in those values and in America as a special place, a nation apart. He wasn't big on *nU*-ance, as he liked to say, drawing out the syllables. And on this day, standing at the podium, Bush bluntly gave voice to a peculiarly American impatience: Will the United Nations serve the purpose of its founding, or will it be "irrelevant"? Rapping out his lines like a prosecutor, Bush declared that Iraqi dictator Saddam Hussein had flouted the will of the international community for more than a decade, defying UN Security Council resolutions that called on him to destroy his weapons of mass destruction. There was no immediate response from the cavernous hall. Staring out at the diplomats, each sitting motionless—not like the raucous political crowds he was used to—Bush thought he was addressing a "wax museum," as he later told aides.* Part of it was the venue, the pretense of the so-called Parliament of Man. The General Assembly's very grandiosity seems foreign to American sensibilities; it is "anti-human," says diplomat Richard Holbrooke, compared to the parliamentary coziness of the U.S. House of Representatives or Senate.

The odd thing is that this strange entity, the United Nations, was conceived, born, and built in America. Its founding was a labor of love for three major twentieth-century presidents: Woodrow Wilson, Franklin D. Roosevelt, and Harry Truman. The UN is as much a New York City landmark as the World Trade Center, of cherished memory, once was. And yet few of us have ever really understood this stranger in our midst. For many Americans, the decaying, giant, green-tinted box on the bank of the East River might as well be a black box in Timbuktu, so foreign do its internal workings still seem. And in this particular era—an era in which the difference in power between America and the rest of the world has grown huge—it has become more difficult than ever to maintain the egalitarian myth, the idea of a community of nations, that the UN was built on.

The gulf of misunderstanding between the American president and the foreign diplomats he addressed that day was really about the tensions between America and the so-called international community. The battles that occurred behind the scenes in the war on terrorism—between the

---

* I am indebted to my *Newsweek* colleagues Martha Brant and Tamara Lipper for part of this account of Bush at the UN.

"allies" who were supposedly fighting on the same side—were as telling as the war itself. The Bush administration struggled internally over how much it needed other nations to help, while many of those nations doubted that America was sincere in wanting to defend the honor of the UN or "civilization," as Bush called it. One reason Bush got a cool reception at the UN was that people didn't easily accept the sudden switch of enemies from al-Qaeda to Saddam. Another reason for the skepticism was that the Bush administration and its supporters had spent months before his appearance hinting that America was ready to make unilateral war to remove Saddam—whose efforts to build biological, chemical, and nuclear weapons were no longer tolerable in a post-9/11 world, Bush said—and suggesting that UN inspections to determine whether he possessed weapons of mass destruction were useless. The Bush team was only now, almost as an afterthought, invoking the UN resolutions Saddam had violated and suggesting it wanted to send UN inspectors back in only to disarm him. This did not do much for Bush's credibility at the UN (though his bellicosity certainly made Saddam more compliant). Even when it came to the real power at the UN, the Security Council—which was FDR's creation, and of which America was one of the five permanent members—the Bush people constantly spoke of the UN as an alien entity. "The UN does not have forever," White House spokesman Ari Fleischer warned over and over as negotiations over Saddam's fate dragged on.

Yet as much as Bush tried to keep the UN at arm's length, by early 2003 the Security Council had become "the courtroom of world opinion" once again, as Adlai Stevenson had described it during the Cuban Missile Crisis. On February 5, in one of the most extraordinary moments of the post–Cold War era, U.S. television networks cut into their morning soap operas for eighty minutes to train their cameras on the larger melodrama inside the Security Council. Bush's much-admired secretary of state, Colin Powell, seated at a giant, horseshoe-shaped table, tried again to make the case for war against Iraq. Powell cited reams of intelligence information, but world opinion did not seem to be with America this time. Millions marched in world capitals against a war (including 200,000 at the Brandenburg Gate, this time mostly anti-American). Bush invaded Iraq almost alone. And polls showed that substantial numbers of people around the globe saw Bush as more of a menace to world peace and security than Saddam was.

So the questions remained: What exactly—and who—were we fighting for? Which side were we Americans on, and who was on our side? Was taking on a rogue tyrant like Saddam the UN's problem or was it America's problem? How much were American interests still a thing apart—a purely "national" issue—and how much were American interests the same as those of the rest of the "civilized" world?

This book is about answering those questions. Although the war on terror and its sequel in Iraq serve as a backdrop to the tale I have to tell, this is really a book about America and us, the Americans. It is about the war within our own hearts and minds over who we are as a nation of the world. This book is my attempt to resolve, to some degree at least, the debate that has been running for most of this country's two and a quarter centuries of existence (with time out for brief periods of national crisis and unity), a debate that for the last decade or so has left us utterly confused about our global role and what's at stake in it.

For most of the period since the Cold War, these issues about American engagement in the world—symbolized by our difficult relationship with the UN and other global institutions—have been dry fodder for policy wonks. They didn't seem to matter a great deal. Today these issues matter urgently. They are about securing the safety of the world that we will leave to our children decades hence. They force us to ask who and what we are as a nation since the new millennium revealed vulnerabilities we never before imagined and powers that we barely knew we possessed. What does it really mean to be the only Great Power left standing at the End of History (as one writer has called the spread of democratic capitalism worldwide) and for that reason the target of every malcontent's fury? Are we a nation that is truly of the world, or are we still, as we have been since the beginnings of the Republic, a people apart, with one foot in and one foot out? What, precisely, is our responsibility as a nation and as individuals?

During the course of the so-called American Century, when the United States came to dominate the world and built, almost by accident, an entire global system, we never really resolved these existential questions about our relationship with the world. Today we no longer have the luxury of leaving so much about our global role undefined. Why? Because today the perception of America abroad is almost as important as the reality. Perceptions, we now know, can kill. Osama bin Laden succeeded in gaining substantial support in the Muslim world because he accurately diagnosed our national confusion about our global role—our willingness to withdraw our troops from Somalia in 1993, for example, at the first sign of trouble—and he built his terror campaign upon it, calling the American soldier "a paper tiger [who] after a few blows ran in defeat." Bin Laden's error, of course, was to mistake America's weak-mindedness about its role in the world—our vacillation over how engaged we really wanted to be—for intrinsic American weakness. In fact, the United States was as strong as ever, and American force was more devastating than ever before. But thousands of us had to die to prove it.

This book argues, finally, that America can vacillate no longer. Circumstances have forced us into a stark choice: either withdraw completely to our borders and watch the international system wither away without us, or fully embrace, at long last, this global system we fathered and yet too often have fecklessly orphaned in our eagerness to retreat home. The first option, withdrawal, is simply not practical, for a whole variety of reasons I will go into further on. And yet we cannot quite bring ourselves to endorse the second option, full engagement, either.

This book is an argument for full engagement, one that unfolds chapter by chapter, with each chapter's conclusions building on the last. The book's argument draws largely on the experiences of the first two post–Cold War presidents, Clinton and Bush, and on my own experiences in covering both of their administrations up close, at home in Washington, and on travels to every continent. Many writers have preceded me in describing how the world *should* work. This book attempts to describe how it *does* work. The value I bring to the table is more than a decade of on-the-ground experience in watching the post–Cold War world evolve—crisis by crisis, war by war, and decision by decision. I have covered in great detail both the political and the economic dimensions of this new world: the Kosovo war, Iraq, and the war on terror on one hand; and the Asian financial contagion and the anti-globalization movement, on the other. I have been privy to the discussions of many high-level officials as they have felt their own way through this period—crisis by crisis, war by war, and decision by decision.

This book is intended to help general readers navigate this complicated landscape—but it is especially for those who are or plan to be parents. The main reason I decided to write this book is that I have two young sons who are growing up in a world that is Americanized and yet often hostile at the same time, a world that most Americans scarcely understand. We parents spend much of our time absorbed in nurturing thoughts about schools and doctors and the perfect play date—but very little time thinking about the world these painstakingly brought-up children will face as adults.

That is not to say that my book should end up on the family how-to shelf with Dr. Spock and T. Berry Brazelton. This book is *not What to Expect When You're a Superpower*. But it is a book that's meant to be readable, even enjoyable, and to help the general reader take part in a debate about America's role in the world that is still too often confined to a foreign-policy elite, whether academics or government experts, and to the ever-yammering TV pundits of the Washington echo chamber. The arguments of these academics and pundits never really end. Nor do the squabbles on Capitol Hill over such critical issues as foreign aid and UN support. I suggest, again, that these arguments have to end—at least in the area of national strategy. But for that to happen, the public that elected presidents like Bill Clinton and George W. Bush must make its voice heard.

# AT WAR WITH OURSELVES

*Introduction*

# The Age of the Überpower

Wandering between two worlds, one dead, the other powerless
to be born . . .

**Matthew Arnold, "Stanzas from the Grand Chartreuse"**

IN THE EARLY DAYS after September 11, 2001, when the Pentagon and
lower Manhattan lay smoking and it dawned on Americans that thousands of their compatriots had died because of something evil emanating
from Afghanistan, the Department of Defense was in a state of confusion
and fear. The heart of America's economic and military power had been
attacked. The terrible images from the twin towers, the caved-in facade
across the way from Secretary Donald Rumsfeld's office, cried out for
decisive retaliation. But the idea of launching a war in Afghanistan seriously worried a military brass still haunted by "Vietmalia" syndrome: a
wariness of suffering U.S. casualties in out-of-the-way places like Vietnam
and Somalia, where both the national interest and the exit strategy were
unclear.[1] Afghanistan was a nation fabled over the centuries for its fero-
cious resistance to invaders. With its treacherous mountain passes and
jutting, knifelike ridges, the country was God's gift to guerrilla warfare,
the place where great powers sent their young men to die. It was where
British and Soviet troops, in two different centuries, were carved up
by fierce warlords—*jang-sallar* in the main Afghan tongue, Dari—in

turbans and black beards who had ambushed the enemy from those mountain redoubts.

Not surprisingly, the naysayers in Washington were out in full force, just as they had been before the United States went to war in the Persian Gulf and Kosovo. Then *Newsweek*'s foreign editor, I was among the legions of the gloomy in those first, shell-shocked days. As a plume of gray-black smoke continued to gush from the Pentagon outside our Washington bureau window, my *Newsweek* colleagues and I trotted out all the things that could go wrong with an American retaliation: there were too few "high-value targets" to strike; Special Forces teams would find themselves fighting in mini-Mogadishus (as in *Black Hawk Down*) around the country; American planes and helicopters would be vulnerable to the Stinger missiles we once supplied to Afghanistan's mujahideen, or soldiers of God, during the Soviet invasion of the 1980s. In an article, I quoted a verse from Rudyard Kipling that, in subsequent weeks, became a cliché of pessimism in the American press:

> *When you're wounded and left on Afghanistan's plains*
> *And the women come out to cut up what remains*
> *Jest roll to your rifle an' blow out your brains.*

What made most of *us* so wrong—what few of us realized at the time—was a central fact that neither the pundits nor many of the Pentagon planners fully appreciated, at least until it was over. The contest in Afghanistan, this time around, was absurdly unequal. These Americans were not the hapless soldiery of the Soviet Union, the cannon fodder of a dying empire. They were not the brave but outnumbered British of the nineteenth century, marching off to do or die for king and country. They were not even the low-tech Americans of decades past, caught in the meat grinder of Vietnam or Korea during the worst days of the Cold War. These were the shock troops of a Cold War–triumphant America, an America reinvigorated by the Information Age, the tools of which had turned into new, finely honed weapons that no one else had, and armed with world-girdling stealth bombers. An America whose global dominance had grown year by year and war by war.

As one of my correspondents on the front lines, Owen Matthews, described the conflict just after the bombing campaign began on October 7, it was almost like *War of the Worlds*, the H. G. Wells novel in which ray gun–armed Martians (the Americans) zap the earthlings (the Afghans and Arabs) with a "mysterious death—as swift as the passage of light." On the ground, U.S. special operations forces, the global SWAT teams of the twenty-first century, didn't have Martian heat rays, but they were armed with equipment almost as effective. They had GPS navigators that used the U.S. global positioning system—a constellation of small satellites that give electronic receivers geographic and altitude information—and laser-targeting equipment with which to "paint" Taliban troops for an armada of B-1s, B-2s, C-130 gunships, and B-52 bombers ranging on high. The Taliban literally never knew what hit them, and bedraggled survivors from the trenches, their faces dirty and their eardrums ringing, told their captors of the otherworldly nature of the war. "You don't hear anything, you don't see anything, and all your best stuff blows up," one U.S. officer related later.[2] "It's like God did it to you—your trenches, your tanks just blow up, cloudy or not, day or night." Afghanistan fell to the Americans and their small proxy forces, the Northern Alliance, in just eight weeks. Yet even then the U.S. military fought with a hand tucked behind its back, reluctant to take ground casualties.

It was, in other words, no contest at all. The experts who had been so skeptical a few weeks before now strained for historical comparison. There was none. On one side stood the most advanced society on earth, brandishing an array of precision weaponry that once more, as it had several times in the '90s, from the Gulf War to Kosovo, stunned the world. On the other side were men who would have looked at home in faded sepia pictures from *National Geographic* magazine a century ago, a regime absurdly backward not only in arms—the Taliban's soldiers rode around in Toyota pickups—but unable to feed, clothe, or house its people. It was a clash, in other words, between the most technologically advanced society on earth and the least; between the champions of the world as we know it —the world of globalization, silicon, and Starbucks—and that world's most stubborn holdouts. It was, as Rumsfeld later said, the moment that "the nineteenth century met the twenty-first century."[3]

Back in Washington, where President George W. Bush, to his credit, had ignored the doom-and-gloomers, the hawks who made up most of the senior level of his administration rejoiced when the last city, Kandahar, fell in early December. As the Bush team saw it, might and right were in one set of hands, and they were thankfully American. For Bush, a president who liked to cast things in simple, easy-to-understand terms, it was sweet vindication. Since September 11, Bush had repeatedly portrayed the war on terror as a black-and-white battle. To be sure, he said, it would be a long struggle, but it would be a clearly defined one, of good versus "the evildoers." This was the kind of leaderly rhetoric that presidents—who are defined by nothing if not tough foreign policy tests—live for. Bush's rhetoric harked back to Ronald Reagan's fight against the "evil empire" of communism, or FDR's global campaign against fascism. For a president who had started out, in the public mind, as a kind of frivolous Prince Hal, a formerly dissolute ex-youth who had never completely shed that youthfulness, the apparent transformation into King Henry V at Agincourt translated, for a while, into soaring approval ratings. It also gave the office of the presidency a gravitas that it had not had all through the Clinton years.

Yet when the bombs stopped dropping on Afghanistan, everything ceased being clear. What did we do now? A shaky peace prevailed, secured by American power. In February 2002 I went to Afghanistan to talk to some warlords and find out whether the peace would hold and the new government would survive. The questions would always elicit the same reaction: a knowing smile, eyes raised skyward to suggest the phantom presence of American planes, the gap-toothed grin of men who appreciate raw force more than anything else, no matter what package it comes in. Those who broke the peace, they said, would suffer "B-52 justice" from the mystifying assortment of precision-targeted weaponry that destroyed the Taliban. "This is happening all over the country," one top aide to a warlord, police commander Abdullah Mujahid, told me. "The B-52 is called 'the peacemaker.'"

But was it really enough to be so powerful from above? We Americans now had vulnerabilities on the ground that we didn't fully comprehend. As American power ranged overhead, down below Afghanistan teetered on the brink of chaos. Because the bombardment had been accompanied by only a minimal U.S. presence on the ground, many Taliban and al-Qaeda had escaped, scurrying into the cracks and gullies of the region to wait out America's patience. Bin Laden's mystique endured as it became clear that al-Qaeda operatives had dispersed around the world. Gingerly the Bush administration began to marshal small numbers of U.S. ground troops to root out the remaining terrorists. But it only grudgingly sent aid and balked at a large peacekeeping force, even as various warlords consolidated control, dividing Afghanistan into private fiefdoms. Whole provinces remained cut off from commerce and international aid as fear of banditry and terror ruled the nation's skeletal road network, which had been 95 percent destroyed during twenty-three years of civil war. Virtually resourceless—its main export was poppies to the world's narcotics gangs—Afghanistan's chances for becoming a unified nation, and part of the global system, seemed small in the near future, according to longtime observers on the ground. Both Afghans and international aid workers feared a repeat of the country's descent into civil war—and ultimate destiny as a harbor for terrorists—in the 1990s.

Bush, self-confident as ever, quickly moved on to other fronts, declaring Iraq, Iran, and North Korea to be a vague "axis of evil" that might support terrorist groups such as al-Qaeda, and making Saddam Hussein's ouster next on his to-do list. He boosted his defense budget to the highest levels since the Cold War. But no one could escape the unpleasant fact that the bristling high-tech equipment that the president was investing in, including $8 billion that year for missile defense, would have done little or nothing to stop bin Laden on September 11. At the same time it was equally clear that what could have prevented that terrible day was an Afghanistan that had never become a virulent host nation for al-Qaeda—an Afghanistan that had been brought into the ranks of "civilization," to use Bush's term. Not the projection of force, in other words, but the projection of values and, above all, our attention and aid, a friendly all-American embrace.

But how involved did we Americans really need to be in places such as Afghanistan and other potential terrorist hideouts, including Indonesia and Somalia? What was the right combination of force and friendliness—

of military power, on one hand, and aid and succor, on the other—in our approach to the world? We got mixed signals from others around the world about how much of a U.S. presence they sought. Other nations seemed to resent our power at the same time as they clamored for the stability it offered; they seemed to deplore the lack of U.S. leadership and then, in the next breath, complain that we were too pushy. This criticism was annoying and all too familiar. As Zbigniew Brzezinski, Jimmy Carter's national security advisor, once remarked to me, "We get damned if we do nothing and we get damned if we do something."[4] If we really had been the Martians of H. G. Wells's fable, of course, we might have been able to shrug off what the rest of the world thought (or perhaps only worry about their germs, the nemesis of Wells's Martians). But we Americans were earthlings too. We still lived in the world; we traveled, worked among, and traded with our fellow human beings, and we were as vulnerable to physical threats from terrorists and other hostile groups as any Frenchman, Russian, or Chinese. Indeed, we were more vulnerable, since we were Americans, and we ourselves had played the decisive role in building the international system that the terrorists hated, and whose open byways they had traveled to kill us. So something was needed beyond the sheer projection of power.

## Power and Vulnerability

The war on terror has brought into focus all the swirling debates about America's global role. The catastrophic terror attacks and their immediate aftermath in Afghanistan, especially, gave us a unique snapshot into the core truth of our time. Over a period of a few months we witnessed both our country's unprecedented vulnerability and its unprecedented power. America's economic and military centers were more vulnerable than anyone had thought possible before September 11, and yet within several weeks Americans were displaying more power than anyone had thought they possessed, and on one of history's toughest battlefields.

To a large extent, this book is about what it means to possess such power and vulnerability at the same time and why that condition will last for a long, long time. What it means, I will argue in the pages ahead, is that America must make use of the full panoply of its tools of "hard" and "soft" power to secure itself. It is clear that the demonstration of U.S. might is needed, both to wipe out the terrorist threat and to send a message to the world. The use of overwhelming force in Afghanistan destroyed al-Qaeda's base and helped to restore U.S. credibility after a decade of irresolution, halfhearted interventions, and flaccid responses to previous attacks. Bill Clinton's sporadic cruise missile strikes only seemed to encourage bin Laden, who had derided the United States as a "paper tiger." But at the same time our vulnerability to the terror threat demonstrates the necessity of bolstering the international community that Clinton believed in and that Bush barely acknowledged, one built on nonproliferation agreements, intelligence cooperation, and legitimizing institutions like the UN, as well as a broad consensus on democracy, markets, and human-rights norms. It also demonstrates the necessity of a values-driven foreign policy—of nation building in places such as Afghanistan under multilateral auspices. All this in turn requires judiciousness in the use of force, which Bush and his team were so eager to employ.

It was no accident that bin Laden saw America as the chief enemy of his efforts to spread Islamic fundamentalism around the world. As the twenty-first century dawns, the United States is no longer a mere superpower. I believe this term should be discarded. It retains too many connotations of the bipolar Cold War world. The United States has become something more. To adapt a prefix increasingly in vogue, America has become the world's überpower, overseeing the global system from unassailable heights, from the air, land, sea, and, increasingly, space as well.[5] America is today the object of everyone's desire, and the target of everyone's ire. American power is the linchpin of stability in every region of the world, from Europe to Asia to the Persian Gulf to Latin America. And now, by putting down what may become permanent post-9/11 bases in Uzbekistan and Tajikistan, it is quietly setting up a new command post in long-neglected Central and South Asia, emulating its dominant role elsewhere.

The sources of this power are at once economic, military, cultural, and intellectual. The United States today spends more on defense than the rest of the industrialized world combined, a pace that has picked up in the post–Cold War period as the U.S. economy, in the 1990s, powered well into the lead of the Information Age.[6] So thoroughly does the U.S. military dominate the skies over the world that even surface-to-air missiles have proven ineffective against it in recent campaigns. New generations of "standoff" weapons—which allow America to attack enemies beyond their ability to shoot back—are expected to make U.S. forces even more like the Martians of *War of the Worlds*. Among them: pinpoint cruise missiles that can distinguish between floors of a building two hundred miles away; a weapon that drops from an airplane and releases numerous projectiles that can sense tanks and other enemy vehicles over a large battlefield; and the Low Cost Autonomous Attack System, a bomb that can "loiter" over a battlefield and search for targets on its own.[7]

Indeed, perhaps the only real weapon left to the rest of the globe, "apart from suicidal acts of terror, is the world's indignation" when innocents on the ground are killed, says author Mark Bowden.[8] "Nothing has ever existed like this disparity of power," writes Paul Kennedy, the Yale historian who a decade ago became famous for projecting that a declining America might soon fall victim to "imperial overstretch." "The Pax Britannica was run on the cheap. Britain's army was much smaller than European armies, and even the Royal Navy was equal only to the next two navies—right now all the other navies in the world combined could not dent American maritime supremacy. Charlemagne's empire was merely western European in its reach. The Roman empire stretched farther afield, but there was another great empire in Persia, and a larger one in China. There is, therefore, no comparison."[9]

Also without historical precedent is America's dominance in the "soft" realm of culture, values, and ideology. The world that Americans once kept at ocean's length has become, to an extent most of us don't realize, *our* world, shaped largely by U.S. values and U.S.-engendered institutions. We are the chief architects of a vast, multidimensional global system that consists of trading rules, of international law, of norms for economic and political behavior. As we will see in the chapters ahead, it is overwhelmingly in our national interest to stay engaged in the global system shaped by these ideas and values, to strengthen and nurture it. Imperfect though they may be, the institutions of this system—the UN and the World Trade Organization (WTO), among others—have been molded by centuries of Western civilization, tempered and informed by past wars and past failures. After centuries in which world affairs have been governed by ever-shifting great power rivalries—leading time and again to war—these are the most powerful and entrenched global institutions ever to exist. And it is entirely appropriate that America, whose founding principles represent the distilled wisdom of Western civilization dating from the Enlightenment, should be their steward.

It is this global "institutionalized order," as the scholar G. John Ikenberry calls it, that was at play after September 11, finding common cause in Bush's war on terror.[10] And for all the reemerging resentment of the rest of the world toward what it perceived as U.S. unilateralism, Bush managed to keep most of the world on his side. More broadly, it is this global order, I will argue, that explains why the worst predictions for the post–Cold War world have not come true, why Samuel Huntington's "clash of civilizations"[11] has not actually happened, and why Robert D. Kaplan's "coming anarchy" has, despite assorted financial crises, wars, and mass slaughters, proved to be less than anarchic.[12] The structure of the post–Cold War world has held together through its many stresses and strains, from financial contagion in world markets to Islamic contagion at the provocation of bin Laden. It does so not least because there is no viable alternative agenda.

Yet it is hardly a foregone conclusion that this international system will survive in Washington's hands. Indeed, if the conservative second Bush administration had one major agenda as it took power, it was to dismantle many of the institutions of this global system as quickly as possible and assert Washington's right to act unencumbered by them. Even after 9/11, only gradually—and half-heartedly—did the Bush team begin to make use of these institutions. On the extreme right, conservatives hate this international system as something that infringes on U.S. sovereignty, and they seek to scale back U.S. involvement in its leading institutions, especially the United Nations. On the extreme left, liberals demonize global institutions such as the WTO as the latest incarnation of undemocratic rule by arrogant elites. And in the middle, polls show that the broad mass of Americans feel in their bones that we should be engaged in this global system—for example, by paying our dues to the UN—but are wary of being pulled in too deeply. They remain tempted by our nation's time-honored wish to distance ourselves from the world—an attitude that traces its long lineage to George Washington's farewell exhortation to maintain America's "detached and distant situation" and Thomas Jefferson's warning against "entangling alliances."

We are, as ever, a schizoid people when it comes to our role in the world. Consider, as evidence, the strange public career of Pat Buchanan. Since his isolationist call to arms flopped with voters in the 1996 presidential campaign, the blustery former Nixon speechwriter and pundit is no longer seen as a viable political candidate. But Buchanan still occasionally makes the best-seller list with the same ringing rhetoric he used on the stump, like this declaration, in *A Republic, Not an Empire:* "If this Prodigal Nation does not cease its mindless interventions in quarrels and wars that are not America's concern, our lot will be endless acts of terror. . . . What is it about global empire that is worth taking this risk?"[13]

The temptation posed by Buchanan's words is still a compelling one. Why *do* we need to burden ourselves with the world's problems? After all, haven't we Americans already performed above and beyond the call of duty in the last century, committing hundreds of thousands of lives to the salvation of Europe and Asia? Having fathered the world order, can't we let it be, like responsible parents? Can we at least establish some kind of threshold of restrained involvement? Is it possible to develop a realistic framework that won't unduly tax U.S. resources or turn Washington into a full-time globocop or global central bank?

Yes, it is possible. But first we must cross a psychological threshold ourselves. We need to grasp what many other nations already understand: the meaning of America in today's world. Despite a century of intense global engagement, America is still something of a colossus with an infant's brain, unaware of the havoc its tentative, giant-sized baby steps can cause. We still have some growing up to do as a nation. One of my favorite movies has always been *It's a Wonderful Life*. Like everyone, I'm a sucker for the sentiment. But I also thought the conceit was ingenious: What if we could all be granted, like Jimmy Stewart's George Bailey, a look at the world without us? I think it's useful to apply the same conceit to the one-überpower world. Suppose, with the end of the Soviet Union, America had mysteriously disappeared as well or, more realistically, had retreated to within its borders, as it had wanted to do ever since the end of World War II. What would a Jeffersonian America, withdrawn behind its oceans, likely see unfolding overseas? Probably a restoration of the old power jostle that has sent mankind back to war for many millennia. One possible scenario: Japan would have reacquired a full-scale military and nuclear weapons, and would have bid for regional hegemony with China. Europe would have had no counterbalance to yet another descent into intraregional competition and, lacking the annealing structure of the postwar Atlantic alliance, may never have achieved monetary union. Russia would have bid for Eurasian dominance, as it has throughout its modern history. Most important of all, the global trading system, which the United States virtually reinvented after World War II (with some help from John Maynard Keynes and others), would almost certainly have broken down amid all these renewed rivalries, killing globalization before it even got started. That in turn would have accelerated many of the above developments. A war of some kind would have been extremely likely. And given the evidence of the last century, which shows that America has been increasingly drawn into global conflicts, the U.S. president would be pulled in again—but this time in a high-tech, nuclearized, and very lethal age of warfare.

America has a unique opportunity to thwart history's most ruthless dictate: that nations are ever fated to return to a state of anarchy and war. It has a unique opportunity do what no great power in history has ever done—to perpetuate indefinitely the global system we have created, to foster an international community with American power at its center that is so secure that it may never be challenged. But this can be done only through a delicate balancing of *all* our tools of power and influence. And it can be done only by bridging the ideological gulf that continues to divide Americans over our place in the world.

The beginning of getting from here to there is to understand that this is a brand-new challenge. There never has been a moment like this in recorded history, with one power so dominant, an international system so all-encompassing, and an array of secondary but rising powers so co-opted by that system. One reason is America's extraordinary military dominance, as described above. Another reason is that, as the scholar James Richardson points out, the global economic order policed by institutions such as the World Trade Organization is also "without historical precedent; earlier attempts to establish international order relied mainly on political and military means."[14] As we will see in subsequent chapters, the overall prosperity provided by this worldwide economic system has created, despite the inequities of globalization and occasional resurgences of protectionism, a powerful and enduring motivation for nations to become part of the global system. That's especially true in an era when so many leaders are elected and must maintain popular support (and therefore prosperity) in order to survive. That is why America's new role also means accepting the necessity of continuity: of perpetuating a century's worth of institution building that has secured and advanced this economic system and, one by one, brought other great powers into the fold of a new international community: Germany, Japan, Great Britain, possibly Russia, and, if we play our cards right, perhaps China and the Islamic world as well. It is a historically lucky accident that the two powers with the greatest potential for causing America trouble in the twenty-first century—China and Russia—are both permanent members of the UN Security Council and are proud of that fact. For that reason alone, it is worth America's time to support and promote the UN. While some authors see the rise of a rival great power in the European Union, and others project that China will play this role, the evidence is to the contrary: there is virtually no evidence these entities are gearing up to challenge American primacy.

And yet, even as we face a future without precedent, too many foreign-policy specialists and pundits devote books to trolling the past for the right American approach to the post–Cold War era. Many of these writers have attacked Woodrow Wilson, whose precepts formed the basis of twentieth-century American foreign policy and transformed much of the world by laying the groundwork for a democratized, free-trading global system. Scholars such as Walter McDougall and Frank Ninkovich have sought to dismantle Wilsonianism, dismissing it as ineffectual "meliorism"

(McDougall) or as a temporary (as in century-long) "crisis internationalism" (Ninkovich) that is no longer necessary. Political realists such as John Mearsheimer, who believe that international relations are defined by a state of anarchy in which nations vie for power, point to the inevitability of past wars and conclude that wars will be inevitable again. Charles Kupchan sees America and Europe developing into rivals as Rome and Byzantium did fifteen hundred years ago. Walter Russell Mead identifies four U.S. foreign-policy "schools" that have defined our thinking about trade, war, American values, and nativism going back to the early days of the Republic, and he urges us to pay special attention to the "Jeffersonian" school, which calls for a pared-down U.S. presence in the world. Max Boot has asked us to hark back to the aggressive way we Americans fought the Barbary Wars or the Philippines conflict in 1899 in deciding how to intervene today. Many of these arguments are interesting and useful—Mead's analysis is particularly so, and we will come back to it—but most of these commentators, I would argue, miss the larger point: A great deal of what Thomas Jefferson or George Washington once thought is just not terribly relevant today, at least as concerns foreign policy. Nor is what happened in the Philippines in 1899, or to Rome and Byzantium.

The tendency to lean too heavily on the past for guidance is hardly confined to experts. Policy makers are always typically fighting the last war or solving the last crisis. The most overquoted epigram in modern times may be George Santayana's remark that those who do not remember the past are condemned to repeat it. I suggest that, in practice, the reverse proposition has proved to be more true: Those who remember the past *too well*, or dwell on it too much, are the ones condemned to repeat it, because they rarely recognize the novelty of the challenges they face. As we will see in the chapters ahead, the hard-liners surrounding George W. Bush spent far too much time refighting the battles of the Cold War and scarcely looked up to see that they were living in a very different world. Bill Clinton too was always casting about for historical models. In his first term he sought to emulate Franklin Delano Roosevelt, whom he quoted in his first inaugural address to the effect that in 1993, as in 1933, America needed "bold, persistent experimentation." He tried a New Deal–sounding doctrine, the "New Covenant," visited Hyde Park, and placed an iconic FDR bust in the Oval Office. In fact there was little need for bold, persistent experimentation: Rather than a Depression, Clinton was handed an economy that, it turned out, needed only a little deficit cutting and was already soaring on its own in the great tech boom of the '90s. Health care reform, Clinton's most New Deal–like plan, flopped. Overseas, instead of facing down Hitler and Stalin, the president shadowboxed with Saddam Hussein and Slobodan Milosevic. In his second term a more foreign-affairs-minded Clinton trended toward the model of Teddy Roosevelt, the first president to test America's newfound greatpower status on the world stage (and to achieve greatness without a major testing crisis). But when TR set about mediating and resolving the Russo-Japanese War in 1905, he was starting down the road to what Clinton, by century's end, would find routine for the president of a United States that was now at the center of global affairs, just as TR once dreamed it would be. Clinton was no TR, but he had a lot more to teach the twenty-sixth president than the other way around. The America of the present has challenges that the America of the past could not have fathomed.

## The Real New World Order

What is the nature of this new global system and of America's role at its center? If the United States has become the world's hegemonic power, then the president of the United States is no longer merely the "leader of the free world," the appellation that dates from the bipolar conflict of the Cold War and yet is still so commonly, and mindlessly, applied to him. He has become, instead, the de facto leader of a U.S.-sponsored global system that we ourselves played the main part in creating, which is organically linked to our national life, and whose stability the president has responsibility for overseeing.

This is not, obviously, a formal post. No president could claim the title of "president of the world" without being laughed off the world stage. No foreign leader, either, could confer such authority on the U.S. president publicly without being roundly ridiculed by his own people and probably dismissed from office for being a stooge of the much-resented Americans. Barring a coordinated attack on earth by aliens, the president of the United States is not likely to ever have sovereign command of the world's military forces or find it in his power or interest to treat other countries like Roman dominions. This critical if informal role as leader of the global system must be practiced with a great deal of subtlety. The president's tasks combine a "soft" role as global arbitrator in chief—for example, mediating conflicts in the Mideast, South Asia, and Northern Ireland —with "hard" leverage, using America's dominant economic and military power to play a global enforcer of last resort, for example, by taking on Saddam Hussein in Iraq.[15] It is a role that is constantly updated, refined, and shaped by world events.

The president of the United States is also the agenda setter at a sort of open-ended global convention of nations and interest groups, a convention that is never quite adjourned, whether the issue is free trade, geopolitics, or terror. It is a convention that, quite frankly, we want to go on forever, because the streets outside its doors are mean. In recent years commentators have tended to focus on the limits to U.S. power—our vulnerability to terror and environmental depredation, the restraints placed on national sovereignty by the explosive growth in NGOs (nongovernmental organizations, or global interest groups, which have quadrupled in number in the last decade to about twenty-six thousand today), by globalized markets, and by the new assertiveness of the developing world over trade rules. It's time to nudge the discussion in the opposite direction. If anyone doubts that the U.S. president is the world's chief gavel banger, consider the way that George W. Bush almost single-handedly transformed the number-one item on the global agenda into antiterrorism—and then Iraq—after America was attacked on September 11.

## A Tale of Two Presidents

Like it or not—and many around the world don't—this broadly conceived role as leader of the international system will be *the* defining role for American presidents in the twenty-first century. And accepting the reality of this role requires a dramatic broadening of what constitutes the national interest. But the devil is in the details. As we will see in Chapter 1, the starkly different approaches that Bill Clinton and George W. Bush— the first two post–Cold War presidents—brought to this new world were really titanic fights over these same issues, over America's place in the world. The end of the Cold War had left a vacuum, and abruptly the United States was left alone on the global stage. The collapse of the Soviet Union in 1991 was only the beginning. It soon became clear that there was no competitor even on the horizon. Japan, which only a few years before had been seen as the up-and-coming superpower—"The Cold War is over, and Japan won," presidential candidate Paul Tsongas joked darkly in 1992—fell into deep recession as its "bubble economy" collapsed. Post-Soviet Russia imploded into an economy smaller than Portugal's. Western Europeans grew even more self-absorbed than Americans over their historic experiment in combining national sovereignty with monetary union. China lumbered forward, a nation in transition, but it remained a developing country with its future as a putative superpower well ahead of it. No one paid much attention to the Arab world. Suddenly there seemed to be a blank slate. And both Clinton and Bush faced very few limits on what choices they could make to fill the blank.

Clinton, who like Bush was little concerned at first with foreign affairs, filled in the blank with the promulgation of globalization and "soft" goals such as economic integration and the spread of democracy and open markets. Hamstrung by his draft-dodging past, scandal, and a conservative Congress that obstructed him for six of his eight years, Clinton shied away from projecting American muscle abroad. He was a military minimalist, resorting too often to a least-offensive approach that eroded American credibility, even in his one war, Kosovo. Overseas interventions that might have been successful had they been more robust and involved more troops—in Somalia, in Haiti, in Kosovo in 1998 (when he refused to send in NATO peacekeepers before the war in 1999)—mostly failed or became bogged down. Clinton got away with this halfhearted foreign policy because most Americans saw these issues as mere annoyances, small-scale wars "in a time of peace," as David Halberstam aptly put it.[16] But the ill effects of this vacillation were adding up: bin Laden, who was relatively unmolested by American attempts to kill or capture him, was quietly making plans in his many training camps in Afghanistan and at his comfortable villa in Jalalabad.

When George W. Bush came into office, he filled in the post–Cold War blank slate by reasserting America's "hard" or military power. Bush tried at first to set his priorities narrowly and to garb a very new world in the old clothes of Cold War–style alliances and raw, Hobbesian might. This was partly in reaction to the perceived weaknesses of Clinton's approach. If Clinton depended too much on the international system, Bush would slight it. Especially after 9/11, the tools of that system—institutions like the UN and the World Trade Organization, and treaties curbing weapons of mass destruction—needed to be used and strongly supported. Only a united effort by the international community could ensnare hostile groups—terrorists or otherwise—operating within the cracks of the global system. But Bush, a conservative, surrounded himself with right-wing unilateralists, many of whom came into power believing that America must remain a place apart, that the demands of other nations and peoples must not infringe on its sacred sovereignty. Bush hesitated in projecting a common global vision of the "civilization" he spoke of defending. He gave voice to only one-half of the überpower equation when he declared America's right to unilaterally and preemptively strike anywhere, such as Iraq, in order to defeat terrorism and threats from weapons of mass destruction. His philosophy of world leadership was simple: "America has, and intends to keep, military strengths beyond challenge, thereby making the destabilizing arms races of other eras pointless, and limiting rivalries to trade and other pursuits of peace."[17]

Perpetuating American dominance is a good policy for the world. If deftly applied, it can even be used to add "calcium" to the backbone of institutions like the UN, as Bush liked to say. But what Bush failed to realize early on was that so much more is needed than the militarization of foreign policy. And as the reality of the global challenge dawned on him, Bush too vacillated over how actively he should be engaged in this international system, just as Clinton did over asserting America's hard power. As sharply divergent as Bush's and Clinton's views of the world were, in the end they found themselves facing similar challenges and needing to make similar responses.

Together, Clinton and Bush represented two halves of what might have made the perfect president—or at least one perfectly suited for the vastly complex task of managing America's role in the global system. Both presidents, I will argue in this book, failed to grasp the full dimensions of this new global system they presided over, especially early in their administrations, and the nature of America's überpower role within it.

For America, at the center of this world stage, our "vital national interest" is no longer just about picking the right allies, guarding certain sea lanes, or preserving our oil supply from the Mideast. It is no longer just about building a military and alliance system of the kind that has sustained great powers throughout history—for example, lining up with old allies such as Britain and Japan to co-opt potential new rivals such as China. Yes, projecting U.S. military power is necessary, as Bush proved in the war on terror and in forcing Saddam to permit UN inspectors back into his country. But leading America today is also about managing, full time, a global system that is sinewed to our national life through deeper markets than have ever before existed, through stronger international organizations and conventions than have ever before existed, and through a historic level of global consensus on the general shape of societies, politics, human rights, and international law.

As I will explain, this global system is what we think of as the "international community." This is a controversial concept: Realists and conservatives still believe the international community is a Wilsonian myth, an empty catchphrase used by presidents and other leaders to line up various friendly nations behind their pet policies. I'd like to put such canards to rest and make a larger point: The international community is not only real, it has become, in fact, America's greatest ally in the twenty-first century.

Acknowledging the full dimensions of America's hegemonic role means understanding that the traditional power relationships that once defined foreign affairs are merely the foundation, the undergirding, of the international community. The superstructure of the international community in turn changes these relationships. It means understanding why America's traditional posture as an ally in Western Europe and Asia, whether to Britain and Germany or to Japan and South Korea, is being reconstituted into that of a regional policeman or stabilizer, and why U.S. generals act as virtual viceroys to keep the peace in Latin America and the Persian Gulf, and now in Central and South Asia. It is also about understanding how America must systematically use international institutions such as the UN Security Council and WTO to co-opt potentially hostile nations, including China and Russia, into the U.S.-led international system—*especially* when at the same time we are riling them by putting down military bases just across the border. It is about understanding why the UN system, so long demonized in Washington, is critical to bending other nations to our will and is the most effective proxy, despite all its flaws, for nation building in places such as Afghanistan and for pressing democratic and market reforms on terrorist-generating nations such as Saudi Arabia and Egypt. It is about understanding why only Washington can organize a global halt to nuclear weapons proliferation, arbitrate the Mideast and India–Pakistan conflicts, or deter a rogue state such as Saddam's Iraq from attacking its neighbors. It is about understanding why, in a globalized world economy in which America is the dominant player, the chairman of the Federal Reserve sets rates for a waiting world as well as for Wall Street and Main Street, and the U.S. Treasury secretary is the only man with the stature to tackle a global financial crisis.

All of this is a lot to worry about. It makes up a complex foreign-policy landscape that I will call, throughout this book, the Permanent Quagmire. Why this rather ungainly and grim term? Simply because no other term will do. The challenge we face is permanent, because there is no escaping our responsibility for the world we have built. It is a quagmire, because in the face of its many complexities, there is no clear way out, no obvious exit strategy. Understanding America's role in managing the Permanent Quagmire is about why it is not only impossible for us to disengage, and why in the present century it will be far more difficult than it was in the last century to pick our fights and determine our interests, simply because there is so much more on our plate.

American involvement in the world has come in three major stages. In the nineteenth century, U.S. foreign policy was governed by the Monroe Doctrine, which warned the European empires to stay out of our hemisphere; this embroiled Washington in small wars mainly in places such as Cuba, Panama, and Nicaragua (with forays into China and Japan). In the twentieth century, Wilson and his successors—especially FDR and Truman—effectively took the Monroe Doctrine global, expanding America's sphere of influence to Western Europe, the Persian Gulf, and most of Asia; this embroiled us in larger wars in Korea and Vietnam. In the twenty-first century, America's sphere of influence has become the great globe itself. And especially in this age of terror, under Bush's new doctrine of preemptive action, we could potentially intervene anywhere around the globe, from Iraq to North Korea to Somalia. As a result, picking and choosing where to apply our enormous resources as a nation may well be the trickiest foreign-policy task we have ever faced. During the Cold War, the eminent foreign-affairs commentator Walter Lippmann fought titanic battles against American overextension; in the late 1940s he called containment doctrine "a strategic monstrosity." Ultimately, containment's bastard child, the Vietnam War, made him look prescient. Today the war on terror could easily become a strategic monstrosity if we are not careful (yes, I too occasionally succumb to historical analogies). That is another reason why we must make full use of the tools and institutions of the international system we have built.

And yet, to return to the idea that this is a new world, the historical parallel is inexact. Lippmann also inveighed, toward the end of his life, against the "foolish globalism" of his Wilsonian youth:[18] "I am in favor of learning to behave like a great power, of getting rid of the globalism which would not only entangle us everywhere but is based on the totally vain notion that if we do not set the world in order, no matter what the price, we cannot live in the world safely."[19] This analysis may have been right when Lippmann wrote it, in the early 1970s, but it is no longer right. Today we simply cannot live in the world safely without setting it in order. Every American president relishes the moment the troops come home, with flags waving and bands playing, and things can get back to "normal." Every president tries to focus on what Bush once called "the big ones"—important strategic countries such as China and Russia. And yet increasingly, because of America's twin burdens of power and vulnerability, every president in coming decades will find himself dragged into what we once considered the margins of our national interest, into the Permanent Quagmire. Even now, the temptation for Americans will be to say that defeating al-Qaeda or taking on the "axis of evil" is a unique challenge—that we can somehow finish up such tasks and then retreat home as usual. But that presupposes there is a distinct "home" to which to retreat. There isn't. If al-Qaeda operated like an invasion of loose cancer cells, then the American-dominated global system whose vulnerabilities bin Laden exploited was like a bloodstream that now extends throughout the world. Terror on the scale that bin Laden conducted, we now know, was probably not possible without a failed-state base such as Afghanistan —the key reason why staying fully involved there for years to come is so critical now. But we also know that the September 11 plot was born in Egypt and Saudi Arabia, conceived in Hamburg, coordinated in Kuala Lumpur, and compounded of dozens of flights, e-mails, phone conversations, and money transactions worldwide. The point is, future threats of any kind could come from anywhere, through the globalized byways we ourselves have created in the push for free trade and open political and market systems. We have a choice: either police these byways in force, using all the tools of the international community, or shut them down.

The international system and its institutions will be critical to another key dimension of the Permanent Quagmire: a strategy of institutional envelopment. This involves co-opting not only the backward nations of the Arab world into the international system but also the putative superpower of the twenty-first century, China, by molding their behavior through such institutions as the WTO and, yes, even the much-criticized UN Security Council. When it comes to Beijing, some neoconservatives would call this policy appeasement; they want to solve the problem of China with "regime change." But they have never offered a practical program: Washington cannot isolate China as it once did the Soviet Union, and it is certainly not going to invade and occupy a nuclear-armed nation of 1.3 billion people. And while we await the advent of democracy there, the international system offers Beijing a real alternative to the old geopolitical power struggle.

Yet for politicians there is no drama in such a plodding, careful strategy—nothing like Richard Nixon's stunning opening of China in 1972, for instance—and probably not too many votes. And so the main temptation for U.S. politicians in the future will be to try to retreat from the Permanent Quagmire. The bottom-line problem American presidents will face here is one of domestic politics, not global politics or diplomacy. No one —especially a politician—wants to manage a quagmire. American presidents still have to worry about their image in the polls, and indecisiveness in a leader typically doesn't rate highly. Yet indecisiveness—and a good amount of ambiguity and fudging as we juggle assorted crises—is built into the Permanent Quagmire. That creates a constant and dangerous temptation: stay out, or at least minimize our role. Because the Permanent Quagmire is so hard to navigate conceptually and so unrewarding politically, American presidents will be constantly tempted to throw up their hands at its complexities. Clinton didn't get many points for ridding Kosovo of Milosevic, just as the first President Bush didn't for crippling (but not taking out) Saddam Hussein in 1991. Even his son's popularity rate began dropping after the "war on terror" became a long series of arrests and covert actions in other countries. Much like their predecessors, presidents of the twenty-first century will be tempted to sacrifice distant foreign threats to immediate political goals at home—to demonize the UN, for instance, in order to neutralize nativist fears of a loss of sovereignty, or to scapegoat our own brainchildren, new institutions such as the World Trade Organization. They must resist this temptation, but only a greater awareness by the American public—a shift of mind-set that would turn such "nonvoting" issues as UN dues or arms control into "voting" issues—can ensure that they do so.

## It's Still Good to Be the King

I have drawn a picture of perhaps unsettling complexity here. But the landscape of the Permanent Quagmire is not entirely bleak. In the end this is an optimistic book—it's still good to be the king, after all, in Mel Brooks's immortal words. Indeed, one of the chief arguments of this book is that we Americans can *afford* a more expansive engagement. We can muddle through. Powered by a still-dominant economy, a fully engaged America can both fight wars and keep the peace. We can combat terror with one hand and build international institutions with the other (using them in turn to get others to help us maintain stability). Even the latest surge in defense spending will amount to a paltry, very manageable 3.3 percent of GDP, one-half of what it was at the height of the Cold War, and a pittance compared to militarized Germany (23.5 percent) and Japan (28.2 percent) in the late 1930s.[20] Yes, we face a budget crunch in decades ahead as baby boomers become senior citizens and our economy grows top-heavy with Social Security and Medicare recipients. But Newt Gingrich, the former leader of the "Republican revolution" of the '90s, estimates that if America were to aggressively embrace all the tasks of the war on terror—including an occupation of Iraq—it would still only cost the nation about 5 percent of GDP.[21] The real problem is not "imperial overstretch"—Paul Kennedy's phrase—but that America is suffering from "understretch," to quote another historian, Niall Ferguson. America can do much more. Perhaps the "greatest disappointment facing the world in the 21st century," Ferguson writes, is "that the leaders of the one state with the economic resources to make the world a better place lack the guts to do it."[22]

*Guts* may be less the operative word here than *awareness*. During the 1990s, as America became astonishingly rich—and a net user of other nations' capital through the magic of Wall Street—Washington chopped the foreign-aid budget by more than half to less than a cent on the federal dollar, or 0.1 percent of GDP (compared to the Marshall Plan–era high of 3.21 percent of GDP), putting America last among twenty-two major nations, and a posse of right-wing legislators nearly bankrupted the United Nations.[23] The free market was the answer, many politicians said; yet at the same time the gap between rich and poor nations widened, and no region was hit worse, apart from Africa, than the Arab world.

We can argue—as Congress and the executive branch assuredly will—over the size of the foreign-aid budget or whether the dues we pay to the UN should be 20, 25, or 30 percent. But we no longer have the luxury, as a nation, of debating whether or not we should pay those dues at all. We can opt to bypass the UN in certain international crises. But we must remain *systematically* committed to supporting and funding the world body and other international institutions we have built. We must be their champion and main cheerleader, as unpleasant as that job may sometimes seem. And American politicians who shirk this global responsibility must be voted out of office.

The very fact that nation building in places such as Afghanistan is still at issue in American politics suggests how far we still have to go in assuming the full breadth of our international role. Nation building is a relatively small task; the United States is already engaged in building a world —continuing the process that Wilson and his successors started—or at least it is the chief contractor in that effort. "Nothing is possible without men, but nothing is lasting without institutions," Jean Monnet, the champion of postwar European unity, once observed.[24] Today we are midway through the historic task of institutionalizing the American global system. But as with the anonymous builders of the Pyramids, little glory will accrue to presidents and political leaders who lay down its foundation, brick by inconspicuous brick. It won't get them on *Meet the Press*, and it probably won't get them reelected. It is a very risky task to entrust to politicians, so we had better make sure they do it.

During the 1990s we Americans had a legitimate national debate over humanitarian intervention in places such as Somalia, Bosnia, and Kosovo. Our connection to those places was indirect—were we just being altruistic? Were we there just because we couldn't stand seeing atrocities on CNN?— and the national interest unclear. In Afghanistan after September 11, 2001, the connection was nightmarishly clear: Here was a state that we Americans had permitted to fail, which was once seen as distant and marginal, and that neglect had led directly to the mass slaughter of Americans. Even the most stalwart conservatives have seen their illusions shattered on that score. As the Bush administration acknowledged in September 2002 in its new national security strategy: "America is now threatened less by conquering states than we are by failing ones."[25] But accepting responsibility for Afghanistan opened up a new dimension of global responsibility. For how do we really know where the next Afghanistan is? Which states are we going to permit to fail now? No longer can we draw a defense perimeter around certain regions and exclude others, as Secretary of State Dean Acheson did in the early years of the Cold War (leaving the Korean peninsula, unfortunately, outside of it; the North invaded the South six months later). Nor can we cut off and quarantine certain recalcitrant sections of the world, somewhat as Rome once declared natural "boundaries" to an empire that did not include barbarian hordes (boundaries that did not ultimately hold). Al-Qaeda may be destroyed some day, but some other threat will follow it, and it will have even greater means to harm us. A former Pentagon planner, one of the smartest men I know, once told me, "Outfits like al-Qaeda have the whole world as their option. They're like water, they're going to go to the lowest place on earth." And from the lowest place on earth they can reach us.

So that's where we Americans must go too, brandishing both arms and aid, both stealth weapons and the seductions of our success—mainly the global system we have built. We are in this world with both feet now. We have achieved our Founding Fathers' fondest dream and, at the same time, their worst nightmare. We are a shining success, the supreme power on earth. And we are entangled everywhere.

# 1

## Navigating the Permanent Quagmire

> You may fly over a land forever. You may bomb it, atomize it,
> pulverize it and wipe it clean of life—but if you desire to defend
> it, protect it and keep it for civilization, you must do it on the
> ground, the way the Roman legions did, by putting your young
> men in the mud.
>
> T. R. Fehrenbach, *This Kind of War*

INVITED TO THE Oval Office shortly after the war in Afghanistan began in October 2001, U.S. senator Joseph Biden had a heart-to-heart with the leader of the free world, the newly engaged George W. Bush. After a white-knuckled month of terror, the mood of the two men was buoyant. America was striking back at last: Taliban and al-Qaeda forces would soon flee from the major cities, signaling the end of the bizarre fundamentalist regime that had harbored Osama bin Laden. The topic of discussion now was postwar Afghanistan. Biden, a garrulous Delaware Democrat who was then chairman of the Senate Foreign Relations Committee, was delighted at what he was hearing from the president. America would do it right this time, Bush told him, not leave some hapless country in the lurch, sowing the seeds of future rage and discontent—and terror. Afghanistan would not be Somalia or Rwanda or even Afghanistan circa 1989, when America discarded the country like a used cartridge after years of supplying and encouraging the mujahideen, who were once our allies, in their successful war against the Soviets.

Bush himself, two days later, would indirectly criticize his revered father, President George H. W. Bush, on that score. Bush senior, who took great pride in having smoothly managed the end of the Cold War, helping along socialist transitions in Eastern Europe and the Soviet republics, had left Afghanistan utterly in the cold—even though Moscow's ten-year bloodletting at the hands of the "muj" may have had as much to do with the collapse of the Soviet Union as any other single factor.[1] America, his son would say at a news conference on October 11, a month after the terror attacks on the World Trade Center and Pentagon, "should learn a lesson from the previous engagement in the Afghan area: that we should not just simply leave after a military objective has been achieved."[2] Now, in the Oval Office, the younger Bush was "going on about the long-term commitment we have to make," Biden recalled. "I said, 'Mr. President, it's going to cost billions of dollars. I think we're going to have to have a multilateral force in there.' And I think he and I are mostly in agreement."

The meeting ended, and Biden was walking down the hallway in the West Wing when Bush's press secretary, Ari Fleischer, came bounding after him. Fleischer asked Biden to stop at the "press stakeout" outside the office in an effort to show that Bush's policies had bipartisan support. Then, in Biden's account, he said to the senator, "'But you're not going to say anything about nation building, are you?' I looked at him and said, 'You mean, what the president talked about for the last hour?'"

For Biden, the brief exchange with Fleischer (who says he can't recall it) encapsulated all the "phoniness" of the endless debate over America's role overseas. The Republicans, Biden said, had "beat the living bejesus out of Bill Clinton for I don't know how many years about nation building [in places such as Somalia, Bosnia, and Kosovo]. Now they're trying to make a fine distinction: We're not putting troops on the ground, we're not going to keep them there. Well, good. But you're coordinating meetings to put a government in place. You're going to insist on elections, and on and on. What would you call that?"[3]

For George W. Bush, managing his own transition to the new world he faced after September 11 wasn't easy. Certainly the last thing this starkly conservative Texan had intended for his presidency was to get involved in such an ill-defined, hopelessly Clintonesque activity as nation building, especially in far-off Afghanistan. Judging from his rhetoric since he first began running for office, it was also the last thing anyone else should have expected of him and his administration. Biden was right: During the 2000 campaign, when most foreign-policy issues scarcely registered with voters, Bush nonetheless made a point of hammering the Clinton administration and his opponent, Al Gore, over the folly of "extending our troops all around the world in nation-building missions," as Bush phrased it in his first presidential debate with Gore. For the "Bushies"—as the Bush team came to be called by pundits—one of the most objectionable things about nation building was that it reeked of Clintonism.

Though Bush scarcely ever mentioned Bill Clinton's name after he took office, the new president made clear, through his actions, that one of his overriding foreign-policy goals was to be the un-Clinton.[4] That Bush would seek to renounce the policies of his predecessor was hardly surprising. Every opposition-party candidate running for office seeks to distinguish himself from the incumbent, whose lack of vision and poor policy choices have, invariably, led the nation to the precipice of disaster. But Bush went about this obligatory political task with a special vengeance in his heart. Clinton, after all, was the man who had deprived his father of a second term, and who then had soiled the great office that the blue-blooded Bush family—with its odd mix of Yankee rectitude and Texas regular-guyness—had worked so hard to dignify. "If I know anything about George W. Bush, it is that one of the psychological themes in his soul is settling scores. Anything to do with Clinton gets his antennae up," says one Republican senator who talked with the president frequently. "I think he took the last eight years as a personal affront to his family."

And it wasn't just the moral turpitude of "Monicagate" that Bush sought to eradicate. Bush and his new team, the most conservative administration since Ronald Reagan's, were determined to leave behind the vacillation, the squishiness of purpose, the liberal promiscuity they perceived in the Clinton administration. Conservatives, out of power for twelve frustrating years (if one counts the first Bush administration, which to true believers was suspiciously moderate, almost turncoat), believed Bill Clinton had been a duplicitous, craven politician without a core of values. They believed he had focus-grouped and polled his way to every policy decision. And they were certain that his foreign policy was fatally tainted as a result.[5]

This chapter is about the vastly different approaches that the Clinton and Bush administrations—the first two post–Cold War administrations—brought to the complex world they faced as the government of the lone superpower. Clinton and Bush each believed he had, more than presidents in the Cold War period, a blank slate on which to inscribe any sort of policy direction he saw fit, unhindered to a large extent by the choices of his predecessors. One thing was clear: American power and influence were preeminent, and the question was how to use them. Each president initially went in a different direction. The reason it is important to delve into these differences is that this book is about how, in the end, two men who began their presidencies so opposite in outlook and perspective faced the necessity of adopting similar policies as they grappled with the realities of the Permanent Quagmire, the world of endlessly multiplying crises and diffuse demands on their attention that I described in the Introduction.

True, the particular challenges the two presidents confronted were very different. While Clinton's eight years were largely consumed with scandal over his personal and political behavior and with budget politics at home, and abroad with promoting globalization while fending off distractions such as Slobodan Milosevic, Bush faced what seemed to be an entirely new landscape. On September 11, only eight months into his term, he was suddenly handed an irreconcilable enemy, the sort of black-and-white challenge that we thought we had transcended in the post–Cold War period, when the great clash of ideologies had ended. For a time this transformed the entire focus of his administration and gave Bush an opportunity to do what Clinton could not: to forge a unifying vision both for the nation and for the world around the war on terror. It also gave him a chance to signal, once and for all, his administration's departure from the perceived softness of the Clinton administration.

## The World According to Bush

Most senior officials in the new Bush administration believed that Clinton and his team had profoundly misunderstood the world. Clinton and his influential foreign-affairs consiglieres—in the first term, Warren Christopher and Anthony Lake; in the second, Sandy Berger and Madeleine Albright—saw a Wilsonian, liberalizing world where no war was inevitable, where almost everything could be negotiated on the premise that international comity was in everyone's interest, where global society was perfectible. It was a world where *things generally got better over time.* "Enlargement of democracy" had replaced containment of Soviet communism, as Lake put it in 1993 in the defining speech of the Clinton foreign-policy era, and until the end the Clintonites hewed to that worldview with striking faithfulness.[6] It was all very positive and benign, especially compared to the stark and dark worldview of the Bush team. Paul Wolfowitz, the resident intellectual in Bush's foreign policy team, led the way in dismissing the overconfident globalists of the Clinton administration who put their faith in the "seemingly benign international environment," as Wolfowitz wrote in 2000. "Thus, we have been told that the really important problem is 'the economy, stupid,' or the environment, or . . . AIDS in Africa. What is wrong with these claims is not that AIDS in Africa and the environment are not serious problems; rather it is the implication that conventional security is no longer something we need to worry much about."[7] Security meant a stout military, and while Clinton had actually increased the defense budget in his later years, Wolfowitz's neoconservative ally, the scholar Robert Kagan, spoke for many hawks when he savaged the president's cavalier attitude toward defense. "Clinton's willful evisceration of the defense budget during his two terms in office is all the more appalling when one considers that he cut while the American economy was soaring and the federal deficit was shrinking and turning into a surplus," Kagan wrote as the forty-second president left office. "Clinton may have left too little time to turn the ship around before the next major international crisis."[8]

It wasn't just what Clinton deemphasized, like defense; it was the kinds of things he emphasized as well. In the view of Clinton's Republican critics, he was a passionate world-hugger and serial intervener who rarely saw a global stage he didn't covet, a conflict he didn't seek to resolve, usually through negotiation. The Bush team also hated what they saw as the dangerously rose-colored globalism and one-worldism of the Clinton liberals. This was the belief in what Clinton's deputy secretary of state Strobe Talbott, an old FOB (Friend of Bill) who acted as a kind of party philosopher for the Democratic administration, once called "pooled sovereignty," the idea that in the new, ever-progressing age of globalization America must give up some of its freedom of action to the emerging international community. Much of this thinking went back to Woodrow Wilson, who originated the crusading U.S. internationalism of the twentieth century and sought, ultimately, to create a global "community of democracies" governed not through might but through international law.

Many key players on the Bush team believed they embodied an even older American tradition than that of Wilson, the despised liberal: a desire to keep the rest of the world at arm's length and to assert America's right to act as it pleases in its own best interests. Bush officials had no problem with democracy—indeed, the neoconservatives among them wanted to be more aggressive than the Clintonites had been in promulgating it abroad—but they believed it would come in the wake of the assertion of American power, not by working multilaterally through international institutions. Even the word *globalization*—the promotion of which was the leitmotif of Clinton's every foreign policy speech—seemed a liberal-tainted epithet to the Bush hard-liners and rarely passed from their lips. As Condoleezza Rice, Bush's future national security advisor, put it in her definitive account of the Bush team's mind-set coming into office, the deluded globalist thinking of the Clinton administration made it hard to define "the national interest." "The 'national interest' is replaced with 'humanitarian interests' or the interests of 'the international community.'" Much of this also went back to Wilson, she said: "The belief that the United States is exercising power legitimately only when it is doing so on behalf of someone or something else was deeply rooted in Wilsonian thought, and there are strong echoes of it in the Clinton administration."[9]

Bush was to a certain extent his father's son, though he was clearly more conservative. Like his father, who was a determined internationalist in the tradition of moderate Republicanism, Bush junior believed in engagement, in projecting American power abroad, and in the transformative powers of free trade and democracy. But Bush was also wary of his father's missteps. The first President Bush had, famously, focused too heavily on foreign affairs at a time when the Cold War was ending and many Americans wanted to turn inward again. George H. W. Bush, a former CIA director and ambassador to China whose patrician restraint was constantly at war with his political ambition, had humbly refused to gloat over the collapse of the Soviet Union on his watch, and he had coasted for too long on his 90 percent approval ratings during the Gulf War. Worse, as a politician he had a tin ear—he was not good at "the vision thing," he once clumsily said with his New England twang—and a young Arkansas governor named Bill Clinton was emerging as the master politician of his generation. As the United States entered a recession in the middle of Bush's term, Clinton pounced. The crystal-clear message of his 1992 campaign—"It's the economy, stupid," a Jeffersonian call to Americans to "take care of our own people first"—made Bush senior out to be a clueless holdover from the Cold War, excessively and needlessly obsessed with foreign policy.[10] Clinton coasted to an easy victory. It was a bitter blow to Bush senior and junior—"Dubya," as he was then known, was a key figure in his father's reelection campaign, and at one point exulted after the Gulf War, "Do you think the American people are going to turn to a Democrat now?"[11]

Yet Clinton, by the end of his second term, had also been pulled into the world, getting bogged down in mediation and peacekeeping in Somalia, Haiti, Bosnia, and, disastrously, the Mideast, presiding over a failed summit at Camp David in July 2000 that led directly to the bloody Palestinian intifada. Clinton had become "the globalization president," the most traveled U.S. leader in history. And that left Clinton and his would-be successor, Gore, vulnerable to a counterattack by the new Bush team over the issue that had so humiliated the new president's father: foreign policy. Bush and many in his administration thought the opportunity was ripe to scale down these Clintonian overcommitments around the globe. During the 2000 campaign, Bush attacked Clinton and Gore for their "open-ended deployments and unclear military missions." Bush also spoke of "a new division of labor" with U.S. allies, especially Europeans, that would not have, as Condoleezza Rice put it, "the 82nd Airborne escorting kids to kindergarten," an allusion to Clinton's nation-building intervention in the Balkans. Rice, who was so close to Bush she virtually became his alter ego, declared that the "attachment to largely symbolic agreements and its pursuit of, at best, illusory 'norms' of international behavior have become an epidemic." She also implied that the Clintonites had lacked "a disciplined and consistent foreign policy that separates the important from the trivial."[12] Even Colin L. Powell, the new secretary of state and the administration's house moderate, had tweaked the Clintonites for their "haphazard" approach to world affairs.[13]

So dramatically different were the worldviews of the second Bush and Clinton administrations that they seemed to occupy virtually opposite poles of the political spectrum, representing classic archetypes that have divided liberals and conservatives for centuries. The Bush team, at least the hard-liners among them—led by, at the most senior levels, Vice President Dick Cheney, Rumsfeld, and Rice—saw the world as a nasty, alien place still largely defined by anarchy, a place where conflict is natural or inevitable and force is what works, as realists and conservatives going back to Thucydides and Thomas Hobbes have insisted. Negotiation and trade are good for America but largely irrelevant to the main task: getting ready for conflict, staying ahead of the other nations, and defining down the national interest to these considerations. "Norms" and international law are a liberal myth, as is the "international community." Treaties and conventions are, as Hobbes wrote, "but words, and of no strength to secure a man at all" without the sword.[14] Any values imposed in foreign policy must be true-blue American values. It was a mixture of traditional realism and a crusading, Reaganite neoconservatism, layered over with Bush's Texas feistiness and Southern religious fundamentalism: If America shows a strong and true face to the world, our enemies will quail in fear and awed allies will draw nearer, America and its values will triumph, and alternative systems will crumble as the Soviet Union did. The attacks of September 11 seemed to bear out their criticism of Clinton—and their dark worldview—in spades.

The Clintonites, by contrast, saw the world as a place that was already *our* place, America's place—the freedom-loving international community, melded through markets and common values and norms, that the heirs to the Enlightenment, liberal dreamers from Jean-Jacques Rousseau to Immanuel Kant to Wilson, have sought to create. (Of course we can build nations—our own is the shining prototype—and we can win over other peoples by drawing them into our peaceful global system.) Charles Krauthammer, perhaps the most hawkish columnist in Washington, summed up the conservative view of the Clinton administration after September 11: "Guided by the vision of an autonomous, active, and norm-driven 'international community' that would relieve a unilateralist America from keeping order in the world, the Clinton administration spent eight years signing one treaty, convention, and international protocol after another. From this web of mutual obligations, a new and vital 'international community' would ultimately regulate international relations and keep the peace. . . . This decade-long folly—a foreign policy of norms rather than national interest—is over."[15] Or as Victor Davis Hanson, a conservative military historian whose work was admired by Cheney and who believes war is "innate to civilization," wrote after 9/11:

> As we have seen in the current crisis, those who are the most educated, the most removed from the often humiliating rat race of daily life (what Hobbes called the *bellum omnium contra omnes*), and the most inexperienced with thugs and bullies, are the likeliest to advocate utopian solutions and to ridicule those who would remind them of the tragic nature of mankind and the timeless nature of war. . . . McClellans—not Shermans; Chamberlains—not Churchills; and Clintons—not Reagans, usually pose as the more sensible, compassionate, and circumspect leaders; but in fact, even as they smile and pump the flesh, they prove far, far more dangerous to all involved.[16]

So at the start, Thomas Hobbes was in, Wilson was out. For the new administration, there would be little attempt at continuity, the hallmark of American foreign policy for a half century. Bush seeded his administration with some of the leading figures of the far right, many of them veterans of the Reagan administration. They took a dramatically different view of the world, not only compared to Clinton but also in comparison to the center of their own party, the traditions of Eisenhower, Nixon, and Ford. Silenced for too long on the world stage, they were suddenly back in power and running things. It wasn't long before they were in full roar.

And Bill Clinton was only one of their victims. Another was the chief representative of continuity in the new administration, Colin Luther Powell.

## The Rise of the Hegemonists

Despite all the harsh campaign rhetoric, Bush had run as a centrist, a practitioner of "compassionate conservatism." Even then he had only squeaked into office, losing the popular vote to Gore in one of the most disputed elections in U.S. history. So as the Bush administration took power it was Powell, a man who always positioned himself in the center, who seemed destined to become the main voice of American foreign policy. The Bronx-born son of Jamaican immigrants, Powell had risen to become the first black national security advisor under Reagan and then the youngest-ever Joint Chiefs chairman, and he was a moderate internationalist in the mold of Bush senior. The new secretary of state was "expected to be the star of the administration, the one who commands every room he walks into, who can silence a strategy session just by clearing his throat," I wrote in *Newsweek* in December 2000, one of many in the Washington media who were somewhat awed by the Powell aura.

Bush himself had tears in his eyes when, greeting the press at a Texas schoolhouse two weeks after the Supreme Court anointed him president, he introduced his new secretary of state. Perhaps Bush was crying for joy at his good fortune in snagging a man who, after all, was more popular than he, one who could have been president himself had he chosen to run, many said, and with far less fuss than his new boss. Bush knew that Powell would lend instant legitimacy to his asterisked presidency by taking the top Cabinet post. Now, stepping up to the podium, Bush called his new secretary of state "an American hero" and evoked Powell's personal role model, George C. Marshall, another ex-general who graced the office of America's top diplomat. Like Marshall, the namesake of that most visionary of American foreign-policy initiatives, the Marshall Plan, Powell possessed the right stuff, Bush said, "in directness of speech, his towering integrity, his deep respect for our democracy, and his soldier's sense of duty and honor." Then the president-elect laid out a line that could have come from Powell himself: "Our next secretary of state believes as I do that we must work closely with our allies and friends in times of calm so that we will be able to work together in times of crises. He believes, as I do, that our nation is best when we project our strength and our purpose with humility."

When Powell got up to speak himself, it was with a notable lack of humility. It was as if he had won the election after all. Ever eloquent, tall and solidly built, with an air of calm command that came from winning his first star at forty-two (at the time, the youngest brigadier in the army), Powell quickly took charge of the news conference. Standing behind him, the president-elect faded into the backdrop, seeming to grow smaller and smaller as Powell spoke. Powell, who had first gained national fame wielding a pointer like a rapier during televised Gulf War briefings, boldly poked fun at the Texas setting—"I'm from the South Bronx," he said, "and I don't care what you say: Those cows look dangerous"—and rather presumptuously gave his endorsement to the already-elected Bush: "He will be a president for all the people, all the time." As the president-elect listened silently, Powell made clear that he intended to run American foreign policy—all of it. He pronounced upon the administration's policy on the Balkans and on the Mideast. "It is absolutely a given that under a Bush administration, America will remain very much engaged in the Middle East," Powell said. When asked about some of the administration campaign rhetoric about scaling down peacekeeping, he was decorously evasive. "Our plan is to undertake a review right after the president is inaugurated and take a look not only at our deployments in Bosnia but in . . . Kosovo and many other places around the world, and make sure those deployments are proper." Powell even pronounced policy on missile defense, though that was more the province of the as yet unnamed secretary of defense. "We're going to go forward," he said.[17]

It might have been a display of overconfidence, but it was also reassuring. The Bush team was clearly more conservative than their predecessors, committing themselves to missile defense, for example, with an almost missionary zeal, but Powell himself symbolized a long tradition of American engagement in the world. On one hand, he was heir to the successful Wilsonianism of the twentieth century, and he echoed Clinton's optimistic view of the forward progress of American ideals: "There is no country on earth that is not touched by America, for we have become the motive force for freedom and democracy in the world." As such, he said later at his confirmation hearing (he was approved unanimously, of course), "We are attached by a thousand cords to the world at large, to its teeming cities, to its remotest regions, to its oldest civilizations, to its newest cries for freedom. This means that we have an interest in every place on this Earth, that we need to lead, to guide, to help in every country that has a desire to be free, open, and prosperous."[18]

Powell was also the heir to another strain of continuity in U.S. foreign policy—the great tradition of pragmatic internationalism going back to Elihu Root (secretary of war under William McKinley and secretary of state under Teddy Roosevelt), Henry Stimson (secretary of state under Hoover and secretary of war under FDR), and Dean Acheson, the Truman secretary of state who was "present at the creation" (his own words) of the postwar world order. Despite his Wilsonian idealism, Powell was, like those men, a hardheaded problem solver unchained to any particular ideology beyond patriotism, breaking through global logjams by virtue of his charisma and intellect. He also exuded a classic American positiveness: "Perpetual optimism is a force multiplier" was one of the thirteen "rules" he lived by and later posted, like a legacy to the nation, at the end of his autobiography. Walter Isaacson and Evan Thomas's description of the "wise men" establishment of the Cold War fit Powell perfectly: "They were equally opposed to the yahoos of the right and the softies of the left. Ideological fervor was frowned upon; pragmatism, realpolitik, moderation and consensus were prized. Nonpartisanship was more than a principle, it was art form."[19] In the 1940s, this described the Ivy League–educated WASP elite; by the multicultural, PC standards of fifty years later, it was no surprise, somehow, that an African American out of City College would be the lineal descendent of this tradition. But Powell was such a man, starting with the fact that no one in Washington could tell if he was really a liberal Republican or a centrist Democrat in disguise.

In other ways, however, Powell was also a product of his own times. If the "Wise Men" were legatees of a victorious World War II America, Powell was heir to the Vietnam debacle. Like so many of his generation—the neoconservatives themselves were mostly ex-Democrats appalled by their party's handling of Vietnam and the Cold War in general, reborn as hawks (though almost none of them served a day in the military)—Powell was burdened by the mistakes of Vietnam. He had done two tours, and, as he wrote in his 1995 memoirs: "Many of my generation, the career captains, majors, and lieutenant colonels seasoned in that war, vowed that when our turn came to call the shots, we would not quietly acquiesce in halfhearted warfare for half-baked reasons that the American people could not understand or support. If we could make good on that promise to ourselves . . . then the sacrifices of Vietnam would not have been in vain."[20]

In 1992, Powell, as chairman of the Joint Chiefs of Staff, gave his generation's answer to the "Vietnam syndrome" by committing himself to a set of principles that later became known as the "Powell Doctrine." While he disavowed hard-and-fast rules, Powell believed that the U.S. military should be astringent in the extreme, applying only overwhelming force when it was mobilized, and then only in situations where victory was near certain and the exit strategy was clear. He defined up America's superpowerhood, in essence, so as to make it almost beyond reach of policy makers. This Vietnam-haunted worldview sometimes led Powell into an excess of cautiousness, and that would come to hurt him later in his battles with the Bush hawks: During the Gulf crisis in 1990, he had notoriously suggested that reversing Saddam Hussein's occupation of Kuwait was not in the U.S. interest. "The American people do not want their young dying for $1.50 a gallon oil," he said.[21] As Serb ethnic cleansing began in the Balkans, he also counseled against a military intervention. In Somalia it was Powell, then in his last months as Joint Chiefs chairman, who urged Clinton to intervene with Special Forces, but with a minimum of air support. Yet when disaster ensued—eighteen U.S. soldiers were killed when they found themselves entrapped by Somali gunmen—it was the defense secretary, Les Aspin, not Powell, who took the fall.

For all his errors, however, Powell had also learned the lessons of post–Cold War America better than many of his generation. He was one of the first military policy makers to recognize the weakness of the soon-to-collapse Soviet Union, and to call for a shift away from the nation's Cold War military posture well before the hard-liners he would later butt heads with in the war on terror, like Cheney (who was secretary of defense under Bush I).[22] If there were lingering doubts about his talents as a strategist—the consummate staff man, Powell was more of manager in the mold of John McCloy, a chief aide to General Marshall and later "chairman" of the "wise men" establishment—he seemed superbly outfitted to run America's foreign policy.

But all this was the view of Powell in the beginning of the Bush presidency. As was said of Hamlet's father, "What a falling-off was there."

Within the first months of the new Bush administration, Powell found himself odd man out, engulfed in a conservative counterrevolution that left him almost alone in George W. Bush's Washington. Not only would there be no continuity from the Clinton administration, there would be a wholesale lurch in the opposite direction. It was quickly clear that Powell would not be the administration's foreign-policy voice. Instead he became the man with a shovel—cleaning up after the diplomatic imbroglios left behind by the hard-liners, who were really making policy. Powell found himself outflanked by the hegemonists, a group of senior officials led by Rumsfeld and Cheney, two conservatives from the American heartland (the former from Chicago, the latter from Wyoming). Shaped by their Hobbesian view that power is what mainly matters, their agenda was one they had been waiting for years to impose: to force others to recognize the reality of America as world's hegemon, or dominant power (though that was not a term they used), to exploit this moment in history to rid the world of rogue threats, and to lock in America's dominance. China, for example, was weak but would one day be strong, so now was the time to shift U.S. forces to the Pacific in order to contain Beijing. Iraq's Saddam Hussein was dangerous but weak, so now was the time to destroy his regime. And it really didn't matter much if Beijing or other U.S. allies squalled about it: America should not be hampered by international law or the nitpicking of other nations. If America leads, the world will follow. "A number of [us] believe that U.S. power is always potentially a source for good in the world," said one of the leading activists and thinkers in this movement, Richard Perle. "The contrast is with people who fear American power."[23] Explained a former senior official of the first Bush administration who was as appalled as Powell by this approach:

> It's about changing the course of history in the sense that we're in a period when a lot of things are in turmoil and unstable, so this is the time to be bold, to kick over the apple cart, then put it back together again in a very different mold. This is no time for caution, it's time to abandon your allies, your friends and just go for it. They think that the United States has been in a Gulliver-like position for a long time, tied down by the Lilliputians [the rest of the world] from doing the things that we think are right. Their thinking is: "We have no world aspirations for hegemony, for territory. When we act in our interests we're acting in the world's interests, and therefore we shouldn't pay any attention to it."[24]

At the same time as they sought to project American hard power outward —especially as the war on terror commenced—many of the Bush conservatives were leery of diplomatic engagement of any kind. If Washington would have an expansive foreign policy, it would still emanate solely from Washington. This was traditional conservative thinking. As we will see in Chapter 2, Americans have always treasured the exceptionalist idea that we are a unique people who could "begin the world again" between our two broad oceans, in Tom Paine's iconic phrase—that, in short, our sovereignty is sacrosanct. And none cherished these ideas more than American conservatives, the putative keepers of our founding traditions. It was no accident that the presidents who led America into the biggest wars of the twentieth century, Wilson, FDR, Truman, Kennedy, and Lyndon Baines Johnson, had all been Democrats—Bob Dole, the 1996 GOP presidential candidate, once sneeringly called these conflicts "Democrat wars"—and that it was a Republican-led Congress that sought to demobilize quickly and leave Europe after World War II. But the titanic struggle of the Cold War, emerging so quickly afterward, forced conservatives to stay engaged in every part of the globe, as far away and as tragically as Vietnam, for another half century. Moreover, they had to be deferential toward the Europeans: The institutions of the transatlantic community were built on the idea of great-power cooperation, a "concert of power," in Wilson's phrase, with America the superpower as first among equals. If the disparity of power between the United States and Europe was just as great at the end of World War II, the limitations of technology and the delicate balancing act of Cold War deterrence, of forward-based missiles and troops in Europe vis-à-vis the Soviet bloc, required real cooperation.

But the new Bush administration marked perhaps the first time since World War II that this engagement policy could be discarded, and the deep-rooted conservative strain in American political thought could dictate foreign policy according to its true impulses. There was no more need for the grand compromise of the Cold War. The old conservative tradition was back, but transmuted by America's extraordinary power advantage—especially in a post-9/11 world—into a stark unilateralism. The Bush hegemonists' mixed message of engagement, *sí*, diplomacy, *no*, was their peculiar way of eating their cake and having it too—exercising global leadership, as America's dominant position and the war on terror demanded, but remaining a nation apart, as America's traditional sensibility also demanded. The new hegemonists brought isolationism back "in a different form," Susan Eisenhower, Ike's granddaughter and a leading moderate GOP figure in Washington, told me in mid-2002. "This isn't the kind of internationalism that has been the bedrock of the Republican Party. It's sort of an isolationist approach to a globalized world." [25] Indeed, for men who came from a long tradition of American exceptionalism, the vast might they inherited was almost like a narcotic to an addict, and the terrorist attacks were an amazing effrontery. America was God's gift to humankind. And they would prove it.

Powell's opposite in this pitched ideological battle was Rumsfeld, who was back at his second turn as defense secretary. Squinty-eyed and square-jawed, a man of ruthless efficiency and endless drive, Rumsfeld was a legendary infighter in Washington, with a long winning streak in policy battles going back to his days as White House chief of staff and defense secretary under Gerald Ford. Not content with running the vast and unwieldy Defense Department, he would shoot "Rummygrams" over to Powell, notes intended to pry loose the secretary of state from his moderate views. "I found it maddening," said one Rummygram recipient from the Ford administration. "It's 'Why don't you do this? Have you thought of that?' He does it just to keep people off balance." Like Powell, Rumsfeld had a résumé that read like a *Parade* magazine hero-profile: wrestling captain at Princeton, Navy pilot, congressman at thirty, White House chief of staff at forty-two, defense secretary at forty-three (the youngest ever), Fortune 500 CEO and turnaround specialist. Friends say Rumsfeld, in fact, failed only once in a big way in his career: when he ran for president. After forming a test-the-waters committee in the late '80s and winning support of conservative editorial boards impressed by his charisma and clarity of vision, the man known to his friends as "Rummy" mysteriously bowed out, complaining that fund-raising was too difficult.

Rumsfeld was not a frothing-at-the-mouth ideologue. Friends and rivals were unanimous on that point. Newton Minow, an old Democratic friend from Chicago (and former Kennedy official), called him "an idealist without illusions" and added that on social issues such as abortion "he's very much in the center."[26] Minow said he once asked Rumsfeld how he got into public service. Rumsfeld promptly pulled from his wallet a tattered copy of an inspiring speech on the subject given to his 1954 Princeton class—by none other than archliberal Adlai Stevenson. "We became friends after that," said Minow. But Rumsfeld's superaggressiveness in all things—tennis, physical fitness (as a younger man he used to do one-armed pushups for money), bureaucratic infighting—amounted almost to a philosophy of life. It seemed to inform his vision of America's role in the world. Well before 9/11, Rumsfeld made clear that his mission as defense secretary was to reassert American power after eight years of flabbiness under Clinton. At his confirmation hearings in early 2001, in between plugging hard for missile defense and hinting that America ought to dominate space as well as the air, sea, and land, Rumsfeld laid out his overall philosophy: "We don't want to fight wars. We want to prevent them. We want to be so powerful and so forward-looking that it is clear to others that they ought not to be damaging their neighbors when it affects our interests, and they ought not to be doing things that are imposing threats and dangers to us."[27]

Rumsfeld, who took power in the Ford administration just as America was reckoning with the failures of Vietnam, was as shaped by that debacle as Powell and others of his generation—but in a very different way. He was a former naval aviator who had missed America's wars—enlisting between Korea and Vietnam—and was "free of irony, postmodern doubt and angst," as a close aide described him.[28] Whether he was an ideologue or not, Rumsfeld almost uniformly sided with the far right on foreign policy. The founding forum of the Bush hard-liners may have come in 1981, when Rumsfeld and Cheney were introduced to Wolfowitz at a Washington brunch and the three had a long discussion. Wolfowitz, then an academic, had been a member of "Team B," a group of like-minded hawks who argued against Kissingerian détente, while Rumsfeld, behind the scenes, had scuttled the SALT II arms control treaty—possibly helping to cost his then-boss, President Gerald Ford, the 1976 election.[29] In 1983, in one of the first shots fired at the international community that true-blue conservatives despise, Rumsfeld persuaded Margaret Thatcher to oppose the Law of the Sea Treaty, which would have handed decisions on exploiting mineral seabeds to the UN. During the '90s, both Rumsfeld and Wolfowitz signed on to a hegemonist policy statement by the Project for a New American Century, formed by Bill Kristol, the quintessential neoconservative, and two years later Rumsfeld led a commission calling for missile defense against the present-day "axis of evil."

Rumsfeld also had an impressive backup team: a group of conservative ideologues—many of them minor figures during the centrist first Bush administration—who were seeded at high levels throughout the administration and had long been waiting for their moment to shift the nation rightward. Among them were Rumsfeld's two top deputies, Wolfowitz and Douglas Feith, a Harvard-educated lawyer with close ties to Israel's right-wing Likud party. Vice President Cheney, Rumsfeld's former assistant in the Ford administration (he once joked at a Washington dinner that Rumsfeld "still treats me like his assistant"), meanwhile brought in other hard-liners, including Wolfowitz's former deputy, Lewis "Scooter" Libby, as his chief of staff. Another key player was Perle, who was known as the "prince of darkness" during the Reagan era for his harsh stand against arms control. Perle, Feith's former boss in the Reagan administration, was named by Rumsfeld to chair the Pentagon's Defense Policy Board, an influential advisory panel stocked mainly with conservatives.

While there were differences in emphasis—neoconservatives like Perle and Wolfowitz tended to give more of a moral cast to the use of U.S.

power, saying it was a force for freedom (it was a kind of hard-edged
Wilsonianism, though they wouldn't describe it that way), while Rumsfeld and Cheney tended to be realist pragmatists—all of them shared this
hawkish, power-is-what-counts philosophy. Rumsfeld had also learned a
great deal from his previous government experience, not least by serving
as ambassador to NATO in the 1970s. "He got to know a lot of Europeans
and he got to know there can only be one leader in the NATO alliance, or
in the world now," says Ken Adelman, Reagan's disarmament chief and a
longtime Rumsfeld friend. "There was an old saying in NATO in those
times: 'You had fifteen chimpanzees and one gorilla, and the gorilla
thought he was a chimpanzee.'" The lesson, says Adelman, was that "if
you wait until a consensus is formed on any issue, you're dead. Because
it's never formed on any issue. And especially a consensus is never formed
to do anything different than you're doing now."[30] The need to assert U.S.
leadership only grew in the post–Cold War period, when the disparity in
transatlantic power left Europe looking like a "pygmy" compared with
America, in the rueful words of NATO secretary-general George Robertson. To his conservative friends, it was no surprise that Rumsfeld
brusquely sidelined NATO immediately after September 11. In a show of
sympathy, the alliance invoked its Article 5 for the first time in its history,
defining the attack on the United States as an attack on all members. But
Rumsfeld simply believed the European nations didn't have much to
offer: they might offer troops, one official said, but then they needed U.S.
airlift. "They would just get in the way," says the official. So Rumsfeld dispatched Wolfowitz to say thanks but no thanks to NATO, that "the mission would define the coalition." In Europe, that snub rankled for a long
time.

What was interesting was how unresolved debates of the past came
home to roost in this new period. The Cold War consensus was, in truth,
always fragile. The Truman Doctrine and containment are now seen as
part of the golden age of American foreign policy, when the wise men,
who of course had the nation's best interests at heart, resolved the great
issues over bourbon and cigars, rather than the acrimonious battle in
Congress that it really was, during which the "politics of personal destruction" ruled the day. (Acheson suffered more from critics, especially on

Capitol Hill, than Powell ever did.) The Korean War and then, catastrophically, Vietnam led American policy makers to question their criteria for
intervention, and in the late 1960s the "wise men" cold-warrior culture
completely broke down in the angry debates over Vietnam. Meanwhile
there was always a split on the right between those who wanted to engage
and contain the Soviet Union and China—Eisenhower, Nixon (as president), and Kissinger—and hard-liners who opposed détente. In fact, what
was most striking about the new post–Cold War era was how the debates
that were always simmering below the surface during the long period of
America's Cold War engagement erupted once again.

## Détente Revisited

The Bush hegemonists sprang from what was often the losing, right-wing
side of this Cold War debate, and they had a historical ax to grind. They
argued that Chicken Little moderates, going back to the 1970s, had consistently underrated the usefulness of U.S. power and overestimated adverse
reaction to it. Nixon and Kissinger orchestrated détente with Moscow—
until Reagan came in, dubbed the Soviet Union an evil empire (to much
hue and cry from U.S. allies), spent billions more on defense, and, lo, the
USSR collapsed. (Though the Reaganite right tends to gloss over the fact
that in his second term Ronald Reagan rejoined the Cold War consensus,
growing fond of arms control and détente with Soviet leader Mikhail
Gorbachev.)[31] During the Gulf War, moderates such as Powell counseled
caution and sanctions (he and Cheney, then defense secretary, clashed
over that view). Yet the war was won, ushering in the "smart-bomb" era
and awing the world (though the hawks complain it was ended too early,
another sin blamed on Powell). And then in the fall of 2001, moderates
fretted over attacking Afghanistan—would it turn into a quagmire? would
the Islamic world erupt?—but the Taliban collapsed in eight weeks with
nary a peep from the "Arab street." The hard-liners also point to the ease
with which they achieved a key goal, the dissolution of the anti-ballistic-
missile treaty in the fall of 2001, despite much fretting from Europeans
and liberals that the ABM was the "cornerstone" of stability between

America and Russia. "We were just scaring ourselves. It was ridiculous,"
says Adelman. "Rumsfeld is keenly aware of track records like that."[32]

Some close observers of Republican Party politics saw the roots of the
present debate dating back to the early Cold War and discussions about
whether America should "preemptively" attack the Soviet Union and
China at a time when they were weak and had few (or no) nuclear
weapons and America was strong. The Committee on the Present Danger,
formed in 1950, urged a more aggressive stance (a later Committee on the
Present Danger was reborn in the 1970s and invoked anew in the definitive neocon manifesto published by Kristol and Kagan in 2000.)[33] Under
this minority view, if the United States had conducted preventive war
against the Soviets when it had the chance, the whole history of the second half of the twentieth century would have been different. These cross-
generational hawks see the 1960s and '70s as wasted decades that could
have been avoided—along with the catastrophe of Vietnam—had Washington not contented itself with containment and opted instead for rollback. (Their view of Clinton was that he too had basically settled on a
squeamish policy of containment of rogue states like Iraq, instead of rollback and "regime change.")

But Dwight D. Eisenhower, in perhaps the critical decisions of his
eight-year presidency, became the first Republican president to sideline the
hawks and embrace the containment policy that Truman had authored. As
he took office in 1953, Ike reined in his anticontainment campaign rhetoric. Later in the '50s, he declined again to pre-empt the Soviets as they
developed a long-range missile capability. "There were many, many policy
discussions," Susan Eisenhower says. "But in the end both the Truman and
Eisenhower administrations stepped back from this [pre-emption]."
Instead, "the kind of internationalism that revolved around the establishment and maintenance of healthy and multilateral alliances" became the
"bedrock of the Republican Party."[34] It is this international set of structures that became, to a large degree, the global system that is so critical to
the nation's future security. Powell, as the emblem of continuity in the new
administration, played the role of Eisenhower in this revived debate.

William Kristol, along with his writing partner and neocon mentor
Robert Kagan, had long been trying to break out of this hidebound world

view and agitating for a forthright American empire. As Kristol and Kagan wrote in 1996, "American hegemony is the only reliable defense against a breakdown of peace and international order. The appropriate goal of American foreign policy, therefore, is to preserve that hegemony as far into the future as possible."[35]

Wolfowitz, the original author of hegemony, took pleasure in crowing over the mistakes of the left and the Powellite and Clintonite moderates. In a spring 2000 article in *The National Interest,* he recounted the outrage caused by "the Pentagon Paper" that his office conceived in the waning days of the first Bush administration. Among the opponents, he noted, was Joe Biden, who "ridiculed the proposed strategy as 'literally a Pax Americana. . . . It won't work.'" Wolfowitz didn't say so, but another of these critics was Powell's policy planning chief, Richard Haass, who declared in a 1997 book, *The Reluctant Sheriff,* that "unipolarity" or the idea that America could continue to be the world's hegemon was unrealistic: "For better or worse, such a goal is beyond our reach. It simply is not doable."[36] Bush foreign policy later took on some of Haass's views—the war on terror was very much fought as a "foreign policy by posse," one of the chief recommendations in Haass's book—but judging from some of the vicious attacks he suffered in the conservative press, he was not forgiven this contrary view against the rising strategic vision of the hegemonists. Hegemony was not only doable, it was happening. "Just seven years later," Wolfowitz wrote in 2000, "many of these same critics seem quite comfortable with the idea of Pax Americana."[37]

The hegemonists' Hobbesian view of the world was always too dark and didn't really comport with the emerging reality of a fairly benign international system, especially as the 1980s rolled around. Cheney, during the first Bush administration, was the last senior official, for example, to acknowledge that Mikhail Gorbachev was a genuine reformer and not just playing games with the West. The Reaganite wing that the Bush hawks hailed from had actually misunderstood the Soviet threat more than the containment moderates had: As Reagan took office in 1981, the prevailing view of the neoconservatives was of Soviet expansion, of the "Finlandization" of Europe (or the spread of Soviet influence), rather than of an empire that was already beginning to implode economically.

Reagan certainly helped that implosion along by confronting the "evil empire," but the mythology of the neoconservative movement is that the Reagan defense buildup almost single-handedly drove the Soviet super-power out of business. And for hawks such as Rumsfeld, Wolfowitz, Perle, and Kristol, who thought America had gone soft, the horrors of September 11 were like a vindication from hell. As some hard-liners saw it, Iraq was in some ways the original sin of the Powellite moderates: Because of too much concern over the sensitivities of other members of "the coalition," Saddam was left in place, and American troops lingered provocatively but inconsequentially on Saudi soil for a decade. That gave Osama bin Laden his casus belli on September 11. It was during the Gulf War period that the first fissures appeared between those in the Bush II administration, such as Rumsfeld and Wolfowitz, who saw the post–Cold War period as a time for asserting U.S. power or hegemony to ward off potential rivals and those who said that was too risky (among them Haass).

Bush's sympathies seemed to lie with the hard-liners. He and Rumsfeld shared the view that Clinton's too-rosy view of globalization, combined with his character flaws, had weakened America during his eight-year presidency. The "word was out," Rumsfeld told President-elect Bush before they both took power, that a soft America had become an easy target.[38] He was right for the most part. True, Clinton had also beefed up the defense budget through the '90s—the war in Afghanistan was essentially won with the military he had left behind—but he hadn't done enough. And he had undercut America's "deterrent" power by responding flaccidly to previous terrorist challenges. Even after bin Laden had struck at America repeatedly, blowing a hole in a destroyer, the USS *Cole*, in the harbor at Yemen and destroying U.S. embassies in Kenya and Tanzania in 1998, Clinton had merely fired off impotent cruise missile strikes without any apparent follow-up. "It was clear that bin Laden felt emboldened and didn't feel threatened by the United States," Bush himself said after September 11.[39] Indeed, in a stream of messages sent from his lair in Afghanistan, the terrorist leader had mocked the Americans for retreating from conflict in Muslim lands since the 1993 debacle in Somalia. "After leaving Afghanistan the Muslim fighters headed for Somalia and prepared for a long battle thinking that the Americans were like the

Russians," bin Laden said in 1998, the year he announced his global jihad against "Jews and Crusaders." "The youth were surprised at the low morale of the American soldiers and realized, more than before, that the American soldier was a paper tiger and after a few blows ran in defeat. . . . The youth ceased from seeing America as a superpower."[40] (Still, the Bush administration was hardly blameless itself; it never explained why it did nothing to retaliate for eight months after an FBI report issued on January 26, 2001—six days after Bush's inauguration—conclusively tied the *Cole* bombing to al-Qaeda.)

Like their forebears at the beginning of the Cold War, the new hegemonists surrounding Bush also brazenly declared Washington's right to "preemptively" attack any country that threatened, especially those with weapons of mass destruction. The administration, still making short shrift of the views of U.S. allies, was cavalier about refining this doctrine at first. That led to a mini-revolt by Republican moderates, who feared it would turn America into an aggressor nation in the eyes of the world for the first time in its history. After all, Truman and Eisenhower had rejected preventive war for much the same reason. Even during the Cuban missile crisis—which posed a far greater threat than bin Laden—John F. Kennedy had worried about attacking Soviet installations in Cuba for fear of appearing the aggressor, like the Japanese on December 7, 1941. "It's a Pearl Harbor thing," Robert F. Kennedy had said, echoing Secretary of State Dean Rusk's worry that America would forever bear the "mark of Cain" if it drew first blood. The latter-day debate took on the same tone.[41] As one former official with the first Bush administration, who shared the centrist, cautious views of Powell, told me in 2002: "We're not talking about preemption in the way we talked about it in the Cold War," namely, a response to an imminent attack. "With Iraq, for example, we're talking about a premeditated attack. . . . I think preemption is the right doctrine for terrorism. But to bring the rogue states into it is a stretch." Another danger was that every country could decide it was a good idea—sort of the political equivalent of *Minority Report,* the Tom Cruise film in which futurist cops eliminate "future" wrongdoers at their whim.

The old debates of the Cold War era haunted the new debate between the hegemonists and the Clintonites/Powellites in another way. Vietnam was back. After the Gulf War victory George H. W. Bush had crowed, "We kicked the Vietnam syndrome for good." In fact, it continued to hover over nearly every military decision made in the post–Cold War era. Clinton had been a draft dodger, and the combination of that and his scandal-plagued presidency undercut his ability to use force. In Haiti, he meekly withdrew a ship when it met protesters at the dock; in Somalia, he quickly retreated after eighteen soldiers were killed in a failed mission in Mogadishu; and in Kosovo, as the impeachment debate was heating up, he felt he didn't have enough support in Congress during a critical period in October 1998 when he might have been able to impose NATO troops without a war.

In a different way, as we have seen, the same ghosts of Vietnam restrained Powell in the policy battles of the new administration. The peculiarities of Powell's psychological makeup—the Stimsonian internationalist burdened by Vietnam—made him ill equipped to counter this onslaught of hegemonists. He was now one of the "civilian leadership" whose mistakes in Vietnam he once lamented, and he was the nation's chief diplomat. ("His job is to talk them to death, and mine is to hit them over the head," Rumsfeld once said of Powell, according to a friend's recollection.) He knew too well the dangers of too much assertiveness of military power by civilians. The problem was that although he was a believer in American engagement in the world—in the Mideast, for example— American diplomacy often works best only when it is backed by the threat of force. But Powell's conservative view of the use of force left him internally conflicted. This strange admixture of optimistic internationalism and Vietnam-bitten caution made him especially vulnerable to the hegemonists' aggressive, unified worldview, and too often Powell ended up giving up the fight too easily on diplomatic intervention. On the issue of peacekeeping in the Balkans, for example, Powell sought to counter the conservatives' disposition to withdraw and quell European fears, saying, "We went together, and we'll come out together."[42] But his earlier counsel against intervention in the Balkans put him squarely on the fence on this issue. Powell admirers noted that for many years he kept a saying from Thucydides under the glass top of his Pentagon desk: "Of all the manifestations of power, restraint impresses men the most." Powell's critics, the hegemonists, saw that as a character flaw. The Rumsfeld crowd, said Kissinger later, was "trying to beat back the attitudes of the Vietnam generation that was focused on American imperfection and limitations."[43] That was code for the mindset of Colin Powell.

Rumsfeld's relentless drive to place Iraq at the top of America's agenda soon after the defeat of the Taliban was very much in line with this clash of ideologies. Confronting Saddam was far more about giving the world an object lesson—teaching the bad guys to fear U.S. power—than making a case that the Iraqi leader was linked to al-Qaeda or the war on terror. One reason was that after the shock of 9/11, the administration's number one nightmare was that a weapon of mass destruction might be used in a similar attack, and Saddam was believed to have them. But it was also simply because America had to do *something* dramatic to reassert itself. The hawks, once again, wanted to seize the opportunity to "be bold." One of Rumsfeld's confidants, a member of his Defense Policy Board, explained the thinking then, only weeks after the 9/11 attacks: "It will be very tough to get bin Laden in the rocky and mountainous terrain of Afghanistan. How do you send the message of strength as Ronald Reagan sent it, that we don't allow these things—you inflict damage."[44] And as the administration grappled with the pathology of the Arab world, a larger, neoconservative agenda began to assert itself: Now was the time to "kick over the apple cart" in the Mideast. Invading Iraq, transforming it into a democracy and U.S. ally, would in one bold stroke marginalize Saudi Arabia and its oil, force Riyadh to open up and discard its virulent brand of Islamism, do the same to Iran, and make Israel stronger.

As Bob Woodward records, it was Powell who again opposed taking on Iraq, and who feared overextension. "What the hell, what are these guys thinking about?" he asked, referring to Rumsfeld and Wolfowitz. "Any action needs public support. It's not just what the international coalition supports; it's what the American people want to support. The American people want us to do something about al-Qaeda."[45] Bush, wisely, held off on Iraq at first. But by early 2002 the hegemonists' views once again prevailed (though they were well disguised: one reason the administration had so much trouble justifying the shift to Iraq is that it could not admit to such a quasi-imperialist strategic vision). Powell, a loyal soldier and internally conflicted as ever, gamely went along.

But not surprisingly, it was mainly the moderate Republicans who had served in Vietnam along with Powell who came out publicly against a war on Iraq. They counseled caution, containment, and alliance building, much as the battle-wise Ike had resisted rollback of the Soviets and involvement in Southeast Asia during the French war in Indochina in the 1950s. "It is interesting to me that many of those who want to rush this country into war and think it would be so quick and easy don't know anything about war," Senator Chuck Hagel, a longtime Powell friend and fellow Vietnam vet, told me that summer as the debate heated up. "They come at it from an intellectual perspective versus having sat in jungles or foxholes and watched their friends get their heads blown off. I try to speak for those ghosts of the past a little bit." Hagel had a point. Cheney, Wolfowitz, and Perle all avoided Vietnam, and Bush was one of the "sons of the powerful" whom Powell, in his 1995 memoir, condemned as a group for managing "to wangle slots in Reserve and National Guard units during the war."[46] For their part these neoconservative "chicken hawks," as the Vietnam-era draft avoiders came to be called, saw the Iraq debate as a test case for whether the military (and its putative voices, such as Powell and Hagel) would finally outgrow their Vietnam-engendered fears.

The hegemonists' dominance in the new administration brought, in one sense, a dose of reality: It forced the world to acknowledge America's new overarching power. No longer would the United States pretend that it was just another chimpanzee. Few Europeans had appreciated the extent to which their relevance to Washington ended when the Cold War did. After the Cold War, George H. W. Bush and Clinton, both of them instinctive multilateralists, made a good show of pretending nothing had changed. But in fact everything had. In a broad strategic sense, when it came to military strength, there was no "concert of power" anymore; there was only a one-man band. NATO, even as it expanded as a political organization, became less relevant than ever to America's strategic considerations militarily. NATO was still useful—as it proved in the latter stages of the Afghan campaign—but as an outpost of American power rather than a partner to it.

These dissonant views of NATO accounted for much of the bad feeling across the Atlantic—recall Rumsfeld's post-9/11 snub of NATO—as the war on terror commenced. The Europeans learned during the war on terror what the Japanese learned in the Gulf War: The only thing vast economic power gives you is leverage in economics, unless the will or structure exists to turn it into something more. Europe can be a big dog at WTO talks and on issues such as antitrust, harrying giant U.S. multinationals including GE and Microsoft. But as Japan found out upon Saddam's invasion in 1990, global security is another matter. Tokyo proved during the Gulf War that it was not ready to be the new Rome of the Pacific Century. And European unity foundered over Iraq, as the EU's leading powers, Germany and France, sought to stop the überpower in its tracks. Rumsfeld's response was to dismiss Germany and France as the "old Europe," and to divide them from his more hawkish supporters in Eastern Europe. This blunt talk didn't help much as Rumsfeld also pressed the western Europeans to "specialize" their forces in areas such as biochemical weapons, airlift, and special operations forces so as to make themselves useful to America the global stabilizer. If America now faced the problem of how to behave on the world stage with too much power, Europe had to confront the fact that its rhetoric too often outstripped its lack of power.

## America Swings to the Right

All this provided the backdrop to the Bush administration's hard swing to the right as it took office—and many of the foreign-policy imbroglios that resulted later on. Upon assuming office, the new administration lost no time in beginning to retreat from nearly a century of American engagement in international institutions, including the arms control regimes of previous Republican administrations. Washington's main message to the world seemed to be: "Take dictation." Quite abruptly, without consulting either allies or Congress, the administration forswore the Kyoto treaty on global warming, a UN draft treaty banning illicit trade in small arms (on the grounds that it would infringe on U.S. citizens' "constitutional right to keep and bear arms"), an inspection regime for biological weapons; and, above all, the Anti-Ballistic-Missile Treaty. The demolition man in charge of making much of this happen was John Bolton, a leading antiglobalist pundit who, in fox-guarding-the-henhouse fashion, was made undersecretary of state for arms control. A year earlier, in a journal article, Bolton had written a call to arms to his fellow conservatives, saying, "The Globalists have been advancing while the Americanists have slept."[47] And, needless to say, the Bush team all but ignored the United Nations in the eight months before September 11. On Bush's mind, as always, were the mistakes of his father. As one of the president's senior aides put it to me, "If we're perceived to be driven by the UN and all these treaties, man, we're going to have trouble with the right the way his father did."[48] Complained one former senior Clintonite, "The deep philosophical underpinnings of what they're doing go back to Henry Cabot Lodge" —the conservative senator who almost single-handedly ensured the defeat of the League of Nations in 1920.[49]

True to the hegemonists' new program, the Bush administration also began setting unilateral priorities, declaring to their fellow Americans— and, quite incidentally, to the rest of the world—what was important and what was trivial. China would be, if not quite yet the new Soviet Union, then America's greatest emerging threat; it would be a "strategic competitor" rather than the "strategic partner" that the soft-minded Clintonites had tried to make it. (So intent were Bush officials on publicizing this realignment that in the early weeks of the administration they hastily arranged a useless Washington visit by Japan's lame-duck prime minister, Yoshiro Mori, and snubbed China's vice premier by putting his trip off.) The depleted Russia of Vladimir Putin would be put in its place, namely, that of a second-rate power. Inside the Pentagon, Rumsfeld began pushing for a wholesale redeployment of U.S. military resources from Europe to Asia, the better to contain China. In meetings with the military chiefs, Rumsfeld also "disparaged the policy of military 'engagement' with other nations as an outmoded relic of the Clinton years."[50] Mexico and Latin America would get a lot more attention than Clinton gave them, harking back to the deeper traditions the Bushies so revered, our nineteenth-century hemispheric concerns. Beyond that, the Bush team would stay out of the Mideast, seek to withdraw from the Balkans as early as possible, and spurn a half-decade of fairly successful nonproliferation talks with North Korea begun by Clinton.

Never mind that one of America's most stalwart allies, the heroic South Korean president Kim Dae Jung—who had made a remarkable journey from jailed dissident to one of the leading democrats of Asia—had staked his political career on opening up talks with the North, what he called his "sunshine policy." Or that negotiations with North Korea were the only way of containing proliferation of its nuclear and missile technology. As the Bush team saw it, North Korea was a key "rogue state," and later part of the "axis of evil." More important—though they never actually admitted this—the continued recalcitrance of the North's strange, somewhat comical leader, the pouf-haired Kim Jong Il, helped to justify the true centerpiece of the new Bush foreign policy: national missile defense (NMD). This was presented as a new strategic framework of defense that, in its grandiosity, was the truest giveaway to the Bush team's worldview and how starkly it contrasted with Clinton's. Still unproven as a technology, NMD was ostensibly meant as a way of deterring small rogue nations from paralyzing U.S. action abroad by threatening to fire off small numbers of nukes. That by itself was not a bad idea; even Clinton had signed on to it in the end, albeit typically halfheartedly.

But the Bush team embraced the untested NMD with an almost religious fervor, casting it as a broad new strategic way of thinking that would replace the deterrence theories that had kept the peace during fifty years of Cold War. They never explained how this squared with the idea that NMD was supposedly aimed at just small rogue states, and, not surprisingly, the notion was roundly derided by allies and rivals alike. The best explanation may be that NMD comported with the Bush team's overarching ideology. While it was technologically futuristic, its underlying concept was as old as human society, certainly as old as conservative thought; it was castle walls done over with guidance systems. NMD was, in other words, only the latest incarnation of the old American dream of apartness, and at the same time of total freedom of action. It had always been an us-versus-them world, and so it would continue to be. Missile defense, in turn, would be accompanied by a new blueprint that would leave the United States freer to develop and deploy new nuclear weapons against such rogue states as North Korea, Iran, Iraq, Syria, and Libya.[51]

The biggest headache, the Bush officials discovered, was in defining who was "us" and who was "them." As it turned out, few of the putative parties to this trumped-up conflict wanted to cooperate. If "them" was supposed to be China and rogue states such as North Korea, then the "us" —mainly America's European allies and Japan, the allies Bush had pledged to restore to their place of primacy—refused to sign on to this view. It wasn't like the Cold War or Gulf War at all. George W. Bush may have been leader of the most powerful country in the history of the world, and our Cold War allies were eager to continue to dwell under our defense umbrella and maintain broad-based ties. But what Bush could not do was impose an outdated alliance structure on a brand-new world order. There simply was no consensus abroad to treat Beijing or even Baghdad, Tehran, or Pyongyang as enemies. Even stalwart pro-American allies complained that the Bush administration was moving into what Christopher Patten, a leading British conservative, called "unilateral overdrive."

Things only grew more confusing after September 11. America had been struck, and while many people around the world quietly expressed an I-told-you-so satisfaction that the arrogant Americans had received their comeuppance, the Bush team was instantly and enormously success-ful in portraying the terror attacks as an assault on "civilization" and the U.S.-led global system, and in building a coalition to roll up al-Qaeda's networks worldwide. The worldwide wave of sympathy for America was not simply altruistic. It was also a recognition, at least among foreign gov-ernments, that a weakened America means a weakened world order. Here too the Bush team found that their ideology no longer squared with real-ity. Suddenly the "us" of the antiterror alliance included China and Rus-sia, while the "them" described old friends like Saudi Arabia, which had pursued its own brand of Islamic fundamentalism as a state ideology (and where fifteen of the nineteen September 11 hijackers originated).

Those on Bush's side now also seemed to include the United Nations, which was doing the main work of building up the new central govern-ment of Afghanistan that Bush was so intent on seeing succeed. Strangest of all, America's main ally in the war on terror turned out to be the inter-national community, which the Bush team had once declared to be "illusory." Suddenly the Bush administration seemed to need this mushy liberal entity to flesh out the president's proudest statement of policy: the "Bush Doctrine," the idea that every nation must take sides between America and "a mighty coalition of civilized nations" (as Bush liked to call the international community), on one hand, or the terrorists and their rogue hosts, on the other.[52]

For someone of the president's Manichean sense of right and wrong and powerful religious faith—not to mention unilateralist instincts—the Bush Doctrine came naturally. It also seemed to express the rage, grief, and grim resolve that many Americans were feeling right after September 11. Bush's message to the world, first delivered in a speech to the nation on September 20, 2001, was this: "Either you are with us, or you are with the terrorists." Either you stand with civilization and good (us), or you stand with barbarism and evil (them). Choose. And those nations that choose wrongly, beware. Bush was, to say the least, less than deft with the English language—and almost all his statements were written for him—but one of his chief advisors says that he came up with the Bush Doctrine himself. Powell and Condoleezza Rice had worked out the language of his speech from the Oval Office, and the speechwriters had written it, but "then the president looked at it, and he's the one who came up with the very straightforward line . . . that's how the Bush Doctrine was born."[53] As Bush later put it, "I think moral clarity is important."[54]

But because of all the ideological baggage the Bush team carried into the war on terror, the president ended up frittering away much of the goodwill he had started out with after September 11. For much of the first year of the war on terror the Bush Doctrine scarcely evolved beyond its original bare-bones formulation. The president kept using the doctrine to justify new calls to action: for example, he asserted that Saddam and al-Qaeda had become allies of convenience. But the "who-is-us?" problem came back to haunt him. What did it mean to be with the United States in the war on terror? Was this a temporary alliance, the "multiple coalitions" the administration vaguely referred to at the start, or did it mean something more? And why were so many of those who were included, in Europe and Asia, griping that they didn't feel a part of any larger cause?

Attempts by Powell's lonely band of moderates to push a more all-embracing global agenda consistently faltered. A speech in the spring of 2002 by Haass calling for a new, suspiciously Clintonesque "doctrine of integration"—its goal, as Haass put it, is "to integrate other countries and organizations into arrangements that will sustain a world consistent with U.S. interests and values"—sank quickly out of sight.[55] As Deputy Secretary of State Richard Armitage, another Powellite, admitted at a congressional hearing that same year, "We are not as far along in a public diplomacy strategy as we ought to be."[56]

The problem, of course—and the theme of this book— was that there was a disconnect between the kind of world order the Bush hegemonists wanted to impose and the one they were handed in the war on terror. The world they wanted to impose was one in which America would have its way, and America's raw might would make the difference. The world they were handed was one in which the most profound cooperation among nations was necessary to snare the terror groups in our midst. As his first anniversary as president approached, there were some signs that Bush had begun to understand that the world he thought he was dealing with, and the one he had been saddled with, were not quite the same. Somewhat schizophrenically, the president began sounding more and more Wilsonian in tone, talking of the common global struggle. As he said at the 2002 West Point graduation, in one of the defining speeches of his presidency, "We have our best chance since the rise of the nation-state in the seventeenth century to build a world where the great powers compete in peace instead of prepare for war. . . . We have a great opportunity to extend a just peace, by replacing poverty, repression, and resentment around the world with hope of a better day." But such speeches were made in a policy vacuum—there was still no real "building" going on, other than of the U.S. military—and that rendered his unilateralist moralism all the more grating on foreign ears. For example, the nations that were part of the global system were all too eager to resume negotiations on nonproliferation agreements to stem the production of nuclear, biological, or chemical weapons material. But although such accords seemed a more direct way of stopping future terror acts than missile defense, the Bush administration, treaty-averse as ever, showed little interest in pushing for them. Instead, it announced in the middle of the war that it was withdrawing unilaterally from the ABM treaty. And Bush continued to describe himself as a "cold-eyed realist."[57]

In fact, the president couldn't seem to decide which worldview he embraced. The hegemonists were dominant, and the overall tilt of his administration remained toward disengagement except in the use of military force. Bush wanted to go on the offense against terror, yet he didn't recognize how valuable a good-will offensive might be. So as the administration kept running into new crises it kept calling on Powell to come to the rescue. When China forced a U.S. surveillance plane to land in April 2001 and detained its crew for eleven days—and Bush, at first, hawkishly demanded they be released or else—it was Powell who concocted a salving letter of near-apology and restored relations. When Bush, prodded by hard-line pro-Israel hawks in his administration, in June 2002 dropped a previous demand to Israeli prime minister Ariel Sharon to withdraw from the Palestinian territories and insisted on Yasir Arafat's ouster—effectively destroying any prospect of peace talks—it was Powell who rescued a shred of U.S. credibility by setting up a "quartet" (the United States, the European Union, Russia, and the UN) to push for political change in the territories. In the end, in other words, Powell's pragmatism often won, but only after his right-wing opponents had staked out hard lines that the administration later had to retreat from. The result was an image of vacillation and a kind of ideological paralysis. The president was trying to lead a global fight that cried out for deep U.S. engagement in the global system. But, held back by the ideological hard-liners in his administration—and, perhaps, his own stubbornness—he barely acknowledged the global system he was ostensibly fighting for. Even after the attacks, when it became apparent (to everyone but the White House, it seemed) that the enmities between the Israelis and Palestinians and between the Indians and Pakistanis would complicate the war on terror, giving radical Islamists a case for saying the West was at war with Islam, the Bush administration was dragged heels first into mediating these conflicts. This was especially true of Afghanistan, about which he had talked so promisingly to Joe Biden. Bush invoked the Marshall Plan in declaring that America will help Afghanistan to develop a stable, free government, an effective education system, and a viable economy. But behind the scenes, the administration's ideologues acted to minimize U.S. involvement. In the middle of all this squalling Bush often seemed genuinely torn. In some ways the president was blindsided by the titanic struggle of world-views in his administration. Bush "came into office not knowing much about foreign policy, seeing the world in pretty simple terms," said Hagel. "I don't think he ever intended to have a big foreign policy debate in his party, but September eleventh forced it upon him."[58]

Bush, in other words, kept getting pulled back into the international system he had spurned and caught up in the "crisis of the day." The president who sought "moral clarity" found himself steeped in the murkiest of circumstances with no exit strategy in sight: keeping a lid on Afghanistan, managing the ever-festering India-Pakistan conflict, moving to mediate in the Mideast (even proposing, as Clinton had, to employ the CIA as monitors on the ground), and planning for a full-scale nation-building effort in post-Saddam Iraq. Condoleezza Rice and even hard-liners such as Cheney began regularly invoking the term "international community" —which if they still considered it illusory, was at least a useful illusion—in an effort to win support in the campaign against Iraq. By late 2002 Bush himself started to use the phrase in a telling way; in his national security strategy, he adapted the line from his West Point speech about building a new world order. Only instead of "*We* have the best chance to build . . . ," he now said: "*The international community* has the best chance since the rise of the nation-state in the seventeenth century to build a world where great powers compete in peace instead of continually preparing for war."[59]

But by then the international community had had just about enough of George W. Bush. A year and a half into his tenure, the president experienced something of an epiphany on the nature of the global system he had spurned. It was the summer of 2002, and Bush was getting savaged in foreign capitals and the world's media over his administration's go-it-alone-style, which even one of his supporters, conservative Yale historian John Lewis Gaddis, likened to that of "a sullen, pouting, oblivious and overmuscled teenager."[60] Anti-Americanism had grown rampant world-wide, especially as Bush began hinting that he would destroy Saddam

Hussein's regime, unilaterally if necessary. For the Europeans especially, there was a sense that the Bush administration was recklessly casting aside the multilateral global system they had embraced as a lifeline after a long and bloody history of conflict. Other nations believed Bush and his team were, in a strategic sense, taking the world in precisely the wrong direction, and that America's awesome power was in the hands of dangerous zealots. "Americans have no idea how much animosity there is toward them," former Israeli peace negotiator Uri Savir told me around that time. "Never has there been a country with so much goodwill that is perceived in the world with such bad will. That hostility is much more dangerous than all the other threats put together."[61] Most worrisome to Bush was that even domestic polls showed that most Americans opposed a unilateral war. They wanted allies, and they wanted him to go through the UN.

So at a mid-August meeting at his Crawford ranch, Bush seized on an idea initially put forward by Powell, his oft-slighted secretary of state. The idea was to issue a muscular challenge to the UN: to make itself "relevant" by insisting on the implementation of its own resolutions calling on Saddam to disarm, or to become "another League of Nations" and stand aside while America acts to secure global peace.

On September 12, 2002, Bush delivered a tough but rousing speech to the UN that surprised most of his critics with its appeal to multilateralism. Bush committed himself to gaining some degree of consensus among the "permanent five" members of the UN Security Council before attacking Iraq. It was a deft move politically, a way of satisfying both his conservative base and his moderate critics (the speech immediately silenced his Democratic critics, having robbed them of their chief argument, that he wasn't seeking international consensus). It was the clearest evidence to date that Bush had rethought his practice of foreign-policy-by-diktat. And, for the moment, it was Powell's most signal victory over the hegemonists in the struggle for the president's heart and mind. "I think some of the people around [Bush] wanted that speech to be: 'You guys at the UN have screwed up. You're weak-kneed. We have to do it ourselves.' But Bush didn't do that," noted the official from the first Bush administration whom I quoted earlier.

At the same time, however, it was clear Bush's commitment to the UN wasn't very deep. And months of uncompromising rhetoric from the Bush team about "regime change" in Iraq had cost Washington a lot of credibility. After slighting the UN, NATO, and international law for a year, Bush now needed the UN, NATO, and international law on his side. But he had a mountain of mistrust to overcome. Following Bush's speech, two months of wrangling ensued in the UN Security Council over how tough to make a resolution demanding that Saddam Hussein reveal his programs to build weapons of mass destruction. The biggest fear among the French and others was that the United States was simply looking for a "hidden trigger"—to use the slightest sign of noncompliance by Saddam as an excuse to invade Iraq. Even UN secretary-general Kofi Annan conceded the Security Council fight was really a proxy war, waged by France, Russia, and China, on one hand, and the Bush team, on the other, over the larger question of how a nearly omnipotent America was behaving, and the rules of the global game. As Annan put it after a 15–0 vote in which Washington conceded it would not attack until the Security Council could consider the results of UN weapons inspections, "I think [the French] feel they have struck a blow for international law and [the primacy of] the Security Council."[62] UN negotiations finally collapsed over this issue in March 2003, and Bush went to war virtually alone.

Yet after citing Saddam for defiance of the Security Council, Bush could not so easily defy the will of the Security Council himself in deciding to go to war. Even in justifying war he invoked UN resolutions, seeking to appease world and U.S. opinion, and fearing a new wave of anti-American hatred (and terror acts). Meanwhile, the hardheaded realists in his administration—including the president himself—began to focus more on the neoconservative (and Wilsonian) agenda of democracy promotion. They saw democracy—an opportunity for self-expression—as the only long-term solution to the endless spiral of anger and quashed hopes that autocracy has brought to the Arab world.

Bush, to his last day as president, would probably never admit that he was evolving. Certainly he would never admit that perhaps Bill Clinton, for all his very real mistakes, had not been so far off the mark as the new president had thought, at least when it came to nation building and acknowledging the international system. If, as the saying goes, a conservative is a liberal who's been mugged, then it is equally true that a liberal internationalist can sometimes be a conservative who's been terrorized.

## Finding a Middle Path

To recap, the real problem that the Bush administration faced in its early years was that both views of the world—that of the Clinton/Powell moderates, on one hand, and that of the hegemonists, on the other—were right. On one hand, the strong assertion of U.S. power was necessary, as I have suggested. On the other, the hegemonist view of the world tended to give short shrift to the tools of an entire global system. Ken Adelman was correct in saying that consensus was hard, and the disparity in power certainly argued for forthright U.S. leadership, as the hegemonists maintained. But in the global system the Bush team was given responsibility for, there was no way around working toward consensus on broad strategic goals such as the war on terror or Iraq. There needed to be a middle path through the Permanent Quagmire.

Perhaps nothing demonstrated the need for a middle path more than the challenge posed to America and the international community by the threat of weapons of mass destruction in the era of terror. If there was any single long-term threat that animated the Bush team, it was that we now live in an era when zealots who value "death over life," as Bush put it, and hate America and Western civilization will only find it easier to obtain and use such weapons. For many years to come, the main threat to Americans will not be nuclear-tipped ICBMs launched from a rogue state that knows it will face massive retaliation; it will more likely be a nuclear or biological or chemical weapon loaded into a trunk, boat, or truck by a small number of hate-filled, "superempowered" people who are not impressed by deterrence theory and lack a "return address." Missile defense won't work here, and a beefed-up homeland defense will only marginally improve our ability to stop them before they are used.

It was this threat that drove the campaign against Saddam Hussein, for example. The Bush team believed that Iraq's relentless attempts to obtain weapons of mass destruction were proof of the uselessness of arms control. "We cannot put our faith in the word of tyrants who solemnly sign nonproliferation treaties and then systemically break them," Bush said in his West Point speech. "The era of arms control is dead," said a senior official. The Bush team believed the only way of ridding the world of these threats was instead to "devalue" such weapons by aggressively taking on states that pursued them. This was a major reason why Iraq so quickly became the focus after Afghanistan, senior sources in the administration say. It was less because of any alleged ties to al-Qaeda than the demonstration effect to other would-be nuclear powers like North Korea and Iran that obtaining weapons of mass destruction would not deter America; on the contrary, it would only invite a devastating response.

The problem was that at about the same time, the administration was confronted with the news that North Korea was secretly building its own nuclear weapons. At a meeting in Pyongyang on October 4, 2002, a senior North Korean official stunned U.S. envoy James Kelly by confirming a U.S. allegation that North Korea was running a uranium enrichment program for developing nuclear weapons, in violation of an accord signed with the Clinton administration eight years before that bound Pyongyang to become nuclear free. Yet the administration was flummoxed about what to do. Threatening war on the Korean peninsula—where Kim kept a 950,000-man army and batteries of missiles just twenty miles from Seoul —was all but unthinkable. Bush tried to keep the news secret—an act of hypocrisy that was widely noted, since at the same moment he was suppressing proof of Kim's recalcitrance, he was desperately trying to marshal evidence that Saddam was doing the same thing. But the news leaked anyway.

The lesson other countries took away from this was hardly the "devaluation" of nuclear weapons. On the contrary: Kim Jong Il had showed that in an environment in which arms control treaties are no longer valid, the Americans don't respect borders, and force rules rather than international law, other countries had better develop their own arms programs quickly and secretly, because that is the only approach that strikes fear into the Americans. The Bush hawks also derided a Clinton-era program designed to pressure North Korea to stop trying to make nuclear weapons in exchange for billions in aid and a civilian nuclear reactor, which the West and Japan would provide. They refused to negotiate. Instead they tried containment and sanctions. The threat of once again being economically cut off angered North Korea, which suggested it might start exporting nuclear and missile technology to other countries.[63]

By declaring he would neither attack nor negotiate, Bush quickly found himself without options. He too would have to play the Clinton game of offering carrots such as food aid as an incentive to get the North Korean dictator to cooperate. The hawks said that the secret North Korean program demonstrated that Kim Jong Il was only extorting the West and couldn't be trusted, and it made the argument for missile defense more powerful. But had the Clinton program not been in place, Pyongyang might have built dozens of plutonium-fueled nuclear weapons by the time the Bush administration came to power. More important, Washington knew it would need the cooperation of surrounding powers, China, Japan, and South Korea, as well as UN sanctions, to pressure Pyongyang. Yet few of the unilateralists in the Bush administration noted the inconsistency: How can you behave unilaterally in one part of the world, Iraq, and then expect full multilateral cooperation in another?

Similarly, as they threatened to invade Iraq, the Bush hegemonists—principally Cheney and Rumsfeld—belittled anew the Clinton administration's efforts to keep Saddam Hussein "in a box" with UN-agreed economic sanctions and UN inspections. Yet they ignored the fact that whatever danger Saddam posed now, the sanctions and inspections had stopped Iraq from becoming a nuclear power for a decade, making it possible to take him on now.

What is my point? That taking a hard-edged approach to rogue states does not negate other approaches, in particular mediation and arms control. All are useful, all can be used, and it is silly and dangerous to let ideology get in the way of that. Bush administration hawks suggested that the secret nuclear programs of Kim and Saddam proved that nonproliferation treaties were, as Hobbes said, "but words." But most countries are not rogues such as Iraq and North Korea; most will observe treaties if others do, especially the United States. And it is clearly in the vital national interest of the United States to reduce, by whatever means possible, the number of weapons of mass destruction proliferating around the world, even in countries that we don't necessarily consider a direct threat, such as Brazil or the Ukraine (where loose controls could prevent containment). That means reducing—or at least holding in place—the number of states that produce them, and curbing the rest. There were, as the Bush administration took office, a whole slew of useful if flawed tools for helping to accomplish the task of cutting back weapons of mass destruction, all of them regimes launched by the United States, all of them regimes that would tend to lock in U.S. military superiority. Among these tools were the Nuclear Non-proliferation Treaty—under which 188 countries agreed to forgo pursuit of nuclear weapons, including technologically ready states such as South Africa and Brazil—the Comprehensive Test Ban Treaty, the Nuclear Suppliers Group, and the Chemical Weapons Treaty. And yet the Bush administration, pursuing its old agenda against sovereignty-crimping treaties much as it continued to resist the nation building that would give terrorists fewer hiding places, discarded most of these tools.

Both power and cooperation, a policy of applying coercive might and muddling through, were necessary. The key again was getting the *details* of the mix right. If the Clintonites veered too far in the direction of optimism about globalization and the value of soft power, the Bush pendulum swung too far back in the other direction, toward walled-off disengagement and the primacy of hard power. The Bush hegemonists, trying to insert a new dose of reality into great-power relationships, sought a division of labor with our European allies—and something like that isn't a bad idea, as we will discuss further—but the unilateralists who dominated policy did little to make this palatable diplomatically. Yet it is precisely because American power is so dominant that Americans must bend over backward to play down, rather than harp on, the disparities. As I have argued in the preceding pages, this was not just a matter of being nice or doing "coalitions for coalitions' sake," as some internal critics of Powell's lonely multilateralist efforts contended. If the Europeans no longer played as much of a part in America's military planning, they were an essential ally in the strategy of institutional envelopment, co-opting the Chinas and Russias into the international system. And if the Bush team genuinely wanted to see a global division of labor that worked, it couldn't expect the Europeans and others to blindly sign on to peacekeeping and nation building without being consulted on overall strategy beforehand. Both our traditional allies, including France, and our putative future rivals, such as China, fear the prospect of falling so far behind the überpower that they appear as mere "ants" to us from on high, as one Washington commentator put it. This is precisely the moment for America to be magnanimous: The payoff in goodwill could be priceless.

Which way these sentiments will ultimately go hangs very much in the balance. "This is a historically defining moment," one European diplomat told me. "The decisive question is how America will manage its dominance."[64] Anti-American elements within countries such as China are even now studying the ways of "asymmetric warfare" to determine how best to take America on, even as Beijing itself is resisting a military buildup to challenge American hegemony. To avoid coming out on the wrong side of history—and engendering anti-American alliance building—we Americans must find the proper balance between reassuring the world of our nation's essential benign nature and yet not encouraging the idea that we've gone "soft" or will withdraw, and warning the world that we will permit no other power to challenge us and yet not being overbearing about it. This is a task of consummate diplomacy that will require, Washington analyst Andrew Krepinevich says, "the virtuosity of a Bismarck to pull it off."[65]

Much of the rest of this book will be about how to find this middle path. Yes, American hegemony is a fact. It is even a historically lucky fact: The world, in truth, has never enjoyed such a benign "imperium." And yes, American hegemony is necessary, as a kind of exoskeleton of hard power that keeps the international system together. But to embrace power alone as a worldview is far too simplistic. The world the hegemonists and realists describe as a mushy fantasy world—the world of the international community, of norms, of values—is now real. While it doesn't follow that the world they thought they were living in—the world defined by hard power—is fantasy, this view does need to be drastically modified, as we will see in later chapters.

At the time of this writing, the hegemonists were still in the ascendancy in Washington, and the Bush administration was only painstakingly, bit by bit, pulled into the international system that many of its principals refused to acknowledge in full. Perhaps the main reason the administration resisted change was that its hard-edged policies continued to be popular with the American people. If the Bush hegemonists were to change their outlook, Americans would have to as well. But to do so is no simple thing: Americans first must change their own frame of reference. Above all, they needed to understand that it's no longer "us" on one hand and the rest of the world on the other, as it has been for most of our two and a quarter centuries of existence. To understand why that needs to change—and how very difficult it will be—requires a journey into the heart of American exceptionalism.

# 2

# The American Temptation

Our detached and distant situation invites us to take a different course.

George Washington, Farewell Address, September 17, 1796

SHORTLY AFTER September 11, General Richard Myers was asked at a congressional hearing why the mightiest military in history had failed to protect the heart of American power from a band of men brandishing box cutters. Why hadn't he "scrambled," or launched, fighter planes? In those early, shell-shocked days, before the spin set in, the incoming chairman of the Joint Chiefs had no ready reply but the unvarnished truth. "We're pretty good if the threat is coming from outside," Myers said. "We're not so good if it's coming in from inside."

The fact that at this late date, in the age of globalization and a borderless world, many Americans still believe threats are divisible into those that are "outside" and those that are "inside" says a lot about the American sensibility. The historian John Lewis Gaddis points out that few other nations have had to worry so little about "homeland security" for as long as the United States.[1] After all, before September 11 the country had not suffered a foreign attack on continental soil since the War of 1812. Other nations, such as Britain, have long accommodated themselves to domestic surveillance with agencies like MI5, because of the infiltration of terrorists. America is just getting started on this very troubling road. It is this confusion that is at the heart of the divisions in America's intelligence community, long neglected but now critical to the war on terror. The old clash of interests between the CIA, since 1947 responsible for the outside, and the FBI, our fabled crime stopper at home, had been getting ever more aggravated in the post–Cold War period. The CIA began moving into the FBI's traditional bailiwick as crime grew more transnational, involving drugs and the proliferation of weapons of mass destruction. As the terror era began, the FBI began elbowing into the CIA's territory, "running" agents overseas in response to the bombings of the Khobar Towers in Saudi Arabia in 1996, which killed nineteen American military personnel, and the USS *Cole*. But these mutual efforts barely improved communications, and the two agencies seemed to feel little urgency about doing so—until 9/11.

Even now, the idea that borders don't mean much anymore is not an easy idea for Americans to stomach. Bill Clinton, the "globalization president," was constantly harping on this. "There is no longer a clear division between what is foreign and what is domestic," he said at his first inaugural back in 1993, and reiterated the point in his final foreign-policy address in 2000. But Clinton himself didn't seem to fully appreciate what that meant. As we saw in the last chapter, Clinton had a too-optimistic view of the globalizing effects of post–Cold War prosperity; he was careless in defending Americans against a threat that had already crossed that line between things foreign and domestic, and which was about to erupt in our faces. Bush had a crash course in the same reality eight months into his tenure, but his harsh, hands-off view of the global system that Clinton put so much stock in meant he had to be dragged slowly into understanding it, just as he had to be pulled, inch by inch, into nation-building in Afghanistan.

Why all this trouble telling the inside from the outside? Because for most of American history, we have thought of the rest of the world as "outside." We have grown used to that. One of the nation's founding myths, after all, is that of exceptionalism, the idea that America is an exception in the long history of nations, a place apart in spirit and physical reality, protected by its broad oceans, cherishing its uniqueness as a country that was founded on a set of universal principles rather than ethnic, racial, or tribal unity (our WASP founding fathers aside). This attitude is the wellspring behind the thinking of the Bush hegemonists. It is enshrined in our Constitution and evident in the sovereign pride we take in that defining document. It is an attitude that is so much a part of our national character that it will never quite go away. But as I will argue in the pages to follow, American exceptionalism needs some serious rethinking. It is time we take the borderless world seriously and, more, that we accept that it has fundamentally altered our national self-identity.

The problem is not so much that globalization and the Information Age have made the world so interconnected. Most Americans understand that. What many Americans haven't come to grips with is that this world system is *their* system. For a century now we have built a global order without quite comprehending what we were doing, bit by bit, era by era, all the while listing homeward, like a guest at a party who's yearning for an excuse to leave politely. But it is our party. Every major international institution—the UN, the World Bank and International Monetary Fund, the trade "rounds" that led to the WTO, NATO—was literally made in America. The open highways and byways of this system, of markets and trade rules, international standards for human rights, and even democracy, are largely American-influenced and secured by American power. And while we would not design it quite this way now—the alphabet soup of agencies from the UN to the World Bank needs to be pared down, for example— taken together, all this institution building has amounted to a workable international system that the rest of the world embraces. This central truth of our times is extraordinarily hard for Americans to absorb because it means allowing the rest of humanity to partake of our sense of uniqueness —which in turn means accepting that we are no longer so unique.

But to understand how this international system came about and why it is still so difficult for us as a nation to reckon with it psychologically, we must understand our history a little better.

## An Evolving Self-Image

Exceptionalism goes back to the very beginnings of our idealized Republic, which was conceived as an apotheosis of the best ideas coming out of the European Enlightenment. "We have it in our power to begin the world again," Thomas Paine wrote in "Common Sense" in 1776; the sentiment (as well as the phrase) became a favorite quote of a number of presidents, especially Ronald Reagan. The implication, of course, is that we would have to leave the bad Old World and all its corrupting influences behind to achieve this. Washington's farewell plea for insularity in 1796, Jefferson's warning against entangling alliances, John Winthrop's famous image of America as the "city on the hill"—all these hopes sprang from the fact that we had a national life of our own, gloriously isolated from Europe and Asia, lording over our hemisphere. We treasured our founding ideals, unencumbered individual and national freedom. We had a lovely continent of our own in which to practice them. We also had the oceanic distance to make sure that our continent and the freedoms it represented stayed ours. Were we a nation of immigrants? Yes. But here immigrants instantly became "Americans" (at least they used to). We were a secular chosen people. We possessed a Manifest Destiny and had all the forces of history—geographic, moral, political—converging on our side. America was unlike all other nations on earth, and unlike any that had ever existed before.

And in the early years of the Republic, as we congealed as a nation and piled triumph upon triumph—the Louisiana Purchase; the annexation of Florida, Texas, California, Oregon, and other territories; the post–Civil War "new birth of freedom"; victory in the Spanish-American War—our national self-confidence only grew. By the late nineteenth century, without even trying, we were already the largest economy in the world. All this imbued our exceptionalism with palpable reality. Our success in building a continental empire only fed into the certainty that we could act with total freedom of action. "Not a place upon earth might be so happy as America," Paine wrote. "Her situation is remote from all the wrangling world, and she has nothing to do but to trade with them."[2] Even during times of domestic upheaval, Americans felt all but immune from the world, at least until the nuclear age. As Abraham Lincoln said in 1837, an era of violent sectionalism when the national debate over slavery was heating up, "Whence shall we expect the approach of danger? Shall some transatlantic giant step the earth and crush us at a blow? Never! All the armies of Europe and Asia could not by force take a drink from the Ohio River or make a track on the Blue Ridge in the trial of a thousand years. If destruction be our lot we must ourselves be its author and finisher."[3]

Not that Americans were isolated from the world. From the earliest years of the Republic, Americans were heavily engaged overseas in one fashion or another, whether it was dickering with Napoleonic France or fending off the British imperium, fighting the Barbary Wars, forcing Japan to trade through "gunboat diplomacy" in the mid-nineteenth century, or opening our borders to vast trade flows from the Old World. Nonetheless, we remained convinced that we were different, both conceptually and geographically, from every other great power in history. Draw a line from the nation's radiant early history, through U.S. dominance after World War II and the triumph over the Soviets during the Cold War, and up through the current period—America's reign as military and economic overlord—and you begin to understand why the Bush administration's unilateralist confidence has deep roots in the American sensibility.

Exceptionalism has shaped our national psyche in profound ways. It is an American creed that our leaders never tire of invoking and that transcends party lines, the endless debates between conservatives and liberals that, in various forms, have shaped our domestic politics. From George Washington to Bill Clinton and George W. Bush, every American president has invoked our American specialness in speeches. The Romans and the Spaniards, the French and the British swept through the world from their tiny home territories seeking markets, land, and booty. They created heroes that were a measure of their imperialism: Odysseus, Julius Caesar, Cortes, Napoleon, and Churchill. Some, such as Britain, were more civilizing empires than others, but all seized territory mercilessly, treated their occupied subjects harshly. Our earliest heroes were farmers and flinty nativists—Washington, Jefferson, Lincoln—men who, ultimately, only wanted to patch together a more perfect union and be left largely alone. True, we were imperialists to a degree. We conquered our own continent, often brutally, and declared a dominion over the Western Hemisphere under the Monroe Doctrine in order to fend off the Europeans. But few Americans, even today, have been comfortable viewing themselves as imperialist; Americans, in the popular self-image that has flourished since the Founders, have never had any ambition but to maximize freedom, secure the region, and go home.

I remember back in the summer of 1991, when I was on a reporting assignment in Iraq just after the Gulf War, a fellow journalist, a Briton, summed it up nicely as we watched American officials roaming around Baghdad: "The British, in their day, walked the earth as if they owned it. The Americans walk the earth as if they couldn't care less who owned it." When he said it, I felt a surge of pride. Yes, that was exactly what it meant to be American. In the twentieth century, the antihero became the emblem of our national greatness because he, in his own way, embodied the same devil-may-care attitude. For Americans, Humphrey Bogart as the detached, ironic Rick in the brilliant *Casablanca*—"There are some sections of New York, Major, I wouldn't advise the Germans to invade"— will always trump David Niven as the prim, take-charge British legation chief in that mediocre drama of Western imperialism, *55 Days at Peking*. And Rick certainly had no intention of getting yanked into someone else's fight unless his vital interests—and ultimately his values—were in dire jeopardy. Then, and only then, did the hero part of the antihero take over. Like Rick, we have always thought there was something *just not right* about cosmopolitanism; the rest of the world, after all, is what most of our ancestors fled. George W. Bush's "trademark smirk" at the United Nations in September 2002 was all too typically American.

This attitude is not the same as isolationism, but the isolationist tendencies that have occasionally cropped up in American history are rooted in this exceptionalism. Up until the day before Pearl Harbor, the small but powerful America First movement was thriving, and numerous senators and congressmen, most of them Republican, were proud isolationists. But on December 7, 1941, almost all of them scurried into the woodwork, and since then no American politician has been able to embrace anything resembling isolationism publicly and be elected to national office. Indeed, today's Republicans typically deny their party is or ever was isolationist, only unilateralist.[4] Yet for the purposes of this discussion it doesn't really matter. Unilateralism and isolationism both spring from the same exceptionalist mistrust about the rest of the world—especially Europe, about which George Washington warned: "Why, by interweaving our destiny with that of any part of Europe, entangle our peace and prosperity in the toils of European ambition, rivalship, interest, humor, or caprice?" The outside world, in other words, would only contaminate and corrupt our grand American experiment. This is still American scripture, cited by our fundamentalists, such as Pat Buchanan and John Bolton, the Jeffersonian libertarian whom we met briefly in the last chapter as a senior ideologue in the Bush administration. If unilateralism is more politically acceptable today, like isolationism it doesn't accept encumbrances on our hallowed sovereignty.

Even today the spore of isolationism, feeding on our exceptionalism, remains very much alive in our national life. During the Cold War, turning back the communist threat and nuclear peril meant we had to be out there, engaged in the world, and when a lone internationalist GOP senator, Arthur Vandenberg, famously crossed the aisle in 1946 to support the Truman Doctrine, leaving his archconservative (and relatively isolationist) colleague Robert Taft behind, it was the start of a new internationalist consensus in Washington. But over the ensuing decades the conservatives never liked this degree of engagement, and again they knew they stood on solid ground with the American people. If our broad oceans no longer protected us during the days of nuclear brinksmanship, we still thought of the threat as "out there," coming from the sky and across the sea—from an alien, less perfect world.

Then the Cold War ended, and for eight years we heard Bill Clinton's gospel of globalization. Clinton knew he had to work hard to justify U.S. engagement overseas to an ever-skeptical American public, which was aware that America no longer faced a major geopolitical challenge and which felt the pent-up yearning to return home that had been thwarted at the end of World War II. So he drew on the "It's the economy, stupid" thesis that got him elected. In his first term, touting exports and jobs growth, Clinton turned U.S. ambassadors into virtual account executives for U.S. multinationals. They would now justify their paychecks by drumming up contracts. In Malaysia, Ambassador John Stern Wolf, a career diplomat, became a "one-man marketing organization," one American CEO told me at the time, landing multimillion-dollar contracts for McDonnell Douglas and General Electric. Walter Mondale, the former vice president, spent much of his two-year tenure as ambassador to Japan plugging for Motorola. Commerce secretary Ron Brown, a close Clinton crony, transformed his backwater agency into a policy dynamo with trade-mission-a-month headlines, and even Secretary of State Warren Christopher declared that global economics was at the top of his foreign-policy agenda. Clinton's combative first-term trade representative, Mickey Kantor, said he wasn't interested in free-trade "theology" and declared that Americans would now behave like the mercantilist Europeans. "For years we have allowed our workers to be hurt and our companies to be left out because we wouldn't pick up the phone and ask for the order. Why shouldn't we?" he explained.[5] But the idea that we should suddenly start behaving like the rest of the world didn't sit well with Americans. In any case, the policy never really produced many jobs—the rules of economics, defined by national investment and savings, still governed—and after Ron Brown was killed on one trade mission too many, crashing in the foggy mountains of Croatia, the new approach petered out. Very few people missed it.

It should have been no surprise to anyone, then, that traditional American exceptionalism came roaring back in January 2001, with the administration of George W. Bush. It took the form this time of a strident unilateralism that, because of the supremacy of American power, could act freely, and of a desire for disengagement. George W. Bush, his conservative impulses unchecked by the need for Cold War engagement, sought to shrink America's presence abroad to a more manageable size. Until September 11, when things got confusing.

## The Grand Shift

Given the persistence of our irrepressible exceptionalism—this national psychohistory, if you will—it may seem strange that a country such as America could ever become engaged enough in the world to build an entire global system. How was it that a people whose natural instinct is to remain apart managed to muster the willpower and sustained application to construct a new world order? This seems a paradox on its face, but it may not be: The same righteousness and self-confidence that fuels our exceptionalism makes us convinced that our way is the right one and that everybody would be better off embracing it.

Yet it was still a long road from believing in our righteousness and seeking to impose it on others. Scholars such as Walter McDougall and John Mearsheimer have argued that America's conduct of foreign policy in the nineteenth century had little to do with exceptionalism or values at all; it was mainly about playing realist power politics with the larger European countries. Indeed, for most of America's first century or so of existence, the desire to see American values spread abroad amounted to cautious well-wishing.[6] "This ball of liberty," Thomas Jefferson wrote hopefully after Independence, "is now so well in motion that it will roll around the globe."[7] "America does not go in search of monsters to destroy," John Quincy Adams said in the classic formulation of America's fare-thee-well detachment. "She is the well-wisher to the freedom and independence of all. She is the champion only of her own. . . . She well knows that by once enlisting under other banners than her own, were they even banners of foreign independence, she would involve herself beyond the power of extrication."[8]

The tendency to move beyond merely hoping others would see the light about American values and to actively go forth and remake the world first really emerged in the twentieth century. The U.S. economy began to generate enormous wealth—by 1910, its GDP was $460 billion, more than twice the size of Britain's—and Europe grew bogged down in the absurd imperialist jockeying that led to World War I. American elites began to realize that Alexis de Tocqueville—and their own sense of national exceptionalism—were on the mark after all: It was our destiny to dominate (at least) half the globe.

Yet in fulfilling that destiny we were still, for the most part, whipped forward by circumstances beyond our control, and we were still quite internally conflicted about it. On one hand, America's enormous power cried out for an expansion of influence on the world stage, according to the inexorable law of great powers described by such scholars as Michael Mandelbaum and Fareed Zakaria.[9] America followed this pattern, to a point: "Manifest Destiny" not only drove the unslakable acquisition of territory on our own continent, but also led in the late nineteenth century to imperialism in surrounding territories, especially under the presidency of William McKinley, who started the Spanish-American War and vacuumed up the Philippines, Guam, and Puerto Rico, among other islands.

And yet the ideological drag of exceptionalism helped to limit American expansion at first. As he took office upon President McKinley's death in 1901, Teddy Roosevelt was intent on becoming the first true internationalist American president, and he was perhaps the most traditionally imperialist-minded of presidents. Initially he confined himself to reasserting American primacy in our own hemisphere. Roosevelt sought to reinvigorate the Monroe Doctrine, mainly in an effort to secure the new Panama Canal for trade and to rid the New World of lingering European claims in Cuba and Latin America (which had led to the Spanish-American War). When the first major global crisis of his tenure erupted— the Russo-Japanese War in the Far East— he declared at first that America would remain neutral. But America had growing trade interests in the Pacific, having recently taken possession of the Philippines and a territory called the Hawaiian Islands, and Roosevelt was a keen student of geopolitics. He predicted Japan's victory over troubled Czarist Russia in 1905, and just as presciently worried about the small island nation's growing power: "In a dozen years the English, Americans and Germans, who now dread one another as rivals in the trade of the Pacific, will have to dread the Japanese more than they do any other nation," Roosevelt said. Eight years earlier, Roosevelt, then the secretary of the navy, had posed this strategic question to planners at the Naval War College: "Japan makes demands on Hawaiian Islands. This country intervenes. What force will be necessary to uphold the intervention, and how should it be employed?"[10] Worried about the rise of the Japanese in the Pacific—and at the same time admiring them—TR stepped in and negotiated the Treaty of Portsmouth between Japan and Russia. It was a first foreshadowing of the U.S. president's arbitrator-in-chief role—a role that, by the Clinton and Bush years, was to press on us from all sides.

Roosevelt, who, like his predecessors, feared excessive American entanglements, later retreated partially from East Asia. He too was held back by exceptionalist drag, admitting after the Philippine war "that

America lacked the stomach for empire."[11] But America's gradual engagement in global, as opposed to hemispheric, politics proceeded in fits and starts from that seminal Rooseveltian moment. Roosevelt's successor but one, Woodrow Wilson, is still seen today, especially by conservatives, as a crusading idealist who parted ways with his predecessors and led America down a path at odds with its interests and nineteenth-century nativist traditions.[12] Wilson *was* an idealist, and he did believe, too optimistically for his times, in the effectiveness of binding arbitration over the use of force, mainly through law-based international institutions such as his League of Nations. It may be that he was overreacting to the failure of great powers to keep the peace—the disheartening lesson of World War I. Wilson was also a difficult man: arrogant and insufferably self-righteous. But in truth the differences between Roosevelt and Wilson were less than is imagined. In many ways Wilson simply picked up on the world stage where TR and McKinley had left off, venturing into the world but with a certain amount of reluctance. The chief difference, I would argue, is not that Wilson abruptly decided to apply exceptionalist values to American foreign policy, as his critics have said; it was that the problems he faced were much more serious, the kind of expansion demanded of him was very different, and so his degree of engagement as well as his solutions were all the more dramatic.

When World War I erupted in Europe in 1914, Wilson, like TR before him, at first responded in traditional American fashion: He declared neutrality. Later he proposed playing an arbitration role not unlike the one TR undertook in the Russo-Japanese War. But in 1917 German aggressiveness provoked an American declaration of war (the notorious Zimmerman telegram, in which Berlin pledged to help Mexico regain the American territory it had lost in 1848 in return for an alliance, was a key trigger). Not long afterward, the czar's regime collapsed in Russia—in part a result of the shattering blow delivered in the Russo-Japanese War. The Bolsheviks seized power and sought to embarrass the other two Triple Entente allies (Britain and France) by publishing secret treaties that revealed Allied plans to carve up territories controlled by the opposing Central Powers: Germany, Austria-Hungary, and the Ottoman Empire. Meanwhile, three years of war had turned Europe into a charnel house; a conflict that the ruling governments had thought would be "over by Christmas" left the best part of a generation of young men butchered in the trenches. Morale among the Allies, now lacking their partner Russia, hit a new low point. "The plunge of civilization into this abyss of blood and darkness," wrote Henry James after World War I began, "gives away the whole long age during which we have supposed the world to be, with whatever abatement, gradually bettering."[13] "Never such innocence again," wrote the poet Philip Larkin in what was an epitaph for the age of progress.[14]

Already committed to the war, Wilson thus faced something very different from Roosevelt—indeed, something brand-new for American presidents: an *ideological* threat. First there was the utter breakdown of belief not only in the Allied cause but in civilization itself; then, later in the war, came the challenge from a newly Bolshevized Russia, which portrayed the conflict as a capitalist grab for spoils. Reflecting on the bankruptcy of the old European order, the failures of the vaunted "balance of power," Wilson fretted that even in America the "Bolshevik seeds found the soil already prepared for them."[15] All there was to do was to put forward a counterideology. Confronted with what seemed an endless downward spiral of hope, Wilson sought to resurrect—perhaps quixotically— the idea of Progress, and what the scholar Frank Ninkovich calls "international society's progressive machinery."[16] And Wilson did it in the only way an American leader could: by invoking the American creed. Justifying greater U.S. involvement, he knew, meant drawing from the deep well of American self-righteousness about our values, our exceptionalist certainty that we had found the Way. The European great powers had demonstrated, once and for all, the dangerous excesses of dictators who are not held in check by democratic consent. America would "make the world safe for democracy," Wilson said on April 2, 1917, in asking Congress to declare war, "for the right of those who submit to authority to have a voice in their own government, for the rights and liberties of small nations . . . and to make the world itself at last free." Jefferson's "ball of liberty" would now have America behind it, actively pushing it along.

But Wilson was as aware as any of his predecessors that he would first have to overcome the other half of America's exceptionalist tradition, our sense of apartness. The former Princeton University president, who had made his scholarly reputation as a political philosopher, consciously sought to bridge the two American eras—the gap between Quincy Adams's warning and what he, Wilson, saw as America's emerging global world role. "You know that the United States has always felt from the beginning of her history that she must keep herself separate from any kind of connection with European politics," he told an audience in England. "But she is interested in a partnership of right between Europe and America."[17] At another point he reassured the U.S. Senate, "There is no entangling alliance in a concert of power."[18]

We will deal later on in the book with the consequences today of Wilson's ideological excesses—his somewhat too sanguine championing of self-determination and international law, and his uncompromising insistence that these values be made universal all at once. But my point here is that his core response at the time was sensible and eminently American: It followed the expansionist impulses that had emerged in the new century but at the same time was fully rooted in the tradition of American exceptionalism. In seeking to make the world safe for democracy, in other words, Wilson was responding in a uniquely American and even somewhat "realist" fashion—some scholars have called it a "higher realism"—to an entirely new challenge as the American giant reckoned with its primacy on the world stage. Richard Holbrooke, one of the leading diplomats of the present era, also believes that to create a sharp dichotomy between TR and Wilson is "historically false and conceptually false. Wilson considered himself a realist."[19] This notion—that Wilson tried to be a realist for his times—will become important later, when we try to bridge the gulf between realism and idealism as a practical solution for American foreign policy today. Even Henry Kissinger, a champion of balance-of-power geopolitics and no fan of Wilson's, concedes that the twenty-eighth president's ideas are still the "bedrock" of American foreign policy. He notes grudgingly, "Whenever America has faced the task of constructing a new world order, it has returned in one way or another to Woodrow Wilson's precepts."[20]

In some ways, in fact, Wilson was the proto–cold warrior. For a century Americans had believed heart and soul in their creed, but before

Wilson they also had the luxury of believing that it would be, for the most part, unmolested by world events. When those circumstances changed in the First World War, it became necessary to do more than merely wish the American belief system on the world; the times called for active promotion of it. The same need arose when the ideological threats from fascism and communism emerged later on. That is why every president from FDR to Reagan fought out those titanic battles of alternative worldviews along distinctly Wilsonian lines, and why George W. Bush has followed suit in the war on terrorism. The reason is that American expansionism has never been able to move too many steps beyond an exceptionalist justification for it. To wit, if we are going to commit our national resources and will to go abroad and fight major wars—nothing like that had been done in the nineteenth century—it must be to remake the world in our image so that other nations will become as nonthreatening as we are, rather than merely to broker or influence foreign conflicts. As John F. Kennedy once said in summing up what was at stake in the Cold War, "The real question is which system travels better."[21] George Kennan, a realist, once condemned this "legalistic-moralistic" tradition as an American disease. But he was shouting into the wind: This exceptionalist, values-driven foreign policy was clearly demanded both by the times and by the peculiarities of the American sensibility. And this "skein" of thinking, as Kennan called it, shows no sign of disappearing today. Quite the contrary. Just as the Bush neoconservatives would later argue during the war on terror—when the president declared that "the twentieth century ended with a single surviving model of human progress"[22]—Wilson believed that his postwar settlement, involving the failed League of Nations, would show "there was to be no difference between American principles and those of mankind."[23]

But out in the heartland, and among their representatives in Congress, many Americans continued to believe there was a difference and that John Quincy Adams was still right. Wilson himself failed, finally, to impose a new international structure; the League went down to defeat in the Senate when Henry Cabot Lodge, the chairman of the Foreign Relations Committee, refused to sign off on Article 10, which obligated all league members to intervene in the event of aggression against other members, and

Wilson refused to compromise. Lodge's objection, of course, was merely the old fear of entanglement, and his unilateralist justification for this stance was very much along the lines of today's unilateralism. Thanks in part to Lodge—and to Wilson's overreaching—American nativism enjoyed a resurgence in the interwar years. The hapless Wilson died embittered, paralyzed by a stroke, to be replaced by a self-described "normal" Republican president, Warren Harding, who never brought up the League of Nations again (and was followed in succession by two other isolationist GOP presidents, Calvin Coolidge and Herbert Hoover). "We have torn up Wilsonism by the roots," Lodge crowed after Harding won in a landslide.[24] That was followed by other abject failures of international law, especially of the 1929 Kellogg-Briand Pact outlawing war. "The effort to abolish war can come to nothing," Walter Lippmann wrote, "unless there are created international institutions, international public opinion, an international conscience which will play the part which war has always played in human affairs."[25] He was right, but American internationalism would lay dormant for another decade—until December 7, 1941.

Whatever expansionist tendencies McKinley, TR, and Woodrow Wilson displayed at the beginning of the century had, by the 1930s, fallen victim to our irrepressible exceptionalism. Henry Luce, in his famous 1941 essay giving a name to the "American Century," lamented that "Americans were unable to accommodate themselves spiritually and practically" to the fact that they were the most powerful nation on earth (an echo of TR's lament that Americans were too "immersed in our own material prosperity" to care about shaping the world).[26] But the horrors of World War II, which Wilson himself had predicted would be worse than those of the Great War, cried out again for a Wilsonian-style attempt to impose a new global order. FDR, who as the vice-presidential candidate in 1920 had stumped for the League of Nations, proclaimed a concept as idealistic as Wilson's—the Four Freedoms—but he and Harry Truman wanted more geopolitically astute, workable structures in order to secure them.[27] The United Nations, with its Security Council designed around Roosevelt's Four Policemen concept—the United States, Russia, Britain, and China each overseeing stability in its region—was the first such attempt combining realist armed might with idealist international law.[28] The UN was also a conscious effort to correct—not eliminate—Wilson's mistakes with the League of Nations. "We will not accept a world, like the postwar world of the 1920s, in which the seeds of Hitlerism can again be planted and allowed to grow," FDR said.[29]

As historian Michael Beschloss shows, FDR's experience in the debates in Wilson's cabinet—he was then assistant secretary of the navy—over what to do with post–Wilhelmine Germany deeply influenced his approach to handling Hitler's Germany a generation later. In a precursor to today's debate over nation building—and just how intrusive America needs to be—Wilson refused to occupy Germany and hoped it would learn from America's moral example. Wilson was still, to a large extent, a man of the nineteenth century, of the ethos of John Quincy Adams. The young FDR, however, was already learning the lessons of America's global role. "Roosevelt thought Wilson should have insisted that the victors occupy Germany and train the Germans to give up their old ambitions," Beschloss writes. "When he saw Hitler come to power . . . Roosevelt realized earlier than most Americans that during his term in office, the United States might be forced to pay for Wilson's mistakes." Hence FDR's insistence on "unconditional surrender" in World War II.[30]

The FDR/Truman administration also imposed a global system of regulated open markets at Bretton Woods, with everyone's currency pegged at fixed rates to the dollar. This was a conscious corrective to both the mindless protectionism of the 1930 Smoot-Hawley Tariff Act—which exacerbated the Great Depression and the fascist spiral afterward—and the equally mindless laissez-faire capitalism that preceded Smoot-Hawley. There were attempts, too—also U.S.-sponsored—at building an International Trade Organization to set rules on trade tariffs and market behavior, but for the post–World War II Republican Congress this proved to be a bridge of engagement too far.

Thus did the one-foot-in, one-foot-out pattern of the American Century play out, a tug of war between engagement and withdrawal unlike that pursued by any other great power of the past. The central tension, I would argue, was always between our "realist" great-power responsibilities and our exceptionalist reluctance to lose our founding sense of apartness and distance. The realists generally won out, but only by giving exceptionalism due deference. This meant, in practice, building all these international structures with a minimum of publicity (while making them very American). While unilateralists like Lodge obstructed international entanglements, and isolationists like Charles Lindbergh and Father Coughlin tempted millions with their siren's appeal to nativism, American institution builders were usually hard at work in quiet places making plans for a more perfect global community. Some of these plans went horribly awry, such as Wilson's League; others have been brilliant in conception and execution, including NATO and the Marshall Plan. In the end, the internationalists have dominated national policy. It's just that since Wilson's failure they have tended to play down their globe building for fear of provoking the other half of the American psyche, the exceptionalist passion so prized by the Bush sovereigntists, where our polity, our Constitution, were sacrosanct. We were inside. The others were outside.

So it is no surprise that American internationalists often worked up their grand plans in the most out-of-the-way places. Even Wilson, in the early days of his peace plan, fretted about the grandiosity of what he intended. In December 1917 he secretly convened "the Inquiry," a group of eager reformers including a young Walter Lippmann, to meet in the basement of the New York Public Library and draw up the Fourteen Points. In mid-1941 FDR, a far savvier politician than Wilson, concocted the Atlantic Charter, the founding document of the postwar UN system, in the mists off Newfoundland while under fire from America Firsters who suspected him of prodding America into war (he sent a double out on his yacht on the Potomac to fool reporters). A village in the remote White Mountains of New Hampshire, Bretton Woods, gave birth to the new American-sponsored system of global market regulation—the IMF and World Bank—in 1944. (Although John Maynard Keynes, a Briton, had a major hand in this effort, the Americans dominated and, critically, fought successfully for an open global trading system against Keynes's efforts to maintain the British empire's protectionist "imperial preferences" system.) And a year later, following highly secretive negotiations between Washington, London, and Moscow, the United Nations came to life within the walled Georgetown estate of Dumbarton Oaks. (So skittish was FDR about negative press leaks that the talks were known merely as "the Dumbarton

Oaks Conversations.")[31] When the International Trade Organization idea failed to gain traction, American internationalists responded by gathering quietly for years to piece together the General Agreement on Tariffs and Trade—which in the 1990s, in the hands of a somewhat more internationally minded Congress, finally became the World Trade Organization.

All this institution building was historic, spine-tingling stuff. Taken together, it amounts to a vision for a workable "international community": a collection of nation-states with very different personalities, but united by a general consensus on democracy, open markets, low tariffs, and disciplined budgets, all of it embedded in international law and institutions. But, again, we took little pride in our handiwork. For Americans, there was none of this business of crowing that "the sun never sets on the British Empire," the pomp and circumstance of celebrating new colonial possessions, the bestowing of titles like "Empress of India," that so marked British world domination.

What does the legacy of low-profile internationalism look like today? It is a world system that is very different from the one Wilson envisioned, but it retains powerful elements of his vision. And it is worth saving. The United Nations, the second-generation iteration of the League of Nations, has performed far below expectations in both the Cold War and post–Cold War periods. As we will see in Chapter 6, its once-proud progenitor, the United States, is constantly seeking trial separations and threatening divorce from the UN. But the co-opting of Russia and China by the UN system, I will argue, may be the surest firewall against war in the twenty-first century. And as we will examine in detail in Chapter 7, the UN's many agencies, such as the United Nations Development Programme, are doing the dirty but necessary work of nation building.

NATO is also a troubled institution, uncertain of its post–Cold War role, but both Clinton and Bush, despite their sharply divergent ideologies, pushed for its expansion eastward into the old Soviet bloc. In an odd way NATO is beginning to look very much like the "community of democracies" that Wilson ultimately hoped to create through the League of Nations (although, as we will see in the next chapter, there is another organization by that name today—invented, of course, by an American: Madeleine Albright). Wary of doing regional policing again after a difficult campaign in Kosovo, NATO seems to be turning into a transatlantic political organization—one that could someday include its erstwhile raison d'être, Moscow. In Asia another Cold War–era institution, the U.S.-Japan Security Treaty, uniting the world's first and second largest economies, remains the keystone of stability in that region, but it is increasingly questioned by the Japanese public. The major economic institutions—the WTO, IMF, and World Bank—are also under attack, both at home and abroad. As we will see in Chapter 5, their very success in achieving global consensus on markets—the so-called Washington consensus—has generated a worldwide backlash. The IMF, especially, has moved far from its founding charter; it has gone from being balance-of-payments stabilizer to a schoolmarmish dictator of developing nations' finances. But these institutions have nonetheless been successful in helping to avert a return to the protectionist anomie of the 1930s and a global depression. The WTO is the world's rule-setter; the IMF its credit union; and the World Bank its principal charity. It's just that few Americans are paying attention to the absence of bad news on this front.

Together these many layers of multilateral cover also serve to take the raw edge off American hegemony, making it acceptable to much of the world, the scholar G. John Ikenberry argues. That is unique in the history of great powers, which in the past have always provoked new rivalries and alliance building against them. "American power is not only unprecedented in its preponderance, but it is also unprecedented in the way it is manifest within and through these institutions," Ikenberry writes.[32] Realists such as John Mearsheimer have sought to argue that Wilsonianism—and consensus achieved through international institutions—has always been mere window dressing. "Behind closed doors," he asserts with little evidence, "the elites who make national security policy speak mostly the language of power, not that of principle, and the United States acts in the international system according to the dictates of realist logic."[33]

Unfortunately for Mearsheimer's theory, the truth is far more complicated. As noted in the last chapter, even during that most "realist" of foreign-policy tests, the Cuban missile crisis, JFK sought the moral or Wilsonian high ground by worrying what the reaction in the UN and international community might be if he launched a preemptive strike on

Cuba. (He defied his hawkish military advisers and opted for a naval quarantine instead.) George H. W. Bush, in strategizing over the Gulf War, spent long hours with top aides such as his national security advisor, Brent Scowcroft, worrying about winning support at the United Nations.[34] Clinton fretted over winning consensus in NATO, and the neo-conservatives in George W. Bush's administration found themselves needing to win over the "international community" by making an evidentiary case against Saddam Hussein in the UN Security Council, much as Adlai Stevenson presented satellite evidence of Soviet missiles before the UN in 1962. The list goes on and on.

## The Accidental Empire

And yet in pursuing this internationalism so furtively and reluctantly we have ended up fooling ourselves. As a nation, we have been sleepwalking through history, to borrow a phrase from the journalist Haynes Johnson. We managed to piece together an international system and then failed to recognize our authorship of it when we awoke to our new responsibilities —though, as I have argued, we are still only partially awake. This is why one argument rarely heard through all the debates that have occurred, especially in the 1990s, over the usefulness of institutions like the UN, IMF, and World Bank is that these institutions are American-made, and therefore we have an obligation to take ownership of them.

It also explains why the greatest fear of our allies has always been American withdrawal, not expansionism. Wilson's commitment to the League of Nations was a specific response to these fears; the implicit pledge of an institutionalized American involvement in Europe was his main leverage in forging the peace treaty at Versailles. But it is noteworthy that Wilson's failure to secure America's entry into the League left him open to the same kind of charges made against George W. Bush today: that his strident moralism was unmatched by commitment and was thus useless. As a piqued David Lloyd George wrote afterward, "The Americans appeared to assume responsibility for the sole guardianship of the Ten Commandments and for the Sermon on the Mount; yet when it came to a practical question of assistance and responsibility, they absolutely refused to accept it."[35]This was the deficiency that FDR and Truman tried to correct, but the Europeans weren't taking any chances. After World War II as well, the British and Europeans also sought to lock the United States into their affairs through NATO, and it was only an American commitment that prevented more draconian treatment of Germany.[36]

Even our greatest internationalist presidents have sometimes deceived themselves—or perhaps believed their own press—about the real depth of American commitment. It is a little-known fact that the Pentagon, built hurriedly in 1942 after Pearl Harbor, was designed with floors to bear 150 pounds per square inch rather than the standard 75 pounds so that after the war it could be used as warehouse space. FDR's War Department assumed it would probably shrink back to its small size, because America would not need to project power worldwide once the war was won.[37] FDR, who never fully escaped right-wing accusations that he had deviously orchestrated America's entry into World War II, was certainly not going to tell his generals to plan for postwar empire. In the early days of NATO, the Truman administration pined for a self-contained European security pact that would allow the Americans to deemphasize or even unwind NATO, provoking Lord Ismay's famous comment that the point was to "keep the Americans in, the Russians out, and the Germans down." Even George C. Marshall, the revered World War II chief of staff and secretary of state of the early Cold War, doubted the wisdom of that most iconic of American foreign policy successes—his own Marshall Plan. In a talk with Paul Nitze, then a State Department aide, in the spring of 1947, Marshall worried too that America was overreaching in its bid to resurrect the economies of Europe, saying, "It's just not the sort of thing we do," according to Nitze's recollection.[38] The Marshall Plan's first administrator, Paul Hoffman, declared dismissively, "The idea is to get Europe on its feet and off our backs."[39] As the war ended, most Americans simply ignored Vice President Henry Wallace's 1942 call for a global New Deal. Americans after the war, wrote historian Robert Divine, "yearned for a magic formula which would permit them to live in peace without constant involvement abroad."[40]

The seemingly existential threat of communism during the Cold War ended that soap-bubble hope. But our uneasiness about the international institutions we fathered resumed in the post–Cold War period. During the war in Kosovo in 1999, NATO supreme commander Wesley Clark found himself treated like a pariah at the Pentagon as he sought to bring more assets to the battlefield. Despite his success in getting Slobodan Milosevic to withdraw from the province after seventy-eight days of NATO bombing, he was later cashiered as NATO commander and treated not to a ticker-tape parade à la Ike but to public obscurity (at least until he became a presidential candidate). This may have had something to do with the peculiar nature of Bill Clinton's humanitarian war—about which more later—as well as Clark's prickly personality. But there was also a gulf of sensibility there. The fissures between Clark and the Pentagon were precisely the fissures between an older view of the U.S. national interest and the new, more diffuse national interest represented by this American-ized international system.

If we built a kind of American empire from our triumphs of the last century—in World War I, World War II, and the Cold War— it was an accidental empire, an "empire by invitation," as one commentator has put it.[41] Accidental empires are not unique in world history; essentially the same thing happened to Great Britain, though for different reasons. Cen-turies of conquest in the pursuit of markets and establishing "spheres of influence" left it willy-nilly with an empire it had not really set out to build. But the British, at least, understood in the end what they had; they adopted not only the pomp and circumstance but also a robust foreign policy commensurate with their empire.

Yet this ambivalence also works for us to a degree. It is why everyone from the Arabs to the Singaporeans, though they gripe endlessly in public about it, secretly prefers American hegemony to any other they can imag-ine. Consider the beauty of the Gulf War, as seen from the emir's palace: America drove the Iraqis out, capped the wells, gave the Kuwaitis back their ungodly wealth, and asked them to throw a few reconstruction con-tracts our way and keep shipping oil. The wonderment of the rulers in Kuwait City was equaled perhaps only by the astonishment of the Japan-ese and Germans when Washington delivered their countries back to them after World War II. We cleaned up Berlin and Tokyo—quite thor-oughly, I might add—and then shipped out (leaving, again, a minimal troop presence behind to secure the peace). That this duality never seems to go away is much appreciated in the world; the anti-Americanism one senses today in most foreign capitals is more that of an unrequited lover, a sense of mussed pride (especially over the Bush team's hard-line unilateralism), than outright opposition.

## Moving Things into Balance

One would think that the war on terror would have been enough, at long last, to jolt us out of this endless cycle of engagement and withdrawal. But Americans today still have not made the basic conceptual crossover into the idea that the world we remade is our world, defined by our structures and, to a large extent, our values. Polls still show most Americans support a strong U.S. role overseas—whether it's a question of paying UN dues or passing the Comprehensive Test Ban Treaty. The difference is that people are just not very intent on seeing that their wishes are fulfilled compared to, say, getting tax relief or prescription drug reform. As Bill Clinton once said in an enlightening postmortem on his presidency, "Your real problem is not that people are opposed to the UN or opposed to us paying our fair share. . . . Your problem is that there's no penalty for not doing it, and there's always other competing claims on the dollar. There are not more than a handful of congressional districts in the entire country where a member of either party would be defeated for standing up and saying, 'We live in an interdependent world, we have to make it more integrated. I want to see us pay our fair share to the United Nations.'" But, Clinton added, "they won't get any benefits for doing it."[42] That permits small, hard-line lobbies in Congress to get away with pet passions, like defeating the Comprehensive Test Ban Treaty in October 1999 with little fear of voter wrath.

The Bush administration, for example, continued its hard-line opposition to reviving the test ban treaty well after 9/11, even though a 2002 poll by the Chicago Council on Foreign Relations showed that a whopping 81 percent of Americans now supported it.[43] Yet Bush's continuing opposition to the CTBT did not cut into his high approval ratings. While Americans were increasingly aware that multilateral control of weapons of mass destruction was needed to keep them safe, they did not yet consider this to be as critical to their lives as domestic issues. They still saw it as an "outside" issue, not an "inside" issue.

We Americans can't expect to change our national personality fundamentally. Our task now is to concede that while American exceptionalism lives on, it can no longer be defined as it has been for two and a quarter centuries, as us against them. We must recognize that American exceptionalism has succeeded, finally, in "beginning the world again." The scholar Ikenberry points out that the "paradox" of Wilson's agenda was that "he wanted to avoid involvement in European politics, so he pursued a vision that entailed the utter transformation of European politics."[44] But as with so much that Wilson did, this also tells the larger tale of America's involvement in the world in the last century: If we were going to be engaged in the world, then, by God, we would remake the world in our own image. We have.

Hence, we Americans must embrace what might seem a contradiction in terms: a more *inclusive* exceptionalism, which recognizes that what binds us to the world is now far more significant than what separates us from it, and that this phenomenon has been largely our doing. Especially in a post-9/11 world, a world in which both opportunities and threats have become globalized, the task of securing freedom means securing the international system. We face, finally, a trade-off of time-honored American ideals, for in order to preserve the most central of our founding principles, freedom, we must give up one of our founding myths, that of a people apart.

Part of what exercised the hard-line ideologues of the Bush administration is the idea that the United States was the nation with the most to lose from an erosion of sovereignty. Why should a country so dominant militarily and economically give up even a slice of its freedom to act? The problem lies in the fact that America is also the country with the most to lose by rejecting globalism. If we are to embrace this Americanized international system, we must understand better how it works—and just how indistinguishable "outside" has become from "inside." Above all, we must accept that the "international community" we had such a large hand in building, and of which we are a part, actually exists.

# 3

# What Is the "International Community"?

Foreign policy in a Republican administration will . . . proceed from the firm ground of the national interest, not from the interests of an illusory international community.

**Condoleezza Rice**

THE INTERNATIONAL community illusory? Yes, it's fairly fashionable to say so. But the international community is real. We Americans helped create it. And if we do a good job of helping it to grow, it could well prevent our children and grandchildren from ever having to hear a shot fired in anger.

But first things first. Let's understand what we're talking about. To do so, let's remove ourselves from the realm of academic abstraction and head straight for the real world. Come witness with me the creation of a new member of the international community.

No, we are not in the well of the UN General Assembly, which U.S. conservatives (among them the Bush hegemonists) most often identify, derisively, with the international community but which is more like a modern-day Tower of Babel, wielding very little real influence or power. Nor are we at one of those big economic gatherings such as Davos, where the global elite meet and greet—somewhat nervously these days, as protesters rail at them from the barricades. Contrary to popular perception, the international community doesn't derive its existence or true power from cacophonous conventions like these.

Instead, we find this new inductee in a place of utter quiet: the town of Xupu, not far from Nanjing, on China's eastern coast. We have come here to observe an important event whose implications have barely begun to dawn on the inhabitants of this cut-off factory town.

It is a cold winter day in 1994. I am being driven along an immaculate, mulberry-lined boulevard. We pass under a large red arch emblazoned with gold Chinese characters that proclaim: Welcome to Yizheng Chemical Fiber Company. We drive by schools, a park, a hospital, restaurants, various day-care centers, and a "children's palace" with a Disneyland-like fairy castle at the center (copyright protection is still weak in China). There are few cars: Yizheng workers on bicycles pedal mutely by us, cheeks reddened by the wind. Posted along the roadside are scarlet billboards inscribed in black with Big Brotherly fiats, such as the "Ten Forbiddens" mandated by the cadres who run China's largest polyester manufacturer. Among the rules: no being late, no reading on the job, no dozing off, no falsifying invoices, and no private enterprise. Eventually we pass by the Yizheng TV station, where every other day a new dose of propaganda is fed by cable to the industrial complex's twenty thousand workers in their neat but uniformly small, centrally heated apartments. For nearly a year this self-contained community—a relic of a past era, of a different world—has been "ideologically prepared," in the words of plant managing director Ren Chuan Jun, for the great event. And now they are ready.

The event is the listing of a $200 million, approximately 30 percent stake in Yizheng Chemical Fiber on the Hong Kong Stock Exchange. Yizheng is about to become the seventh of China's historic First Nine state companies to be privatized after growing up as Communist entities. And, despite the outward calm in the streets, the privatization is a revolution that is literally cleaving the "perfect" world of Xupu in two.

On one side of the Xupu River, which divides the town, is the impressive plant complex itself: a four-factory money machine that cranks out more than half million tons of polyester a year. Back in Hong Kong, a major financial center hooked into the global marketplace (and at this time still a British colony), Western-educated investment bankers are salivating over the Yizheng listing. The company has some of the newest technology and best management in China's state sector. And it faces a future of almost unlimited demand in the world's most populous nation, where in some impoverished provinces "one-pants families" (rural households so poor the males must share a single pair of trousers) still exist, but which is rapidly developing—and where almost the first thing people do when they get a taste of prosperity is to buy clothes and commodities made from or packaged in polyester fiber. Factory workers swell with pride over the listing. "We feel a great sense of responsibility," a quality control worker, Li Kai Yin, twenty-eight, tells me when we finally arrive at Plant No. 1.

But there is little joy on the east side of the river, where the main part of the town and all its services are. Once subsidized entirely by plant operations and indistinguishable from the production crews, these maintenance men, waitresses, doctors, nurses, and teachers have been cut out of the listed portion of the company under the careful ministrations of S. G. Warburg, the Hong Kong–based investment bank that is sponsoring the stock issue. Some seven thousand of these workers are learning that despite all the positive propaganda, they have been judged and found wanting. In a society that is still officially classless, they are about to become second-class citizens. For the first time since the Yizheng plant-city was conceived in 1978—as the last gasp of communist command planning before former supreme leader Deng Xiaoping's market reforms —a value is being placed on their work. After the listing they will be connected to their listed brethren only by the thin tissue of a service contract. A contract that could, at some future date, expire.

It is a fate most of them dimly comprehend. "I'm afraid we will become poorer than the others," a sullen salesgirl at the Pai Sa Department Store tells me. "But they're not taking any more staff." "I feel bad about the listing, but I don't quite know why," says a young female teacher at a day-care center. Da Kiou Hua, the director of the center, who is standing next to her, quickly chimes in: "We trust Mr. Ren. He will not forget us." The unlisted workers are also painfully aware that they live in a fragile protective bubble. Company homes are available to them at just 16,000 yuan ($1,800), but the town's streets are so bare because autos, sold in nearby Nanjing at free-market prices of 200,000 yuan and up, are out of everyone's range. And now most of the subsidies that once made

Yizheng a worker's paradise—if a rather spartan one—are being dismantled. Workers must start paying rent and buying homes at market prices, paying hospital and utility bills, and so forth.

To help the workers get a leg up, the injunction against private enterprise on the aging sign at the gates of Yizheng is no longer in effect. Bits of entrepreneurial greenery are already beginning to sprout from the gray-slab confines of Xupu. At drafty Yizheng Hospital, patients are getting charged "market rates," says director Zhang Changlai, who adds that market discipline will make him a "better doctor." "We are having a lot of meetings, discussing how to improve service," he says. "And we're opening up a cancer ward." At the library, a shop has been started; at the movie theater, a fast-food restaurant. "I will try to do my best in the business cycle," says restaurant owner Hu Xing Quan, as if reciting from a capitalist phrase book.

Aubrey Li, a handsomely tailored Warburg director who took the lead in preparing the company for privatization, says the unproductive workers were the single biggest headache of the Yizheng listing. He says managing director Ren quickly understood what had to be done: They would be "reallocated." There was surprisingly little resistance even from Ren's Communist overlords in Beijing—and little sympathy for the fate of the unlisted workers, says Li, a typically fast-talking Hong Kong Chinese. In fact, the listing was held up for three months while China International Trust and Investment Corporation (CITIC), Beijing's main investment arm and a 30 percent owner of Yizheng, battled with the National Textile Council, the Communist Party entity that held the other 70 percent, over spoils from the listing. CITIC insisted that it not take any responsibility for the unlisted portion, and that its 30 percent stake be converted entirely into listed stock. So much for communism. "CITIC is also a commercial entity, and it definitely had its self-interest in mind," explains Li.

Ren himself, a quiet, bespectacled man with slicked-back hair who wears a beige Mao jacket, still has a lot to learn. Warburg's Li tells me of the near-disaster a year earlier, shortly before the investment bank was awarded the Yizheng "mandate" by Beijing. "We took Mr. Ren to Shanghai to introduce him to some [Western] fund managers. One of them asked him, 'Why should I consider Phase 3 [a plan to expand the plant based on revenues from the stock sales] a viable project?' His only answer was,

'Because [Premier] Li Peng approved it.'" The response was a groan from the audience, and that was the last time Comrade Ren mentioned Comrade Li. Ren admits he's learned a lot since then about his new masters, the international financial markets. "Our goal before the listing was to make money for the enterprise, and therefore for the state," says Ren. "After the listing our goal is to make money for the shareholders."

### A Two-Stage Process

Events such as the Yizheng listing, repeated thousands of times in small and large ways around the world since the Cold War ended, constitute some of the basic building blocks of that sprawling work-in-progress, the international community. Scholars and thinkers have generally done a poor job of explaining this vast, untidy, and nebulous concept, which is at the heart of this book. Instead they tend to describe bits and pieces of the international community, like the proverbial blind men groping various parts of the elephant. Journalists such as Thomas Friedman, John Micklethwait, and Adrian Wooldridge have deftly described how the economics of "globalization" have changed the world. Such scholars as Joseph Nye, Robert Keohane, and John Gerard Ruggie have spent their careers brilliantly explaining "globalism," the political process by which the international economy and international law and institutions have made nations interdependent. But very few observers have given a full picture of what today's international community is and how it works on numerous levels at the same time, economically, politically, and socially.

The process of building this global system consists of two stages: disintegration—as one part of Yizheng is torn away from the other, and the old domestic system loses its insularity—followed by reintegration into the larger global community. And yet it is not an either-or phenomenon: The international community is not completely destroying national borders or leading to world government, as right-wing caricatures would have it. Ren and his workers now hold a kind of dual citizenship. Today they owe fealty both to what remains of China's domestic "socialist-market" system and to the international community.

This process of creating dual loyalties is constantly occurring under the auspices of the American-secured global system. Very often it starts out of economic self-interest. Sleek investment bankers like Aubrey Li, hungry for profits, are the laborers who are putting in the infrastructural girders of the international community, like construction workers on a vast convention center who never see the overall blueprint. Equipped with little more than smarts, spunk, and no small amount of bravado, they are poking their way into the world's emerging economies, advising, signing contracts, setting up transnational production, and teaching the locals "due diligence," the basic rules for assessing market value, and international law. In so doing, these emissaries of capital are playing an almost evangelical role, exerting a universalizing influence not seen, perhaps, since the heyday of the Christian missionaries who combed the globe centuries ago. If their latter-day gospel is about making money, not saving souls, it is finding a receptive audience in former communist cadres such as Ren and his masters in Beijing, all of whom want a piece of the action.

Beneath the headlines about globalization, about new privatizations and the ebb and flow of trade and market movements, the creation of a common value system is steadily pulling managers like Ren and his "productive" workers into a relationship with the international system, forcing others such as the service workers to rethink their relationship with the traditional community, and unwinding the inbred system seen in hermetic industrial towns like Xupu. It is a process not terribly different from what happened to many U.S. factory towns beginning a generation ago.

The creation of dual loyalties—to the traditional community and to the international community—is one of the great phenomena of our time. Consider what has happened to China's neighbor, Japan, over the course of the last century. Japan is a country that for most of its history has epitomized insularity and anomie. After cutting itself off from the world entirely for 250 years, in the late nineteenth century Japan was finally pulled into the world, but in a confrontational way. Tokyo's feudal aristocrats swiftly threw off their samurai robes and created an industrialized economy and a modern military. Japan's first response to the challenge from the West was to launch a war of aggression in the 1930s and

'40s. When that failed they waged war again, this time with trade as a weapon, by creating the fabled "Japan, Inc." of decades past. This was an entire social system, not just an economic system. Japan's giant banks acted as public utilities, dispensing cheap capital to corporate *keiretsu*, which in turn could afford to grant lifetime employment to most of their workers, thus "privatizing" Japan's welfare system. The system was paid for, and its costs were widely distributed, by pricing goods high at home for a compliant Japanese public—and keeping many foreign products out —while "dumping" cheaply priced products abroad. The nation's corporate, public, and private interests all conspired to create an unstoppable manufacturing sector in order to keep the system running. In the 1970s and '80s, during the heyday of Japan. Inc., Japan-bashing became a national political pastime in America. Under union pressure, Washington constantly threatened trade sanctions. President George H. W. Bush famously took the chairmen of the Big Three automakers to Japan in 1992 to press their case for open markets. Back home, a group of U.S. congressmen once took a sledgehammer to a Toshiba stereo on the Capitol steps to make the same point.

But in the early '90s, after years of relentless pressure from both Washington and a burgeoning global marketplace to open up Japan's markets and change its practices, Tokyo's bureaucratic and business elite began touting the concept of *kyosei*, or "symbiosis" with Western economies. Japanese multinationals began setting up production abroad—in the United States to avoid trade sanctions on exports and in Asia to escape the high-priced labor of their own maturing economy. The result was that Japan began losing its Inc. The interests of the nation and its giant corporations started to diverge. The Mitsubishis, Toyotas, and Matsushitas—the pride of Japan's postwar rebirth—began joining the great multinational diaspora, and the international community. Japanese companies, to a startling degree, have become "us" rather than "them." Consider Japanese auto exports, which made up the majority of the trade deficit: They plunged from 3.4 million units in 1986 to just one-third of that a decade later as automakers quickly moved manufacturing to the United States. Though the Japanese retained virtually the same market share overall, the shift in production had an enormously calming effect on U.S.

public opinion. Indeed, in the late '90s and early '00s, when the U.S. steel industry—one of the last holdouts to this trend of transnationalized production—began agitating once again for tariffs to protect their workers, they found they had less company: The United Auto Workers union no longer had an angry base of disenfranchised workers from which to create a protectionist movement. Even in Detroit, where in the 1980s one was likely to find one's parked Toyota gouged by someone's keys, people aren't ruffled any longer by "foreign" cars. "I don't think people are motivated by the nationality of the makers of the vehicles they buy," Ford's then-CEO, Alex Trotman, casually remarked to my *Newsweek* colleague Dan McGinn at one point in the late '90s. That was a striking confession coming after years of Ford-sponsored "Buy American" campaigns.[1]

The impact of this shift has been enormous back in Japan as well. Today the biggest Japanese companies obey a new taskmaster: They are paying less attention to Tokyo's fractured alliance of bureaucrats, businessmen, and (often corrupt) politicians and far more attention to a global marketplace changed fundamentally by lowered barriers to capital, goods, and services, by ever more complex and expensive technology requiring cross-border strategic alliances—witness the "multimedia" blending of Japanese electronics and American software—and by the need to send production abroad to meet challengers in local markets. In the era of the outsourced global corporation, many *keiretsu* relationships at home—the traditional "convoy" system whereby Japanese companies and their supplier chain organize around a single large bank that supplies them with cheap capital—are now less important than the multinational's linkups around the world. Japan's economy, to a remarkable degree, has followed the pattern of U.S. industry. It has undergone a "hollowing out" (known as *kudoka* in Japanese) that has left Japan increasingly "a headquarters economy where the design and marketing is done, while the manufacturing is performed elsewhere"—mainly China, where wage levels are only 5 percent of Japan's.[2]

After the Asian financial contagion of the late 1990s—a broad-based collapse of currencies and stock markets—I talked with Tsunenari Tokugawa, a shipping executive who also happens to be the Man Who Would Be Shogun. An urbane man educated in the West, Tokugawa is the scion of the family of shoguns who ruled Japan for 250 years before the country was forcibly opened up by the appearance of U.S. gunships in Tokyo Harbor. (You may remember his ancestor, Ieyasu Tokugawa, portrayed as the victorious Toranaga in James Clavell's megaselling 1980s novel *Shogun*.) But the present-day Tokugawa, who is a deeply conservative nationalist, believes this new "threat" from the West—the international community— is more fundamental than the one faced by his great-great-grandfather Yoshinobu Tokugawa, the last shogun. In the late nineteenth century, after the Meiji Restoration that toppled the shogunate, Japan adopted Western technology and practices to ward off foreign invasion. Opening up to Western markets, however, is different, says Tokugawa. Financial markets, especially, are invasive, like a computer virus that can subvert a whole system. They demand openness throughout an economy, and a level playing field. They require shareholder returns—not in a generation but in the next quarter—and, maybe, job cuts. And that strikes at the heart of Japan's still-protected economy and its promise of social harmony, low crime, and relatively equal income distribution. Japan, a country so isolated that it managed to keep out Christian missionaries entirely —Tokugawa's shogun ancestors used to crucify them—now finds itself in a pitched battle with these even more subversive forces. "The world is becoming so small," Tokugawa said. "Communications and money movements are so rapid today. I don't think we can maintain our beloved Japanese form of capitalism." As of this writing, Japan, though severely hit, was still holding on to its antiquated banking system and the price-it-high-at-home-and-dump-it-abroad system that was the heart of Japan, Inc. But this rump Japan, Inc., had fallen into a long period of slow growth and appeared to be fighting a losing war.

One by one, even those who most combatively resisted the encroachment of the "West" are giving up ground and accepting the reality of the international community, or at least of a globalized value system that encroaches upon and compromises their indigenous sense of community. Before the Asian financial crisis, for example, the foremost champion of "Asian values" was Lee Kuan Yew, the autocratic and near-legendary senior minister who almost single-handedly transformed Singapore from a mosquito-ridden backwater into an economic paradigm. In a 1994 interview in *Foreign Affairs*, he even lectured Americans on the relative failures of their loose values and too-open society. "We [Asians] use the family to push economic growth," Lee said. "We were fortunate we had this cultural backdrop: the belief in thrift, hard work, filial piety and loyalty and the extended family, and, most of all, the respect for scholarship and learning." But by 2001, the white-haired sage was repudiating a good deal of what he'd said back then. "Confucian" values—the term he came to prefer —have become all but obsolete under the demands of the global economy, Lee asserted with exactly the same soft-spoken serenity he displayed in 1994. Indeed, Singapore and Hong Kong performed best in weathering the Asian financial crisis not because of Asian values but because of British colonial ones, especially transparency and the rule of law, Lee said at a conference in Davos, the annual "globalization fest" in Switzerland. In much of East Asia, Confucian values "led to excesses," especially family cronyism—in other words, investing on the basis of whom one knows rather what they can do with the money. And in most of those countries, investment flows are only back to between 40 and 60 percent of pre-crisis levels, whereas Singapore has fully recovered "because we aggressively went out to meet global standards." In its own way, Lee's recantation was just as striking as that of Alex Trotman, the Ford executive.

## *So What Is It?*

Still, we have a ways to go in defining the international community. Until now we have looked at it mainly as an economic phenomenon, because that is how it began. The economic linkups that we know today as globalization really started with small gatherings of like-minded Western businessmen: the Trilateral Commission, a group of very Republican businessmen; the annual Bilderburg meeting (which resembles Davos but is far more secretive and exclusive); the annual G-7 gatherings of the United States, Japan, Britain, Germany, France, Italy, and Canada, which started in 1973 as an informal meeting over exchange rates in the White House library. Yet the modern international community only really took off when it began expanding beyond these elites—when, as Thomas

Friedman puts it, technology, finance, and information all became democratized, broadening the accessibility of the pathways opened up by the elites. The convergence in thinking and values that results is typically evolutionary rather than revolutionary, a sort of culture creep that makes you sit up one day and say, "Hey, whatever happened to . . . ?" Do you ever wonder, for example, why we don't hear about "Japanese-style" and "American style" ways of doing business anymore, as we did ad nauseam in the 1980s? Because now everybody has adopted such practices. While national differences remain—accounting practices continue to be a sharp issue, for example—there is now a fully global way of doing business.

By the 1980s in Silicon Valley, the journalist G. Pascal Zachary writes, "The big story wasn't about which companies won and lost or which technologies conquered global markets, but rather how a new breed of talented people were redefining national identity and global competitiveness. . . . The valley was also about how new ways of being human and new human communities were growing in the shadows of older forms."[3] Another specialist in the cyberworld, scholar Lawrence Lessig, compared the development of a global sense of identity today to the congealing of the American identity in the nineteenth century. He refers to Daniel Webster's famous comment on the floor of the U.S. Senate, as the great national debate over slavery heated up, that he spoke not as a representative of Massachusetts or the North, but as an American. "We stand today just a few years before where Webster stood in 1850," Lessig writes. "We stand on the brink of being able to say, 'I speak as a citizen of the world,' without the ordinary person thinking, 'What a nut.'"[4]

But it is one thing to talk about globalized cybercommunities of software engineers or an internationalized economic system that draws in companies such as Yizheng and Japanese multinationals. It is another thing to say this constitutes a social and political "community" on a worldwide scale. And it is reasonable to ask: If the international community really exists, shouldn't it have a certain structure? What does this structure look like? Does the international community behave like a nation, or a city, or a village? And if the president of the United States is the ultimate source of authority within this community, or at least its most influential member, and the UN Security Council and other international agencies and conventions confer some legitimacy and order on it, then how would the organizational chart look? Clearly there is no single constitution or charter or treaty that sets out its parameters. And how can it be a community when it speaks so many different languages, and when we Americans really don't trust or understand many of the people, such as the Chinese or Russians or Europeans, that we supposedly share this "common social space" with?[5]

Even many Democrats from the Clinton administration who call themselves globalists consider the international community to be little more than an ever-shifting alignment of governments and interest groups, or ad hoc alliances that are sometimes broad in base, as in the war on terror, and sometimes narrow, as in pursuit of, say, an international ban on land mines. As Charlene Barshefsky, Clinton's second-term U.S. trade representative, puts it succinctly, "Is the international community an adjective or a noun?"[6] In other words, does it merely describe, like an adjective, the international context in which decisions are made, mainly by nation-states and markets, or is it a noun, a true entity unto itself? Plainly, something that remains so inchoate leaves itself open to perpetual second-guessing.

Just as important, to what extent is the international community built on the troubled but still vibrant institutions such as the UN and WTO, and to what extent is it more a matter of the mutual self-interest of markets, as in the case of the Yizheng privatization? In other words, is it defined more by globalism or by globalization?

Globalization, as typically described, is mainly an economic phenomenon. Thomas Friedman, in his generally excellent *The Lexus and the Olive Tree,* goes so far as to identify the international system with globalization. "The defining document of the Cold War system was 'The Treaty.' The defining document of the globalization system is 'The Deal,'" Friedman writes, as if one "system" has superseded the other.[7] He says the challenge ahead consists of whether the integrating forces of globalization (the Lexus of his title) can overcome the nativist pull of old communities, of tribes and ethnic allegiances (the olive tree). Friedman is right to say that globalization is creating a new internationalized identity that doesn't displace national identity but adds another dimension to it. But it is misleading to look at globalization as a lone phenomenon. Globalization is a process that is taking place within the international system; it is not a system unto itself. There is clearly more tying together the post–Cold War international system than deal making. The Cold War system of treaties and international institutions and law, what is generally known as globalism, is still out there, alive and operating even if ailing. The process of globalization has occurred on the back of the stable international political environment that globalism helped to bring about, and which American power has secured. As Friedman himself notes, globalization is possible only in an international system of generally accepted norms of behavior, especially of legal and accounting practices; it goes without saying that globalization would have been impossible in an international environment of anarchy and war.

## Have We Been Here Before?

The other stock response of skeptics is that this sort of globalization has all happened before, and the tenuous interconnections and meager "norms" of the international community turned out to be a gossamer protection when the going got rough. Realists point to the shocking demise of the pre–August 1914 era of globalization, a halcyon time when, as Keynes famously wrote, "the inhabitant of London could order by telephone, sipping his morning tea in bed, the various products of the whole earth." And they point to catastrophically wrong predictions such as that of Norman Angell, who argued in *The Great Illusion* in 1911 that economic interdependence would prevent another major war. As Micklethwait and Wooldridge point out, "In one vital way, the world was probably more integrated then than it is today: the movement of people. Citizenship was granted freely to immigrants, and people moved between countries without the bother of a work permit, much less a passport. America allowed access to anybody who was not a prostitute, a convict, a lunatic or, after 1882, Chinese."[8]

In other respects too, today's international community seems a work in progress at best. As the author George Packer observes, our globalized, twenty-four-hour media tend to transmit largely superficial images that often only reinforce national stereotypes and biases. "What America exports to poor countries through the ubiquitous media—pictures of glittering abundance and national self-absorption—enrages those whom it doesn't depress," he writes. "And how does the world look to Americans? Like a nonstop series of human outrages. . . . On the whole, knowing is better than not knowing; in any case, there's no going back. But at this halfway point between mutual ignorance and true understanding, the 'global village' actually resembles a real one—in my experience, not the utopian community promised by the boosters of globalization but a parochial place of manifold suspicions, rumors, resentments and half-truths."9

Today economists publish endless papers comparing and contrasting the earlier era of globalization with the present one. Most agree there are significant differences, but there is little consensus on why. Certainly we can't know if there will be another war, and Condoleezza Rice, whom I quote at the beginning of this chapter dismissing the international community as "illusory," and others like her are probably right in saying that America's power will probably be more decisive than international norms in preventing a major conflict. But at the same time it is disingenuous to compare this international community to the loose, European one, with its elites trading capital and its huge flows of hungry refugees, that defined the pre–World War I era.

The truth is, despite the far stricter limits on immigration and the fact that, as Packer notes, superficial images often misrepresent different parts of the globalized world to each other, this international community is far deeper than its predecessor. It is also far more secure under the overwhelming aegis of American power than its predecessor, which was kept alive by the precarious balance of European powers. Indeed, what is happening now in the world has never happened before.

In the 1990s we worried about "transnational terrorism." But a more powerful force is transnational production. (In the wake of September 11 we learned, in fact, that a state like Afghanistan was critical to the success of al-Qaeda by supplying government-protected safe houses, training camps, visas, and so forth.) "What you had in the past was a shallow integration of trade flows," Karl Sauvant of the UN Conference on Trade and Development told me back in 1995. "Now there is an emergence of an international production system organized by transnational corporations." The reason for this has mainly to do with the many brand-new advantages of a globalization powered by information technology. Consider, for example, the use of time zones for competitive advantage, which in the late '90s became routine. George Everhart, the American president of Fujitsu PC in Milpitas, California, told me his team worked literally nonstop for months to develop the BIOS, the basic input-output system for the firm's new series of Lifebook notebook computers. "When the work had been done in Japan, they would ship it here in the morning, our time. We did validation testing, wrote it up and shipped the results back to them in the evening," he says. "I would say we gained probably three quarters of an extra month that way."[10] Paul Ray Jr., a New York headhunter, recalled a mid-'90s search for a top executive by a semiconductor company. "They were looking for someone with enough experience abroad to understand that the chips were designed in India, water-etched in Japan, diced and mounted in Korea, assembled in Thailand, encapsulated in Singapore and distributed around the world," he says.[11] The transplantation of production is true not just of Japan but of other major industrial countries. German chancellor Gerhard Schroeder likes to point out that German companies in the United States do six times as much in sales as German exports to the United States. As a result, even Washington's trade hawks have been forced to compromise their views. "We're in a global economy," Democratic majority leader Dick Gephardt told me in 1998, when I asked him why he had moderated his formerly protectionist views, "and you have to deal with it."

Another factor that is dramatically different from the earlier period of globalization is the convergence of political and social values. If the foundation of this system is built on the mutual self-interest created by markets, very much as Adam Smith once said it should be—and on the obvious lack of a viable alternative system—it has also yielded what former assistant secretary of state Harold Hongju Koh calls "an emerging global culture of democracy."[12] As David Halberstam writes, the great insight that came out of the collapse of the Soviet Union was that "freedom was indivisible, and that the freedom to speak openly and candidly about political matters was in the long run inseparable from the freedom to invent some new high-technology device."[13]

The link between economic freedom and democracy—whether the two necessarily go hand in hand—is not crystal clear.[14] Certainly the question of whether economic openness leads to democracy is still at issue in China. But the preponderance of evidence in the post–Cold War world is that this idea, a central tenet of Wilson and his successors, is true. One by one, developing nations that have created a middle class, as in Taiwan, South Korea, and Thailand, have democratized. I saw that borne out in one of the lesser-noted codas to the Cold War, in late June 2000, during an extraordinary gathering of representatives from 108 nations in Warsaw, Poland, inaugurating the Community of Democracies, which I attended. The Community of Democracies was largely a feel-good conference, intended as a kind of group therapy for emerging democracies, which would share "best practices" on how to create and adhere to universal standards on elections, the rule of law, and freedom of religion, speech, and the press. Indeed, what was important about it was not the conference itself. It was that enough countries felt the same way about the way they ran their societies that they thought holding a conference was a good idea.

The founding conference was largely the brainchild of U.S. secretary of state Madeleine Albright and her old friend, Polish foreign minister Bronislaw Geremek, and their own relationship said a great deal about this emerging international community of values.[15] The day before the democracies conference Albright had flown from Warsaw to Gdansk, the shipyard city where the Eastern Bloc's revolution against communism began in 1980, to receive an honorary degree from the local university. Seated next to Albright, dressed like her in a blue academic gown and four-cornered cap, was the bearded, gentle-faced Geremek, whom she had first met when he was a dissident in Gdansk in the early 1980s and she was an aspiring academic researching her Ph.D. thesis in Poland. Geremek had been a close advisor to Lech Walesa in the early days of the Solidarity movement and imprisoned, and yet, like other dissidents such as Vaclav

Havel of Albright's native Czechoslovakia and Kim Dae Jung of South Korea, had completed a miraculous journey from a jailbird to a giant who helped create his nation's post–Cold War history. Albright and Geremek's close friendship had been forged in their common lifelong passion: opposing totalitarianism. During the ceremony in the University of Gdansk's newly built lecture hall, the two laughed and exchanged kisses, and Geremek complimented her "vision" by quoting from her thesis, a book on the early struggles of the *samizdat* Polish press during the Solidarity movement. Though martial law had forced Solidarity into hiding, she wrote in 1983, "the beginnings of the new earthquake are just under the surface." In this observation, of course, she proved brilliantly correct, and one of the great pleasures of her tenure as U.N. ambassador and then secretary of state was nurturing the newly born democracies of Eastern and Central Europe in the '90s. The personal bond between Albright and Geremek evolved into a political one: America as a kind of benign Big Brother, helping to nudge nascent Polish democracy to stability by bringing it into international organizations like NATO. Out of that came the idea for the Community of Democracies. And yet, just as important, few participants saw it that way. Albright made a point of taking a back seat to Geremek at the conference, posing as just another delegate.

The Community of Democracies was the kind of event that journalists write about—if they bother to pay attention at all—in dismissive tones. The *New York Times* and the *Washington Post* buried the story of that first gathering deep inside the paper. Even CNN, with its twenty-four-hour news appetite, declined to send a camera crew to Warsaw. This was not surprising, because it hardly fit the old definition of news. There was no particular war or crisis that brought it on; there was no great-power clash at the heart of it. Instead it seemed to be another ill-defined conclave of countries professing to have something in common, in this case democracy. Albright's French counterpart, foreign minister Hubert Védrine, sniffily dismissed the gathering's goals as "oversimplistic"—the French, inventors of the word *nuance,* love to sound this theme about U.S. policy—and he refused to approve the so-called Warsaw Declaration that emerged from it. And yet many of the 107 other participants that did sign considered the gathering a milestone. The Community of Democracies, some said, is a concept that's quite new: an acknowledgment that democracy—now most nations' form of government—is no longer an internal affair. "People were practically beating down doors to be invited to this," Albright said.[16]

At the conference, Geremek quoted Wilson to the effect that "democracy is not so much a form of government as a set of principles." But he built on that with an insightful observation of his own, born of his bitter experience of Poland's and other nations' vulgarization of the term in the brutal days of "democratic socialism" behind the Iron Curtain. "There is only one concept of democracy," Geremek declared in a forty-five-minute speech opening the conference. "There are not different models of democracy, there are only different forms and flavors. . . . The acceptance of this idea of democracy is as important as its practical application." Democracies, the delegates said in the Warsaw Declaration, must now be held to a set of universal standards: They derive their power from the will of the people, through free and fair elections. They ensure equality under the law. They obey the rule of law and create an independent judiciary. They respect freedom of association, religion, speech, and the press—and that includes, as the confined Burmese democracy leader, Aung San Suu Kyi, poignantly said in a videotaped speech at the conference, "freedom *after* speech and freedom *after* association."

Many critics predicted the Community of Democracies would expire with Albright's tenure, but it survived, if shakily. A second gathering was held in Seoul in 2002, and in the post-9/11 environment even some conservatives saw it as a good way of reinforcing the global coalition against terrorism. Secretary of State Colin Powell, originally dubious about attending a conference begun by his Democratic predecessor, opted to go (even though he had to back out at the last moment). Even William Safire, the *New York Times* columnist and arch-hawk, endorsed it, if only as a "a more creative reaction to the domination of the U.N. by dictatorships, oligarchies, kakistocracies [government by the least qualified] and rogue nations."[17] The sense of community in the international community was evolving.

## Defining the International Community

Clearly all that has been described in the preceding pages—from the privatization of Yizheng to the emergence of a common set of values represented by the Community of Democracies—adds up to *something*, a growing nexus of markets, governments, and peoples. There are old working institutions such as the UN Security Council that sometimes speak for these common values, and new businesslike institutions such as the WTO that adjudicate disputes when the nexus breaks down. There are inspirational if somewhat mushy forums such as the Community of Democracies that help to fortify all these trends, if only because democracies, unlike autocracies, generally don't like to go to war; casualties cost elected leaders too many votes.

For the present, the best definition of what this all adds up to—the international community—must be a negative one. By this I mean its existence can be proved by the *absence* of anarchy in the international system. It can be seen in the failure of other major powers, in the face of U.S. dominance, to build up alliances against the United States despite the many predictions by realist scholars of international relations that they would. The existence of a compelling alternative global system—what I am calling the international community—helps to explain why none of the major powers, the European Community, Japan, Russia, even China, is engaged in a major military buildup and the geopolitical power games of the past. Scholars going back to Thucydides have argued persuasively that great economic powers inevitably try to convert that power into influence on the world stage. Countries such as China and Japan and new hybrid structures such as the EU should swiftly try to convert their economic power into military and strategic power. They all occasionally make noises about doing so, but on the whole their defense spending has remained steady and small. The challenge now is to say why. I suggest it is because there is an intervening structure, the global system backed by America's stabilizing power, that has provided prosperity and security to most countries that are part of it (or at least has persuaded them that it will provide prosperity and security) and has made the old path less necessary.

Despite the war on terror and the fearful imbroglio of the Islamic world, one would have to be seriously blinkered to deny that the forces of order are much more powerful than the forces of chaos in the world today. In the last decade or so financial markets collapsed several times, yet the global economy has remained intact (so far). Terror struck down the World Trade Center, yet the clash of civilizations has not ensued (to date). Antiglobalization protests raged, yet protectionism has not returned (for the most part). If there is a coming anarchy, then the burden still lies with those who believe in it, such as Robert D. Kaplan, to prove that it is coming, because one sees barely a glimmer of it on the horizon.

Conservatives and realists would argue that this could still change at any time, proving the international community to be, once again, a thin veneer of civility over the seething power struggle that has defined international relations for centuries. A chief argument of the most hard-line hegemonists, for example, is that a new threat could emerge from anywhere. Before he took office, Paul Wolfowitz harked back to the rapid changes in global power balances from 1905 to 1915 (the rise of imperial Germany and Soviet Russia), 1929 to 1939 (the rise of Nazi Germany and militarist Japan), and 1981 to 1991 (the final collapse of the USSR and the rise of America) in arguing for a new vigilance. "If that was true in earlier decades, how much truer is it today when the tempo of change has increased so dramatically?" he asked.[18] The problem with this view is that the world's major powers—whose consent is most needed to maintain the international community—have shown very little dissent about one thing: They want to stay in it.

Consider the fact that two of the major parties to the international community, Japan and Germany, never fully regained their sovereignty from America after World War II. Even more remarkably, there is little evidence that they are seeking to do so now. Long after the Cold War, neither shows serious signs of wanting to change its status as semisovereign powers whose security is permanently affixed to the U.S. defense umbrella. Germany, which has increasingly come to dominate France in the European Union, has relinquished a double dose of sovereignty—in a security sense, to the United States, and in a financial sense to the EU. After inflicting the worst atrocities in history on humankind in the last century, the bloodlust of Frederick the Great, Kaiser Wilhelm, and Adolf

Hitler appears to have been cauterized from the Teutonic sensibility. And even if German chauvinism has not entirely disappeared—in recent years, German xenophobia, even neo-Nazism, has been reawakened to some extent against its huge immigrant population—Germany is today so organically linked to a greater Europe that there would be no route by which a Hitler could emerge from the bowels of a great city to drag the nation into anomie again. Young Germans scarcely even think of themselves as German any longer. "When we travel through Europe, we say we are Cologners, not Germans," one student told me during a visit to that city in 2000. German chancellor Schroeder, a liberal social democrat, parted ways politically with George W. Bush over an attack on Iraq in 2002 (mainly because he was in a tough reelection campaign, and anti-Americanism was on the rise in Germany in the face of the Bush hegemonists' hawkishness). But those differences did little to damage the overall relationship. Far more telling than Schroeder's election rhetoric was a poll conducted in mid-2002 by the Chicago Council on Foreign Relations and the German Marshall Fund, which showed a striking convergence of views between Americans and Europeans over the basic tenets of world order. As the *Washington Post*'s veteran European correspondent described it, the poll results indicated

that politicians on both sides may be badly out of touch with the true sentiments of their constituents. On a broad range of issues, the survey suggests, Americans and Europeans still share similar visions, values and objectives. They see each other as dependable friends in a treacherous world and yearn for policies that will be mutually reinforcing. Americans are clearly uncomfortable with a go-it-alone attitude and want the Bush administration to work within the framework of the United Nations and international law. Europeans, meanwhile, would rather be seen as an equal partner with the United States, and not as a rival power.[19]

Even Schroeder, when I asked him a year before his campaign whether the U.S. role in Europe was today the same as it was during the Cold War—a guarantor of peace—responded that it had gone way beyond that. He spoke of a "great confluence" of "intrinsic values" shared by the two countries.[20] This from a nation that, more than any major power—except perhaps militarist Japan and Stalinist Russia—epitomized alienation in the twentieth century. It required what was effectively a transplant of societal DNA largely performed by U.S. occupiers, but it worked, as it did in Japan. Because Germany is the largest power in the EU, and the EU itself is so structurally infantile, it probably takes Europe out of the competition for a long, long time to come. Maybe for good, if Washington handles the relationship right. The historic Maastricht Treaty has unified Europe's currencies, but the European Union is still its old cacophony of voices, without a unified power structure on foreign policy. "The [U.S.-European] relationship depends a lot on Europe," German foreign minister Joschka Fischer told me in May 2002. "I do not think that there is too much America. I think there is too little Europe. We are two hundred years behind you. . . . In an institutional way we have just now reached the level of the Federalist Papers." But even this humble description strained common sense: there seems a lot more dissent within the European Union today about forming a "United States of Europe" than there was in Philadelphia 225 years ago.

Charles Kupchan, in his book *The End of the American Era,* joins a long line of previous authors who have predicted superpowerdom for the EU and therefore a return to great-power rivalry with the United States. What these scholars consistently ignore is that for a nation, or an international entity, to become a great power, there must be a willingness to aggressively use force. That is the sine qua non of sovereignty. Germany, the heart of the new Europe, has lost that willingness. Just as important, almost no one else in Europe wants Germany to regain it. Indeed, the EU itself was partially conceived to contain Germany's age-old aggressive tendencies, and the EU is likely to continue to see its mission this way. It is difficult to imagine Brussels sanctioning EU militarization, or anything more threatening than the rapid-reaction force currently envisaged, if for no other reason than that would require German remilitarization.

Japan is a more complicated case. Unlike Germany, Japan has never fully owned up to the horrors it inflicted on Asia in the 1930s and '40s. In the schools, several generations of young Japanese have been kept well

wadded in ignorance about the feral behavior of their fathers and grand-
fathers (even as their more distant forefathers' swordplay is glorified in
daily samurai dramas that appear with the same numbing frequency as
buddy-cop shows do on American TV). Racial chauvinism about the
inferiority of other Asians lingers more palpably beneath the surface in
Japan than is the case with the comparable phenomenon in Germany,
occasionally still cropping up in the comments of right-wing politicians.
But pacifism—a better term may be what the Japanese have come to call
it, *heiwa boke,* translated as "peace lethargy"—is now almost as totalitar-
ian in the Japanese mind-set as prewar militarism once was. Under the
U.S. defense umbrella, "the postwar generation has grown up without any
consciousness of the need for military strength," Minoru Hirano, a high-
school principal in Tokyo, told me when I lived there in the early '90s. In
the Diet, despite an increasing willingness to militarize, Japan's famous
constitutional prohibition against using force overseas is still treated as if
it were divine will. In a sense it is, since it represented the will of the
nation's last "shogun," General Douglas MacArthur. As Kazuo Ogura, a
Foreign Ministry official, put it in an essay, "No longer is there any patriotism so intense that people would gladly give their lives for the sake of
their country's pride; all that remains is a slender sense of pride in the
aesthetic sensibilities and artistic spirit of the Japanese." As we suggested
above, Japan seems to have resigned itself to trying to maintain what it
can of its distinctive, socialistic form of capitalism even at the expense of
its global profile, with one foot in the international community and one
foot out. If it remains, as ever, an insular place, its insularity has grown
rather harmless, except to the extent that Japan continues to be a drag in
the global economy. Increasingly, pundits in Tokyo say an aging Japan is
headed into international retirement as an Asiatic Switzerland or Austria;
it has become known as "arthritic Japan" and "the lifestyle superpower."
"Japan could be like Austria someday," a senior aide to Prime Minister
Junichiro Koizumi said in 2002. "Stagnant, lacking strong dynamism but
with a high living standard. And why not?"[21]
    And as long as other countries feel safe within the U.S.-secured inter-
national community, the ongoing process of disintegration and reintegra-

tion described above will continue. Hence Serbia and Croatia tear away or are torn away from Yugoslavia, enter a nightmarish period of anomie and ethnic cleansing, but then gradually—and eagerly—are reintegrated into the international community. The Baltic states join NATO. The governments of China and Russia also find themselves torn between two worlds, beholden both to their traditional mulish independence and to the global system. Putin straddled the fence for a while before he seemed to make the crucial decision that Lee Kuan Yew did, to conjoin his nation's fortunes with the West. Now even Russia, whose modern history is defined by its existential struggle over whether it is mainly European or Asiatic, is likely to fall to the trend. As Dmitri Trenin argues in a recent book, the emergence of Chinese power to Russia's east and the political instability to its Islamic-dominated south, including Chechnya, mean that Russia must cast its lot with the West, integrating with the European Union and allying with the United States. One key to making this happen, he says, is a proactive approach by America and Europe to enfold Russia into their central institutions, NATO and the EU.[22] The Bush administration's national security strategy expressed hope that this integration was already happening. Citing efforts to get Moscow into the WTO and the new NATO-Russia Council—perhaps a halfway step to Russia's inclusion in the alliance—the administration said: "We are already building a new strategic relationship based on a central reality of the 21st century: the United States and Russia are no longer strategic adversaries." At the same time, the strategy noted: "Russia's uneven commitment to the basic values of free-market democracy and dubious record in combating the proliferation of weapons of mass destruction remain matters of great concern."[23]

America won't be occupying China or Russia anytime soon, as it once did Japan and Germany, but I would argue that we don't need to. The disruptive forces of the international community are doing that for us. It is the international community, too, that for very different reasons offers the Chinese and Russians a real alternative to the old geopolitical structure of power, both by holding out the possibility of achieving national prosperity and pride within such a system and, related to that, giving them a face-saving way to say they have another choice but to bow to the American hegemon.

## Reckoning with China

China is the most complicated case of all. In fact, I believe it will prove to be the real test for whether the international community has staying power or ultimately falls like a house of cards in some distant decade, which is why I began this chapter with the example of the Yizheng Chemical Fiber Company.

When al-Qaeda is a distant memory and Saddam Hussein is in his grave, China is likely to be the handiest bad guy for American strategic planners decades into the future—and to supply the chief argument that old-style power politics, and not the international community, is what defines global affairs. George W. Bush, far more conservative than his pro-engagement father, came into office displaying an ideologue's view of China as a long-term future enemy. Andrew Marshall, the Pentagon's near-legendary chief of "net assessment" who was the last of the Truman-era cold warriors, directed a study that called for a wholesale reallocation of military assets away from Europe and toward Asia. In the view of Pentagon planners, the new Fulda Gap—where Soviet troops were poised to invade Western Europe during the Cold War—would be the South China Sea, a key choke point that the Chinese might some day seek to control. Taiwan, as conservatives see it, is the essential element in Chinese strategic thinking to controlling a chain of islands that will give it effective military dominance over the region. Wolfowitz, in an article before he took power, cited "Admiral Liu Huaqing's assertion that 'the Chinese navy should exert effective control of the seas within the first island chain,' defined as comprising the Aleutians, the Kuriles, Japan (including the Ryukyu), Taiwan, the Philippines and most of Indonesia."[24] An incident early on seemed to confirm the conservatives' worst suspicions: On April 1, 2001, a Chinese fighter pilot collided with an American surveillance plane monitoring China's coast over the sea. That touched off an eleven-day standoff during which China detained the American crew.

Bush's right-wing political base, meanwhile, grew increasingly vociferous about containing China, slowing China down, disengaging from it—anything to prevent what seemed to them the inevitable rise of a rival superpower that will either behave roguishly or, at the very least, challenge American power in Asia, under the age-old dictates of great-power politics. The realist scholar John Mearsheimer argued that if China "continues modernizing at a rapid pace," it "would surely pursue regional hegemony, just as the United States did in the western hemisphere during the nineteenth century."[25] Engagement with China, he argued, was misguided "because a wealthy China would not be a status quo power; it would be an aggressive one determined to achieve regional hegemony—not because a rich China would have wicked motives, but because the best way for any state to maximize its prospects for survival is to dominate its region of the world." Mearsheimer's prescription was that America should not only withdraw from engagement but somehow slow down China's growth—as though Aubrey Li, the Warburg banker, and the tide of Wall Street's influence could be outlawed. They cannot be, nor should they be. Even if, as some skeptics believe, Beijing's long-term plan is to avoid the mistake of the Soviet Union, which depleted itself economically with an arms race and a closed-off economy, and to build a powerful economy that will allow it to confront the United States many years from now, it is unlikely to succeed with this strategy. Why? Because in taking part in the international economy it is subjecting itself to the same forces that Japan did. And these forces are dividing it internally. Like Yizheng, even many companies affiliated with the People's Liberation Army are getting into the globalization game, subverting the strategy directed by Beijing's Committee of Science, Technology and Industry for National Defense (Costind) to obtain "dual-use" technology. As Bates Gill, a China scholar, told me, many Costind factories would prefer to manufacture consumer goods like refrigerators and motorcycles: "They don't make any money in military research and production."[26] They want to integrate themselves, in other words, into the international community.

Indeed, conservatives who see China as America's next superpower rival find themselves utterly unable to deal with phenomena like these. Lawrence Kaplan, a neoconservative commentator, argues that trade won't bring democracy to China because, in contrast to other market systems that have flourished amid autocracy, China's system derives "from a pathological model of economic development," and private ownership is not allowed. Leaving aside for a moment that Kaplan is wrong on many of his facts—increasingly, large segments of the market economy are owned privately, as at Yizheng—he misses the larger point: that even marginal capitalism and openness integrate and enmesh China into the global system.

In a world in which basic clashes of interests and national chauvinism still exist, the future of U.S.–China relations will be a race between the co-opting effects of the international community and the demands of big-power politics. It may well be, as some hard-line analysts of China suspect, that the Communist mandarins in Beijing, having studied closely the failures of the Soviet Union to keep up in the weapons race, have a hundred-year plan to take on the United States using our own economic methods. But I would suggest that at any number of points along that road they will face a fork: join the international community or don't. And at any number of points along the road those considerations could alter or temper such plans. It was a striking coincidence that on September 17, 2001, less than a week after the terrorist attacks on America, the World Trade Organization in Geneva finally agreed on terms to admit China after fifteen years of negotiations. The agreement locked China into a program of open markets and a long-term commitment to play by global trade and financial rules. As Supachai Panitchpakdi, the current head of the WTO, and journalist Mark Clifford put it, "The timing [served] to highlight those who support a liberal, open world and those who would destroy it." China seemed to throw its lot in with order rather than chaos. [27]

Above all, it is anachronistic in the extreme to assume that great powers will simply resume the path toward hegemony pursued by their predecessors in history. As the scholar and diplomat Adam Watson noted back in 1992, "Modern industrial technology makes the possession or imperial control of large territories a much less important factor of economic power now than when land and raw materials were the principal sources of wealth, so long as an orderly economic system ensures that high concentrations of technological skill in a small area have access to supplies of food and raw materials on the one hand and markets on the other." [28] If the more hawkish Pentagon planners see the South China Sea as a key choke point that Beijing might try to control, one must ask: to what point?

What precisely would they seek to choke off—their own trade? In fact, more sober-minded China analysts say there is no characterization of the South China Sea in this sense to be found in any Chinese military litera- ture, and they point out that for most of its history—aside from occasional bullying of neighboring countries such as Vietnam, and an insistence on planting its flag on pebbly China Sea atolls such as the Spratly Islands— China has never been an imperialist power.[29] The preponderance of experts also agree that to the extent China is building up its military, it is to become a regional power (and to forestall a U.S.-supported move toward Taiwanese independence), *not* a global rival to America. "I don't see these capabilities as the leading edge of a more comprehensive, long- term plan either to supplant U.S. military power in the Western Pacific or to challenge U.S. power on a global basis," said Jonathan Pollack, director of strategic research at the United States Naval War College.[30] Almost all of China's military R&D is for defensive purposes—for example, how to counter moves like the U.S. militarization of space. Much like the Euro- peans, the Chinese "don't like to fight anymore," Pollack says. "Their last big conflict was in 1979 [with Vietnam]." Ironically, the most reliable source of this view has become the U.S. military, which has a somewhat better vantage point than the armchair generals inside the Washington Beltway. "When I look at the Asia Pacific region, I don't see any ideological or geographical or ethnic big causes of a future conflict," said Admiral Dennis Blair, who until his recent retirement was commander in chief of U.S. forces in the Pacific. "We're just not lined up for . . . a big war ."[31]

The "enveloping" effect of the international system is furthered along by what my colleague Fareed Zakaria has described as the weakening of the strong state, which he says "will make the once-straightforward rise and fall of great powers a complex, friction-filled process." Zakaria cites Japan and Germany: "Consider Germany today, with its federal structure, weak central government, and fiercely independent central bank; many of the government's powers have been delegated to Brussels, others have slipped out of its hands as Bonn has loosened its grip on the economy and the welfare state. Japan is trapped on one hand by its postwar consti- tution, which restrains its military might, and on the other by its entan- glement in the world of international institutions."[32] It is just such entanglement, of course, that American sovereigntists fear for their own country. But next to the relatively small loss of sovereign freedom, the gain in international stability—and American security—is enormous.


## What's in It for America

Co-opting the other major powers will, however, clearly require that they feel both unthreatened and protected by the United States. And—to return to the main theme of this book—this can happen only if Washington itself embraces the international community that other nations now see themselves as part of at the same time as Washington projects its power. As we saw in Chapter 1, that was not the message the incoming administration of George W. Bush wanted to convey. Many conservatives wanted to roll back what they saw as the rabid globalism of the Clinton years; they deplored the extent to which this globalized society sought to influence issues they wanted to reserve for U.S. sovereignty—from land mines to international war crimes tribunals to taxes.

Most significant of all, many of these so-called sovereigntists at senior levels of the Bush administration, like John Bolton, renounced international law altogether. If they did not accept the international community, it followed that they failed to see that international law is the backbone of the international community, since it binds foreign leaders to the dictates of the system (and gives them a face-saving way to tell their domestic constituencies that they have no choice but to, say, support U.S. efforts against al-Qaeda or Iraq under a UN Security Council resolution). The Bush administration's dismissive view of international law was especially damaging after 9/11, when the president announced his new doctrine of preemption. Preemption may have been necessary against an enemy, such as al-Qaeda, that could not be deterred through traditional means, but, as discussed in the last chapter, to embrace such a doctrine without the mitigating effect of binding it to international law and norms recklessly invited the rest of the world to adopt preemption as a universal precedent. Above all, the abjuring of international law put the United States, legally at least, in the same camp as al-Qaeda: outside the international community.[33]

In truth, by the time they took office, well before 9/11, the Bush sovereigntists were already putting their fingers in a very leaky dike. The international community had extended into America's national life in myriad ways. The U.S. economy had become directly hooked in, like an addict, to the Wall Street–centered international financial system. Indeed, America had become a net user of other nations' capital—and this figure includes the foreign aid we send out—enabling Americans to habitually buy more goods from abroad than we sell to others. The antiglobalism of Bolton and other conservatives was, more than ever, in direct conflict with the interests of their party's business base. U.S. businesspeople knew they had to compete on the playing field of the international community, and under the same rules. For example, when it came to postwar Iraqi oil, U.S. companies feared Iraqi revenues would get tied up in litigation if Washington failed to operate through the UN.

But nothing argues more that the international community is in the national interest of the United States than the war on terror. Indeed, the hostility of bin Laden and his Islamic fundamentalist sympathizers can be properly understood only in the context of the ever-widening circle of Westernized international society. His jihad, remember, was launched against "Crusaders and Jews" and the "iniquitous United Nations" as well as America. Bin Laden may have been personally upset by the presence of U.S. soldiers in Saudi Arabia, his home, but the problem is not that the Arab world is surrounded by Western armies. The problem is that it is surrounded by a global society that is vastly richer and more successful than the Arab world. The terrorists represent the ragtag fringe of a region that is itself on the fringe of what remains a growing and vibrant international community. The Islamic scholar Bernard Lewis traces today's Muslim rage to the final decline of Islamic society after a millennium-long war of primacy and self-esteem with the West: "Compared with its millennial rival, Christendom, the world of Islam had become poor, weak, and ignorant. . . . The dominance of the West was clear for all to see."[34]

This struggle of civilizational identity has occurred on other fronts as well, and always the West has triumphed. In a brilliant essay, Ian Buruma and Avishai Margalit argue that in the history of what they call "occidentalism," or repeated attempts to organize a hostile resistance to Western-ization, Islamists are only the latest incarnation. Today's fundamentalists were preceded by Japanese nationalists in the early twentieth century, early German nationalists, and Slavophilic Russians.

Like Islamism, both German fascism and Japanese militarism were born as resistance movements to the perceived corrupting tendencies of the West. In Japan, fealty to the emperor and *kokutai*, loosely translated as "national essence," were the cardinal values; it is no accident that even as Japan, in the late nineteenth century, adopted the technology, the political systems, and even the dress of the West, the unifying slogan of the Meiji Restoration was "expel the barbarians." As Buruma and Margalit point out, "Similar language—though without the neo-Shintoist associations—was used by German National Socialists and other European fascists. . . . Nazi ideologues and Japanese militarist propagandists were fighting the same Western ideas." Yet one by one, either by war or influence, these resistance movements have been not only overcome, but usually funda-mentally transformed.[35]

America faces a terrible conundrum in deciding how to heal the pathology of the Arab world, but I believe it is only a matter of time (his-torical time, to be sure, which could mean decades or even a century) before the rabid occidentalists of the Arab world are crushed by the tec-tonics of Westernization as well. If the demands of the moment make it nearly impossible, as a matter of U.S. policy, to impose democracy and open systems on the Arab world, the historical trends are so powerful, and the ability of these weakened societies to resist is so deficient, that at some point they too will be absorbed by globalization. As Lewis writes in *What Went Wrong?*, his trenchant analysis of the long decline of Islamic civilization from its medieval glories, "If the peoples of the Middle East continue on their present path, the suicide bomber may become a metaphor for the whole region, and there will be no escape from a down-ward spiral of hate and spite, rage and self-pity, poverty and oppres-sion."[36] They have only one real choice: join the international community —or be contained or even destroyed by it. The West is making them an offer they can't refuse.

The tactics of the war on terror also required that Washington make use of the international community. To fight what became, at least after the al-Qaeda leadership was partially destroyed in Afghanistan, disaffiliated cells, the United States desperately needed information on terror groups from Berlin to Kuala Lumpur. That cried out for a much more conciliatory attitude by the Bush administration, but again it was slow in coming. Washington was even reluctant to share intelligence information with key countries like France and Germany. Not surprisingly, cooperation in shutting down terror cells and rolling up their financial support networks quickly flagged. The Bush administration's antiglobalist mind-set also delayed the formulation of a new international regime, developed during the Clinton years, to stop money laundering. This allowed the continuation of activities as varied as the quiet funding of terrorist groups through Muslim charities and Saddam Hussein's weapons acquisition efforts (through laundering schemes in places such as Liechtenstein) to continue.[37]

The arcane but critical issue of the proliferation of weapons of mass destruction is another reason why we must work to flesh out a fuller international community. The president's answer was to say "we will oppose [proliferation] with all our power." Yet raw power doesn't work to stop nations from passing on the knowledge of how to build such weapons. It doesn't work well to stop other nations from seeking to obtain these types of weapons, especially if they know that America is working to enlarge and improve its own nuclear arsenal and that it cares little for international law and organizations. The irony was that after years of Washington's trying to bring potentially rogue powers such as China into this system of norms —to stop Beijing from transferring nuclear know-how to Pakistan, for example—Bush left many of these governments flummoxed. "We used to chastise the Chinese for being outside that process," says Pollack of the Naval War College. "So they made a major investment in training people for arms control. They're all set up and ready to go at a time when we're peeing all over arms control." Some of the administration's policies actually seemed to welcome a world of more nuclear weapons; the nuclear posture review leaked in March 2002 went several steps beyond Clinton's presidential decision directive in 1997 (PDD-60, which first broached the use of nuclear weapons to take out terrorist states).

Well into the war on terror, the administration continued to pitch for more missile defense money to defend against "terrorist states," even as it slighted more cooperative programs such as the Nunn-Lugar nuclear materials reduction plan, which sent millions of dollars to Russia to help it dispose of Cold War–era weapons. In a traditional strategic, set-piece way, the Bush administration's pursuit of missile defense could prove to be smart, long-term thinking, if it works. But continuing to make it the centerpiece of an ongoing defense strategy post-9/11 while slighting multilateral efforts to contain proliferation was nothing less than delusional. Keeping nuclear, biological, and chemical weapons from terrorists requires international cooperation in the most profound way and justifies anew one of the fuzziest, most derided elements of Woodrow Wilson's old program for peace: arms reduction.

This means it is worth compromising on other aspects of our sovereignty—especially since the claims of the sovereigntists are wildly overstated. That the Bush sovereigntists attempted a counterrevolution is not surprising: For a while in the late '90s there *was* a sense that everything was becoming transnationalized, since financial markets and the explosive growth of NGOs meant there was a new force out there that had broken free of governments. But governments and nation-states still plainly define the world in which we live. The international community, as real, powerful, and growing as it is, shows no signs whatever of fostering a world government. The idea is absurd on its face: Even as George W. Bush beefed up his defense budget levels near those of the Cold War, about $390 billion, the *total* world budgets of all the major multinational organizations put together—the UN, IMF, and World Bank—amounted to less than $20 billion a year. Newer institutions, such as the WTO, are not giant supranational bureaucracies but dispute-resolution forums attended by states. The nation-state is a basic, irreducible unit of the international community, much as the household is the basic unit of the local community. Yet no one argues that because households don't merge into communes or cooperatives, or because some households take part in local government and community activities and some don't, the local community therefore doesn't exist.

By midway through his term, as noted earlier, President Bush had begun to acknowledge the reality of the international community—and, just as important, the universal values that define it. He began to recognize that he needed permanent allies in the war on terror, that something more was required than the spare "Bush Doctrine": You're with us or against us. Bush also began to see that if America was going to build a "soft" empire—one that depends on common values rather than Roman-style conquest—he needed to move beyond the hubristic views of the neoconservative hawks in his administration. Increasingly if gingerly, Bush sought to define the contours of the international community by saying that America was not necessarily the model for others. In his speeches, for example, he made a point of saying that "freedom is not America's gift to the world; it is God's gift to the world." The invocation of divine will wasn't exactly the right touch, especially to secular Europeans who derided Bush as a born-again cowboy and to Muslims who feared a Christian "crusade." But the president's emerging approach, said one of the drafters of Bush's 2002 national security strategy, was "to rebut American exceptionalism, to say we are not the exemplar here. We are not the city on the hill. This path is not America's alone. There are many ways of achieving" what the strategy called "a single sustainable model for national success: freedom, democracy, and free enterprise." This statement was taken as more American arrogance, but it squared with what Bronislaw Geremek had said (quoting Wilson) at the Community of Democracies forum, that there is only one concept of democracy. And perhaps that also meant one international community.[38]

## Rethinking Realism

Yet the notion that the international community was mostly myth lived on. People expected a tidy structure, and there was none. As with so much of the Permanent Quagmire, the truth about the international community lies somewhere murkily in the middle, somewhere between the sovereigntists' overwrought fears of global government—symbolized by a favorite fantasy of the far right, that UN "black helicopters" overfly U.S. territory—and the fears of the left that global capitalism is an untrammeled juggernaut heading toward "some kind of abyss . . . with no one at the wheel," as the writer William Greider put it.[39]

There are no black helicopters, and little sign of an abyss either, despite all the problems of globalization. And we are, in truth, fairly comfortable with dwelling on this "isthmus of a middle state / a being darkly wise and rudely great," as Alexander Pope famously described the lot of humankind—all the while edging forward, ever so gradually, as we saw in the last chapter when FDR and Truman consciously corrected the mistakes of Wilson. We are muddling through. Louis Henkin, a theorist of international law, began his classic book *How Nations Behave* by writing, "In relations between nations, the progress of civilization may be seen as movement from force to diplomacy, from diplomacy to law."[40] It's not turning out that way—nor is it likely to. There is no orderly progression. If international law is indeed more highly developed than ever before in history, we still need deft mixtures of all three—force, diplomacy, and law —to preserve the progress of civilization, at least as long as Washington is overseeing matters.

This state of being more or less in between perfect order, on one hand, and chaos or anarchy, on the other—while seeing a general forward motion to civilization—suits modern sensibilities just fine. If we are, as a species, predisposed to thinking that we can master chaos, we are also predisposed to being skeptical about too much order. For much of the twentieth century, from the failure of progressivism to the collapse of civilized Europe into World War I to the rise of totalitarianism, it became intellectually unfashionable in the West to talk at all about an international order that works, and of course an international community. After the two world wars, such thinking smacked of utopianism, or more often dystopianism; anything orderly was Big Brotherly, Stalinist, or Hitlerian. But in recent years two major books have sought to rescue human history from the drift and confusion of postmodernism (which, distilled down from its gaseous ubiquity in contemporary thought, is the concept that human society can't be explained by overarching theories). Those books are Francis Fukuyama's *The End of History* and Robert Wright's *Nonzero: The Logic of Human Destiny*. I won't go so far as to endorse Fukuyama's seminal if somewhat overwrought declaration of global victory for liberal democracy, perhaps the most thrashed-out thesis of the last decade or so. Nor do I subscribe to all of Wright's conclusions, which are less familiar.

Using the tools of game theory, Wright argues that human society has evolved toward "non-zero-sum results," meaning greater and greater integration as a means of securing peace, stability, and prosperity for as many people as possible. The gradual "loss of sovereignty," he says, "is a fact of history, one of the most fundamental, stubborn facts in all of history."[41] Wright's conclusions are far too blithe: "In 1500 B.C., there were around 600,000 autonomous polities on the planet," he writes. "Today, after many mergers and acquisitions, there are 193 autonomous polities. At this rate, the planet should have a single government any day now."[42] In fact, there is no reason whatever that the current number of polities could not represent some kind of end state—or that, given the forces of ethnic devolution we will discuss in Chapter 5, they will not increase further. But Fukuyama and Wright are correct about the overall idea: The centuries-old growth of the international community proves that there is indeed a progressive motion to human affairs. The mistake that leads to dystopia—and totalitarianism—is to think that just because there is a progressive motion that it must lead to perfect order rather than the controlled chaos that characterizes the Permanent Quagmire.

Following the lead of Fukuyama and Wright, it is not too much to say that the pathways of globalization that ultimately led Aubrey Li and Ren Chuan Jun to each other at Yizheng Chemical Fiber evolved as the tail end of a much longer-term project. Li and Ren were both Chinese. But Aubrey Li, the investment banker, was also the emissary of an Anglicized Hong Kong, and therefore of the West. The message of globalization he brought to his fellow Chinese, Ren, was the product of the social and political communion of the West that began with ancient Greece and Rome and the Magna Charta and moved on to the Glorious Revolution, the Enlightenment, the Industrial Revolution, and then the American and French Revolutions. This tradition, in the twentieth century, conquered "outnations" such as Germany (which had stopped the advance of Roman civilization at the Teutoburg Forest in A.D. 9 but could not stop the Allies) and Japan and brought them into the fold. It's been one long bucket brigade down the centuries. If, as historian David Landes writes, Europe bequeathed to the world "nothing less than the invention and definition of modernity," then it was America that principally globalized that modernity and transmuted it into a set of universal values.[43] The international community we feel somewhat a part of is an outgrowth both of that European tradition and, in the past century, of America's exceptionalist crusade, and is today kept intact by the global sinews of the American überpower.

In understanding this evolving world system, the ones who have even more explaining to do than Fukuyama and Wright are the realists, and unlike those two, they still represent the mainstream. I will not burden the reader with a detailed account of the mind-bending debate between realists and Wilsonian internationalists, and their many spawned schools: neorealists and neoliberals, institutionalists, constructivists, and structuralists. The debate, boiled down, still revolves around the central problem of how to create international order. The bedrock belief of the realist school is that while nation-states have constitutions, laws, and hierarchies of authority, relations between states are still governed by anarchy, and states have fixed interests based on a zero-sum game of material gain. Since there is no global government, how do states manage their affairs amid that state of anarchy? The answer is that the interests of nations and peoples must be "defined in terms of power," as one of the fathers of realism, Hans Morgenthau, wrote—whether balance of power in a multipolar world of roughly equal states, or hegemonic power by one dominant state, as with the United States today. The more powerful states, in other words, dictate terms to the less powerful. In a world still haunted by the failures of Wilsonianism after the First World War—and the nuclear balance of power between the United States and the USSR—various forms of realism still shape the thinking of most scholars of international relations. As a result, most of the burden has fallen on the liberal, Wilsonian crowd —those who believe in an emerging international system—to prove that something exists beyond mere anarchy. The litmus test again is: What is keeping the peace? What is maintaining stability?

I think my own conclusions must be fairly clear. If the classic flaw of Wilsonian liberalism is that it believes too much in change—overestimating the perfecting possibilities of human nature—the classic flaw of realism is that it lacks "a theory of change."[44] And what we have had in the last century or so is change, lots of it—if not of human nature then of globalized society. That is why the emerging existence of the international community, as described here, must utterly alter the traditional debate over U.S. foreign policy. It is why we, as Americans, must destroy the wall that still exists in our own minds between our national life and the international community —a wall that is all but gone in actual fact, though psychologically we haven't grasped that yet. On the realist view, the "West" and its construct, the international community, should have disintegrated after the Cold War, not expanded, as it has. Multilateral conventions that kept other powers down, like the Nuclear Non-Proliferation Treaty, should have suffered wholesale defections years ago, rather than a few rogue violators such as Saddam and Kim Jong Il or unique rivalries such as Pakistan and India. As Owen Harries wrote in 1993, "the political 'West' is not a natural construct but a highly artificial one. It took a presence of a life-threatening, overtly hostile 'East' to bring it into existence and to maintain its unity. It is extremely doubtful whether it can now survive the disappearance of that enemy. The 'West' has lost much of its definition and raison d'être."[45] For years the realists have desperately tried to reckon with the failure of predictions like these and to keep up with the growth of international society, to the point where they are no longer able to explain the world well at all and their theories have fallen apart.[46] But the realists haven't given up. As the United States geared up to take on Saddam Hussein's Iraq, and many Europeans balked, the realists seized on the transatlantic dispute to launch another counterattack against Harries' "artificial" construct, the West. "It is time to stop pretending that Europeans and Americans share a common view of the world, or even that they occupy the same world," wrote Robert Kagan (though he was more of a neoconservative). He argued that Washington's emphasis on military strength as a means of keeping order contrasted so greatly with European reliance on international law and institutions that "Americans are from Mars, and Europeans are from Venus."[47] But his argument ignored the central fact that America itself had the biggest hand in creating the global institutions the Europeans wanted to hang their hats on. And in the end Bush—tentative though his embrace of the international community was—succeeded in making a compelling case, at least to some U.S. allies, that the United Nations' credibility was threatened by Saddam. As much as many Europeans viscerally wanted to make a new, hegemonic America their enemy, the inconvenient truth was that America was not really such a terrible hegemon and that some threats, such as terror and WMD proliferation, were still worse. The result was that European leaders, faced with an embarrassing new iteration of the Bush Doctrine—do you stand with Saddam Hussein, or with George Bush?—squabbled more among themselves over Iraq than they did with Washington. Far from projecting the common European view, Gerhard Schroeder was even branded a "unilateralist" by some European commentators for his resolutely dovish views, and the conservative, pro-American governments in Italy and Spain sided with Bush, as did a host of new NATO members from Eastern Europe. Victor Davis Hanson even suggested that Schroeder's "sudden outbursts"—renewing as they did age-old fears of German nationalism—meant that "Holland, Italy, and the eastern Europeans are more likely to strengthen, not enfeeble, their American ties."[48]

So the international community continued to defy the realists and to lurch forward, in fits and starts. It is interesting that even Hans Morgenthau did not preclude the possibility that his theory of realism would be eclipsed by such developments. He ended his seminal book, *Politics Among Nations*, by saying that internationalist solutions to the problem of order, like free trade and collective security, "presuppose the existence of an integrated international society, which actually does not exist."[49] Perhaps it did not when he first wrote those words (the book came out in 1948). It does now.

How could it be that the dominant school of American political thinking, realism, misses so much of the reality of our world? Well, it's not completely out of touch, because obviously raw nation-state power still counts. If the U.S. military had not trounced the Taliban and its dominance was not utterly clear to every would-be rival, bin Laden might well be leading a horde of Islamists into New York and Washington right about now, China might be already seeking hegemony in Asia, and Russia might be causing trouble for Europe. And even within the international system, states still jostle for power and influence, as realists predict they will. But clearly realism has been unable to adjust to the overarching reality of our time: While one set of battle lines in the war on terror was between America and bin Laden, the broader battle lines were between two nebulous nonstate actors: the international community, and that community's remaining holdouts, the Islamist terror networks.

True, the United States was doing most of the actual fighting. And of course many conservatives, even now, still will not be persuaded that this fight is about anything other than raw power—the power of the American hegemon against the "asymmetric" threat of the terrorists. For American unilateralists, military power is still what counts. That's at least partly true, as I have said. But as we will see in the next chapter, even America's all-powerful military—the source of our unilateralist pride—draws much of its vitality from the international community.

# 4

# *The Argument from Hard Power*

America's defense industrial base is now global.

John Hamre

LIEUTENANT GENERAL Michael V. Hayden has the peculiar problem of running the world's most secretive spy agency in the world's most open society. Situated about midway along the busy industrial corridor between Washington and Baltimore, the National Security Agency is both visible and invisible. The "Crypto City" complex lies just a few miles off Interstate 95, one of the most traveled arteries in America. But thick, dark green–tinted windows guard its secrets, and at its gateway the NSA has prevented county officials from laying down a rubber traffic-counting hose to determine how many employees pass over the roadways.[1] Hayden tries his best to bridge the parallel universes of secrecy and openness that he inhabits. Many of the NSA's thirty-five thousand employees are forbidden from telling their spouses exactly what they do; yet the agency has its own website, with a "kid's page" for aspiring young code breakers.

And once you get through the multiple security checks—where waiting NSA public-affairs officials seem a bit stunned at greeting an outsider—Hayden, a native Pittsburgher who quaffs diet Dr. Peppers in his office through the day, is friendly and outgoing in manner, even jovial. As a bobble-headed Pittsburgh Pirates doll peers over his right shoulder, the NSA director sits before a glass-topped map of central and south Asia and the Mideast, where his agency is engaged in a life-and-death struggle in tracking the movements and communications of America's terrorist enemies.

The NSA is the überpower's eyes and ears, a vast network of spy satellites, surveillance planes, computers, and telecom equipment around the world that monitors terrorist or other threats on cell phones, radio transmissions, and Internet communications the world over. The gathering of this signals intelligence, or "Sigint," is now even more critical to the nation's future in an era when the government must preemptively take on threats like terrorism, and must pinpoint who is planning what action. In 2003 the public got a rare glimpse of Sigint when Colin Powell revealed electronic intercepts that showed Iraqi officials were evading UN inspectors. But rarely is there such a Perry Mason moment. More than a year after September 11, U.S. intelligence officials admitted that despite all the clues that an attack was imminent, they simply could not gather enough detail in time to avert it.

In a few short sentences, Hayden sums up why. The transformation from the endless arms race and spy-versus-spy skullduggery with the Soviet Union to the present challenge for America's national security apparatus could not be greater, he says. "We have gone from chasing the telecommunications structure of a slow-moving, technologically inferior, resource poor nation-state—and we could do that pretty well—to chasing a communications structure in which an al-Qaeda member can go into a storefront in Istanbul and buy for $100 a communications device that is absolutely cutting edge, and for which he has had to make no investment in its development. That's what we've got to deal with."

It's much worse than that, actually. Tracking the Soviets involved listening in on a few well-known communications pipelines—microwave transmissions, say, from Moscow to an ICBM base in Siberia. Now the NSA has to deal with billions of conversations worldwide on many different media. "NSA downsized about a third of its manpower and about the same proportion of its budget in the '90s," Hayden told Congress in 2002. "That's the same decade when mobile cell phones increased from 16 million to 741 million—an increase of 50 times. That's the same decade when Internet users went from about four to 361 million. . . . In that same decade of the '90s, international telephone traffic went from 38 billion minutes to over 100 billion. This year, the world's population will spend over 180 billion minutes on the phone in international calls alone."[2]

That's a lot of "chatter," as raw intelligence is called. Almost immediately upon taking up his post in 1999, Hayden met with charges that his agency was "going deaf" and couldn't keep up with the bad guys. And so it was around that same glass-topped table in Hayden's office that he and his senior staff decided there was only one way to battle this new enemy and its state-of-the-art technology—with the same technology. His answer has been a major strategic shift from traditional defense contracting to commercial technologies, in order to make use of the best America's high-tech companies have to offer, and to learn better how to "bug" commercial transmissions. Signals intelligence "has to look like its target. We have to master whatever technology the target is using [to] turn his beeps and squeaks into something humanly intelligible," says Hayden. "If we don't, we literally don't hear him."[3] In only a few years, Hayden has so outsourced the agency—giving contracts to companies such as IBM for "data mining"—that by 2003 the amount of spy technologies the agency still builds on its own was expected to drop below 20 percent. He has set up a facility at a nearby office park where would-be commercial contractors can come in and "surf" an unclassified NSA computer, looking through the kinds of contracts it has to let. All of which brings us back to the paradox of Hayden's life: He must depend on the openness of the American economy—and the globalized nature of its top companies—to accomplish the most secretive work. Hayden is philosophical about working his way through the paradox. "The way a nation makes war, the way a nation protects its security, is as much a product of its culture as the way it writes poetry, or literature, or creates art," says Hayden. "So why then would we as an agency try to do something different from what our society writ large was offering to us?"

But this marks a profound shift in America's defense apparatus from the Cold War era. During most of the Cold War, the U.S. defense industry was sequestered in lone, top-secret grandeur. What Eisenhower famously called the "military-industrial complex" spent untold billions on weapons designed exclusively for the Pentagon (with older-generation models for our Cold War allies). You never saw their products in stores. Today the pride of America's military is also the pride of America's economy: Many of the best defense technologies that are giving America its military edge, such as satellites, computers, avionics, electronics, and command-and-control telecommunications, come in large part from the booming commercial high-tech sector. And here is the crucial point: Many depend far less on Pentagon dollars than on the international marketplace to survive.

If the heroes of the wars of the twenty-first century are U.S. Special Forces units, the U.S. Air Force, and intelligence gatherers, the unsung agents of their heroism lie in Silicon Valley and other hotbeds of information technology. Not only have these IT companies transformed the U.S. economy, they have made America, quite literally, the überpower— delivered the world's commanding heights to our military and intelligence apparatus. This is hardly just limited to Hayden's astonishingly accurate eye-in-the-sky satellites and ears-in-the-ether spy planes, which bristle with supersensitive listening equipment. The decisive edge in recent U.S. military campaigns also has come from the use of "systems integration" equipment—which enabled communications between Special Forces on the ground and pilots in the air, and made the laser- and satellite-guided bombs possible—far more than from "platforms" (Pentagon jargon for big war-fighting machines such as planes, ships, and tanks). And the most dramatic improvements in military effectiveness over the last decade have come in communications, especially between military services. "In the Gulf War, our Air Force and Navy couldn't talk to each other," says Don Hicks, a Reagan-era Pentagon official who has become a campaigner for commercialization. "That's all improved a lot."[4] Much of this critical information flow was coordinated through satellites, which transmitted laser targeting or GPS navigation data through ground stations and even allowed pilots and Special Forces and CIA targeters in the trenches to communicate in real time in secure computer chat rooms. "Ask a general or admiral for thoughts about the Afghan campaign and they are more likely to talk about 'bandwidth' [processing power] than bombs," the *Washington Post* reported.[5] Especially after Afghanistan, the Pentagon was quick to take this lesson on board. "The challenge of the future isn't building a great infantry carrier or artillery piece," said Lieutenant General John

Riggs, the officer who was heading up the Army's modernization effort. "The challenge is building a system that ensures we get the right information to the right place at the right time on the battlefield."[6]

That's one challenge. Another is to recognize that the industrial base that will produce this system—and keep America on top—is today fully globalized, and to understand the implications of that. The companies that constitute this vibrant industrial base are those same transborder corporations that, to recall Pascal Zachary's comment in the last chapter, are redefining national identity. Most of these companies, in other words, get substantial portions of their revenues from overseas sales, and to stay ahead of their foreign rivals they must compete freely and in a stable, expanding marketplace. Supercomputers, for example, are necessary to twenty-first-century warfare—determining everything from Hayden's success at surveillance to warhead design to weather patterns in the event of an air strike—and every U.S. supercomputer company now gets at least half of its revenues from sales abroad. In a world defined by generally open markets and comparative advantage—the idea that every economy manufactures and sells what it is best at—it is often these "dual-use" goods (high-tech products with both commercial and military uses) that America is most proficient at making and which underpin our economic health. What that means is that maintaining America's hard power depends, as never before, on a stable and open international system. "You have to confront the fact that America's defense industrial base is now global," said John Hamre, a former deputy defense secretary under Clinton. Or as Major General Robert Scales, a key mover behind the Army's modernization program, called "Army After Next," puts it: "Like it or not, the advantage we are going to gain in the future over a potential major competitor is going to come from the commercial sector. . . . We ought to just step back, relax and be prepared to exploit it."[7]

The problem is that many officials in Washington have not yet accepted this. Especially on Capitol Hill, few legislators have made the leap from the Cold War–era mind-set. The idea of outsourcing to the commercial sector still doesn't sit right with many of the hard-liners who run America's national security apparatus. The result is a damaging gap between reality and perception that in recent years has hurt key defense

industries, among them the makers of encryption, satellites, and computers. Many government officials, such as Hayden, admit that even now the
U.S. national security apparatus is still not making use of the best U.S.
technology. Today, "we're behind the curve in keeping up with the global
telecommunications revolution," Hayden says.[8] The hegemonists in
Washington still believe, to a disturbing degree, that the world they live in
is one in which America can protect its prized technologies simply by
unilaterally imposing export controls that are no longer viable, not least
because other countries won't agree to them. The harsh truth is that such
controls are effective only with full cooperation from allies and the international community. And the result of these antiquated attitudes in
Washington is that in a world increasingly defined by savage competition
between technology companies worldwide, the nation that rose to power
based on its relative openness—the United States—is among the more
closed economies when it comes to some important dual-use technologies. Because that undermines our industrial base, almost nothing is
more dangerous to our national security.

Take just one example, software encryption, which is necessary for
securing battlefield transmissions as well as a plethora of other internal
Pentagon communications. For most of the postwar period, encryption
was highly classified, subject to multilateral restrictions under the Cold
War–era COCOM, the Paris-based Coordinating Committee on Multilateral Export Controls, which required export licenses for any sensitive
technology transfers. But in 1990, as the Cold War was ending and the era
of the personal computer and the Information Age was taking off, America's European allies decided to lift export restrictions. America retained
its own restrictions unilaterally. "It was like a cowboy holding a gun to his
own head to make a threat," said Bruce Heiman, an industry expert and
lobbyist. The result was that U.S. companies basically stopped investing in
R&D capabilities in the United States. Investors plowed their money into
foreign companies. During the 1990s other countries, including Israel,
Russia, and the Scandinavian nations, began to take the lead in encryption technology. By 1997, one industry survey found, 653 encryption
products were available from twenty-nine different nations. "What that
did was dramatically lessen the CIA and Defense Department's ability to

be in touch with the best encryption," says Kenneth Kay, a Washington-based computer industry lobbyist. The Clinton administration finally liberalized the controls in 1999, but "in a post 9/11 environment, we're just realizing the longer-term costs because our computer networks are not as secure as they might have been," said Heiman.

The vibrancy of America's industrial base was also key to winning the Cold War, of course. The Soviet Union was essentially bankrupted out of existence, not defeated on the battlefield. But during the Cold War arms race, when America maintained a "hothouse" defense industry and most big-ticket equipment was developed and manufactured mainly for the Pentagon (and there was a striking degree of international consensus on who was the enemy), it was far easier to keep technology out of foreign hands. The relationship between economics and national security was then an indirect one in that a strong U.S. economy produced the taxes needed to supply the trillions of dollars plowed into this sequestered defense industry. Because they were so protected and had only one customer, many defense contractors grew inefficient and didn't develop economies of scale. Recall the hundreds of contractors who infamously slurped up billions from the public trough, selling the Pentagon $2 billion stealth bombers and $264 hammers. Why were they so expensive? Well, you have to charge $264 for a hammer if you design and manufacture them only for the Pentagon and it buys only a few hundred of them.

The commercialization of the defense industry is, in fact, mainly a return to the old ways. During the Civil War and World War I, commercial companies were contracted with—or, in the case of World War II, drafted—to build armaments. Military transport vehicles were commercial trucks with a coat of olive-drab paint slathered on. The difference today, of course, is that these commercial companies are globalized. And despite the big boosts in defense spending during the post-9/11 era, the huge expense of developing high-tech products and the sophistication required mean the government is likely never going to catch up with Silicon Valley and other civilian sectors. "Once upon a time we had the resources in this department to lead the field," says Paul Kaminski, a former undersecretary of defense for acquisitions. "So if something interested us like the development of transistors or computers in missiles, we led the pack in developing it." Hence, for example, the Internet, which famously began as a highly classified Pentagon project, a data-transmission network linking U.S. nuclear weapons labs. But three decades ago or so, that balance began to shift. Now it has just gotten too expensive for the Defense Department to build new technology from scratch on "milspec," or military specifications. "I think the amount spent on research in the Department of Defense was surpassed commercially in 1965," says Kaminski. "The disparity has grown ever more since."[9]

As Michael Hayden describes the transformation of the NSA, "We were America's Information-Age enterprise during America's industrial age. Therefore we had built up a habit of saying if we need it, we're going to have to build it. [But] while we were doing that, in the outside world there was a technological explosion in those two universes that had been at the birth of the agency almost uniquely ours: telecommunications and computers. The Internet began as a combination of those two. You could probably draw a good history as to what we did to help create the American computing industry back in the '50s. But now for their own reason, not any industrial policy by us or the government, those industries have outstripped our ability to be as innovative and revolutionary in many areas." Take just one key sector, telecommunications. A quarter century ago about 40 percent of the dollars spent on R&D came from the Defense Department. By fiscal 2000, the Pentagon was providing only 2 percent of the funds spent on information-age technologies.[10]

Pentagon planners are also finding that the commercial sector is far cheaper and more efficient. JDAMS, the smart bomb guided into Taliban positions by Green Berets bearing GPS navigators or laser designators in Afghanistan, costs only about $20,000 a bomb thanks in large part to its use of commercial technologies. Standout performers of the Afghan war, for example, were unmanned aerial vehicles such as the Predator and Global Hawk, which were used to great effect in scouting out al-Qaeda for air strikes. A large percentage of the Global Hawk is made up of off-the-shelf commercial technologies. After the war the Pentagon budgeted more than $1 billion to buy thirty-seven more of the high-tech aircraft in the next year. "It's going to take years for us to get there. But the end point, the vision we want to accomplish is unlimited bandwidth with global access," said Pentagon acquisitions chief Pete Aldridge.[11] The military sometimes still orders its own specially developed microprocessors for weapons systems, but very often by the time they are ready the commercial microprocessors available have gone two generations beyond that.

Kaminski told of sending a Defense Science Board task force to Bosnia in the mid-'90s to examine how the U.S. military was doing in supplying intelligence to forward-based troops. "They said, 'pretty badly,'" he recalled. "They said there were better modems in the corner store. So we put in place a fix, leasing a transponder on a commercial satellite. There was a three-thousand-fold improvement. The only thing we needed was encryption." In 2001, the U.S. military began testing the Land Warrior sensing system, intended to "create the world's first digital soldier." The idea was to give the army the same dominance on the ground that the air force enjoys in the skies, according to a newspaper account. But the system started working only when Silicon Valley entrepreneurs threw out a clunky predecessor developed by Raytheon, a traditional defense contractor, and redesigned it, reported *USA Today*. "The firms—Pacific Consultants, Exponent, Pemstar, and Computer Sciences—ignored rigid Army specifications and brainstormed ideas," the newspaper said. "They lightened the Land Warrior computer harness, wrote new software and worked closely with soldiers. . . . 'We made it the classic Silicon Valley way: quicker, cheaper and better,' says Hugh Duffy, a former Pacific Consultants executive."[12]

A further quantum leap in this trend will come with the "revolution in military affairs"—a further shift away from big platforms such as carriers and forward bases, which are increasingly vulnerable as missile technology gets cheaper and more widely available, and toward long-range U.S. bomber and missile capability guided by cutting-edge information technology. As Bush said in a speech at the U.S. Naval Academy commencement on May 25, 2001: "I'm committed to building a future force that is defined less by size and more by mobility and swiftness . . . one that relies more heavily on stealth, precision weaponry, and information technologies."

Some military strategists lament the advent of what one has called "the fragile battlefield," wherein enemies could jam or disrupt commercially accessible systems like the GPS satellites that are now so central to

U.S. battle plans.[13] U.S. military planners, as a result, have to develop new antijamming devices to counter such asymmetric threats. Officials like Hayden have installed CIA counterintelligence units in their acquisitions department and are conducting polygraph and security background checks on all their vendors. He admits the transnational production networks described in the last chapter—where different components are made in different countries—are a huge problem. Some core high-tech items are so sensitive they will continue to be produced exclusively for the NSA and Pentagon. "This is something to be managed," Hayden says. "This is risk management, not risk avoidance."

But these problems will not slow the shift to dependence on commercial companies. Another factor driving the revolution in defense technologies—one that is also irreversible—is that more and more countries produce the same dual-use equipment. Many of these technologies are widely shared as multinational corporations develop strategic alliances across borders, and the militaries in other countries make use of *their* best commercial stuff. Consider one controversial export case involving supposedly state-of-the-art machine tools made by McDonnell Douglas that were diverted to a Chinese military plant. The Americans forced the Chinese to return the tools—which were actually old and inaccurate—but "ironically the U.S. action led to an improvement in China's industrial capabilities, as the Chinese replaced the worn-out stretch press they were obliged to return with a more modern and sophisticated stretch press bought in Europe," said James Lewis, a former official in the State Department under George H. W. Bush.[14] As we saw in the last chapter, Japanese multinationals have been shifting production abroad, largely to China, to escape their maturing, high-wage economy, but more recently they have begun transferring research and development and design facilities as well —especially when it comes to semiconductor design and production, the building blocks of supercomputers.[15] Economic necessity, combined with a lack of international consensus about withholding technology from China, has made America's old export-control regime all but obsolete. Once again, the international system of open markets that we ourselves promoted has limited our policy choices, illuminating the unpleasant realities of the Permanent Quagmire. "There's going to be a lot more slippage and leakage," says former assistant defense secretary Joseph Nye.

"This technology is broadly shared, and the sense of threat [about China] isn't broadly shared."[16] Norman Augustine, the former head of Lockheed-Martin, says that much of the state-of-the-art technology that drives defense is "fungible. I think it's just not possible to keep it in the box anymore."[17]

## The Seeds of Self-Delusion

Among those who saw this revolution coming was Paul Kaminski. Now a white-haired Pentagon veteran, Kaminski was present at the creation of the precision-guided weapons that are today the pride of the U.S. military, the envy of the world, and the key to maintaining American hegemony long into the future. And he was one of the first to discover that commercial technologies could be the crucial building block.

A talented former Air Force officer who later got a master's degree in electrical engineering and aeronautics from the Massachusetts Institute of Technology, Kaminski was working at Holloman Air Force Base in New Mexico in 1967 when he and his fellow technologists began experimenting with what they then called "television-guided missiles." "We were trying to knock down bridges in Vietnam. Sometimes you dropped hundreds of bombs and missed the bridge," Kaminski recalls. The team outfitted C-130s with cameras and tried flying them like a missile. But the TV images couldn't capture the fast-moving target. The "critical breakthrough" came, he says, when the videotape recorder was invented commercially, enabling the missile to zoom in on its target and adjust as it approached. Only two companies, an American one, Ampex, and a Japanese one, Sony, built such recorders. "After one firing, we bought Sony's; to our surprise, it worked much better," says Kaminski.[18] That commercially produced TV-guided system, called Maverick, was eventually outfitted with infrared imaging so it could be used at night, and then in the late '60s with laser-targeting capabilities.

Other teams were working at the same time with Texas Instruments to produce the first laser-guided bombs.[19] The result of all this activity by technologists like Kaminski was that in the late stages of the Vietnam War —too late to make a real difference, given the public's eroding support for the war—America gave its enemies the first taste of the precision-guided weaponry that later proved so devastatingly effective in Iraq, Kosovo, and Afghanistan. The Thanh Hoa bridge over the Red River outside Hanoi, for example, had been subjected to seven hundred strikes and never destroyed using conventional bombs during Operation Rolling Thunder. Eight American fighter-bombers had been lost. But the first attack with laser-guided bombs in 1972 destroyed the bridge. "It was the beginning of a new era of warfare," former NATO supreme commander Wesley Clark wrote.[20]

For Kaminski, that first experience of deploying commercially available technologies to improve military capability was an epiphany. Later Kaminski joined up with another Stanford Ph.D., William Perry, to lay the foundations for the Stealth program, and became Perry's undersecretary for procurement when Perry was named defense secretary by Clinton. The two decided that in many cases Pentagon-developed and -ordered devices and systems were inferior. At one point, Kaminski recalls, when a Pentagon report insisted that the Defense Department needed expensive ceramic-protected chips to put on its missiles, he and Perry visited a General Motors semiconductor facility in Kokomo, Indiana, where GM was installing plastic-packaged chips on its engine blocks. The Pentagon bought them and saved millions of dollars.

But it wasn't until the Cold War was truly ending that the civilianization of the defense industry really began to take off: President George H. W. Bush declared in 1990 that he intended to remove dual-use goods from control by the go-slow State Department (though encryption controls stayed). A few years later, when Perry became deputy defense secretary and then defense secretary under Clinton, he conceived a strategy that would keep America's defense edge in an era of declining budgets and an increasingly beleaguered military-industrial complex. It was Perry, then deputy defense secretary, who one night in 1993 gathered the biggest names in the arms industry and announced, at what became known as the "Last Supper," that about half of them would soon disappear from the Pentagon's payroll, victims of post–Cold War budget cuts. Defense companies, no longer sustained by Pentagon contracts, increasingly had to go commercial, especially with information technologies. Then, in June 1994, Perry issued a momentous memo making commercial specifications, rather than military specs, the norm for Pentagon purchases. That same year he oversaw the dissolution of COCOM and opened the way to the overseas sales of almost all computer and telecom equipment without export licenses.

Perry, based on his long experience in the field, had simply realized before anyone else that in the post–Cold War era it was all but impossible to halt the global flow of dual-use technologies, and that America had to join that flow to keep its industries alive. If many of these new exports dovetailed nicely with, say, Beijing's high-tech wish list, that was also all but unavoidable in the era of globalization. "I think the criterion [for export control] is whether or not we are sole possessors of the technology," Perry explained in an interview in 1997. "There was a consistent effort during the whole time I was in the government to reach agreement with Western countries on a unified approach to technology control. . . . We did not have much success." The government did replace COCOM with something called the Wassenaar Arrangement, a less stringent accord among Western countries for curbing weapons and dual-use goods. But with a few exceptions, such as targeting Libya, that has proved to be mostly a porous wall. In 1994 the European Court decided that dual-use industrial exports were a matter of trade rather than security and fell under the jurisdiction of Brussels (the individual nations continued to control their arms transfer policies)—the equivalent of handing purview to the Commerce Department in the United States.

Today, in the age of terror, multilateral monitoring regimes like Wassenaar must be beefed up, at least when it comes to barring dangerous dual-use technologies from terror-supporting states. But the only way to do that is a concerted effort by Washington to work with the international community to develop new agreements. And the only thing standing in the way of this is the self-delusion of unilateralists who continue to believe they can just shut America's technology trade down.

### A Case Study: The China Scandal

All these issues converged in a late '90s scandal that has been largely forgotten during the war on terror, even though the aftereffects continue to damage our national security to this day. On March 5, 1999, I was pecking away in my *Newsweek* office in Washington, finishing up a business story on a somewhat arcane but, I thought, important subject. It was Friday, the day before the magazine's "close," and a typhoon of controversy was about to erupt over the sale of U.S. supercomputers to China, I believed. The reason, I wrote, was that a congressional commission headed by Representative Christopher Cox of California, a Republican, would soon come out with a report alleging that Chinese espionage had ferreted out important secrets from America's nuclear arms program. And because supercomputers were used to build and test nuclear weapons, U.S. business executives feared that a Sinophobic Congress would restrict sales to one of their biggest markets, China, which also happened to be the country that U.S. politicians most feared would become America's principal superpower rival in the twenty-first century. So volatile was China as a political issue that I knew it was highly likely that the Cox report, bits of which had already been leaked, would become fodder for demagogues on Capitol Hill, of which there is no shortage.

Worst of all, this was happening at a time when computer executives were about to start lobbying Congress for *looser* export restrictions on dual-use goods such as supercomputers. The companies were motivated by more than greed; they had a very good argument that goes to the heart of my arguments in this chapter. Semiconductors were improving so fast that juiced-up PCs could now run as fast as a supercomputer could just a year before, so the current export limits were already obsolete. An industry report to be issued the following week, I wrote, would conclude that some three hundred new computers sold abroad each day now qualified as supercomputers because of their increased chip power, and would need to go through a tedious, four-to-six-week process of obtaining export licenses from the government. Normally federal regulators processed that many licenses in a year. "If we end up in a situation where 40,000 license [requests] are dumped at the Commerce Department, we're going to be out of markets," I quoted Richard Lehmann, a spokesman for IBM, as saying. The imminent collision of congressional grandstanding and industry interests was a train wreck waiting to happen. My story, written in the compressed newsweekly style that can sometimes sound overheated, began by describing how congressional investigators, in "a search for the guilty," were treating top U.S. executives like spy suspects.

The next morning, however, as my story was being edited, the *New York Times* came out with a story that seemed to put mine to shame. There, bannered across two columns of the front page of the premier newspaper in America, was the headline "China Stole Nuclear Secrets for Bombs, U.S. Aides Say." The *Times* had gotten wind of specific allegations stemming from the Cox report. The paper reported that federal investigators believed that one of America's most important nuclear weapons secrets, the design for the Trident II missile warhead, the W-88, had been stolen from Los Alamos, and authorities were focusing on a suspect, a Chinese-American scientist who worked there. A former CIA official, Paul Redmond, was quoted in the story as saying, "This is going to be as bad as the Rosenbergs," referring to the spies who helped the Soviets steal bomb secrets from the Manhattan Project. But what really raised the temperature were the strong suggestions in the story that the Clinton administration had further jeopardized U.S. national security through irresponsible actions. White House officials, the story said ominously, "continued to advocate looser controls over sales of supercomputers and other equipment [to China], even as intelligence analysts documented the scope of China's espionage." The implication was that Clinton had sold out U.S. national security to Beijing to make Silicon Valley (and his campaign donors) richer.

By the time the Sunday morning talk shows rolled around, Republican congressmen and senators leaped, like thirsty men for water, on what seemed to be another big Clinton scandal, one that would make up for the disappointment of Monicagate (Clinton had been acquitted in his impeachment trial just two months before). The *Times* kept up the momentum: The Chinese-American scientist was identified as Wen Ho Lee, who was fired, then arrested and charged with spying. Follow-up stories in the paper reported that Lee had downloaded America's "legacy" codes—the digitized history of the U.S. nuclear program—from his computer. On May 25, the Cox report came out. Its conclusions were every bit as alarming as the *Times* stories: For more than twenty years, it said, China had stolen secret information on every nuclear weapon in the

United States arsenal, enabling Beijing to build missiles capable of reaching America. China "has leaped, in a handful of years, from 1950s-era strategic nuclear capabilities to the more modern thermonuclear weapons designs" that took the United States decades to achieve, the report said. No fewer than nine congressional committees were formed to probe the espionage charges in the Cox report.

### The Scandal That Wasn't—and How It Still Hurts Us

One of the things that bothered me about that first *Times* story on March 6 wasn't just professional jealousy. I knew that the same reporter who had co-authored the Wen Ho Lee stories had, a little over a year before, set in motion another great China scandal, one that led directly to the spy allegations. In 1998 the *Times* broke the news that two U.S. satellite companies, Loral Space and Communications and Hughes Electronics, were under investigation for allegedly transmitting important missile guidance data to the Chinese without government permission as part of an insurance-company-ordered probe into the failure of a Long March rocket. All true. But then the story had swiftly moved, again, to raising questions about Clinton's role in the matter. The paper quoted anonymous officials as saying that Clinton had hurt the investigation by signing a special waiver letting Loral launch another satellite in China, even though the Justice Department had advised the president that such a waiver would undercut their case. (The waivers were needed because of post–Tiananmen Square arms sanctions that barred U.S. satellites from being launched on Chinese rockets unless it was deemed in the national interest, but the waivers were routinely granted—George H. W. Bush signed nine of them; Clinton eleven.)[21] In the story the *Times* juxtaposed the fact that Loral's chairman, Bernard Schwartz, was the largest personal contributor to the Democratic National Committee next to the fact that Clinton had signed the special waiver, so that the facts together reeked of corruption. In follow-up stories the *Times* wove in a tale about a Chinese military officer named Liu Chao-ying, who had allegedly funneled tens of thousands of dollars from Chinese military intelligence to the Democratic Party and was "one of the beneficiaries" of Clinton's satellite decision.[22] The cumulative effect was to suggest, again, that Bill Clinton was sacrificing U.S. national security for corrupt reasons, just as a year later the spy stories suggested that the Clinton administration had obstructed the espionage investigation.

In fact, while there were legitimate concerns about how much the Chinese were learning about our best dual-use technology, there were also solid policy reasons why Clinton's decision to allow Loral to launch its satellites in China was "supportive of our national security," as the president himself claimed in addressing the *Times* stories.[23] Similarly, there were solid reasons why Clinton would continue to support super-computer sales to China. The reasons are, of course, the ones I am laying out here. And it's not as if these reasons weren't known at the time. In 1997, a year before the *Times*'s Loral-Hughes stories appeared, my *Newsweek* colleague Melinda Liu and I had been the first to detail the dabbling of the infamous Liu Chao-ying in Democratic campaign financing. In a 3,300-word story, we too suggested that her presence in the United States might have something to do with a covert program to obtain state-of-the-art defense technology from the United States.[24] We also raised the issue of whether lobbying by big Democratic donors such as Loral and Hughes had influenced Clinton's decisions to loosen export controls. Our answer, however, was far murkier. There were, unfortunately, no good policy choices. Stemming technology flows in a globalized economy in which the Europeans and Japanese refused to stop selling to China had become nearly impossible, we said.

But carefully hedged, ambiguous conclusions don't make news. In contrast to our *Newsweek* article, the incendiary allegations in the *Times* stories about Clinton, Loral, and Bernard Schwartz's donations quickly became the topic *du jour* in Washington. The GOP-controlled House of Representatives voted overwhelmingly to ban satellite sales to China. The theme was familiar: America's national security, declared some politicians, was being sacrificed at the altar of commerce. "What we now have is the second-largest country in the world, it is a communist country, that has 13 missiles pointed at the United States with nuclear warheads on the end of them, and because of our technology, they can now navigate those missiles to hit any city in the United States. President Clinton bears that responsibility," Republican national chairman Jim Nicholson said in a fit of hyperbole.[25] Republicans and even some Democrats on Capitol Hill accused the Clinton administration of carelessly liberalizing high-tech trade with China—encouraged, perhaps, by campaign donations from the likes of Loral's Schwartz—and "engaging" Beijing with a stream of deals that were helping to turn China into a twenty-first-century superpower and rival. Schwartz, a longtime Democratic activist, was demonized in the media and in public. He received hate e-mail saying things like "I hope the first Chinese missiles fall on your grandchildren." At one New York dinner party, Schwartz recalls, a woman stood up, called him a traitor, and stalked out.[26]

The *Times* stories touched off a two-year hunt for Chinese spies in America's national security apparatus. The investigation snowballed endlessly: The Loral-Hughes scandal so intrigued Newt Gingrich, then the Speaker of the House—who stopped just short of publicly accusing Clinton of committing treason for money—that he set up a $2.5 million commission to look into it. Witnesses told the Cox commission that America's nuclear secrets were as much at risk as its missile technology, and when the Loral-Hughes indiscretion proved to be a singular event, rather than evidence of a broad trend of delivering U.S. defense secrets to the Chinese, they led reporters to Wen Ho Lee.

The point of this digression is that both big China scandal stories ultimately collapsed, as did most of the charges in the Cox commission report. No charges were ever brought against anyone in the Clinton administration, and no one resigned. Bernard Schwartz was exonerated of all wrongdoing when the Justice Department "turned up not a scintilla of evidence—or information—that the president was corruptly influenced by [him]." In the fall of 2001 Loral paid a $14 million fine in a civil settlement for its inadvertent transmission of rocket guidance information to Beijing—though the company paid even that under protest since it pointed out, accurately, that there were no clear rules for what could be sent, it had immediately reported the mistake, and the report in any case had been demanded by its insurer.[27] Franklin Miller, a deputy assistant secretary of defense, later said on the record at a Senate hearing that "I do not believe that there has been any improvement to Chinese ICBM capability" because of the information transmitted by Loral and Hughes, and the CIA agreed with him.[28] It turned out that the main source of charges that there had been serious harm to U.S. national security was the Defense Technology Security Agency, a Reagan-era body within the Department of Defense whose raison d'être was to prevent the export of dual-use goods, and which was known to be largely manned with hardline Sinophobes. It also turned out that, unmentioned by the *Times* in its first story, the one that triggered all the excitement, Clinton's State Department, Defense Department, and top national security aides had all recommended that he go ahead with the Loral waiver. While the *Times* had reported that Clinton had "quietly" approved the waiver, it was in fact fully on public record.

Similarly, the story that erupted a year later, the Wen Ho Lee saga, ended without a communist espionage case. It turned out this wasn't "like the Rosenbergs" at all. Not only was it utterly unclear what the Chinese had learned about America's nuclear program, but FBI officials realized that the "exclusive" secrets Lee had allegedly passed on from Los Alamos were actually "available to hundreds and perhaps thousands of individuals scattered throughout the nation's arms complex," as the *Times*'s own science reporter, William Broad, later wrote,[29] and that the Chinese could have learned much of what they knew from public sources.[30] Though it was clear he was playing fast and loose with sensitive information, Wen Ho Lee was exonerated of the spying charges; he pled guilty to a single count of mishandling classified data and received an apology from the judge for having been shackled and jailed in solitary for a year. Congressional charges that the Clinton administration had been remiss in pursuing the spy investigations petered out as well—especially as it became clear how troubled the Wen Ho Lee case was and that the president had in fact ordered a revamping of nuclear security the year before, in 1998. The Cox report was discredited for its over-the-top allegations about the dangers of a Chinese spy network. And both the great China Scandals became minor historical footnotes.

And yet beneath the headlines, in ways that most people can't see, the damage to America's national security from both scandals persists.[31]

Since then, defense companies have lost business because of too-stringent export controls created as a result of the scandals—commercial satellites were put on the munitions list, and licenses became the province of the ultracautious State Department—and the best scientific minds are no longer as eager to work for U.S. nuclear labs.

The malign consequences of harsh, unilateral U.S. export controls became clear only as the months passed and the public—not to mention Congress—stopped paying attention. In the aftermath of the Loral-Hughes scandal, the Chinese scuttled a contract to buy a satellite from Loral and made a deal instead with France's Alcatel. Included was a $50 million provision whereby the Chinese paid the French for technology transfer—detailed information about rockets and satellites—of the kind the Chinese never would have gotten from the Americans. Satellite makers reported aggressive tactics by overseas competitors to take advantage of America's defensive crouch. The new export restrictions hampered sales to friends as well as to China, obstructing the ability of the United States and its NATO allies to operate equipment together. For example, in 2000 Orbital Sciences, a company based in Dulles, Virginia, lost an $80 million contract to build part of a radar satellite for the Canadian government. Though Ottawa just wanted to monitor the movement of ice floes —not troops—the part was considered sensitive military equipment under the new export restrictions. The State Department, chronically understaffed and made hypercautious by the atmosphere of fear that, even as the China scandal petered out in public, still infected the government bureaucracy, dithered over the licensing for a year. Under U.S. law, Orbital's engineers found they couldn't even talk about the details of the deal with their own subsidiary handling the deal across the northern border. Finally the Canadians gave up and delivered the contract to an Italian firm. In December 1999, sixteen NATO ambassadors wrote a letter to then secretary of state Madeleine Albright complaining of a "serious impediment to defense cooperation," and DASA, the German aerospace giant, ordered its purchasers to look for non-U.S. suppliers after years of co-production with U.S. satellite companies.[32] Two years after Congress imposed new restrictions on commercial satellite sales, the U.S. share of this global market had dropped from 75 percent to 45 percent. By the end of 2000, the *Los Angeles Times* reported, orders for U.S.-made geostationary satellites, the most widely used kind, had dropped, while orders for European satellites rose from six to sixteen. The U.S. satellite industry, which is dominated by Hughes, Loral, and three other companies, made a comeback in 2001—largely because the European manufacturers were fully booked—but found that by 2002 it was again getting outcompeted by European, Israeli, and even Russian satellite makers. And at the same as it was hit by new export controls, the industry was hurt by competition from an alternative technology, fiber optics.

The U.S. satellite industry also found itself in the crosshairs of the strategic planners in the European Union. While Washington was crimping the U.S. satellite industry, the European Space Agency announced a $400 million plan to fund two French companies, Alcatel and Astrium— the main U.S. competition—for the next generation of commercial satellites. "What they did with the Airbus and with Ariane—with the launch technology—they are targeting to do in the commercial satellite business," said Loral's Schwartz. Industry analysts said that to achieve the global sweep from the skies that it wanted, the Pentagon might have to rely someday on European satellites—which would hardly be joyous news to the unilateralists in the Bush administration. Such a system also might not work very well, since the European Commission, increasingly disinclined to work with Washington in the face of U.S. unilateralism, has been pushing to build its own distinct network of satellites rather than work with the United States to upgrade the existing GPS system.

In curtailing America's satellite industry in order to secure America, Congress had weakened America. Rather than responding to the reality of the globalized marketplace, in which such technologies were available from many different sources, Uncle Sam had cut off his nose to spite his face. The *reaction* to the scandals did far more damage to our national security, by harming America's globalized defense industrial base, than the original allegations made in the scandals. Congress had taken "a sledgehammer to something that required a jeweler's tool," said Joel Johnson, a vice president at the Aerospace Industries Association.[33] It was very much like what we did to our encryption industry.

Satellites are perhaps the best example of how dramatically the Cold

War order has been overturned. Once developed largely for spying and command and control, satellites have become the building blocks of an immense new commercial space industry, which is now producing the best stuff. Nearly 70 percent of the imaging used by the government, for example, comes from commercial satellites.[34] There are side benefits to America's commercial dominance as well: U.S. intelligence, for instance, is helped far more if the Chinese military uses U.S. commercial satellites than it would be if China developed its own hardwired, secure military alternative.

It was no surprise that the phrase "as bad as the Rosenbergs" resonated in Washington, because it was a fear that we all could immediately place. Our enemy-in-the-making, China, was learning our most precious secrets, just as Moscow did during the Cold War. But it is also no surprise that when the spy case bottomed out, the truth was that many of these secrets were already circulating out there in the global economy, especially on the Internet. The same goes for ballistic missile technology (even North Korea, as isolated as it is, managed to develop a system largely on its own).[35] As we have seen, old belief systems are not easy to discard.

The question remains: How did the great China scandals of the late '90s grow to such proportions when they had so little substance? While it is clear that overwrought reporting—on both the original satellite and Wen Ho Lee scandals—helped to ignite the hysteria, and both anti-Clinton fervor and Sinophobia fed the flames, the more profound problem was that we were witnessing, yet again, a collision of Cold War–era thinking with a new, far more ambiguous global reality.[36] And once again, realists who still imagined that the world consisted of unitary nation-states that build up individual power bases and vie against one another failed to grasp that this was no longer true. Borders are simply too porous in this open global system we have built, technologies too fast-flowing and widespread, the economy too globalized.

## Understanding the Globalization of Defense

To reiterate the central point: America, which took the lead in the Cold War era because of the openness of its markets and the attractiveness its freedoms held for foreign scientists, is today at great risk of falling behind because it is compromising those very advantages. If we endured the McCarthy era despite the witch-hunt that rid the government of some of our best minds, it was largely because conditions in other countries— principally the Soviet bloc—were even more repressive. But that is no longer true. In the open international system that we have created, the danger is that we are becoming among the least free, or the most restricted, when it comes to the kind of high-tech products that are America's most competitive exports. In the case of China, for example, the average waiting time for U.S. companies to get a State Department export license in 2001 was three months to a year, "with many high-tech licenses taking closer to one year. In contrast, the Japanese government approves a high-tech export license to China in two to three weeks, with a maximum of one month. Germany's maximum is 30 days," the *Far Eastern Economic Review* reported.[37]

A similarly dangerous dynamic was at work after the nuclear lab scandals, when a kind of Asiatic McCarthyism took hold, casting suspicion on any scientist of Chinese origin. As Cox explained to me sagely before the scandal story broke, "The Chinese use sleeper agents longer than anyone else. A paradigm is a Chinese who gets, say, a Cal Tech Ph.D., then goes to work for TRW. Twenty years later he's activated."[38] By that standard, just about every Chinese working in American industry might be deemed a potential spy—and in fact the Cox report concluded just that. More than a year after the scandals, the *Washington Post* reported that Los Alamos was suffering a brain drain, with its number of postdoctoral fellows dropping by 10 percent. And after a steady increase in the hiring of Asian-American scientists over the past eight years, Asian Americans all but stopped applying for jobs at Los Alamos.[39]At one job fair in California held at Cal Tech, no one at all came to the Los Alamos booth, the Center for Strategic and International Studies found in a study released in mid-2002. That mood began to change after 9/11, when Arab Americans rather than Asian Americans became a suspect quantity, but the chill at the labs persisted. "A scientist doesn't want to have to leave his cell phone, his personal digital assistant, and his laptop outside," says James Lewis, who was one of the negotiators of the Wassenaar Arrangement.[40] So profoundly harmful were these effects that some observers even postulated, some-what whimsically, that the scandal itself was what Beijing had intended all along in order to create an atmosphere of fear in the United States that would draw its best scientific minds back to China. (It was a double agent working for Beijing, after all, who first suggested to U.S. intelligence that Beijing had obtained knowledge of the W-88—a central fact of the Wen Ho Lee scandal that has never been explained.)[41] Whether or not Beijing ever conceived such a convoluted plot is unknown. But the effect was the same. If true, it was certainly a nice bit of asymmetric strategizing—oddly similar, in fact, to Osama bin Laden's boast that his inexpensive targeting of the World Trade Center and Pentagon had set in motion a panic that cost the U.S. economy dearly. The question, as always, is how *we* respond.

Well into the Bush administration, this shut-the-borders mind-set continued, even though, ironically, one of the few Clinton programs the Bush administration decided to pursue was to reach out to the commercial sector for defense technologies and know-how. "We want to attract people like Hewlett-Packard, Lucent and other people who don't do business with the Department of Defense to bring that technology over to us," Pentagon acquisition chief Aldridge said in 2002. "Therefore we are going to remove some of the intellectual property restraints and all the burdensome paperwork to make it attractive for them."[42] But Aldridge's superiors, both Donald Rumsfeld and his deputy, Paul Wolfowitz, had come out in favor of tighter export controls in some areas, and the State Department continued to resist change. Nor did Bush, with his unilateralist bent, do much of the diplomacy that would be necessary to forge a needed consensus with Europe and Japan on how to defy Beijing's technology-acquisition tactics. "The U.S. has not been able to explain to its allies how China is a threat to Europe and it has not advanced a coherent strategic rationale for continued controls on many dual-use items," says James Lewis.[43] Paul Kaminski believes the United States can succeed with very narrowly targeted export controls. For example, rather than requiring an export license for all supercomputers that perform over a certain number of MTOPS, or millions of theoretical operations per second (a measure of computer speed), the United States could restrict sale of the embedded algorithm that drives the logic of certain of these computers.

But as Kaminski sees it, tough export restrictions are only forcing more and more companies out of the defense industry. "We have to create a set of incentives for our system to run faster," he says. "We need to remove impediments for companies that don't want to become involved in defense contracting."

At the same time, Washington must bring Beijing into the system of trade rules represented by the World Trade Organization, and work closely with European nations and Japan to continue to limit weapons systems as well as the riskiest dual-use goods. While there was no means of forcing China to decide to whom it would award contracts, the WTO agreement signed in 1999 by then-U.S. trade representative Charlene Barshefsky forbade China from demanding that foreign companies transfer their technology, and it equally forbade the Chinese from closing their markets if companies didn't. One reason Japan, for example, began shifting the pride and joy of its high-tech industry to China was that WTO rules afforded it new intellectual-property rights and patent protections. Similarly, on the nuclear front, there is clearly so much nuclear weapons information circulating out there now that only agreements such as the Comprehensive Test Ban Treaty can truly ensure American nuclear primacy. (The Clinton administration, it must be said, fostered this situation itself by declassifying hundreds of nuclear secrets in the early '90s on the theory that this would inspire nations to sign the test ban; unfortunately the administration failed to anticipate that certain nonsignatories, such as al-Qaeda, might benefit from it as well.)[44] Indeed, one reason Clinton wanted to free up exports of supercomputers—in addition to the market pressures—was that only with a supercomputer-run "stockpile maintenance program," which involves simulating nuclear tests on a computer, can nuclear powers be persuaded to maintain their weapons without actual testing. He hoped to induce Beijing to accept the Comprehensive Test Ban Treaty—which in 1996 it did, and it has not conducted a nuclear test since then. But the Bush administration, with its aversion to any infringement on U.S. sovereignty, resolutely opposes reviving the treaty. Unfortunately this stance has left the administration without *any* viable means of containing China's nuclear and weapons program, given the self-defeating nature of export controls.

America could still just throw government money at the problem of maintaining its still-huge defense edge—as long as it doesn't mind a permanent return to Cold War–era defense spending, of course. In the aftermath of September 11, Bush requested more for defense R&D, once again leaving the Europeans in the dust. Funds set aside in the Defense Department's 2003 budget for research, development, testing, and evaluation amounted to more than $50 billion. This was more than the combined sum that other industrial nations earmark for developing new military technology (the fifteen European Union countries spent a total of only $9 billion on defense R&D in 2001). But as a senior Defense Department official put it to me, that still doesn't come close to the trillions spent on R&D in the private sector. The best course, he said, was still to "buy the 80 percent solution rather than spending a gajillion dollars and several million man-hours in creating the 85 percent solution."[45] And Bush, faced with new, record budget deficits midway through his administration, no longer had the wherewithal to create the 85 percent solution.

The real key to maintaining America's defense edge indefinitely is to maintain the vibrancy of our commercial industrial base at the same time as we work anew on multilateral regimes. And like so much else about the Permanent Quagmire, that again means working with the international community.

As we have seen, American policy makers still have not fully grappled with the realities of America's twenty-first-century power base. In the next chapter we will examine the pitfalls of another old way of unilateral thinking: the idea that America can trumpet its values abroad as it once did, and expect the world to follow. Much as America's defense base has now become globalized, so American ideas about democracy and open markets have become globalized. Much as our technology is spreading in an open system, the dissemination of these American ideas has meant they are taking on a life of their own. For a long time we have deemed this to be an unalloyed benefit, like the global marketplace. But it's not that simple.

# 5

## When Ideas Bite Back

There is no country on earth that is not touched by America, for we have become the motive force for freedom and democracy in the world.

Colin L. Powell

In word and deed, we must be clear and consistent and confident that our values are real.

President-elect George W. Bush, December 16, 2000

IF AMERICANS KNOW one thing for certain, it is that their values are right not just for them, but for the world. This is a bedrock belief that unites left and right, the Wilsonian internationalists of the Clinton administration and the powerful neoconservatives of the Bush administration. It is a sense that they can make the world a better and safer place by asserting America's power and spreading cardinal American values such as democracy and free markets, if only the world would stand back and let them do it. This chapter is about why this practice is likely to fail in the future—ironically enough, because it has succeeded so well in the past. It is about why we Americans must depend on the institutions of the international system we built, such as the UN and WTO, to do the main work of continuing to promote these values, even though this rubs against our national grain. The alternative is that we will find ourselves caught up in endless self-contradiction and accusations of hypocrisy—at war with our own ideas.

Here's why. The world has already heard an earful from America. And it has listened well. In the last century the United States did an admirable job of vanquishing fascism and spending (most) communist regimes out of existence. We succeeded not just because we were militarily or economically stronger, but because we prided ourselves on having stronger ideas, among them democracy, self-determination, and free markets. Not only did we want to defeat our enemies, but beginning with Wilson we insisted they adopt our philosophy as well, pursuing what Henry Kissinger has called the "age-old American dream of a peace achieved by the conversion of the adversary." Washington achieved this to an astounding degree, presiding over the conversion of most of the former Soviet bloc to democratic capitalism, nurturing similar transitions in Japan, South Korea, and Taiwan, not to mention most of South America—and along the way making some form of democratic capitalism the standard to which other peoples aspire. As we saw in previous chapters, this American evangelism has helped create a vibrant international community. But the international community has a down side that we have only just begun to reckon with. Now American ideas, having saturated the globe—as much as McDonald's hamburgers and Disney movies—are coming back to haunt U.S. policy makers. And since the Cold War ended, the biggest headaches have come from two of our nation's most powerful ideological exports, Wilsonianism and free markets. Most of these ideas have been accepted in principle; now it is the flaws and inconsistencies of these ideas—and America's inconsistency in applying them—that rule the scene.

I call this phenomenon "ideological blowback." The biggest threat to stability in other parts of the world was once tyranny, but today it is more often Wilsonian self-determination, in other words, new separatist bids for legal statehood. Indeed, some of America's knottiest foreign-policy problems involve the threat of "a state too far"—the unilateral declaration of independence in places such as Taiwan, Tibet, the Palestinian territories, Chechnya, Kosovo, and among the Kurds in Turkey and northern Iraq. In each of these cases Washington, in order to prevent conflict, is actively seeking to avert a declaration of independence (in Kosovo, Taiwan, and Tibet, and among the Kurds), is trying to avoid the issue altogether (Chechnya), or has been covertly blocking attempts to make it happen too soon (Palestine). In the global echo chamber, we are finding, these movements tend to study and cite each other as precedents, and often invoke Woodrow Wilson's promises. One of the crowning ironies for U.S. policy makers today is that the right we asserted so eloquently for ourselves in the opening words of the Declaration of Independence—the right of a people to "dissolve the political bands which have connected them with another"—is no longer something we recognize for other peoples in practice.

But the problem goes well beyond Wilson's promise of self-determination. The biggest drag on the world economy is no longer the inefficiencies of communist-style command economies. It is the excesses and instability caused by the free markets we ourselves triumphally imposed in the 1990s. The untrammeled nature of these markets has left many of the world's poor poorer and resulted in an unstoppable job drain from our shores. Behind the Oz-like curtain of American power, we find we're barely able to rein them in. Much as Wilsonian ideas are uncappable, private markets have simply grown too large and too determinative of nations' fates. Yet having won the world over to markets, the United States is conflicted about admitting they don't always work for the common good.

George W. Bush, for all of his conviction that America's salvation lay in promoting democracy and free markets abroad, quickly discovered the pitfalls of ideological blowback. Waging the war on terror, for example, meant propping up Pakistani autocrat Pervez Musharraf, who was desperately trying to tamp down Islamist movements in his country, and doing the same for Arab regimes that have cracked down on fundamentalist violence. It meant grappling with the uncomfortable fact that the rest of the world had noticed all too acutely our reluctance to press democracy and openness on the Arab world. In 2002 Bush declared that democracy was the answer to the ills in the Palestinian territories and to the problem of Iraq. The hypocrisy was all too apparent: The world's most powerful leader was calling for one set of standards for two Arab leaders he didn't particularly like, another for Arab leaders (the Saudis, the Jordanians, the Egyptians) he did like, or at least tolerated. The Bush neoconservatives also began to take a harsher line against the autocratic regimes in Egypt and Saudi Arabia—at one point, the administration announced that further aid to Egypt would be tied to political reform— but this policy was drowned out by the greater need to maintain regime stability in order to gain consensus for an attack on Iraq's Saddam Hussein. Despite growing support in Washington for democracy as a long-term solution, in the short- and medium term Bush stuck by the Arab autocrats because of a plethora of fears that were, unfortunately, fairly sound: In this particular part of the world instant democracy would only mean Islamism, which in turn would mean anti-Americanism and even more antagonism toward Israel, America's number-one ally in the region. Entrusting such Islamized regimes with the world's main source of oil would be too risky, and in an era when weapons of mass destruction are becoming cheaper and easier to make, the wealth that would accrue to such new fundamentalist regimes would give them an arsenal of "Islamic bombs." The rest of the world, and terrorists such as Osama bin Laden, have taken notice of this hypocrisy. In an odd way, our eagerness to continue trumpeting our values abroad *weakens,* rather than strengthens, our moral leadership in the world when we are seen not following through. And as the world's hegemon—in other words, its chief stabilizer—very often we cannot follow through. Our dependence on a functioning international system means we want stability, not revolution.

Bush, like previous presidents, also promoted free trade, but at the World Trade Organization a newly energized developing world, embracing free markets as never before, focused on Washington's hypocritical persistence in maintaining its own tariffs and subsidies, especially in agriculture. There was, in other words, no "moral clarity" here whatsoever. Yet the Bush administration never acknowledged such contradictions in its national security strategy, which committed America both to fighting terrorism and to "encouraging free and open societies on every continent." "What it leaves out is that these two goals often conflict," a Brookings Institution critique noted. At the same time as the strategy calls "the demands of human dignity" "non-negotiable," the Bush administration "criticizes no country of consequence to the United States in the war on terrorism for specific human rights abuses—not Russia for its war on Chechnya, not China for its suppression of Tibet, democracy activists and religious minorities, not Pakistan for its support of Kashmiri separatists or its suspension of democratic institutions."[1]

The problem is that our new role as the world's hegemon is often in direct conflict with our old, treasured self-image as the world's chief promoter of values. American hegemony is now about keeping order in the world. True, to a large extent keeping order still involves isolating and destroying the remaining holdouts in the international system, such as Saddam Hussein or Kim Jong Il (although in the latter case, democratizing North Korea could remove the justification for a U.S. troop presence in the South, which in turn could have destabilizing effects in Asia). But the more enduring challenge will be in fighting the disorder inherent in American ideas. As Walter Russell Mead writes, "On the one hand, as global hegemon, the United States is by definition a status quo power. But to the extent that we are exporting Wilsonian values, we are a revisionist one as well."[2]

It won't help if we decide *not* to export Wilsonian (and free-market) values. Thanks largely to the American Century, these values are already out there. Wilsonian principles, like free markets, cannot be put back in the box. Once promulgated, they are forever available to be invoked—or at least as long as America remains the world's dominant power. They are abstract ideals made real by the American experience and given an American imprimatur as the world's hegemonic power, as the Bush administration's national security strategy indirectly acknowledged: "The great struggles of the 20th century between liberty and totalitarianism ended with a decisive victory for the forces of freedom. . . . No nation owns these aspirations, and no nation is exempt from them."[3] Even if Washington quietly tries to shunt self-determination aside, the principle will endure of its own momentum, a kind of last train out of obscurity for the world's insulted and injured. And U.S. policy makers will find that such principles are constantly flung back in their faces. Timorese activist Jose Ramos Horta succeeded in bringing independence to East Timor, for example, as we will discuss further in the next chapter; since then he has advised delegations from Tibet and Aceh (another separatist Indonesian province) on how they can agitate for independence most effectively.[4]

Not that Washington hasn't tried to tamp down Wilsonianism. Today, with a few signal exceptions such as Palestine, U.S. diplomats have all but banished the term *self-determination* from their lexicon. The United States simply does not want more devolution into statehood. The reason is purely pragmatic. As Richard Holbrooke, the former UN ambassador, put it: "There are some 3,000 ethnic groups in the world, and only 189 members of the UN. If every ethnic group had its own country, you would have war after war."[5] But it's too late. Most of the rest of the world is insisting on fulfilling Wilson's dream, or invoking his principles against us. And that has become, for the United States, a policy nightmare.

## A Case Study: Kosovo

The neoconservatives of the George W. Bush administration were hardly the first policy makers to crusade for American values in the post–Cold War environment. Madeleine Albright, Colin Powell's predecessor as secretary of state, had similar views. A Czech-born refugee from Hitler and Stalin, Albright, née Korbel, came to believe heart and soul not just in the reality of American power but in its forthright use—in the leverage of what she liked to call the "indispensable nation." Becoming American was "the big, defining thing in my life," she once told an interviewer.[6]

Somewhat like the Bush neoconservatives, Albright brought to her policymaking a little too much of the zeal of the converted. And like them, Albright had had her own problem with the pragmatic caution of Colin Powell. In 1993, as the United States dithered yet again over intervention in Bosnia, Albright upbraided Powell, then chairman of the Joint Chiefs, in a principals meeting. "What's the point of having this superb military you're always talking about if you're not going to use it?" she said. ("I thought I would have an aneurysm," Powell wrote in his autobiography. "American GIs were not toy soldiers to be moved around on some sort of global game board.")[7] Albright's words also earned her lasting enmity at the Pentagon, but as she later pointed out, she may have been right about Bosnia: Bombing had helped to bring about the Dayton pact in 1995. As Albright explained to me just before the war in Kosovo in 1999, "You have to understand, for me, Americans liberated Europe. When Americans weren't in the action, that's when bad things happened. That is my political philosophy."[8]

In the fall of 1998 and early winter of 1999, bad things were happening in Kosovo, a province of Serbia inhabited by ethnic Albanian Muslims who had suffered terribly at the hands of Yugoslav president Slobodan Milosevic, one of the last remaining autocrats in Europe. And Albright, true to her interventionist creed, set her team to devising a plan to save Kosovo. It was a good plan, brimming with the highest of America's ideals and values. It was clear and consistent and confident. What is most telling, however, is how badly it worked.

I remember the day it all started to go wrong. It was February 23, 1999. I was traveling, as *Newsweek*'s diplomatic correspondent, with Albright as her French-escorted motorcade sped, klaxons keening, toward Rambouillet, a sleepy French village thirty miles south of Paris. The secretary of state had come to France to negotiate an end to the violence. Brutish Serb paramilitary gangs had been driving the Kosovars into the hills and murdering them. A ragtag group of Kosovar guerrillas calling itself the Kosovo Liberation Army had resisted, killing Serbs in night raids.

Albright's mood had been confident as she alighted in Paris following a redeye flight from Washington aboard her new Boeing 757. Her role at Rambouillet was supposed to be simple and straightforward. For long weeks Albright's diplomats and lawyers had sweated over the plan for Kosovo's future, eighty pages of American promises that read like the distilled wisdom of our Constitutional Convention. Not only did we intend to drive Milosevic's forces from the province, but the plan provided for a Kosovar president, a legislature, a Kosovar judiciary and schools, and a Kosovar police force. This entire scheme for a new democratic society was minutely timed, to the day, to Serb troop withdrawals from the province, a key demand of Albright's. In an attempt to save the Kosovars from the Serbs, Washington was pledging total "autonomy" to this hitherto obscure group of Muslims—a year before, few people in the motorcade would have been able to say where Kosovo was—and it was putting the full faith and credit of NATO behind that pledge, including about four thousand American peacekeeping troops on indefinite loan.

Wearing her black "cowboy hat," as the Europeans snidely called it behind her back, Albright strode up the steps of the fourteenth-century chateau at Rambouillet where the talks were being held. The sixty-two-year-old secretary, who often wore rakish Stetsons and brooches the size of small weapons to distract from her grandmotherly looks, had been told by her aides that she was there merely to give the Kosovars a final shot in the arm. Hashim Thaci, the lead negotiator for the Kosovo Liberation Army, was balking at putting his signature on the plan and needed just a little high-powered arm twisting. And Albright, in turn, needed his signature to round out her January ultimatum to Milosevic: Stop killing Kosovars, agree to the autonomy plan, and accept NATO peacekeepers in your backyard, or be bombed by the mightiest alliance in history. Only with a KLA sign-off would the more reluctant NATO allies, including France and Italy, back air strikes on Milosevic.

But as we reporters waited on the pebbly driveway outside Rambouillet's black wrought-iron gates, shivering and bouncing on our feet in the February cold, we could see that something was going wrong. The talks inside dragged on for hours, then well past sunset. It was only later we found out that the biggest problem Albright was having inside wasn't Milosevic, the appalling "butcher of the Balkans"; it was the Kosovars, the people whom America was trying to save. The KLA was being more than balky. They were adamant, absolutely dug in. Albright's proffer—an all-expenses-paid relationship with the world's sole superpower—apparently wasn't enough for them. The Kosovars were, the American negotiators had come to realize, living in Wilsonian la-la land. They now wanted full independence, a UN seat, world recognition—the Hollywood ending, geopolitically speaking. Once satisfied with autonomy under Serb rule—they had enjoyed a limited version of it before Milosevic canceled it in 1989—the Kosovars decided to take matters into their own hands after the fate of their province was left unaddressed by the 1995 Dayton peace agreement on Bosnia, just as it had been by Woodrow Wilson eighty years before at the Palace of Versailles. They were insisting on the full Wilson: a state of their own. Mere autonomy wasn't enough. To get what they wanted, they had even enlisted private U.S. advisors, including Paul Williams, a former State Department lawyer who advised the Kosovars at Rambouillet that "under customary international law, if you act as a reasonable political entity, you will earn the right of self-determination."

Albright's problem at Rambouillet was that America could no longer let the Kosovars possess Wilson's dream, true self-determination and independence. Never mind that Milosevic, even then, was widely considered a war criminal for having fomented the ethnic cleansing in Bosnia. The Clinton administration, along with its European allies, feared that independence for Kosovo would incite Albanians in Macedonia, Greece, and Albania to form a "Greater Albania," a new state that could start a whole new cycle of instability in the Balkans and upset the tenuous integration of Bosnia next door. It might even inspire the Kurds in nearby Turkey, who wanted to slice off a portion of that NATO ally for themselves and create a new nation, perhaps even joining up with their brethren across the border in Iraq. Washington desperately wanted to keep national borders intact, and Milosevic, as monstrous as he might be, was the man with control over those borders. He was, as Albright herself often said through gritted teeth, "the address in Belgrade."

But the Kosovars decided not to be mere pawns in that larger game. For Albright, the emblematic moment of Rambouillet came just before she finally left for home. She put in a call to Thaci's mentor at the time, Adem Demaci, a squat, sixty-three-year-old former novelist with Coke-bottle glasses who briefly emerged as the key figure in the shadowy Kosovo Liberation Army. All she wanted was that Demaci, who had refused to attend the talks, agree not to stand in the way of the NATO-backed autonomy agreement. But Demaci refused to discuss it, telling Albright that a phone call couldn't solve such a "bloody and serious" problem. "Basically, he stiffed her," one stunned U.S. official close to Albright said at the time. "Here is the greatest nation on earth pleading with some nothing-balls to do something entirely in their own interest—which is to say yes to an interim agreement—and they defy us the whole way." It was, Albright later told friends, one of the most humiliating experiences of her life.

Quite simply, no one on the U.S. side had prepared at all for the idea that the Kosovars might decline to accept what, to the Americans, was an offer they couldn't refuse. As a NATO official explained to me later: "There was a strategy if both parties signed. There was a strategy if the Kosovars signed and Milosevic didn't [in other words, to bomb]. But there was no contingency plan if the Kosovars didn't." When the news got back to Capitol Hill, Senator John McCain tartly summed up the awful asymmetry of Rambouillet—scruffy guerrilla band versus end-of-history superpower—by saying, "Something is seriously wrong with this picture."

Eventually, American power being what it was, Albright did get what she wanted, which was to launch air strikes against Milosevic.[9] Flying back to Washington, Albright launched a major lobbying effort to bring the Kosovars on board. She gave a loving embrace to the KLA, sidestepping the fact that only a year before, her Balkans special envoy, Robert Gelbard, had joined Milosevic in branding it a "terrorist group" and that no one—neither President Clinton nor the European allies—supported its aims.[10] Albright invited the guerrillas to Washington for meetings. She dispatched Senator Bob Dole, a supporter of the Kosovars, to tell them America sympathized with their cause. She also sent her top aide and tart-tongued janissary, Jamie Rubin, to placate Thaci; the two of them, both handsome and well-dressed men about town, began lunching together in Paris (Rubin himself had, a year earlier, called upon Kosovar Albanians "to condemn terrorist action by the so-called Kosovo Liberation Army.")[11] On March 15, 1999, the KLA finally gave a grudging, conditional okay to the plan. That was a small victory, but at a huge price: The U.S. had effectively made allies of a group of guerrillas whose goals it actively and resolutely opposed. "The price of saving Rambouillet," conceded one U.S. official right afterward, "was to tie ourselves more and more closely to the Albanians."

Milosevic could scarcely believe the Americans were taking the side of a group that they, like him, once dismissed as terrorists. He refused to make a deal. He was then subjected to a seventy-eight-day bombing campaign that left NATO in tenuous command of Kosovo for what may well be decades. A year and a half later, the weakened Serb dictator was toppled in a tumultuous popular uprising, to be replaced by the democratic and not as virulently nationalist Vojislav Kostunica. But the Kosovo imbroglio is still festering today, even as it has faded from the front page. And the main reason is that, even now, no one can agree on the political future for the province—especially the NATO allies who spent billions of dollars to save it. Indeed, the new Yugoslavia under Kostunica is now working *with* NATO to suppress a new generation of Kosovar guerrillas— or "terrorists," perhaps. The Kosovars still want independence, but the NATO countries still don't want to give it to them for the same reasons. Yet in going to war for the Kosovars against Milosevic—who was later actually placed on trial as a war criminal in the Hague—NATO robbed its own position of much of its moral legitimacy. Independence looks to be in the cards eventually, and other guerrillas and independence movements around the world will be watching the outcome and drawing lessons from the way the Americans stepped in on the side of the Kosovars at Rambouillet.

Wesley Clark, the NATO supreme commander who directed the campaign in Kosovo and was summarily dismissed from his post after the war, described the outcome best in his memoirs: "Though NATO had succeeded in its first armed conflict, it didn't feel like a victory.... Even in the end, many were questioning what had been accomplished."[12]


## How This Is Different from the Cold War

U.S. policy makers, of course, have long been aware of the ideological Pandora's box created by Wilson's pledge of "self-determination" at the beginning of the last century. After Wilson declared in May 1915 that "every people has a right to choose the sovereignty under which they shall live," his estranged secretary of state, Robert Lansing, lamented that the term *self-determination* "is simply loaded with dynamite. It will raise hopes which can never be realized. It will, I fear, cost thousands of lives." Lansing proved to be right, most dramatically in the 1990s, when the disintegration of the Soviet bloc and Yugoslavia reawakened old ethnic conflicts frozen in place during the superpower standoff. Wilson himself, stunned by the number of delegations that applied to him for statehood while he, British prime minister David Lloyd George, and French prime minister Georges Clemenceau were negotiating peace in 1919, later admitted he had used the term *self-determination* "without the knowledge that nationalities existed, which are coming to us day after day."[13] It was just this sort of fuzzy-headed utopianism, of course, that so annoyed practitioners of realpolitik when it came to Wilson. And it should come as no surprise that Wilsonianism has often been honored more in the breach.

During the Cold War, containment doctrine for the most part recognized the status quo of a world half free and half Communist (as we saw in Chapter 1, the hard-right conservatives never quite accepted this, right through the era of détente). Wilsonianism was flouted most publicly in 1956, when the Eisenhower administration failed to voice support for the Hungarian rebellion at a crucial moment, probably sealing the fate of the Iron Curtain countries for the next thirty years. Wilson was spurned numerous times in covert actions such as the U.S.-approved Diem coup in Vietnam, and in Kennedy's quiet complicity in Khrushchev's construction of the Berlin Wall (JFK thought the alternative might be nuclear war). This was especially true in Latin America where, under the double hammer of the Monroe Doctrine and the policy of global containment, Washington often secretly propped up anticommunist strongmen such as Manuel Noriega and Augusto Pinochet over more democratic but pinkish alternatives—even to the point of promoting the assassination of democratically elected leaders such as Chile's Salvador Allende.

But there is an important distinction between our hypocrisy then and now. During the Cold War we were, for the most part, forgiven. We could point an accusing finger at an alternative value system—that of the Communist bloc—that was less compelling than our own, for all our inconsistencies. In a world engaged in a pitched battle for survival against Communist internationalism or fascism, those self-righteous Americans were always the lesser evil. With Kaiser Wilhelm and Adolf Hitler snarling at them, the French were much less inclined to sniff at American moralism, as they do today. Had German chancellor Gerhard Schroeder faced Stalin or even Leonid Brezhnev across the Fulda Gap rather than Vladimir Putin, he would have been far less likely to turn anti-Americanism into a campaign issue, as he did in the fall of 2002. The same goes for South Korean president Roh Moo-hyun, who was also elected on an anti-U.S. platform. U.S. presidents during the Cold War, even as they compromised their principles occasionally, were cheered on when they persistently identified victory with freedom, from Kennedy's 1961 vow to "pay any price, bear any burden" for liberty to Reagan's famous 1987 challenge: "Mr. Gorbachev, tear down this wall!"

The difference is that today, in Kosovo as elsewhere around the world, Washington really does not want to tear down any more walls. Everyone knows it, and there is no bipolar rival (like Moscow) at which to point a finger to distract people from our hypocrisy. Today when we betray our principles, enemies pounce, as bin Laden did. Washington is finding that the shadowy threat of global terror falls somewhat short of supplying a new Cold War–style excuse for suspending our principles at will: No one has mistaken the "Axis of Evil" for the Axis Powers of World War II. Dancing with dictators is not so easy. In the fall of 2002, when Pakistan's Musharraf finally held parliamentary elections (he had seized power in a bloodless coup in 1999), Islamist fundamentalists won a surprising number of seats. Their victories, especially in border regions such as Baluchistan, where terror groups still found harbor, were a worrisome setback to the war on terror. U.S. officials swallowed hard but, eager to cast Musharraf in a positive light, lauded the elections as "fair and square." The problem, however, was that the elections were not fair and square. And it was left to an election observer from the European Union, John Cushnahan, to point out that there were "serious flaws" in the elections because Musharraf's government had unfairly directed state resources to his party and created laws intended to prevent exiled former leaders Nawaz Sharif and Benazir Bhutto from taking part (one reason the Islamists triumphed). Washington was, quite noticeably, silent on this point.

America's experience with ideological blowback is not unique in the history of great powers. The education of Gandhi, Nehru, and Jinnah at Great Britain's Inns of Court in the late nineteenth century imbued those Indians with the ideas of justice and freedom that later helped topple an empire.[14] But surely ideological blowback has never been experienced before on such a scale as we Americans must now face. And it's not just a matter of having to deal with the ill effects of these ideas; it is *how* we must deal with them as well. We must adopt a foreign policy of pretense. We must secretly stymie ideals that go to the heart of our self-identity but which we no longer can afford to implement. Colin Powell, upon being named secretary of state, invoked the old Wilsonian tradition, saying that America is the "inspiration for the world that wants to be free, and we will continue to be that inspiration."[15] But by withholding statehood from the Kosovars, or democracy from the Arabs, we will provide a less-than-inspiring example, especially next to the self-image we have long cultivated as a beacon to the rest of the world. Albright once told me, when I asked her how it felt for Washington to be fighting its own ideals, "I'd rather be fighting those than a centralized economy [and] dictatorship."[16] But, unlike the Cold War, the battle against our own ideas is one we can never completely win. It will go on as long as America extends its hegemony, a key feature of the Permanent Quagmire—the endlessly spiraling crises we face.

Some have argued that, after a burst of secession—Georgia, Ukraine, Kazakhstan, the Baltic states, and Yugoslavia, among others—the world has seen the worst of ethnic devolution. Apart from Kosovo, Taiwan, Chechnya, and a few other hot or potentially hot conflicts, many other separatist movements remain at a low simmer (like the Basques and Catalans in Spain, and the Quebecois in Canada) or are even petering out, as in the case (possibly) of the Kurds and Cypriots of Turkey. According to the Stockholm International Peace Research Institute, the number of major armed conflicts around the world—almost all of which are internal to states, involving separatist movements—has remained steady at an average of about thirty a year since 1990. The phenomenon of globalization, meanwhile, may help to take the edge off the desire for sovereignty as it becomes apparent that, for small countries especially, traditional state structures are less central to economic success than they used to be.

But in a world in which so many developing countries exist along colonial borders that often cut across ethnic lines, the flames never quite go out. A post-Saddam Iraq, for example, could potentially disintegrate into its three constituent parts (a Kurdish north, a Sunni middle, and a Shiite south), and that could reignite Kurdish claims. Europe may not be finished either: Timothy Garton Ash writes that "any European state with a less than 80 percent ethnic majority is inherently unstable."[17] "Like some unstoppable process of fission, 'self-determination' continues to generate yet more sovereign states," Niall Ferguson writes. "From Scotland to Montenegro, would-be nation-states are waiting in the wings."[18] And while the advent of democracy arguably prevents wars *between* nation-states—to recall Wilson again—democratization also seems to foster self-determination movements *within* nation-states. "In Rwanda the massacre of around 800,000 Tutsis by Hutu [gangs] in April-July 1994 took place *after* international efforts to democratize the regime. In Indonesia, the most bitter fighting in East Timor came *after* the collapse of President Suharto's dictatorship in May 1998 and the island's democratic vote for independence in August the following year," Ferguson notes.[19] Afghanistan itself is a separatist volcano that is ready to erupt if the country ever gets back on its feet democratically. The British-drawn Durand Line, which in the late nineteenth century demarcated the boundaries of Queen Victoria's empire, cut off huge sections of the tribal Pashtun regions—known as Pashtunistan—for Imperial India, and they became part of Pakistan when it broke off in 1947. Pashtun Afghans, who make up the majority ethnic group in Afghanistan, have long yearned to reincorporate Pashtunistan and Baluchistan. That could lead to civil war, and war with Pakistan. And so what the scholar Stanley Hoffman has called "the crumbling of the Westphalian floor"—referring to the 1648 Peace of Westphalia, which founded the modern state system—promises to continue.[20] And so will Washington's need to compromise its ideals.

## The Many Guises of Ideological Blowback

As the twenty-first century begins, ideological blowback has cropped up in many different places and takes many different forms. Consider the problem of markets. Now that the global system is ruled by very much the kind of free markets we Americans have always said we wanted, they are clearly not as pretty in practice as they once seemed in theory. Governments today are under constant threat of surprise attacks from the markets. Multinational corporations, grown gigantic from a decade of record mergers and acquisitions, have often used their transnational production networks to evade local tax authorities—meaning that the biggest beneficiaries of globalization often pay the least to make up for its inequities. Multinational businesspeople and financiers have formed a kind of globe-girdling seditious class, undermining national freedom of action and sovereignty in the interest (they say) of the worldwide economy.[21] They have also grown filthy rich: By 1999, the combined wealth of the world's top two hundred billionaires hit an astonishing $1.1 trillion, nearly ten times the combined incomes of the world's least developed countries.[22]

Maybe these vast inequalities are inevitable, but they are largely the outcome of ideas we Americans promulgated. As we have already discussed, a penchant for reshaping the world order has been a constant theme of modern American history, beginning with Woodrow Wilson. In the 1990s this same shaping spirit filled another group of talented American elites with purpose: our economic policy makers. These elites were the keepers of the "Washington consensus"—the four-block bastion of economic orthodoxy that lies physically on Pennsylvania Avenue between Fifteenth Street, home of the U.S. Treasury Department, and the Nineteenth Street headquarters of the International Monetary Fund, with the Federal Reserve a couple of blocks to the south.

Animated by the free-market evangelism that grew out of the dramatic Cold War triumph over statism, the elites of the Washington consensus spent much of the '90s busily creating a new world order of their own, premised on the overarching idea that free markets around the world will work to create prosperity for all. The operating assumption of the Washington consensus was that more market openness was always better, whether it was a matter of capital or goods. In the 1990s, on the advice of the U.S.-dominated IMF and World Bank, newly reformed nations began dancing to the tune dictated by the victor of the Cold War. Foreign exchange controls were lifted worldwide, and the IMF sought to make capital liberalization a part of its charter. In an astonishingly short period of time, a stream of private capital began girdling the globe, fed by giant mutual, pension, and insurance funds and freed to roam at will by a worldwide telecommunications and computer network. These elites forbade alternative approaches, including the East Asian model of maintaining partially closed economies and subsidizing exports during a country's development phase, before the nation hits full industrialization. This approach was used to differing degrees by such major nations as Japan and China (as well as by the United States itself during its own developmental period in the nineteenth century).[23] Yet it was mostly banned under WTO rules largely dictated from Washington, and remains so today. The result is that developing countries find themselves hampered by the system we created in trying to catch up.[24] The Bush administration's national security strategy was once again fairly clueless about the ironies inherent in this brand of blowback. The document praises free trade as "a moral principle" and calls unambiguously for greater "international flows of investment capital" to emerging markets—as if the 1997–98 Asian financial crisis, in which untrammeled "hot money" helped to cause a disaster in these markets, had never happened.[25] The elites of the Washington consensus failed to appreciate fully that free-flowing capital, with its constant manias, is far more problematic than the free trade of goods. But even goods trade has caused headaches for Washington. In the '00s, as the rest of the world did begin to accept the inevitability of global free trade, developing countries began to attack the Americans and Europeans as never before for maintaining large agricultural and other market protections in their home markets. Again, our hypocrisy was noticed.

## International Law: A Growth Industry

The problem of ideological blowback infects the very foundations of the international system that is in America's care. In the last chapter, for example, we examined the problems of "containing" a China that is cleverly using the openness of this international system to accumulate new technology and know-how and build its power. And as we saw in Chapters 1 and 2, the hegemonic role of the United States regularly places us in situations of friction not only with international institutions such as the UN but with international law, on which Wilson implicitly based the right to self-determination. America may have fought a humanitarian war to save the Kosovars, but for years now the United States has been the laggard government in approving many UN-sponsored human rights conventions. In July 1999, fearing a compromise of its sovereignty, the Clinton administration was virtually alone in opposing the International Criminal Court (ICC) it originally championed and which was later endorsed by 120 nations. The Bush administration went a step further, actually "unsigning" the United States from the treaty in the middle of the war on terror and, at one point, threatening to withdraw money for U.S. peacekeeping if the UN Security Council did not exempt U.S. troops from ICC prosecution. Washington's desire to be permitted to act freely was natural—after all, America, as the überpower, is the nation most often called upon to do robust intervention that might leave its troops open to war-crimes claims. The International Criminal Court, intended to prosecute genocidal acts, could conceivably (though it was highly unlikely) accuse American officials of being war criminals for dropping Special Forces into another country's borders or bombing—in contravention of the UN charter—in order to kill people deemed dangerous to Americans. But to flout the ICC and international law so brazenly at a moment when Washington was trying to identify itself with "civilization" blurred the difference between Washington and the terrorists it was trying to isolate. It also set a worrisome precedent that opened the door to unilateral withdrawal from any number of treaties by any number of nations.

The problem lies in the fact that the more powerful America has become relative to the rest of the world, the more compelling has become the need to break the rules that we would like to apply to everyone else. Principles that sounded good when we were an emerging power don't work as well when we are in charge of global order and need to occasionally knock some heads. Washington has begun insisting on, in effect, a double standard. At the same time, paradoxically, America needs to further the development of international law as a critical sinew of the international community—especially at a time when the international community, in turn, has become Washington's chief ally in the war on terror.

And as international law evolves, America grows ever more uncomfortable with the burden our Wilsonian progeny has placed on us. International pressures are increasing in favor of championing human rights, a favorite theme of both Democratic and Republican administrations. George W. Bush himself, echoing FDR's Four Freedoms, called these "non-negotiable," and UN secretary-general Kofi Annan, who is for the most part admired by U.S. officials, has envisioned a future in which the rights traditionally allotted to sovereign powers to manage their own affairs give way to more universal human-rights concerns. "The sanctity and dignity of every human life," he said in accepting the Nobel Peace

Prize in 2001, "will require us to look beyond the framework of states." This, of course, was the thrust of both Wilson's and FDR's dream too, to achieve such a universal consensus on human values. The push from the international community to intervene in humanitarian disasters, empowered by images from CNN and the explosive growth of activist NGOs and other transnational actors, will only grow stronger. As noted, the Bush administration developed its own standard granting it the right to breach other nations' sovereignty, mainly involving, once again, states that support or harbor terrorists.

But this new body of trans-Westphalian international law runs up against the protection of sovereignty of which America, as the world's dominant power and overseer of the international system, is now prime guarantor. That's another sticky problem that Woodrow Wilson left us with. It is not new, but the pressures placed upon us as a result have only grown more acute. While raising self-determination to "an imperative principle of action"—his words to Congress in 1918—Wilson also demanded respect for the integrity of borders under international law. This is a circle no one has been able to square. Even the UN charter contradicts itself: Article 1 guarantees the "equal rights and self-determination of peoples," while Article 2 vouchsafes the "sovereign equality" of all member states and asks them to refrain from "use of force against the territorial integrity or political independence of any state."

This also was the nub of Albright's problem at Rambouillet, of course. Albright may or may not have mishandled the negotiations—in delivering only ultimatums to Milosevic, she never left a true diplomatic solution open, and in cuddling up to the Kosovars, she encouraged them in unrealizable ambitions. But the hardest problem was something she could not help. The fact was, elements of international law existed on the sides of both Milosevic and the Kosovars. The latter wanted statehood, but Milosevic made a compelling Wilsonian counterclaim—based, of course, on the language of the UN charter. In a wartime interview with a Houston TV station, even as he repeated his outrageous contention that he did not order the ethnic cleansing of Kosovo, Milosevic ran down the list of the various separatist movements that haunted many of his NATO antagonists. "If that became practice," he said in his broken English (the

Serb dictator once took great pride in having been a Communist "banker" in New York during the Cold War), "no one country will be safe." Later, during his trial in the Hague, he made the same points with great effectiveness.

Milosevic knew his audience, for NATO in fact was dragged kicking and screaming into intervening in Kosovo. Consider: From the moment that NATO threatened in October 1998 to bomb Serbia for the first time, every one of NATO's members resisted the idea, as did the UN Security Council. No one wanted to set a precedent for intervening in another country's separatist troubles. As a senior administration official said back then, "The Chinese didn't like it because of Tibet. The Russians hated it because of Chechnya. France and Spain have Corsica and the Basques. No one liked it, but in the end we were able to rationalize it because it was not considered a precedent. It was because of the threat to regional peace."[26] Milosevic also knew he had nothing less than the United Nations charter, the ultimate fruit of Wilson's attempt to build a League of Nations, on his side, backing his claims to sovereignty.

The upshot is that Clinton and Albright took America to war in pursuit of one noble Wilsonian goal, rooting out tyranny and oppression, only to run headlong into other keystones of Wilsonianism. Milosevic was at once an enemy and an anti-separatist ally; the KLA was at once an ally and a pro-separatist enemy. We fought a "war" that we didn't dare call a war (because we wanted only to "persuade" Milosevic to treat his own people better) over an entity, Kosovo, that we didn't dare define. Welcome to the twenty-first century.

Indeed, in 2002, as Milosevic went on trial in the Hague for war crimes, America found itself back in bed with its unlikely partner in sovereignty from Kosovo. When Milosevic insisted that his forcible transfer to the Hague violated his sovereign rights, lawyers for the Netherlands successfully argued that the UN charter, which authorized the war crimes tribunal, superseded national law.[27] The Bush administration, which opposes such UN tribunals for the same reason as Milosevic—to protect its sovereignty—could only sit on the sidelines in embarrassment. In effect, it agreed with the Serb.

## The Taiwan Trap

Of all the Wilsonian traps that await U.S. policy makers worldwide, few have become more dangerous or frustrating than the problem of Taiwan. In another time and another place, the victory of Chen Shui-bian in the Taiwanese presidential election of 2000 would have been considered a historic victory for America and its values as well. It was the first time in five thousand years of history that a Chinese state had democratically elected an opposition leader—displacing, in this case, the long-ruling Kuomintang, or Nationalist Party, of Chiang Kai-shek. The election also seemed to vindicate a decades-old U.S. policy by which Washington has nurtured and protected Taiwan while warding off Beijing, which has always considered Taiwan a renegade province whose fate is to be reunited with the motherland. The Taiwan of Chen Shui-bian is a triumph of the American model: After years of military rule, Taiwan is today a full-fledged democracy like South Korea and Japan and has a roaring Western-style economy with relatively open markets. "I've never seen anything like this," former ambassador to China James Lilley, who was in Taipei as an election observer, enthused to me after Chen's victory. "Here a man of the people has won a democratic election in a very convincing way, in a campaign full of gusto and life."[28]

Instead, back in Washington Chen's victory has become the triumph that dare not speak its name. For three decades, Washington has kept a lid on Beijing's claims to Taiwan by maintaining a policy of "strategic ambiguity," meaning it kept both sides guessing about the extent to which America might intervene in a conflict. This was designed to discourage Beijing from aggression at the same time as it discouraged the Taiwanese from provoking China. For a long time it was an easy policy to maintain: The aging mandarins of the Kuomintang always insisted on the fantasy that they would someday take China back, and Taiwan, as an autocracy run by these mandarins, drew little sympathy in Washington, except for a small knot of hard-core supporters known as the China lobby.

But the more democracy takes hold in Taiwan, the more the Taiwanese agitate for self-determination—and the more difficult strategic ambiguity becomes. Before Bill Clinton's trip to Beijing in June 1998, pro-independence groups in Taiwan addressed an open letter to the U.S. president, reminding him pointedly, "The right of self-determination by the people, proclaimed by [Wilson], has taken deep root in the political tradition of the U.S." But administration officials, worried about having to repeat the dangerous standoff of 1996, when Beijing fired off missiles prior to the previous Taiwan election and Clinton sent carriers to the Taiwan Straits in response, caved to Chinese pressure to squelch the emerging activist sentiment in Taipei. In a remarkably frank concession by a U.S. president that he no longer countenanced self-determination, Clinton declared openly while in China that Washington would not support independence for Taiwan. This was longtime policy, of course, but it had never been voiced before by the "leader of the free world." Clinton, the same man who had once berated George H. W. Bush for kowtowing to Beijing, had sent a clear message to Taipei (and, by the way, to Tibet, another restive province of China): Don't stir the waters. We Americans may still make noises about human rights, but ultimately, for strategic reasons, we've decided to cast our lot with the Chinese leadership, not Woodrow Wilson.

Not surprisingly, like so much else that Clinton did, this approach outraged the new administration of George W. Bush. Conservatives have long hated the compromise language of the Shanghai Communiqué, which was drawn up by Nixon and Kissinger in 1972 and essentially sacrificed America's relationship with Nationalist China to the new Cold War alliance with Red China, acknowledging that Taiwan was part of China. The Bush team was also upset that Clinton, at a sit-down with Chinese leader Jiang Zemin at the APEC summit in Auckland in 1999, had failed to respond forthrightly to an aggressive diatribe on the subject of Taiwan. They sought to set things right. Bush told ABC's *Good Morning America* that the United States would do "whatever it took" to defend Taiwan from Chinese aggression, including using the full force of the U.S. military. That appeared to throw strategic ambiguity out the window, but the administration later denied that it did. Indeed, by late 2002, as he faced the necessity of making China an ally in the war on terror, Bush forthrightly opposed independence for Taiwan in a statement that could only be called Clintonesque. "We intend to make sure that the issue is resolved peacefully, and that includes making it clear that we do not support independence," Bush said.[29]

Yet such is Taiwan's success as a democracy and open-market economy that pressures for independence are likely only to grow. An increasing number of politicians in Washington say it is time to ditch strategic
ambiguity and stand with the Taiwanese. The policy may have been
strategically correct during the Cold War and morally palatable at a time
when Taiwan was ruled by authoritarian Nationalists, but times have
changed. The emerging debate in Washington, and Taiwan's growing
desire for and right to independence, are bound to run up against China's
new nationalism. And now China is embarked on a steady program of
upgrading its military to enable it to project power in Asia. There's no
doubt that "a lot of the military technologies they are developing are
directly linked to solving the problem of the U.S. Navy and an attack on
Taiwan," says one U.S. government source. At the same time Washington
has signaled it is willing to bolster Taipei's missile defense. For now Chen
Shui-bian has been content to make small moves toward independence,
such as issuing passports marked "Taiwan" instead of "Republic of
China," and renaming its de facto foreign embassies Taiwan Representative Offices. In polls, a majority of Taiwanese consistently oppose provoking China unnecessarily. Beijing also alternates between fire-breathing
rhetoric and moderation, and its new leader, Hu Jintao, is unlikely to do
something so foolhardy as attack Taiwan unprovoked. Nonetheless, the
historical shifts are there, though they may take decades to play out.
China has clearly become more nationalistic—a trend encouraged by the
Chinese Communist Party in order to replace the failures of Maoism.
And in Taipei, the very real danger is that once the younger, Taiwan-bred
generation comes into power in a world in which democracy and self-
determination are the dominant ideals, they will force a crisis over statehood. Washington will no longer have the luxury of ambiguity.

## Meddling with Moscow

During the 1990s, Washington's relationship with its former Cold War
adversary, Moscow, was badly damaged by both forms of ideological
blowback—political and economic. This was an outcome that both

Republican and Democratic administrations had wanted to avoid. Soon after the Soviet Union disappeared from the map in the early '90s, Moscow heard a lot of blithe pro-market rhetoric from the elder Bush and Clinton administrations, and it was the subject of much high-minded tinkering by the free-market consultants at the Harvard Institute for International Development, as well as the IMF. Citing their Western-trained advisors, both former Soviet leader Mikhail Gorbachev and his successor, Russian president Boris Yeltsin, confidently predicted a two-year transition to a market economy. But Washington didn't provide much help or support in institution building; its rather poor substitute was to ally itself with the power base of an increasingly addled Yeltsin. Privatization of the former Communist production system quickly degenerated into what the Russians called "grabitization," the unfair seizure of old state assets by party apparatchiks with insider connections, who now saw themselves as oligarchs. When the West did finally send over boatloads of IMF money, things were so far gone that the aid only led to massive capital flight. World markets attacked the ruble, and Russia fell into a long economic slide. "By paying insufficient attention to the institutional infrastructure that would allow a market economy to flourish—and by easing the flow of capital in and out of Russia—the IMF and Treasury had laid the groundwork for the oligarchs' plundering," wrote the World Bank's former chief economist, Joseph Stiglitz, in one of the harsher accounts of Western culpability.[30] Even the eminent Milton Friedman, who fathered many of the free-market ideas that drove Russia's privatization revolution, concedes that it went overboard. "In the immediate aftermath of the fall of the Soviet Union, I kept being asked what the Russians should do," he told me in 2002. "I said, 'Privatize, privatize, privatize. I was wrong. [Stiglitz] was right. What we want is privatization, and the rule of law.'"[31]

Simultaneously, Moscow suffered a virtual epidemic of self-determination. After the Soviet Union's collapse in 1991, the former Soviet republics declared independence one by one, along with the Baltic states. Moscow's sense of self-deflation was exacerbated in the spring of 1999, just before the Kosovo campaign, when Washington expanded NATO to include Poland, Hungary, and the Czech Republic. These two forces together—economic desperation and decimation by self-determination—contributed to a growing sense of anger among Russians and chariness of Western advice. The outcome was the election of a strongman, ex-KGB colonel Vladimir Putin, whose meteoric rise to popularity had much to do with his nationalist promise to keep Russia "whole," as he demonstrated with a savage war against Chechen Muslim separatists. Today, even as President Putin declares his willingness to become part of the West, Russia may be retreating into a quasi-authoritarian regime under his rule, one that bears uncomfortable reminders of the Soviet years, like the growing Putin personality cult. And given the failures of American advice in Russia over the past decade, we no longer have the credibility to resist that trend.

## The Way Out

As we have seen, various forms of ideological blowback have muddled U.S. policy from Russia to the Arab world to the use of international law. We just look silly if we don't acknowledge this and instead simply continue to promote our wondrous values of democracy and freedom to a world that has already acknowledged their validity and is wearily trying to apply them. The principles aren't really in doubt, but in practice they need considerable tweaking, fudging, and fixing. The question now is how to ensure that our values are still promoted, but with a minimum of friction and self-contradiction. The answer, for those who have followed me this far, shouldn't be too much of a surprise. The saving grace of the problem of ideological blowback is that America no longer has to work as hard at building up an international system based on our values. That system now exists—we only have to make use of it. And that is where international institutions come in. Rather than being the sole source of the values we hold dear, we must let the institutions of the international community take the heat for us.

This will not be easy, nor will it be consistent; as we see in the application of international law, there is potential for direct clashes between the U.S. national interest and the interest of other countries. But on the whole the U.S. national interest now coincides with that of the international community. Many Americans, especially conservatives, still blanch at the idea of promoting true-blue American values through a checkered institution like the UN. Indeed, if there is one thing that most bothers conservatives about American fealty to the United Nations, it is that the UN charter makes no difference between dictators and democrats among its membership. Both have equal votes. And the UN's consensus-based system can sometimes produce appalling results, like naming Libya to head its Human Rights Commission in 2003. In the eyes of conservatives, that tends to delegitimize the world body.

In practice, however, the majority of nations in the UN are now democratic to some degree. And in recent years, the United Nations has decided to cast its lot with democracy promotion after decades in which it remained value-neutral on forms of government (during the Cold War, democracy was code for "pro-U.S."). Secretary-General Kofi Annan boldly took this step at the original Community of Democracies meeting in Warsaw in 2000 when he declared, "When the United Nations can truly call itself a community of democracies, the charter's noble ideals of protecting human rights and 'social progress in larger freedoms' will have been brought much closer." For UN officials, democracy promotion has already gone well beyond such rhetoric. The UN's annual Human Development Report in 2002 declared itself in favor of "governance that is democratic in both form and substance." And like the Community of Democracies' manifesto, the UN report actually spelled out specific practices that had to be carried out. The UN Development Programme, which issued the report, had once focused on constructing water wells. But now, said UNDP administrator Mark Malloch Brown, "democratic governance is our biggest business. This is what countries were asking of us. There are now 140 countries that have competitive multiparty elections. That's 80 countries that have changed columns [from authoritarian rule]. That creates a huge demand [for advice] that's got to be met by somebody."[32]

In the spring of 2002 the UNDP also issued an unprecedented report that harshly laid out the failings of Arab societies. Calling them "rich, but not developed," the report detailed the deficits of democracy, economic modernization, and women's rights that were favorite targets of the

American neoconservatives, who (rightly) view these deficiencies as the real cause of the societal rage that can lead to terrorism. It noted that the Arab world suffers from a lower rate of Internet connectivity than even sub-Saharan Africa, and that education is so backward and cut-off that the entire Arab world translates from other languages only one-fifth of the books that Greece does. The report was not exactly the kind of thing that would have come out of the Bush administration, which was peopled with pro-Israel hawks—its introduction was sugarcoated with a pandering section that blamed Israel for many Arab ills—but nonetheless it rocked the Arab world, said Malloch Brown. "Nothing we've published in my time has been as influential." One reason the report had impact was that it was *not* another diktat from Washington. Quite the contrary. It added several layers of buffer: Not only was the report commissioned by the United Nations, of which the Arab world was a part, it was authored and overseen by an all-Arab advisory group and the former deputy prime minister of Jordan. Of course, the news was not all good, since the report was also supported by many opposition Islamist parties.[33] But that's a reminder that institutional sluggishness and bureaucracy can sometimes work in our favor. Democracy by committee is a glacial process—and, frankly, that's how we want it to happen in the Arab world. When it comes to self-determination, the need to forge consensus in the international community will also slow down new movements for statehood.

Even regional organizations—which, as we will see in the next chapter, have become increasingly pertinent to America's national interest—have grown Americanized in terms of their values. The Bush administration discovered this to its embarrassment in April 2002, when a coup appeared to topple Venezuelan President Hugo Chávez. Administration officials, who were intensely frustrated with Chávez because of his maverick views and courting of Cuban leader Fidel Castro, were less than forthright in insisting that he be restored to power. It was the Organization of American States—a U.S.-founded organization that once was toothless and permissive of dictatorship—that insisted that Chávez's democratic legitimacy be observed. He was restored to power. In Africa, the last continent that could be considered a refuge of dictators, national leaders in 2002 created the new African Union to replace the old Organization of African Unity and declared their objectives are to "promote democratic principles and institutions."[34]

So, as unpleasant and messy as it may seem, the best alternative is to work through the international system we have built, even in values promotion. That is why, ultimately, the Bush administration's disavowal of international norms and new institutions such as the International Criminal Court was so self-defeating. The problem of international law working against us—as it might at the ICC—will have to be finessed. But that, after all, is what lawyers are for. The key is to finesse from within, rather than have oneself branded as a rogue from without. To paraphrase Thomas More in *A Man for All Seasons,* if we cut down all the laws in the land to get at the devil, we will find ourselves vulnerable when we ourselves try to apply the law—as Bush did against Saddam Hussein in Iraq. Having abjured international law and begun his campaign against Saddam by threatening unilateral war, Bush never really regained his credibility at the United Nations when he invoked Saddam's violations of UN resolutions as a way of justifying a campaign against him.

But for many Americans the United Nations still represents the worst of ineffectual multilateralism and relinquished sovereignty. So we must go into some detail about what is wrong with the UN—and there is plenty —and what can still be made right.

# 6

## Rethinking Multilateralism

The United Nations was set up not to get us to heaven, but only
to save us from hell.

**Winston Churchill**

RICHARD HOLBROOKE is known in diplomatic circles as "the bulldozer," and he looks the part. Six foot one and broad-shouldered, with a
square jaw and a plowlike nose, Holbrooke naturally dominates any room
he walks into. He is smart and supremely self-confident, with an unin-
flected, insistent way of talking that is like a verbal handcuff, captivating
listeners whether they're inclined to agree with him or not. An A-lister on
the dinner-party circuit in New York and Washington, the career diplomat and sometime investment banker is a shameless cultivator of the
media. (How many assistant secretaries of state get a full-length profile in
*Vanity Fair,* as Holbrooke once did, albeit a negative one?) Holbrooke is
also, like Madeleine Albright and the Bush neoconservatives, a fervent
believer in the essential goodness of American power. And he's happy to
apply it unilaterally, if push comes to shove.

Not surprisingly, Dick Holbrooke's rather undiplomatic qualities
earned him a lot of enemies in places high and low, especially in that last
refuge of multilateralism in Washington, the State Department. While he
rose fast as a young Foreign Service officer, taking part in the Paris peace
talks of 1968–69 and becoming Jimmy Carter's assistant secretary of state

at thirty-two, Holbrooke was often stymied in his bid for senior-level office by jealous or mistrustful rivals—especially when it came to his dream post, secretary of state. But Holbrooke was not a man to be denied the spotlight, and during the mid-to-late 1990s he finally came into his own. The emerging age of brutal ethnic and tribal conflict cried out for heavy-handed diplomacy and creative tactics, and everyone recognized that Holbrooke, whatever his personality flaws, was perhaps the toughest, most talented negotiator in the U.S. diplomatic corps.

Holbrooke was the blunt instrument to whom Bill Clinton turned when the president wanted to tackle the stickiest foreign policy problem of his tenure, Bosnia. Holbrooke, a kind of diplomatic Green Beret at home in the ethnic jungles of "post–Cold War conflict resolution," as he liked to call it, was adept at making use of the threat of American force to forge patchwork diplomatic solutions to the nearly insoluble problems that so characterize the Permanent Quagmire. And he loved trying the impossible—one reason the Balkans were tailor-made for the man. Yugoslavia began disintegrating in the early '90s in an orgy of self-determination. Bosnian Serbs were slaughtering their Muslim brethren and humiliating UN peacekeepers. While the Europeans squabbled among themselves and Clinton's courtly first-term secretary of state, Warren Christopher, dithered, Clinton raged that he was "getting creamed" in the media.[1] Holbrooke, who had been among the earliest and most passionate advocates of intervention, was given the job of negotiating a solution after NATO bombing sent the Serbs to the bargaining table.

Holbrooke proved especially effective at handling Slobodan Milosevic, the Serbian autocrat who reintroduced genocide (euphemized as "ethnic cleansing") into the European lexicon in the '90s and was the true power behind the Bosnian Serbs. The Yugoslav leader's ruthlessness in pursuing the most primitive kind of ethnic politics, coming at a time when Europe was planning its great postwar shift to a "postmodern" union that no longer wanted to wage war and lacked a consensus voice, had stumped European negotiators. Milosevic had also stymied Christopher, who had sought a multilateral solution by forging a common front with the Europeans but had slunk back to Washington with nothing. And needless to say, Milosevic made mincemeat of the UN's timid and underequipped peacekeepers. Only Holbrooke, with his haranguing, let-me-handle-it approach, could match Milosevic bluster for bluster and bluff for bluff. And he did it not through multilateral consensus building but by going head to head with the Serb, backed by the implicit threat of American hard power.

Holbrooke was skilled not only at brass-knuckle negotiations but at the stagecraft of diplomacy. In Dayton, Ohio, where he was the lead negotiator in resolving the Bosnian war in 1995, he escorted Milosevic through a hangar bristling with U.S. planes and missiles at Wright-Patterson Air Force Base, where the talks were held, to drive home the brute actuality of American might. Holbrooke also made a point of banning the UN—which had lost all credibility with the Serbs—from most of the negotiations. "Telling the UN that its involvement would weaken the search for peace was painful," he later wrote, "especially for those of us who had grown up believing in the importance of the world body."[2] Three years later, in October 1998, when Milosevic was balking at a deal to force him to stop trying in Kosovo what he'd once done in Bosnia—oppress and kill the Muslim minority—Holbrooke also opted for an approach that emphasized U.S. might. He flew to Belgrade with General Michael Short, the air force commander who would actually carry out threatened NATO air strikes. They walked into the palace of Milosevic, who barked out in greeting, "So, General, *you're* the man who's going to bomb us." Short, a no-nonsense former fighter pilot, responded with a line that Holbrooke had concocted: "Mr. President, I've got U-2s [surveillance planes] in one hand and B-52s in the other. And I will use whichever I'm ordered to. . . . The choice is yours." Once again, as he had at Dayton, Milosevic settled with Holbrooke. He allowed international monitors into Kosovo—a patchwork deal that lasted until the following year, when Albright, an archrival of Holbrooke's, took over negotiations. Before Holbrooke, commented Gojko Beric, a Sarajevo political analyst, the Balkans were a "graveyard for diplomats. . . . Nobody had been able to achieve anything."[3]

A year later it fell to Holbrooke to save the institution he had once banished from the bargaining table, to turn his unilateralist skills to the task of rescuing a failing ideal in the post–Cold War world: multilateralism. All of his "special talents"—as Jamie Rubin, Albright's spokesman, would sometimes refer to them with a smirk—were needed in the late summer of 1999, when Holbrooke became Clinton's ambassador to the United Nations (he had just missed out being appointed as Clinton's second-term secretary of state, losing the job to Albright). And it was there that he faced his toughest test of post–Cold War conflict resolution. The hot spot was New York, the issue the widening war of sensibilities between the U.S. government and its prodigal child, the UN. Holbrooke's opponent this time was a man who was at least as resolute as Milosevic in his opposition to Clinton administration policy: U.S. senator Jesse Helms, the North Carolina archconservative who was the champion of antiglobalism during the Clinton years.

This chapter is about coming to terms, as Holbrooke and others of his generation did, with the failures of multilateralism as embodied in institutions such as the UN, and yet at the same time recognizing, as he did, that for all their deficiencies they are more indispensable than ever to American interests in the world. As Edward Luck has observed, the tensions between the United States and the poor relation it hosts on its soil, the United Nations, have surfaced in the same form "generation after generation."[4] We must now, at long last, forge past a tired debate that for many years has turned on the fact that the United Nations and other postwar institutions, such as the World Bank and IMF, do not work as they were originally envisioned. They do not; that dream is gone. They are also, as many critics have said, bloated bureaucracies that chronically resist reform. But opponents of these institutions, on both the right and the left, continue to use this gap between the ideal and reality to argue that they should be marginalized or even disbanded. What must be confronted is the fact that they remain, as we suggested in previous chapters, the institutional pillars of the global system, as well as critical instruments for managing world order. And they are adapting to the one-überpower world: Whether we Americans like it or not, these institutions serve now as the chief transmission belt for American values in the world, the chief vehicle for securing the American-led international system and, not least, for making the brute fact of American hard power acceptable to other countries. And they are critical to the policy of institutional envelopment of China and Russia that will help prevent a hegemonic challenge in decades to come. But first let's confront the reasons why they *don't* work well.

## How the UN Failed

By the time Holbrooke took over at the U.S. mission to the UN, the deepening gulf between the United States and the United Nations had become, for many American internationalists, the keenest disappointment of the post–Cold War period. Part of the reason was that, only a decade before, hopes had been so high as the Cold War ended. During the Cold War the world body had been all but written off. The Security Council had been mostly a football of the superpowers, a forum for confrontation and stalemate, where the Soviet Union, using the powers granted to it by Roosevelt in 1945, vetoed nearly everything in sight (with the signal exceptions of the Marshall Plan and the Korean War resolution —Soviet delegates were absent both days—and a few minor truce oversight missions in places such as Cyprus).

But in 1991 the Cold War paralysis finally ended, and Moscow, the shoe-banging, propaganda-droning obstructionist, became an attentive if troubled pupil of Western reform. And Washington seemed eager to help the United Nations take on the task of world peace. In September 1991 George H. W. Bush told the General Assembly that the end of the Cold War gave the world, "for the first time, [a] chance to fulfill the UN Charter's ambition." On the eve of Bill Clinton's election, then-UN secretary-general Boutros Boutros-Ghali proposed an activist Agenda for Peace that won kudos from the Bush administration, the *New York Times,* and the *Washington Post,* as well as some top commanders in the U.S. military. His vision: a robust "peace enforcement" capability for the United Nations, a rapid-reaction force that would fill the gap between the United Nations' traditional peacekeeping role as a lightly armed buffer—the kind of duty it had performed for decades in places like the Middle East and Kashmir—and the large-scale war-making capability left to the United States in the Korean and Persian Gulf wars.

Boutros-Ghali's concept seemed to dovetail nicely with the new administration's agenda: "Enlargement" of democracy had replaced containment as America's basic foreign policy doctrine, declared Anthony Lake, then national security advisor. The United Nations would not be central to this, but that was fine; it would take care of the world's basket cases—a kind of World Bank for political conflict—while the rest of the globe prospered on a diet of open markets and democracy. Madeleine Albright espoused a pro-UN policy of "assertive multilateralism" that would combine forthright U.S. leadership with extensive use of UN peacekeepers. "The time has come to commit the political, intellectual and financial capital that UN peacekeeping and our security deserve," she said.[5] Clinton himself, in a September 1993 speech to the UN General Assembly, proclaimed that "UN peacekeeping holds the promise to resolve many of this era's conflicts." Taken together, it was the last time anyone offered up a coherent plan for the hopefully named and never realized New World Order.

It never happened, of course. Instead, mission by mission, UN "blue helmets" who had served low-key roles as monitors of peace agreements during the Cold War failed at peacekeeping in the new era of tribal and ethnic strife, when so many situations seemed to hover precariously between peace and war. In Somalia, a UN humanitarian mission turned into a debacle, as twenty-five Pakistanis and then, later, eighteen U.S. soldiers were killed—one of whose bodies appeared on CNN, getting dragged through the dust of Mogadishu by cheering Somalis. In Rwanda in 1994, a gun-shy Security Council failed to reinforce the UN contingent, opening the way to genocide. The mother of all peacekeeping disasters was Bosnia, where Dutch peacekeepers were held hostage by snarling Serb forces and meekly handed over seven thousand Muslims at Srebrenica for slaughter. By the time Dayton rolled around, after what Holbrooke called "the triple disaster" of peacekeeping failures in Somalia, Rwanda, and Bosnia in 1993–94, he himself had little use for the UN, which is why he put on such a harsh display of realpolitik; instead NATO would supply the solution and the peacekeeping muscle. This was the same Holbrooke who, as a New Yorker born of immigrant parents, had more than once tearfully described the moment when his father took him, as a boy, to the banks of the East River to gaze upon the UN building and see the great hope of the future.

By the late '90s, nothing seemed to be working. Not only was peace-keeping failing, it was getting very expensive. The overgrown UN secretariat, some ten thousand strong, was a "really swollen, sloppy awful bureaucracy," says Holbrooke, often peopled at its senior level by aging, tenured aristocrats from developing countries who lived well in New York while bashing their host nation, America, in the media. As John Micklethwait and Adrian Wooldridge put it, "Look around the whole UN, and you find a haze of duplication among the manifold funds, programs and agencies. Even when set alongside national governments, it seems bloated."[6] What's worse, by 1994, the United Nations was running seventeen different operations employing some eighty thousand peacekeepers, and its peace-keeping budget had leaped from $600 million to $3 billion per year.

Holbrooke later described his feelings about the collapsed hopes surrounding the UN, symbolized by the futile "talk factory" that the UN General Assembly had become. Once apotheosized as the Parliament of Man, it had become a place paralyzed by regional politics, the droning speechifying and petty clubbiness of small or backward nations, as symbolized most infamously by an Arab-railroaded resolution identifying Zionism with racism. The General Assembly's one-nation, one-vote structure was also an exercise in the worst sort of multilateral utopianism: the pretense that small, insignificant countries such as Zambia or Laos could vie for influence with the major powers. Of course it never worked. "The very physical structure of the GA room, which when I was a kid overwhelmed me with its power and majesty, now as I visited it today and sat in it and even spoke from the podium, seemed to do exactly the opposite," Holbrooke recalled in an interview in mid-2002. "It was no longer a majestic noble parliament of human beings. It was a room whose very size and acoustics deadened human interaction and minimized human beings. If you compare the architecture to the House of Commons or the Senate and House of Representatives chambers, you can see how antihuman it is. The General Assembly became something useless. My parents truly believed the UN was the last, best hope of human beings. Their views were obviously dashed by the reality of how a great idea becomes a bureaucracy, and how the bureaucracy becomes corrupted by its own self-serving nature and very weak leadership and inherent conceptual problems and limitations."[7]

But the worst was yet to come. All this disillusionment with the UN—especially the surge in peacekeeping duties and peacekeeping debacles—coincided disastrously with the Republican takeover of Congress in 1994. In the absence of a true foreign threat to the United States, the sharply rising numbers quickly came to the attention of Helms, the Senate Foreign Relations Committee chair who made an obsession with "UN reform" and slashing foreign aid the focus of much of his vision of a scaled-down U.S. presence in the world.

They called him "Senator No," and Jesse Helms said he was "proud of the title."[8] Conservative to his North Carolina tobacco roots, the courtly but dogged Helms was infamous for using any procedure to block initiatives or legislation he didn't like, and he consciously sought to emulate Henry Cabot Lodge, the bane of Wilson's League. Helms himself was more a unilateralist than an isolationist, but his objections to the UN followed the old isolationist line going back to Senators William Langer and Henrik Shipstead, the lone two Republicans who voted against the UN treaty in 1945 on grounds that it would create a superstate. Helms, like his hawkish successors in the Bush administration, opposed almost any encumbrance on American sovereignty—and in fact he paved the way for them by leading the fight against the nuclear test ban and other treaties. Another of his main targets was foreign aid—much of which, Helms said, had "lined the pockets of corrupt dictators while funding the salaries of a growing, bloated bureaucracy."[9] But rather than a nuanced diagnosis of the problems of foreign aid—which was needed, given the harsh military cast U.S. aid took on during the Cold War—Helms and a small posse of neo-isolationist allies on the Hill tried to kill the patient. They chopped the foreign-aid budget to less than a cent on the federal dollar, or 0.1 percent of GDP (compared to the Marshall Plan–era high of 3.21 percent of GNP), putting America at dead last among twenty-two major nations.[10] The free market was the answer, they said, along with private aid groups like the Christian "Samaritan's Purse" (a Helms favorite). Yet at the same time the gap between rich and poor nations widened, and apart from Africa, no region was hit worse than the Arab world. Now, taking on the UN, Helms decided that Boutros-Ghali and his dangerous plans for empowering the world body had to go (Albright obliged him by denying Boutros-Ghali a second term as secretary-general). Helms also decided that the United States would cut its burden, then about 30.5 percent of the overall peacekeeping budget and 25 percent of the general operating budget, to 25 percent and 20 percent, respectively. Largely as a result of Helms's efforts—and ancillary attacks by Capitol Hill antiabortionists on UN family planning programs—the Republican-dominated Congress held U.S. dues hostage to its whims; indeed, by the late '90s, the United States was responsible for more than half of the world body's $3.24 billion in arrears, including both the general operations budget and the separate peacekeeping account, says Joseph Connor, the UN undersecretary for finance.

Holbrooke's boss, Bill Clinton, faced with an unremittingly hostile GOP opposition, barely fought the slashing of his peacekeeping and foreign-aid budget. One reason was that for Clinton, the disaster in Somalia, coming less than a year into his presidency, left him with a bitter taste for UN peacekeeping that he never got over. What began as an innocent humanitarian relief operation—U.S. forces hitting the beach as TV cameras awaited them—turned into a dangerous manhunt after a Somali warlord, Mohammed Farah Aidid, ambushed UN peacekeepers and Boutros-Ghali prodded the Security Council to authorize "all necessary measures" against Aidid. It was an unusual case of aggressiveness for a UN secretary-general, but Boutros-Ghali, after all, was eager to carve out a new UN role. The problem was that the Clinton administration signed on to the idea of sending in Special Forces to do the job without adequate backup, especially AC-130 gunships (which were later so effective in Afghanistan). The TV images of the lone dead U.S. soldier getting dragged through the dust of Mogadishu by cheering Aidid supporters haunted Clinton for the rest of the decade. This was largely the fault of U.S., not UN, command and control. But the experience so traumatized Clinton—and he was so leery of spending his dwindling political capital on humanitarian issues—that it set in motion a wholesale retreat from UN-sponsored commitments. This included a Clinton/NATO decision not to vigorously pursue Bosnian Serb war criminals after the 1995 Dayton peace accord for fear of a Somalia-like result. (That, in turn, later emboldened Milosevic in Kosovo.) In May 1994 Clinton signed Presidential Decision Directive 25 as a way of blunting Republican opposition to U.S. involvement in UN interventions; by setting a high threshold for action (it required, for example, not just a local atrocity but a "threat to or breach of international peace and security"), PDD 25 made it very difficult for the United States to take part in UN peacekeeping.

And as the 1990s rolled on, the leader of the free world willingly sacrificed the United Nations' reputation to domestic politics. Clinton made the UN yet another victim of the "triangulation" strategy whereby he co-opted key Republican ideas. Silly right-wing demagoguery about the threat to U.S. sovereignty of UN "black helicopters" went unanswered by the administration. While Clinton often voiced support for the UN in principle, he never championed it in actual fact.

By 1999 U.S.–UN relations had sunk to a new low. Both Congress and the Clinton administration treated the world body with a deepening contempt. Recounting tales of UN incompetence became water-cooler sport on Capitol Hill and at the Pentagon. As Stanley Hoffman wrote, there was "a kind of obscene convergence between an administration whose retreat from multilateralism in peace and security matters was signaled by its directive on peacekeeping . . . and a Republican majority in Congress whose foreign policy consists largely of denouncing, hampering and financially starving the UN."[11] The organization that Wilson, FDR, and Truman once dreamed would bind the world into a new structure of international relations had become an orphaned agency, a forlorn Dickensian urchin begging among the political elite.

"No one in Washington seemed to care about it enough," Holbrooke said. "As a result, the initiative passed to the Republicans in Congress." Helms was only too happy to grab hold. As one of his aides describes it, after provoking the ouster of Boutros-Ghali, who had aroused Helms's ire by trying to grant the UN new taxes, the senator decided to box the UN in. At a meeting with the new secretary-general, Kofi Annan, he abruptly proposed a deal: He would sponsor the payback of some arrears (albeit at a reduced dues assessment for the U.S.) in return for drastic reform. "The UN's organizational chart was so big you couldn't fit it onto a poster board," the Helms aide recalls.[12] The result was a compromise forged in 1997-98 with Biden, then the ranking Democrat on the Foreign Relations Committee and one of the few vociferous UN supporters in Washington: the Helms-Biden reform package. "It proceeded from one correct assumption: the UN was a mess," recalls Holbrooke, "but instead of being a carrot and stick, what Helms-Biden said was, 'If you reform we'll give you less money, and if you don't reform we'll give you even *less* money.' It was a stick and a stick, rather than a carrot and a stick."[13] Biden joked that "it was one of the few times that a member of Congress didn't want to see his name on a bill." Other members were in an uproar; even the Canadians—among the firmest of U.S. allies—described Helms-Biden, which was passed that December, as "a lump of coal in the Christmas stocking."[14]

By the time Holbrooke came into office, in August 1999, I wrote in an article that his task was akin to taking over the *Titanic* after it had struck the iceberg. Resurrecting some degree of mutual respect, said one UN official at the time, would require "a piece of almost Dayton-like shuttle diplomacy." "The men and women involved in this in New York and Washington are not evil people," Holbrooke later said, but "at opposite ends of the shuttle, people viewed each other as malignant."[15]

Once again, Holbrooke used his talent for hardball negotiations—and diplomatic stagecraft. The UN ambassador orchestrated a visit by Helms to New York and, in an old negotiating tactic, simply let him vent his views until he had nothing left to say. Helms spoke before the Security Council, which accorded him (at Holbrooke's direction) all the pomp and circumstance of a visiting head of state. The aging senator did not disappoint. "A United Nations that seeks to impose its presumed authority on the American people, without their consent, begs for confrontation and— I want to be candid with you—eventual withdrawal," he lectured the Security Council.[16] The appearance was widely reported at the time as another bashing by Helms, but the press accounts missed a key point: By going to New York, Helms was showing that it was safe for conservatives to work with the UN. With critical help from Biden down in Washington and veteran diplomat Tom Pickering up in New York, Holbrooke met with more than a hundred members of Congress and brought a score of them to New York. He also sent the Security Council down to meet with key congressional leaders in Washington. "Personal connections matter on the Hill. It helped to show they were real human beings," says

Holbrooke. At the same time he bent over backward to reassure the right wing in Congress that he agreed the UN needed a major overhaul. "The only way to buy any running room with the Congress was to show that we were sympathetic to their position," he said. "There were plenty of kill-the-UN people in the Congress. The only way to move them was to say it's in the national security interests of the U.S. to have the U.N, but the UN wasn't at the center of our foreign policy. I had a three-word mantra: 'flawed but indispensable.'" One somewhat comical encounter between Helms and the UN delegate from Namibia helped to break the ice. "The Namibian declared to Helms that he had been a SWAPO guerrilla, and that he was also one of Helms's constituents. So Senator Helms is confronted with this enormous, imposing Namibian," Holbrooke recalls. "Remember, SWAPO [the South West Africa People's Organization, a former communist-affiliated group] were the bad guys. And then the Namibian says, 'My wife is from Greensboro [North Carolina].' I'm watching Senator Helms trying to embrace the fact that a SWAPO guerrilla has in-laws in Greensboro." Helms rolled with the punch, smiled, and turned to Holbrooke, saying, "You know, I have constituents."[17]

While Biden worked the cloakrooms and pressured the Clinton administration for help, Holbrooke and his team spent long days badgering other key UN members to adjust their dues higher to make up for the U.S. reduction he had pledged to Helms, from 25 percent of the total UN budget to 22 percent (a key victory for Pickering, who persuaded Helms to drop his original demand for 20 percent). This was made more difficult by the highly complicated ratings system by which dues are determined based on per capita income. "Each country had its own special problems. Singapore was particularly difficult. They had a per capita income of $29,000 a year, but they refused to give up the deep discount they had on peacekeeping because they said they were still a developing country," said Holbrooke. He remembered a book on his shelf and brandished it in the Singaporeans' faces: *From Third World to First World,* by Lee Kuan Yew, the island-state's legendary senior minister. Holbrooke also dragooned treasury secretary Larry Summers, defense secretary William Cohen, and U.S. trade representative Charlene Barshefsky into a telemarketing campaign. Each phoned counterparts in countries such as Brazil and Singapore to tell them the dues issue was important to the administration. The subtle effect was to make these countries wonder whether their trade or military-to-military relationships might suffer if they didn't fall into line. Holbrooke also presented foreign ministers with a laminated card listing every country's payment in order to remind them that the nearly thirty-year-old system gave steep discounts to some of the richest countries in the world, among them Brunei and the United Arab Emirates.[18]

In the end, a shift into multilateral diplomacy put Holbrooke over the top. He decided to recast the goal of the lobbying campaign: Rather than a unilateralist pay-up-or-else approach, he gave the UN delegates cover by issuing a broad call for reform of the UN dues system. (Meanwhile, to persuade Helms of his sincerity, he set up an operation to tackle the more legitimate aspects of Helms's objections: an overgrown bureaucracy.) He obtained a pledge from the UN Secretariat for reform and zero-budget growth, and other nations' delegates agreed to reduce the U.S. share of the overall operating budget to 22 percent. Holbrooke also gained an agreement to reduce the U.S. share of peacekeeping to 27 percent from 30 percent. But Helms was placated, and U.S. money began flowing in. (It still required a last-minute chip-in of about $34 million by media mogul Ted Turner—a passionate UN advocate—to tide over the UN for that year, 2000.) Together, the amounts saved were just under $75 million the first year, a pittance. "The amount of time and energy spent was disproportionate to the ultimate savings," laments Robert Orr, Holbrooke's deputy, who suggests that time could have been better spent negotiating peace deals abroad.[19]

With the fight over, even Helms seemed to undergo something of a battlefield conversion, won over by the Holbrooke bulldozer and, perhaps, a sense that he had gone too far in his antiglobalism campaign. Late in the game he called Holbrooke and asked if UN secretary-general Kofi Annan, a charming Ghanaian whose soft-spoken but firm manner had done wonders to improve the UN's image, might be prevailed upon to give the commencement address at Helms's alma mater. As Holbrooke recounts it, "I said, 'Mr. Chairman, he might just do that. Give me an hour.' I called Kofi and said, 'On May 13, in the year 2002, you're going to be in North Carolina. I don't care what else you're doing." Helms softened too on foreign aid. In mid-2002, not long before he left office, he came out for more public funding of AIDS prevention programs overseas, which happened to be another pet Holbrooke project. Helms, who a year earlier had led a failed fight to abolish the U.S. Agency for International Development, called for giving $500 million more to USAID to make HIV treatment available to pregnant women, especially in Africa. "Perhaps, in my 81st year, I am too mindful of soon meeting Him," Helms said, "but I know that, like the Samaritan traveling from Jerusalem to Jericho, we cannot turn away when we see our fellow man in need."[20]

### What the UN Is Good For

Before Holbrooke left office, he gave testimony one last time to the Senate Foreign Relations Committee, and Helms led the senators in a standing ovation for the indefatigable negotiator. It may have been the crowning moment of Holbrooke's career. Yet Helms, however tenderized he was by the force of Holbrooke's diplomacy, did not go into retirement a liberal internationalist. And the bitterness of the UN dues fight, along with the failures of UN peacekeeping in the '90s, should teach us some stark lessons about our relationship as a nation to the world body and its future role. Holbrooke had done just about all that could be done. But Holbrooke's solution was, in the end, a patchwork solution not unlike Dayton: It instituted a shaky peace, barely touching the underlying tensions.

Let's examine those tensions a bit further. The central complaint of the Helms-led right wing—that the UN can somehow eclipse American sovereignty if we are not careful—has, in truth, always been a canard. FDR and Truman built the UN around a great-power council, with each of its five permanent members getting sacrosanct vetoes. In practice, except for the obstreperous talking shop of the General Assembly—to which hardly anyone pays attention—the UN has rarely been more than an adjunct to U.S. power. Far from threatening world government, the United Nations has never gone to war in the name of collective security unless the United States has orchestrated such action. And this has happened just twice in a half century—Korea in the early '50s, and the Gulf War in 1990–91. In 2002–3, even the UN-averse Bush administration realized that it needed allies to supply bases, overflight rights, and, above all, help in rebuilding post-Saddam Iraq, and that those allies in turn needed UN cover if they were to accept Bush's aggressive move to confront Saddam.

Even today, the UN is largely what America decides to make it. Again, it's simply not true that the nation-state is giving way to transnational forces, like nongovernmental organizations. Especially after al-Qaeda turned out to be "the ultimate NGO," in Strobe Talbott's words, and it became clear that bin Laden had hijacked a failed state to work from, traditional state security and government hierarchies were seen in a new light. The bulwarks of a state—guarded borders, a strong military, intelligence, and police oversight—were as necessary as they had ever been.

That is good for the UN, because it justifies its basic structure—that of united *nations*—but troubling for its future significance in a one-über-power world. Indeed, during the post–Cold War period there was a deeper structural problem that underlay anti-UN attitudes, one that characterizes the kind of überpower tensions we are examining in this book. As I've said, the Security Council was devised as a Big Four solution of more-or less equals (except for Chiang Kai-shek's China, which both Britain and Russia wanted to exclude as a minor power but which FDR, thinking he might build it into a counterbalance against Japan in the Pacific, wanted to prop up). Later, during the Cold War, even if the Security Council was often paralyzed by the Soviet veto, it was at least a forum for more or less civil discussion across the nuclear divide. But during the '90s, as U.S. power relative to the rest of the world grew and Americans faced no existential threat, the equalizing mythology of the Security Council became harder and harder for U.S. presidents to accept, just as the one-vote-per-nation principle of the General Assembly had earlier turned that forum into a joke. Both Clinton and George W. Bush resented having to defer to now-second-rate powers such as Russia and France in the Security Council. Washington has tended to see the council as a stagnant pool of lost great-power ambitions, a place where a country such as Russia could puff itself up into an image of its former self. Those powers, in turn, resent Washington's high-handedness. In 2002–3 all these tensions came home to roost once again in the debate over Iraq.

The tensions will inevitably continue. But they can be eased. One reason for all this mutual acrimony is that none of the major powers has honestly confronted the changed international environment and the failures of the '90s. The solution, in my view, lies in doing so—in deflating the mythology of the United Nations and facing some very harsh facts about U.S.–UN relations. First, we must accept that the UN has utterly failed in the role some internationalists still believe it was designed to fulfill. Global collective security under UN auspices, involving the creation of a supranational combat force, is unlikely in the extreme to happen. That central element of both Wilson's and FDR's vision is gone forever, especially in a one-überpower world.

Even the UN's more humble post–Cold War hopes for peacekeeping have been dashed. Blue helmets, those polyglot troops whose brief used to be to stay out of fights and act as treaty "buffers," are not going to be terribly effective in most cases in the looser era of non-state conflict, as demonstrated by every major ethnic and tribal war from Bosnia to Sierra Leone (they worked in the latter case only when British troops were present as well).[21] This too is a fundamental structural problem. John Gerard Ruggie notes that there is no constitutional basis for robust peacekeeping in the UN charter: The gap that continues to persist between robust enforcement and peacekeeping is a "doctrinal void."[22] And as Hoffman says, the UN suffers from "a grave discrepancy between its own structure, defined in a fifty year old charter, and the structure of the international system. . . . The UN is simply not equipped to deal with collapsing states or with rulers who systematically violate human rights."[23]

This, in fact, was what Holbrooke himself recognized when he pushed Clinton into Bosnia. "To a certain extent the UN has become a way for governments to pretend they're solving a problem when in fact they're just putting a Band-Aid on it. That is the most dangerous part of the UN system," he says. The pretense of action occurred most dramatically in the Balkans where, as Boutros-Ghali later wrote, for more than two years "the United Nations had been used to 'internationalize' the United States' and NATO's desire to avoid the war."[24] The policy ended only when Clinton finally authorized air strikes in 1995 and sent Holbrooke to Dayton. "Bosnia was a scandal which on the heels of Somalia and Rwanda almost took the UN down," says Holbrooke. "The UN was used to dump the problem and pretend it was being dealt with until it reached such a level that the very people who dumped it in the UN then blamed the U.N. . . . And if you add to this Rwanda, when the United States actively insisted on the removal of the peacekeepers—I think it's one of the most shameful episodes in modern American history."[25]

But for all that, Holbrooke and others argue—and I agree—that the hopes of an international system still depend on the UN, and especially the Security Council, which is the chief source of multilateral "cover" for American hegemony. The growing body of UN Security Council resolutions is what gives American values the heft of international law, rather than the stigma of a diktat from Washington. This will never be a smooth system. Another example of ideological blowback is that America must veto or ignore some Security Council resolutions (like those that bitterly condemn Israel) while invoking others (like the ones condemning Iraq). The Security Council's image might benefit if other major powers, such as India and Japan, were made permanent members, thus ridding it of its World War II–era mustiness. But flawed or not, the Security Council remains the sole repository and source for international legitimacy. One of the ironies of George W. Bush's standoffish attitude toward the UN in 2002–3 was that, in the end, it was defiance of UN Security Council resolutions that gave him his best case against Saddam Hussein. By 2003 Bush was no longer asserting, as he once had, that he had to take on Saddam because the "smoking gun" might be a "mushroom cloud." Bush did not have the evidence that Saddam was building nuclear weapons. What he *did* have was a UN imprimatur declaring that Saddam could not build them. And he had evidence that Iraqi officials were defying that imprimatur. In an era of vast and growing resentment of the only superpower, and at the same time democratic leadership in most major nations, working to get UN legitimation also gives foreign leaders the face they need to sign on to U.S. initiatives. The role of the UN Security Council "is huge," says Wesley Clark. "Because it enables your friends to do what you want them to do in their own domestic politics."

But getting from theory to practice isn't easy. The UN dues fight was also instructive in how to mix unilateralism and multilateralism in a one-überpower world. So resented is U.S. power that America "rarely wins arguments inside a multilateral meeting room," says Suzanne Nossel, a top Holbrooke lieutenant during the dues fight. "No country wants to be publicly seen to buckle under U.S. pressure. During the dues battle, formal meetings at the UN were bruising for the United States, with country after country taking the floor to demand that America pay its back dues 'in full, on time, and without conditions.'" The key to Holbrooke's success, she says, was that his team took on the countries individually—"for every one diplomat in the UN seat, ten others should be working the corridors"—while it dressed up Helms's harsh unilateralism as a more universal push for reform. "Although the U.S. government did not care at first about true 'reform' of the UN's dues structure, U.S. diplomats made this goal their rallying cry, recognizing that—unlike a stand-alone U.S. dues reduction—it was an agenda to which other governments could subscribe" and save face, Nossel says.[26] The end result was that the structure *was* made more fair.

But to make this the model of the future and leverage America's power in multilateral negotiations on a consistent basis, Washington needs to reorganize how it conducts business. Today, when it comes to U.S. diplomacy, one hand rarely knows what the other is doing. "The U.S. government maintains no central ledger in which bilateral relationships are tracked. There is no place to turn to find out what the United States has done for a particular country lately, or what a country may want or fear," says Nossel. During the UN dues fight, "at the end of a long and contentious meeting with the Singaporean delegation, one of their diplomats pulled from his briefcase a press report announcing a U.S.–Singapore free trade agreement. '*This* is what matters,' he said, dismissing the importance of the dues issue while steadfastly maintaining his country's refusal to pay more," says Nossel.[27] Holbrooke's team didn't even know about the trade pact, and it was only as talks grew intense that he began bringing in other Cabinet members to exert pressure. But there is no reason why Holbrooke's impromptu game of hardball can't become standard policy. In a one-überpower world, America's unique dominance of both the security and economic agendas often makes it necessary that we "tie" such issues together, especially during multilateral negotiations.

## Bringing in the Regional Cops

If America needs to practice multilateralism itself more skillfully, it also needs to persuade the international community to embrace a new kind of multilateralism, especially when it comes to hard-power issues such as peacekeeping. Let's quickly clear away the underbrush of the old debates: The fact is, the UN will never by itself have sufficient muscle for aggressive peacekeeping. Washington does not have the will for it, and the UN does not have the way, largely thanks to the stinginess of the United States and other nations. Plans like Boutros-Ghali's for a more robust UN force, including combat-ready "standby" units, have been bruited about for decades, and there is little reason to think they will succeed now where they have failed in the past.[28] American exceptionalism may need to be revised, as I argued in Chapter 2, but it still retains certain unshakable beliefs, and Americans will always refuse to relinquish even a smidgeon of U.S. hard power to international organizations. Other major powers have followed Washington's lead. But this means that Washington "must erect a system of systems by which other actors—states and international institutions—deal with [crises] instead," as the commentator Adam Garfinkle argues. "The United States does not have to lead every posse, but it does have to build the decision-making system whereby posses are formed."[29]

In fact, there is already emerging, crisis by crisis, such a system of systems, imperfect though it may be. Call it the rule of the regional cops. It is a hybrid system, often dependent on both UN legitimation and local or regional muscle. To work, the new system needs regional powers and organizations to do the dirty work of peacekeeping and peacemaking that the UN has largely failed at. But such regional forces need to be trained and pressured to act in accordance with UN norms, and they will usually be far more effective if they go in under the auspices of Security Council resolutions. Without the imprimatur of a UN resolution, most interventions by regional powers would be seen as mere invasions and carry with them the threat of regional hegemony.

In addition to authorizing war, as in Iraq or Afghanistan, this is the most important role the Security Council can play in the future—along with authorizing aid and engaging in "nation-building," to be examined in the next chapter. The peacekeeping model for the future, in other words, will often not be collective security using UN forces but *collective approval* from New York—with American power overseeing things from the shadows —and with regional powers, often U.S.-trained, -advised, and -supplied, doing the dirty work. Or, in cases where regional powers are not available or trustworthy, with U.S. civilian/military peacekeepers in the mix. In some limited cases such as Afghanistan, UN peacekeepers should also be used. But on the whole, the UN needs to become a more flattened and out-sourced organization, much like the modern corporation.

## A Case Study: East Timor

Holbrooke himself came to see this during the 1999 crisis in East Timor, which I regard as a model for how, in the future, American leaders will be drawn into what we once considered "other people's problems" but can often negotiate their way out of them by using the institutions we built, including the UN. In September of that year on the faraway island of East Timor, which lay at the furthest reaches of the faraway nation of Indone-sia—in other words, about as distant as you can get from what was once considered America's national interest—Indonesian-backed militias who didn't want the East Timorese people to declare independence were hack-ing separatists to death with machetes. People were dying by the thou-sands, in the full glare of the international media.

The last thing that Bill Clinton, then president, wanted was for East Timor to become another imbroglio on his to-do list. By then his admin-istration was long in the tooth, seven years old, and tired of its crisis-a-minute pace. If the Balkans were pushing the outside of the envelope of America's "national interest," few people in his administration thought East Timor had much to do with the U.S. national interest at all. And of course the Clintonites were not eager to be sponsoring new independence movements (though East Timor had a more legitimate claim than most: It had been occupied only in 1975, and the UN had never recognized Indonesia's sovereignty). So while Holbrooke and others in the adminis-tration sought to resolve the crisis behind the scenes, mainly by pressur-

ing the Indonesian military, the White House affected a public indifference. Asked about the crisis that week, the president's national security
advisor, Samuel R. Berger, flippantly told reporters that he didn't "intervene" every time his daughter messed up her room at college. Berger, an
avuncular, good-natured man, apologized the next day, calling his remark
"an awkward way of saying we can't obviously go everywhere, do everything." But he didn't take back the point. Clinton and Berger were avow-
ing the kind of hard-fibered realism that would have done George W.
Bush, Donald Rumsfeld, and their ilk proud.

Then a strange thing happened. Clinton found that, no matter how
hard he tried, he could not get away from the East Timor crisis. By coincidence, just as East Timor was exploding in controversy, the president was
heading to nearby Auckland, New Zealand, where he would be the leading presence at the Asia-Pacific Economic Cooperation summit. APEC
was a relatively new forum begun by George H. W. Bush in order to assert
America's role in Asia, both as the region's leading power and to forestall
an East Asian trade bloc that might exclude Washington, and which Clinton himself had endorsed. Meanwhile, on the ground in East Timor, the
UN was in jeopardy of losing its credibility altogether after its previous
peacekeeping debacles in the '90s. The UN compound in East Timor,
established to monitor a referendum on independence, was under siege
by the same Indonesian-backed militias. Annan ordered an evacuation.

Indonesia, where it was all happening, was also one of those places
that, like Afghanistan, had fallen willy-nilly into Washington's care, without us really noticing. This exotic archipelago nation, which straddled
many important shipping lanes in Asia, was near collapse economically
thanks to the East Asian financial crisis. (This was precipitated, at least in
part, by ideological blowback: a rapid market-opening promulgated by the
"Washington consensus.") The Americans were still sending large-scale
financial aid to Jakarta as a result. Perhaps worst of all for Clinton, the horrors in East Timor were getting blared all over cable and satellite worldwide, twenty-four hours a day, and eventually dominated the discussions
at APEC (where Indonesia, of course, was present). This twenty-four-hour
TV culture—the "CNN effect," as it came to be called—was also an essential
element of the international community, molding it, shaping consensus

and common opinions among very different countries. Jose Ramos Horta, an East Timorese underground activist, recalled for me how different this was from his early years. During the Cold War Ramos Horta, who still sports what looks like a permanent three-day stubble, was an obscure, ragged presence who used such comical tactics as pasting bumper stickers on bathroom stalls at conferences to call attention to his people's plight. But suddenly, he recalls, it all came together for him under the glare of international media, and "the Indonesians were caught off guard."[30] By 1999 Ramos Horta had won a Nobel Peace Prize and world recognition, and Clinton was on the spot. As Berger himself noted glumly to our traveling correspondent corps in Auckland—a week after his clumsy remark about intervention—East Timor had "riveted the region's and the world's attention." Ultimately, Clinton realized, he no longer had full control over the decision to intervene. Returning to the themes of Chapter 3, the international community was making the decision for him. Clinton was caught in a "web of mutuality"—to quote a favorite phrase of his—of America's own making. He had a stark choice: He would have to take the lead in stopping the killing, or he would have to jeopardize the credibility of the UN, APEC, and the global leadership role that American presidents, whether Democrat or Republican, love to evoke.

And so the president, at long last, acted. During a refueling stop in Hawaii en route to Auckland, Clinton announced a suspension of military assistance and sales to Indonesia. Quietly he also pressured the IMF to withhold money. This was given the heft of international law a few days later, on September 14, when he directed Holbrooke to push through UN Security Council Resolution 1264, which authorized a peacekeeping force, at a special late-night session of the Security Council. (Interestingly enough, China, never eager to approve violations of national sovereignty, approved the intervention after getting assurances that it would happen only if the Indonesians themselves wanted it.) The Australians, meanwhile, fearing an onslaught of boat people across the Timor Sea—and perhaps coveting an inside track on the rich oil and gas deposits that East Timor would gain—volunteered a peacekeeping force. In the face of all this opprobrium marshaled by the lone superpower, Jakarta finally yielded to an Australian-led troop landing. U.S. forces were involved only at the margins, in a support role, but the mission was a notable success after years of peacekeeping failures. There were no UN troops.

Humanitarian crises are not as central now as they were during the Clinton era. But the resolution of the East Timor crisis showed that when Washington shows a strong hand, the UN system can be a powerful channel through which the opprobrium of the international community and an array of threatened sanctions can be turned into a single hammer blow of pressure. It also showed that when there is a reliance on regional actors such as Australia—who are often more motivated by "national-interest" considerations than countries elsewhere around the globe—"blue helmets" may not be necessary as long as the peacekeepers have the imprimatur of the UN Security Council. Holbrooke, after the crisis, said in a somewhat self-congratulatory way that "it was almost a textbook example of how the UN Security Council is supposed to work as envisaged by Churchill and Roosevelt."[31]

Regionalizing conflicts is a messy solution (as are almost all solutions in the Permanent Quagmire). Australia was a rare First World country situated next door to a Third World hot spot. Other regional players may not behave as uprightly as Canberra did. And there are plenty of places where UN-approved regional solutions would prove impossible, or problematic at best. The Security Council's permanent five members, with their sacrosanct vetoes, are obviously immune (forget intervening in Russia's Chechnya, or China's Tibet). In some parts of the world, such as East Africa and Central and South Asia, no regional actor is strong or trusted enough to do the task. In other cases, such as the Mideast—where Israel understandably does not trust the UN—ad hoc groups such as the "quartet" formed by the Bush administration, consisting of the United States, the European Union, Russia, and the UN, may work better. This means that in select spots, Washington must fill in the gaps. As we will see in the next chapter, in Afghanistan, the simmering tension between India and Pakistan, and the deep mistrust of neighboring powers such as Iran and Russia, cried out for a U.S.-led or UN-led peacekeeping effort, but none was forthcoming. In central Africa, regional actors are still doing battle in the Democratic Republic of the Congo.

But there are emerging regional paths out of many of these nettles.

Washington must pursue and develop them. Whereas in the past many regional players indulged in a kind of geopolitical *schadenfreude* over their neighbors' misfortunes (and often exploited them), today, with their national economies increasingly regionalized and globalized, few governments want to risk the economic dislocation and refugee flows that result from nearby conflict. Hence the growing strength of regional organizations across the globe, from the new African Union to the once-toothless Organization of American States, which in recent years has helped to preempt a war between Ecuador and Peru, helped to pressure Peruvian President Alberto Fujimori from office after election fraud, and to restore Venezuelan president Hugo Chávez to office after a coup.

Few of these organizations are "security"- or hard-power oriented, but here American power can help in beefing them up under the Pentagon's watchful eye. Interestingly, America does have a military structure in place to bolster regionalization and to ensure that it works for U.S. national interests. U.S. military forces abroad are divided into four major regional commands: East Asia, the Near East (including Central Asia and the Mideast), Europe, and Latin America. The American generals who run these commands already act as virtual proconsuls around the world, as the *Washington Post* noted in 2000. In Asia, Dennis Blair, then commander of America's Pacific forces, was "promoting military alliances or 'security communities,' as he calls them, within his region," the newspaper said. Blair was conducting foreign policy, trying to get countries to "forge disarmament policies and security pacts among themselves."[32] Wesley Clark, the former NATO commander who was himself such a proconsul in Europe, told me that the regional commanders "have the resources. And the defense department has a budget where we can provide training. By contrast, when an assistant secretary of state comes to the region he flies on commercial aircraft, arrives with a couple of staffers. He doesn't have a separate line on resources."[33] In Latin America, for example, the Pentagon could easily insist that its extensive joint military exercises come under regional OAS auspices. It is even conceivable that in Southeast Asia, the ASEAN Regional Forum, known as ARF, could gain more bite with greater Chinese participation and take up the UN mission in still-troubled Cambodia. As retired U.S. Marine Corps general Anthony Zinni, who was once a proconsul, running America's Central Command in the Near East, says, "There is no single model."[34] But in places where regional powers or groups can't handle things, U.S. training and equipment are necessary.

In a world of shrinking UN hopes for collective security, but in which an expanding international community is bringing in more like-minded regional players, the system of the future is likely to be regionalizing conflict under UN auspices and the American hegemon's watchful eye. Yet, again, regionalization remains ad hoc and unformalized, and the U.S. government has done little to change this. The State Department is still built around bilateral rather than regional relations. U.S. ambassadors to nations are far more powerful than their counterparts to regional organizations; within the State Department, weak desk officers run most regional policy. And decision making tends to follow the organizational structure. (By contrast, more personnel—about eleven hundred—work at the smallest regional military headquarters, the U.S. Southern Command, than the total assigned to the Americas at the State, Commerce, Treasury, and Agriculture Departments, the Pentagon's Joint Staff, and the office of the secretary of defense put together.) According to Clark, the civilian U.S. government "is not structured properly to deal with the outside world. The committee structure in Congress doesn't reflect the existing division of responsibilities [in the world]. The executive branch doesn't have in it the kinds of organization required to build American security facing outward. The State Department is not just bilateral. It essentially deals with information collection and purveyance. Only in rare cases does it try to influence and act. And even when it does, it doesn't have any real mechanism to do so other than the personal charm of the ambassador. We don't have any action agency in cases where states are failing."[35]

Regionalizing hot spots, an old U.S. dream going back to the Nixon Doctrine (minus the UN back then), may be the only option in an era when the United States quite reasonably seeks a new "division of labor" in the world and is unwilling to put down peacekeepers itself or beef up the UN to do so. There is already a wrenching record of missed opportunities. Had Bill Clinton recognized the possibilities of regional action earlier, for example, he might have exploited the offers from Nigeria, Tanzania,

Ghana, and others to send peacekeepers to Rwanda in the early stages of the 1994–95 genocide. In the end, those troops stayed home because they lacked U.S. transport and equipment. As Samantha Power notes, even small numbers of peacekeepers might have had a deterrent effect: "The Hutu were generally reluctant to massacre large groups of Tutsi if foreigners (armed or unarmed) were present."[36]

So when it comes to failed states and humanitarian disasters, it's time for the proponents of realpolitik and the Wilsonian idealists to get into bed together. In practice, one mind-set has, in many situations, become impossible without the other. Both UN legitimation and the raw force supplied by larger regional actors are needed. It is noteworthy that one of the few areas where Bush and Clinton were in clear accord was in pushing for more regionalization of conflict resolution. Indeed, George W. Bush found something nice to say about Clinton's foreign policy only once, in the second presidential debate in 2000, when Bush praised the administration's decision to train Nigerian troops for intervention in Sierra Leone. Condoleezza Rice also, in her few words of praise for the Clinton administration, wrote that humanitarian interventions "might be better carried out by regional actors, as modeled by the Australian-led intervention in East Timor. The U.S. might be able to lend financial, logistic, and intelligence support."[37] In June 2001, Secretary of Defense Rumsfeld authorized a study that recommended establishing "regional joint forces" that could undertake a wide variety of small-scale operations in Europe, the Middle East or in Asia, in addition to full-scale combat.[38] And even as Rumsfeld's Defense Department sought to disband its own Peacekeeping Institute—designed to train U.S. troops— it continued to fund Clinton's African Crisis Response Initiative, another attempt to organize regional resources for peacekeeping.

Interestingly, the regional cop approach was used ultimately in Kosovo as well. After the failures of Bosnia, the United States went into the Kosovo crisis with a bone in its teeth, brazenly determined to run the campaign through NATO alone. The UN at first was given almost no role at all (merely a UN Security Council resolution, 1199, that vaguely authorized a humanitarian response). Albright, herself a former ambassador to the UN, decided to bypass the UN Security Council altogether and to use

NATO. All this had changed by the end of the seventy-eight-day NATO bombing campaign, however. Milosevic had stood more firm than anyone had expected, and Clinton faced the politically nightmarish prospect of ordering a ground invasion. Washington needed the help of Moscow, Milosevic's only remaining ally, to persuade him to stand down. To get Moscow on board, it needed the cover of the United Nations. Backed by a Security Council resolution and a UN-sanctioned peacekeeping force, the Russians proved crucial to finally forcing Milosevic to cave in. NATO, the mightiest regional power in history, still had to resort to UN legitimation to get what it wanted.

Regionalization is a rediscovered rather than a new idea. The "regional impulse," as scholars Townsend Hoopes and Douglas Brinkley call it, was there from the UN's founding moments. Deputy Secretary of State Sumner Welles in 1943 proposed to supplement FDR's "four policeman" concept with seven regional organizations.[39] Later Churchill pitched three regional councils for Europe, the Pacific, and the Western Hemisphere to supplement what was then called the Supreme World Council and later in practice became the Security Council.[40] Making use of regional actors is also provided for in the UN Charter (in the long-ignored Chapter 8). But few observers have connected the dots between that section and the more commonly used Chapter 7, which dictates responses to threats to the peace. Churchill was enthusiastic about the regional councils because he said "only the countries whose interests were directly affected by a dispute . . . could be expected to apply themselves with sufficient vigour to secure a settlement."[41] He was right.

As we will see in the next chapter, the United Nations also acts as a clearinghouse for a farrago of aid projects that Washington has no interest in orchestrating. Consider Iraq: The major humanitarian effort under way there consists of the 46,000 local officers of the UN oil-for-food program. "The specialized agencies do indispensable things. The world needs these. Now you could argue that many of these specialized agencies would exist anyway and could function just as well or better divorced from the UN. But that isn't the case," says Holbrooke. Exemplary UN agencies such as UNHCR (the UN High Commissioner for Refugees), UNICEF, and the World Food Program "leverage" the U.S. contribution by bringing other nations' pledged money into the mix. "If they didn't exist, there would be less international coordination and the cost to the U.S. would be greater," says Holbrooke.[42] Indeed, the U.S. government does less direct aid today than it once did—say in Vietnam in the 1960s; the U.S. government doesn't have operating programs for refugees and food distribution anymore. In Afghanistan in the winter of 2001–2, for example, it was the World Food Program that managed to get food—much of it supplied by U.S. aid—to hard-to-reach regions as the war was still going on. The WFP averted, to little notice or acclaim, a famine. Hence, the absurdity of George W. Bush's declaring in the fall of 2002 that the UN was in danger of "becoming the League of Nations" if the Security Council did not back his plans to confront Iraq. Behind his rhetoric seemed to be little comprehension of the deep role the UN habitually played in the infrastructure of nation building and keeping failed states from spiraling into chaos. "The administration is implicitly expecting the UN to just show up," said Victoria Holt, an expert on UN security issues. "To donate people and resources for refugee work, reconstruction, and so on."[43]

By midway through his presidency, as Bush increasingly waxed Wilsonian in the war on terror, his administration began to awaken to some of these issues. For one thing, it began to look at using institutions such as the UN and regional organizations to spread democracy. At the 2002 Community of Democracies meeting in Seoul (see Chapter 3), participants talked about getting the Organization of American States to sit down with the new African Union to discuss democratic "best practices"— the kind of cross-pollination that would be a "prototype" for the future, as Paula Dobriansky, Bush's undersecretary of state for global affairs, called it. And the administration began to hesitantly consider an idea it had once pooh-poohed: forming a new "democracy caucus" to help counter one of the chief power blocs still operating against U.S. interests in the General Assembly, the "non-aligned movement," a Cold War–era caucus of developing countries that today have little in common but their institutional history as a bloc.[44] Yet the administration, for the most part, continued to keep the UN at arm's length.

The larger point here is that Washington must get past its now-settled bias that the UN and its sister agencies are hopeless, effete institutions, recognize where they have value, focus on improving their performance in those areas, and fund them accordingly. Is the UN's bureaucracy still "bloated" (that ever-present word)? Yes, Helms was right about that, and Washington must continue to play the scold. Should the penalty for this failing be death? Hardly. It is no exaggeration to say that during the dues fight of the late '90s the UN's actual existence was threatened by American intransigence. We cannot afford to be so cavalier about the future of the world body—especially when it comes to the UN's role in preventing failing states from becoming terrorist harbors.

# 7

## The Dirty Work

Geography ... tells an unpleasant truth, namely, that nature like
life is unfair, unequal in its favors; further, that nature's unfair-
ness is not easily remedied.

**David Landes, *The Wealth and Poverty of Nations***

THE SHAMALI PLAIN north of Kabul, nestled in the foothills of the
Hindu Kush, was once Afghanistan's breadbasket. A broad expanse of
shimmering green lushness set against white-shrouded towers of rock,
the Plain was famous for its beauty as well. As recently as the 1960s—a relatively rare interval of peace for Afghanistan—it had a sylvan loveliness
reminiscent of Japanese rice fields, says the author Rod MacLeish, who
visited there during the reign of Zahir Shah, the lately returned king.
Babur, a seventeenth-century descendent of Genghis Khan and Tamer-
lane who became the first Moghul emperor and, by the end of his life,
master of south-central Asia, kept a villa in those foothills. A poet and
devoted diarist, Babur once wrote that in all his vast domain it was this
region that he pined for most. "If there is a paradise on earth," he
exclaimed, "this is it! This is it! This is it!" But the Shamali's golden age
was the age of empire, and this is the age of failed states and political disintegration. If you are one of the sour skeptics who still believes that history has no forward progress, don't invoke Europe in 1914; better to
compare the Shamali Plains of Babur's time to what they look like now.

By the early '00s, when I visited, the Elysian fields of Babur's rapture were not only gone but rendered into their opposite. The paradise on earth had become just about the worst place on earth. Mud-walled farm compounds lay blasted, and the road was pitted with holes caused by bombs and Russian tank treads; the fields on each side were mined, yet dotted by refugee tents as in early '02 people sought gingerly to return home, risking life and limb (literally). The road through the Shamali Plain is also the road to the major northern city of Mazar-i-Sharif; it is an eroded ribbon of asphalt littered with old hulks of Soviet tanks and so narrow at points that a single heavy rainstorm could wash away the link between Afghanistan's north and south. The whole nation is like that, a collection of almost medieval city-fiefs run by warlords that barely have anything to do with each other, tenuously linked by a pitted road network ruled by highwaymen and bandits.

At this point, many readers will be fairly familiar with the catalogue of horrors that brought Afghanistan—and the Shamali Plain—to this state: twenty-three years of war played out in stages, first Soviet invasion, then U.S.-backed jihad and civil war between the mujahideen, and finally, when Afghanistan lay at its weakest and most desperate, the bizarre, opportunistic disease of Taliban rule. What is less apparent is why Afghanistan, in particular, was the victim of these successive ills—why it was this country and not some other, why these wars went on so long, and why the fighting remained so unresolved until the deus ex machina of American intervention in the fall of 2001.

Based on my years of reporting around the world, I have long believed, with historian David Landes and others, that geography is often the key to national character and therefore the fate of nations. As we saw in Chapter 2, the American landmass, protected by broad oceans, helped define our devil-may-care attitude toward the world. Similarly, Japan's spare, spidery home islands, packing 140 million people into a small place, have defined the collectivist character of that country, as well as its insular outlook. A nation subject to some one thousand earthquakes a year, its sense of geologic and climatic instability is also, some Japan scholars believe, key to the stoic fatalism of the Japanese and their cardinal virtue of *gaman,* or endurance, as well as their industriousness—an ever-present zeal to tame volatile nature. Numerous scholars have observed that in Europe, the close-quartered competitiveness of a patch-work of kingdoms in a relatively open space drove the continent to constant technological innovation and, ultimately, world dominance.[1] The nations of hot climates to the south, ridden with disease, were fated to poverty largely by geography, as Landes has written.[2]

The unyielding dictates of geography have shaped Afghanistan's fate as well. It is too easy to say Afghanistan was too often in the wrong place at the wrong juncture of history. True, once it was a pawn in the great game between the British and Russian empires for dominance in South Asia; a century later, Afghanistan had the misfortune to adjoin the dying Soviet Union and be made the unlucky instrument of Zbigniew Brzezinski's obsessive anti-Soviet realpolitik as he began the U.S. policy of funding the mujahideen in 1979 in order to bleed Soviet troops. ("What was more important in the world view of history?" Jimmy Carter's Polish-born national security advisor once said when he was challenged about this policy. "The Taliban or the fall of the Soviet Empire? A few stirred-up Muslims or the liberation of Central Europe and the end of the Cold War?"[3] Brzezinski delivered these comments, of course, before a few stirred-up Muslims killed thousands of Americans.)

But the real key to understanding how Afghanistan came to this lies partly in those mountains that shadow the Shamali Plains. Afghanistan's problem is not just that it has been vulnerable to war; it is that war works so well there. It is Afghanistan's soaring mountains and ungodly, arrowlike ridges that explain why war has been so enduring and successful, why Afghanistan could not just lie down to a conquerer as other lands have, and why warlords continue to control separate regions today. For much the same geographic reasons, Afghanistan is also a place defined by ethnic and tribal disunity. The country is the size of Texas; if its deep mountainous folds were somehow ironed flat, it might be as large as Russia, some Afghan experts have suggested. To the east, the way from Kabul to Jalalabad is even worse than the road north. So steep are the rock walls as one heads out of Kabul, switching back and forth amid great leaden sheets of upward-shearing stone, that one feels encased in natural armor, almost like being in a roofless cave. Shredded scrap metal from Taliban trucks that didn't quite make their escape lie alongside the switchbacks, and in the forbidding ravines that line the roadways gunmen can still appear at any time. Long before Thomas Friedman spoke of the superempowered individual, Afghanistan's ridges and mountains created superempowered warriors. As Larry P. Goodson writes, "The Hindu Kush and its various spurs not only limited Afghanistan's enemies in their offensive tactics but also provided almost unassailable bases from which rival guerrillas could operate. . . . Neither the British nor anyone else has been able to penetrate the tribal strongholds of the Afghans."[4]

What is my point? That in Afghanistan, more than in most countries, war and disorder are easy; peace and order are hard. As chaos and disorder are rooted out worldwide and sent packing through the forces of globalization and integration, a place like Afghanistan is their natural hiding place. So we discovered on September 11, and so it will be again if we don't do something about it. And as relatively simple as destroying the Taliban turned out to be, making Afghanistan part of the global system is simply too hard a problem for the United States to take on alone without a full-scale Japan- or Germany-like occupation that Washington is clearly not ready to undertake.

To the same extent as Afghanistan's natural environment bodes well for war and national disunity, it doesn't favor nation building or global integration. We Americans could drive out the unpopular Taliban from the skies, but we can drive out the culture of war only from the ground. Nation building in Afghanistan is a task like creating farmland out of a desert; it means making something from nothing, requiring years of sweat, willpower, and, above all, help from the international community. Recognizing the full dimensions of the task and our responsibility for it epitomizes the challenge facing the United States at the beginning of this already troubled century. At this writing, top Taliban and even some al-Qaeda terrorists were still hiding within the folds of Afghanistan's natural disorder. They, or angry successors bent on revenge against America, could easily reemerge were Afghanistan to be left to what is arguably its natural state: war. All that argues for only one course of action: that in a place as resistant to global integration as Afghanistan—in terms of its geography, its backwardness, its lack of competitiveness, its predilection for war—nothing less than an all-out effort by the United States and the international community will be required to set things right. But as we will see, the Bush administration, despite much glowing rhetoric about doing Afghanistan right this time, was scarcely paying attention. And efforts by the UN and World Bank to make up the difference, valiant as they often were, were not by themselves enough.

In the months after the Taliban fell, no one was more acutely aware than the Afghans themselves that their nation was a poster child for international anomie. When I visited, I was struck by how desperately even this proud people wanted the Americans, and the international community, to intervene, to occupy their country. It was because they knew, better than anyone, how easily Afghanistan could fall back into its long-entrenched habits. As Ismail Qasimyar, an Afghan aristocrat who became head of the *loya jirga* commission designing Afghanistan's future government, told me, his countrymen saw that "a window of opportunity has been opened for them." Afghanistan, said Qasimyar, has become "a baby of the international community."[5]

It is only when you have been among people who most acutely feel the absence of the international community that you appreciate how real a thing it has become. One night in February 2002, in the tiny town of Gardez, Afghanistan, I sat talking with my translator, Faisal, in what passed for a hotel. This hotel had no name, and there was no running water or electricity, save for a balky generator that ran for a few hours each night in the back. Outside our room to the west, patrons relieved themselves on the packed-mud roof, leaving piles of feces scattered in no particular septic pattern, and outside our other window a pack of wild dogs howled and yammered through the night. (Only a week before I had been at the Waldorf-Astoria in New York, complaining to the headwaiter about the lateness of a steak while attending the World Economic Forum.)

Gardez is just three hours away from the capital, Kabul, along a rutted road, but now it was one of the most cut-off places on earth. No foreign aid workers would drive along that road, fearful of a simmering rivalry between warlords, which had erupted in a gun battle a few weeks earlier and which we had come to investigate. The cold, unheated local hospital had few medicines and no anesthesia, and a few days before, a two-year-old boy had died of a chest infection because there was no oxygen. A U.S.

Special Forces helicopter had tried to drop supplies, including oxygen tanks, but one of the chutes had failed to open and the equipment shattered, the doctors told us. This was southern Afghanistan, not far from the Pakistani border, where small bands of al-Qaeda and Taliban still roamed or hid, usually for cash paid to desperate villagers (in fact, two weeks after we left, a large band regrouped near Gardez, triggering a major battle).

As we sat drinking tea and smoking (everyone in Afghanistan smokes), Faisal spoke of the desperation of his fellow Afghans for some sense that the international community—a term he used without irony or cynicism—cared. Raised and educated in India, sophisticated about everything having to do with regional politics, Faisal had a naive, convert's sense that the international community simply and powerfully existed. He said a new bin Laden would surely arise unless his people had some sense of a lifeline to the outside world, of being joined to the international community, where access to good TV and newspapers would teach them "that bin Laden stands for the wrong things."

The conversation brought to mind other experiences I had had over the years in cut-off places of the world. I thought of the government "minder" who accompanied me during my reporting trip to authoritarian Burma in 1992. He brought me home to meet his wife, laughing nervously when I pointed to the banned photo of democracy leader Aung San Suu Kyi on the wall; with considerable fear in his eyes, he then slipped me the address of his family in a cheap lacquered container when we parted, hoping I would be a lifeline. I thought of the startling flight I made with Albright from Pyongyang, North Korea, to Seoul, South Korea, in 2000, when I discovered that, compared to the black hole that was North Korea, the neighboring country I had written peevish economic critiques about for so many years—South Korea hadn't opened up fast enough, its banking system was corrupt, and so on—looked and felt like paradise on earth, with its Hilton Hotel, sumptuous restaurants, and (no small thing) hot showers. (It wasn't paradise, of course: it was just part of the international community.) I thought of the Chinese minder who, like his counterpart in Burma, was supposed to make sure I didn't ask the wrong questions or talk to the wrong people—but who ended up asking me, at the end of our week together in 1993, if I could get him a job with Arthur Andersen (back when that firm still represented the glories of American capitalism and not their failings). This longing, this yearning to be part of something larger than their meager, circumscribed worlds is made so much sharper by the images of the information revolution, which give the have-nots a plangent sense of what they're missing. In all these places, not only is the international community real, it is all they have to rest their hopes on.

### Bush Gets Dragged In

For many months the Afghans anxiously awaited some sense of direction from the international community—and from Washington. "Everybody knows who the real muscle is," said Sayed Hamed Gailani, the son and spokesman for a powerful warlord in the south, Pir Gailani. "The people who contact the B-52s should show their faces. I want the Americans here as much as possible to give me back my country." But watching the Bush administration's learning curve was almost painful. The president knew that in Afghanistan he was confronting the bedrock bias of his election campaign: no nation building. Yet from the start Bush's ideology seemed at war with his instincts. "Can we have the first bombs we drop be food?" he asked his national security team, suggesting that he was very concerned that America be seen as a beneficent liberator, not as a conquerer. He later recounted to Bob Woodward that Rumsfeld, too, grasped that the war had this larger humanitarian dimension. "He's a very softhearted man in many ways. He understood it immediately," Bush said.[6] If so, neither man was paying much attention to Afghanistan's longer-term future. After an initial, largely superficial drop of 37,500 food packages from C-17s in the opening hours of the bombing campaign—each a yellow plastic packet reading, in English, "humanitarian daily rations, food gift from the people of the United States of America"—humanitarianism took a back seat. Rumsfeld quickly disclaimed any concern over postwar Afghanistan, and went ahead with his plans to dismantle the Defense Department's Peacekeeping Institute, the agency used to train U.S. troops abroad for such missions. "I don't think this leaves us with the responsibility to try to figure out what kind of government" Afghanistan has, he told reporters in the fall of 2001. As the weeks passed, the administration did decide to help create a new interim government. Even then, however, the White House and Pentagon shot down a plan to expand peacekeeping beyond Kabul and continued to insist that the new Afghan national army would do the job—though that was at least two years off.

Into that vacuum stepped the warlords. Like all Afghans, they also declared they were tired of war. But in Afghanistan, this was the political equivalent of a Capitol Hill legislator who says he is tired of partisanship— and then quietly signs off on an attack ad. In the eastern city of Jalalabad, warlord Hazrat Ali, who helped the Americans crush al-Qaeda at the nearby Tora Bora cave complex, used his U.S. pull to defy Afghan president Hamid Karzai's appointed governor, Abdul Qadir. In the western city of Herat, Ismail Khan proudly hosted U.S. Special Forces soldiers on his compound and conducted his own foreign policy with neighboring Iran. Another warlord, Padcha Khan Zadran of southern Paktia, was known to stop a meeting, pull out his radio handset, and threaten to call in the Americans if he didn't get his way. For many months Zadran openly defied Karzai, shelling Gardez and killing dozens of people in hopes of installing himself as governor. When I interviewed him, Zadran, a burly man with a jet-black beard who sported a bandolier of bullets, declared that "Karzai is misusing his power" and that he, Zadran, had broad support in his defiance of the central government. Bush had relied on these warlords as his proxies in Afghanistan—and, for a brief period, when the Taliban were being ousted, they were America's principal allies. Zadran later lost power when he overreached, killing innocents in rocket attacks on Gardez. But well after the war ended, the administration continued to undercut the legitimacy of the government it sought to shore up by persisting in its support of other warlords. "The warlords have been in fact doing their business as usual: the persecution of minorities, the usual patterns of looting humanitarian resources," an aid worker told me in mid-2002. In the first year after the Taliban's defeat, the warlords collected about $300 million in taxes and duties that should have gone to Karzai's government; meanwhile many government officials went unpaid for months, and schools were robbed of supplies.[7]As Colonel Wayland Parker, who led the tiny U.S.

observer contingent in Kabul—just thirty-six strong—conceded to me when I visited there, the warlords were really just "thugs." "You fundamentally don't have militias. You have gangs. That's what we're dealing with," said Parker. Without physical security, fear continued to paralyze an economy already ground into the earth. Longtime observers feared a repeat of the country's descent into civil war in the early '90s.

The key was to use America's supreme leverage to take back the country from the warlords as quickly as possible. Nonetheless, for months after the victory over the Taliban, top officials in the Bush administration were still betting that "B-52 peacekeeping" from on high—and a minimal U.S. presence on the ground—would be enough to establish the new government and stamp out remaining Taliban and al-Qaeda in Afghanistan. With the help of a 4,500-strong, European-led international peacekeeping force inside the capital city, Bush apparently hoped to be spared the ignominy of taking back much that he said when running for office: that employing U.S. troops as peacekeepers isn't America's job, that nation building doesn't work, and that the world's only superpower should focus on big strategic tasks, like taking on the "axis of evil," and leave the scut work to smaller nations.

The scant American presence in this bomb-pocked country was only a microcosm, of course, of how the Bush administration saw the U.S. role throughout the world as it came into power. Like an amputee who continues to probe for his missing limb months after it's gone, the Bush team continued to grope after their old stay-out-of-it ideology. Privately, administration officials would confidently declare that if terrorists took root in Afghanistan again, they would simply rout them again. This hubris ignored a few salient points—that it would probably take another terrorist act against Americans to alert us to the terrorists' renewed presence, that Washington's previous efforts had been only half successful, and that al-Qaeda and their sympathizers were now dispersed across Pakistan and the world. Oddly, the logic that the Bush administration used to justify an attack on Saddam Hussein—that he needed to be preempted before some terrible act stemming from his collaboration with terrorists was visited on America—was the same logic that should have been applied to nation building in Afghanistan.

But men and women who spend entire careers embracing one belief system don't easily discard that for another, no matter what the evidence. The United States, Condoleezza Rice had said during the 2000 presidential campaign, "is the only power that can handle a showdown in the gulf, mount the kind of force that is needed to protect Saudi Arabia and deter a crisis in the Taiwan Straits. And extended peacekeeping detracts from our readiness for these kinds of missions." The U.S. military, she said, "is lethal, and it is meant to be. It is not a civilian police force. It is not a political referee. And it is most certainly not designed to build a civilian society."[8] America, Rice said, does not want to "have the 82nd Airborne escorting kids to kindergarten."

Yet not all Americans subscribed to this point of view—beginning with the 82nd Airborne. Visiting division headquarters in Fort Bragg, North Carolina, I found that the 82nd was raring for a mission, even a peacekeeping mission. Asked about peacekeeping, General Dan McNeill, the commanding officer of the 18th Airborne Corps, which includes the 82nd, talked proudly of his division's role in the Balkans. His men would prefer to fight, said McNeill, who later commanded U.S. forces in Afghanistan, but they recognized their responsibilities were broader than that. Special Forces officers also told me they see their global role as one of nation building and peacekeeping, even diplomacy. Retired marine general Anthony Zinni called Rice's comment "an oversimplification. When you look at hard peacekeeping missions, you need the 82nd Airborne. You need well-trained NCOs [noncommissioned officers] at checkpoints and road blocks."[9] Other officers said Rice simply didn't know what she was talking about: The U.S. military already plays a role as referee and society builder around the world, especially in Afghanistan. Said Bruce Yost, a Spanish-speaking Green Beret colonel working to train his counterparts in Peru, "Peacekeeping with us is pretty much standard." Colonel Parker, the U.S. military liaison to the international peacekeepers in Kabul, was even more blunt: The U.S. military must be revamped to do even more broad peacekeeping and civil service missions, he said. "I would argue our role has changed. We're a global leader. We police the globe. It's unfortunate we are in this position. But if we are not here long enough we'll be back here."[10]

Even Andrew Natsios, President Bush's director of the U.S. Agency for International Development—the chief foreign aid agency—suggests the U.S. military must carry much of the burden of nation building and reconstruction. "The only institution in the U.S. government that has done exceptionally well in organizing very large, complex operations in very remote locations under very difficult circumstances is the military," Natsios says. "And it doesn't have to do with weapons. It has to do with companies and battalions and who does transportation. And then how they coordinate with each other."[11]

Back in Washington, the civilian leadership was mostly intent on taking America into another war—in Iraq. And they were missing a historic opportunity. The world was watching how the United States handled postwar Afghanistan, whether traditional American friendliness and aid and support would follow the exercise of America's phenomenal hard power. The world was watching especially closely because the administration was talking so forthrightly about regime change in Baghdad, which everyone knew would be at least as messy as Afghanistan. Winning support for a preemptive attack on Iraq, or anywhere else for that matter, would depend on how well or badly the Americans were handling this first campaign in the war on terror.

And if the Bush administration, and many conservatives in general, believed that nation building was too complicated and messy, many Afghans said that, in truth, the first-stage solution to Afghanistan's problems was surprisingly simple: money, directed to the right people. Corrupted by two decades of lawlessness, Afghans had become notoriously susceptible to the purse. Funds had bought the Taliban their way into power, and funds would buy off the troops still loyal to the warlords. All it required was the will from Washington and an awareness of what was at stake. But in the first months after the war—a critical time for the future direction of Afghanistan—aid only trickled in, with little guidance from Washington. Some $4.5 billion was pledged in aid to Afghanistan at a UN conference in Tokyo, but little of that money made it to the country quickly. Critical programs involving electrical power, the training of police and teachers, and the building of roads—95 percent of which had been destroyed—went unaddressed for months. Midway through 2002, six months after the fall of the Taliban, the only major road rebuilding project was occurring in the western city of Herat—under *Iranian* supervision, says Julia Taft of the UN Development Program.[12] (Washington, embarrassed by this, later funded a major road project from Kabul to Kandahar.) In addition to the security problem, this too left Afghanistan's nonexistent economy on hold—and it was an economy, of course, any kind of economy, that would be the engine pulling Afghanistan together as a nation.

While the Bush administration dithered, Afghanistan's political future was being set in the stony landscape. The *loya jirga* process, involving the selection of nationwide delegates to a traditional tribal council in Kabul, was beset by warlord tampering. In picking the delegates who would decide on the form of Afghanistan's new government, Qasimyar and other members of the *loya jirga* commission tried to exclude warlords and stack the deck with educated Afghan elites. Dr. Mir Mahfouz Nedai, a former minister in the Afghan government and chairman of the *loya jirga* committee on criteria, brandishing a stack of guidelines in his Kabul living room, told me flatly that "people who killed other people, according to our new norms, cannot be part of the *loya jirga*."[13] Later one delegate, Omar Zakhilwal, wrote that "at least 80 percent of delegates favor excluding all warlords from the government."[14] But the UN, despite valiant efforts to implore villagers to select their delegates freely, didn't have the U.S. muscle behind it on the ground to put in election monitors. As a result, many villagers simply ended up voting for the only paymasters they knew, their local warlords.

Participants in the final *loya jirga* conference, held in June 2002, described their gradual disillusionment as it became apparent that this new birth of representative democracy, Afghan-style, was also a U.S. tool for maintaining the status quo—a Pashtun puppet in Kabul, Hamid Karzai. He was surrounded by a Tajik "troika" of former Northern Alliance officials running the Defense, Foreign, and Interior Ministries, and rendered nearly powerless by America's warlord allies in the provinces. "When I complained about [the delegates'] restricted role, a top UN political advisor told me in no uncertain terms that the *loya jirga* was not intended to bring about fundamental political change, such as ridding the government of warlords," wrote Zakhilwal. "On the first day of the *loya jirga*, we were filled with hope and enthusiasm. Most of us stayed up past midnight in spirited debates about the country's future. By the third day, a palpable demoralization had set in. Our time [was] being wasted on trivial procedural matters" as the real decisions were made behind closed doors. The long-term outcome of this is not clear, except that this Afghan government now appears to be as thinly legitimate as previous ones—the same weak governments that paved the way for the Taliban and terror.

Ever so gradually, the Bush administration got pulled into postwar Afghanistan. In April 2002 the president began discarding his doctrinal baggage, at least rhetorically, and talking of a Marshall Plan for Afghanistan. "We know that true peace will only be achieved when we give the Afghan people the means to achieve their own aspirations," he said in a speech to the Virginia Military Institute, the alma mater of George C. Marshall. "Peace will be achieved by helping Afghanistan develop its own stable government. Peace will be achieved by helping Afghanistan train and develop its own national army. And peace will be achieved through an education system for boys and girls which works."

It was only a step from there, of course, to having the 82nd Airborne "escorting kids to kindergarten." Yet even after Bush's speech, his administration continued to flick its attention at Afghanistan in tiny doses and to oppose any expansion of peacekeeping. It was another lesson in how an administration's policies are largely determined by the political appointments a president makes; in this case Bush had shifted his views, but he had already seeded his administration with ideologues whose beliefs *hadn't* changed and who still were making policy beneath the public radar. Mitchell Daniels, the chief of the Office of Management and Budget and a conservative known for his high-handed ways, quietly slashed a congressional request for educational and agricultural assistance to Afghanistan from $150 million to a paltry $40 million, though it caused little controversy in Washington. The administration, in its 2003 budget proposal, included no funds for Afghanistan at all. Rumsfeld, asked at one of his regular news conferences about sending more peacekeepers, argued that the international community had not offered up enough volunteers —without noting, of course, that without American leadership and support no one was likely to. In October 2002, nearly a year after the defeat of the Taliban, Foreign Minister Abdullah Abdullah said, "The real reconstruction efforts in Afghanistan have not started yet."

It wasn't that Rumsfeld was just being mulish. He believed that until the "war" ended, more peacekeepers would just get in the way of U.S. troops. And as a matter of philosophy, he believed that large peacekeeping forces "deform" countries like a broken leg that isn't set right, causing the subsequent growth to depend on such a presence. But a U.S. Army senior officer involved with the U.S. military presence in Afghanistan said the real problem was that Rumsfeld's Defense Department continued to fight the war long after it was over, hunting down al-Qaeda who had already fled (mainly to neighboring Pakistan, which was also getting scant aid). That was costing a lot of money: about $1 billion per month. And the Pentagon's civilian hawks, also beholden to their pre-9/11 ideology, could not bring themselves to embrace the U.S. military's broader role. The issue wasn't so much whether to expand peacekeeping, the army officer said, as it was the necessity of shifting the U.S. military into a civilian nation-building role in coordination with the peacekeepers in Kabul, replacing the warlords with civilian leaders in the provinces, to be overseen by U.S. brigade commanders. "The problem is that guys like Rumsfeld don't have any sense of the moral dimension of the war. They're just not interested," he said. "They're there to fight the war. They see [nation building] as a bridge too far. What they forget is, the thing you really need to do to make Afghanistan inhospitable to terrorists is to dig some wells and provide some school books."[15]

## Bringing International Organizations In

By late 2002, even Rumsfeld had begun to grudgingly concede that his view of the military's role was too pared-down, too spare. Responding to months of pressure, the Pentagon chief finally authorized the dispatch of small military teams to Afghan cities to help in civilian reconstruction, and at the same time ensure stability. But for the most part the nation-building task was left to the United Nations to handle on its own, along with the World Bank, which worked on the country's financial and power infrastructure, rebuilding schoolhouses and hiring teachers (with help from a scattering of institutions such as the Asian Development Bank and the Islamic Development Bank). Asked to describe the UN's role, the UNDP's Taft, a former career State Department official who joined the UN only in November 2001, pounced with glee on the question and laced into her erstwhile U.S. government colleagues—as well as her fellow Republicans. "When I think of growing up in the U.S. with Jesse Helms saying how bad the UN is, they don't realize how hard we all work," she said. "The UN is the premier burden-sharing institution when other countries don't want to own the problem. In Afghanistan, the U.S. doesn't want to own the problem." It was Lakhdar Brahimi, UN secretary-general Kofi Annan's special representative for Afghanistan, who conceived and organized the Bonn conference setting up the interim Afghan government, she says. The UN set up a trust fund, co-managed with the World Bank, that paid eighty-four thousand civil servants after the first month (the United States contributed just $5 million to this in 2002, less than Canada, which gave $6.5 million) to get the economy going. The UN provided the database for the Tokyo conference of donors to Afghanistan, held in late 2001. Malloch Brown's UN Development Program installed computers and other infrastructure in government ministries. The UN's office of refugees coordinated the return of Afghan exiles, many of them educated elites critical to the country's future. "The whole network of humanitarian coordination, of what shipments need to go where, and what people are moving where, was done by the Office of the Coordinator for Humanitarian Affairs," says Taft. The World Food Program "gets more food to more places in a better way and has saved lives all over the world." And UNICEF coordinated a huge project to build a series of health clinics so that, as Natsios described it, "every person in the country will be within a four-hour walk." (UNICEF, Natsios added, "did a very good job.")

The UN was also the shadow power behind the *loya jirga*, which, despite its less-than-perfect outcome, was a historic step forward politically for Afghanistan. Michael Semple, a shaggy-haired Irishman who speaks almost every Afghan language, was one of the unsung heroes of Afghanistan's ambitious bid to match its medieval sensibilities with modern democracy. A UN civil affairs officer and former Oxfam activist who tended to Afghanistan's sick and wounded throughout the '90s, Semple put his deep knowledge of the country to use, piecing together village conferences on delegate selection almost single-handedly—and traveling without security on Afghanistan's bandit-riddled roads. When I tried to track him down during my visit to Afghanistan, he was a phantom presence, darting ahead of my efforts day after day until I finally located him at the UN-administered *loya jirga* commission headquarters, breathlessly in between village meetings. Semple was energized by his frenetic perambulations, but he was not naive about the country's future. "I'm quite stunned by how you can step ten minutes out of Kabul and the international presence is invisible," he told me, seated Afghan-style on the floor in his office. The success of the *loya jirga* "is a fifty-fifty thing for me. The Afghans have gotten the message that this is their last chance. But they also need to see results. They have to be able to eat the peace, to be clothed by the peace, to be given shelter by the peace." The soft-spoken, bearded Semple bravely faced down warlords at town gatherings. In the village of Sayagerd in north-central Afghanistan, he turned to the local warlord, Amir Sattar Khan, and said, "I request you should not interfere. You should let the people choose their own representative to the *loya jirga*."[16] When I asked Semple how the process of keeping the *loya jirga* free of warlordism was going, he gave his fifty-fifty shrug. "The good warlords accept our political actions. The bad warlords are still saying 'me, me, me.'" Without more security throughout the country, and a sense among Afghans that the warlord era was truly behind them, the future could go either way, he said.

The UN was responsible for actually moving more than a thousand delegates to the *loya jirga* to Kabul in June. "What we did on the loya jirga you'll never hear about," said Taft. "We designed all the requirements: getting the tent, getting the food, the food tasters, the security arrangements. How we got people to Kabul is in my mind absolutely miraculous: Fifteen hundred people were moved in two days from all over Afghanistan, by helicopter and fixed-wing planes in our airlift. We got them there all safely and, more importantly, got them home safely. It was the biggest airlift in UN history. And every time we kept saying, this is really great, we really pulled this thing off, we were told, 'Well, give the credit to the *loya jirga* commission, to boost their standing.'" The UN also engaged in a host of "invisible" efforts undergirding Karzai's government—for example, by putting him in touch with donors and installing Internet connections. These under-the-table efforts were directed at the Bush administration's goal of creating the image of self-reliance. "We are trying to make sure that in every opportunity the government itself is setting priorities and is responsible for the implementation," says Taft. Naturally, none of these efforts made headlines for the UN, which might have helped to counter all the anti-UN sniping still going on back in Washington.

## Miserly Wilsonians

The world I have described in this book is a Wilsonian world—a world, in other words, of more or less universal values. But as we can see in Afghanistan and elsewhere, it is also a world of miserly Wilsonianism, one in which America and other rich nation-states still treasure their sovereignty and the corollary illusion that they can still live in a bubble, where no nation wants to commit major resources to peacekeeping or other supranational duties. It is a world where the UN is mainly seen as a large, unwieldy bureaucracy but is filled with committed people who rarely hear more than complaints about their work from the great powers that drop it into their laps. Fleshing out this too-meager internationalism requires, above all, a recognition and commitment by the United States that the global system as a whole is its responsibility. And in an era when the American hegemon seems readier to go to war than it has in a generation, it is more critical than ever for Washington to drive home the point that these wars are for the world's good by setting a good example afterwards—in other words, by cleaning up the mess. No, Washington can't be everywhere at once—hence the need for UN agencies and regional cops—but as long as we accept responsibility for failed states, it is easy to conclude that places such as Afghanistan, which ooze evil for decades, whether as hideouts for al-Qaeda or as narcotics producers, should be priorities. As we have seen, those evils can now stream unnoticed through

mountain passes and travel the open byways of our international system
like a miasma. They must be dealt with at their source.

The tragedy is that America can easily afford these additional tasks. For
the average American, committing more than the paltry amount Washington sent to Afghanistan and other failed states would amount to no more
than a few dollars per year per person. Yes, there needs to be a healthy
rethinking of the uses of foreign aid. A plethora of economic studies in
recent years has concluded that there are scant links between aid and economic growth. But one authoritative study by World Bank economists
David Dollar and Craig Burnside showed that in countries that had successfully controlled inflation and managed their budgets, aid could help enormously.[17] Those criteria were cited by Bush when, in 2002, he announced a
new foreign aid program, his Millennium Challenge Account, through
which "responsible" governments would get to partake of an increase of
about $1.5 billion a year in U.S. aid. But even now the United States is still
spending less than it did in the 1950s, when we were much poorer. In any
case, failed states, the ones that really need our help, are hardly in line to get
gold stars for fiscal discipline. As Gregg Easterbrook argues, "Asking
whether foreign aid has brought growth is the wrong question, since Western governments often do poorly in picking and choosing winners in their
own economies, too. The morally realistic standard is whether foreign aid
brings humanitarian gains. And by that standard, it has been a success."[18]
Among its achievements: small pox eradication, population reduction
through birth-control distribution, and worldwide famine relief.

Andrew Natsios, the USAID administrator, has argued to me that the
world doesn't have the "absorptive capacity" to put to good use much
more than the $10 billion or so in foreign aid that Washington distributes
annually. "It would distort the economies in the Third World to an
extraordinary degree," he says. Natsios adds that many NGOs, especially
in Afghanistan, can't handle the money "responsibly."[19]

Natsios is a tireless, dedicated official who is as passionate about saving Third World children from starvation as any liberal (he's a conservative)—he as much as anyone was responsible for getting enough food to
the Afghans in the first winter of the war. Yet here Natsios misses the
major point. America must do much more to *build up* the absorptive

capacity, to aggressively lead building efforts like Afghanistan. It is true that foreign aid programs usually don't work very well. And loads of money, ill used, often just breeds resentment—recall Russia's cantankerous relationship with the IMF in the 1990s, as discussed in Chapter 5. But that doesn't mean that such programs *can't* work. And governments, Sebastian Mallaby writes, "have to do some things even if they are not particularly good at them. A large part of the defense budget, for example, is wasted on bases and weapons that the Pentagon neither needs nor wants, but that is not a reason for getting out of the defense business."[20]

In any case, the American way of war, and diplomacy, has always been one of excess and extravagance, not efficiency. We fought and won both World War II and the Cold War with many a boondoggle. Historians and economists have debated the true economic efficacy of even that signature foreign aid program, the Marshall Plan. What no one doubts is that its payoff in goodwill was priceless. It created an enduring sense of gratitude and community that, even in these rocky times for the Euro-American relationship, helps to sustain it. And now, as then, this is no time to be dickering over the economic wisdom of overseas development aid. That critique has run amok in Washington for a decade or so, and it has done untold damage. Foreign aid is an insurance program. As Scott Feil, a former army colonel and post-conflict specialist, puts it, "Every day you get in the car and don't die, you've wasted your insurance premium."

The task we face now is much harder than the Marshall Plan. That was a strategy to refuel First World economies that needed only capital to recover. Challenges like Afghanistan mean a fundamental reorienting of impoverished societies toward modernity. Yet the analogy should not be entirely dismissed. Back then we worried about war-torn Europe tipping toward Communism; now we could be at a critical juncture in the struggle between secularism and Islamism.

It's no counterargument to say, as many conservatives do, that Americans buy more Third World goods than anyone else and therefore we are helping through the magic of markets; being the world's buyer of last resort does nothing to generate goodwill. On the contrary, it only deepens America's image as selfish and self-interested. Free markets are not a foreign policy; they are a private practice.

And there are real consequences to simply withholding foreign aid.

What if we withhold it from the wrong place at the wrong time? Bill Clinton, in an enlightening postmortem on his presidency in 2002, made a direct link between the cutoff of foreign aid to Pakistan (which he helped to preside over) and the growth of Islamic fundamentalist schools, or madrasas, which generate pro–bin Laden sentiment and recruits. "We've been treated to a lot of dismal stories about the over thirty thousand madrasas in Pakistan since September the eleventh," Clinton said. "But it's important to note that less than twenty years ago, there were only three thousand of them. They grew because the government of Pakistan became unable to support its public school system. . . . We continued to reward our Cold War ally, Pakistan, with good military equipment, but we never gave them any money to keep their schools open. Had we done so, it might have made a big, big difference."[21]

Again, it is not practical for America to be out there rebuilding every failing state, even with UN help. The key to maintaining the U.S.-shaped international system will mean keeping a low profile even as Washington manipulates the major agenda behind the scenes. Our strategic planners still need to be quietly at work, examining in a cold, realpolitik way which places can hurt us most and focusing our resources there. But now that we know we can be hit "asymmetrically" from a lot more places than we once thought, we need to be paying a lot more attention to humanitarian problems, especially to the fired-up Islamic world. Realpolitik must now include nation building. And yet even as the United States has rethought its "internal" security by creating a Homeland Security Department, it has done nothing to organize a response to failed states in more than the ad hoc, chaotic way seen in Afghanistan. There is no "czar" for failed states as there is for homeland security or the war on drugs. Perhaps there should be.

Somalia was once bin Laden's hideout, and it too is a lawless place of warlords; U.S. Special Forces began operating there early in the war on terror, but, as with Iraq, it remained unclear whether the Bush administration had any further plans to help the country. Indonesia, the sprawling archipelago that is the world's largest Islamic nation, has been in constant danger of disintegration since the Asian financial crisis; if it is not yet a failed state, it has become a permanently "messy state," as one diplomat describes it. Its president, Megawati, a low-energy, politically cautious daughter of the former dictator Sukarno, has been slow to take on Islamic radical pockets in her country. Despite Washington's clear responsibility for at least some of Indonesia's ills—remember the Washington consensus—Secretary of State Powell told Congress just before he took office that Australia should "take the lead" in dealing with Indonesia's problems, adding that Washington doesn't have to jump at "every 911 call that's out there."²² All of which sounded uncomfortably like Sandy Berger's earlier disavowal of responsibility for East Timor under the Clinton administration. Each of these countries could easily harbor another 9/11-like plot, if not targeted at home then on U.S. targets abroad. In October 2002, Indonesia proved that it had indeed become a gathering place for elements of al-Qaeda and its franchises, when a horrific car bomb killed more than two hundred people—most of them Australian—at a night club in Bali.

The bottom line is that, as he faced this new world, George W. Bush needed to drop his old bias against nation building and to make his military more than a mere war-fighting machine. Yet as the Bush team geared up to transform Iraq, it again sought to minimize the role of U.S. troops. Rumsfeld halved the number of troops his military brass had wanted for the invasion—from 400,000 to under 200,000. His obsession with doing a quick in-and-out operation left Iraq's cities and its myriad arms caches open to pillage, and these weapons later armed the insurgency that killed hundreds of U.S. soldiers. Meanwhile the Defense secretary did almost nothing to train his soldiers in peacekeeping, civilian reconstruction, or counterinsurgency. The result was a pattern of arbitrary arrests and killings by U.S. soldiers that hardened the Iraqi population against the U.S. occupation.

Perhaps Afghanistan will, in the end, manage to lift itself up and pry its way into the international community. Even a war-ordained land gets tired of war, and the tragic and splendid Afghan people are desperately tired. But well into the Bush administration America was still casually rolling the dice with the future of this hard-luck land. The United States had missed an enormous opportunity, at a time when the entire globe was watching, to answer the anti-American virulence of 9/11 with a blast of good will. Yet by 2003, as Bush switched his attention to Iraq, no one remembered that he had once wanted the first bombs he dropped in Afghanistan to be food. American policies were not changing fast enough. America was not changing fast enough.

*Conclusion*

# *Toward a New Consensus*

> I dread our *own* power and our *own* ambition; I dread our being
> too much dreaded...We may say that we shall not abuse this
> astonishing and hitherto unheard of power. But every other
> nation will think we shall abuse it. It is impossible but that,
> sooner or later, this state of things must produce a combination
> against us which may end in our ruin.
>
> Edmund Burke, "Remarks on the Policy of the Allies
> with Respect to France," 1793

THE INTERNATIONAL community, with America at its center, is history's unfinished masterpiece. It remains a work in progress, both conceptually and practically. And our vacillation over whether to embrace it comes at a critical moment when the rest of the world is watching how well we, the primary authors of the post–Cold War system, negotiate the same divide between sovereign and global interests that they must.

The challenge of navigating this divide takes different forms for different countries. For Americans, forging past our founding myths and reaching a national consensus that the global system is in our vital national interest—and accepting the vast responsibility this entails—is the main imperative of the twenty-first century. We must get over the idea that our unprecedented power is a panacea. The paradox of being the überpower is that we exist, and always will, on two dimensions, as a nation and as individuals. As a nation, we can oversee global stability from the skies, apart, removed, and nearly omnipotent. But as individuals, we need everyone's help on the ground, where we are as fragile and vulnerable as other people—indeed, more so, since we are Americans, and since the system we want to maintain, one of open borders and trade, makes us prey to those who want to do us harm. "Like in Roman times, they have no diplomacy," a peeved Boutros Boutros-Ghali complained of the Americans after he was summarily ousted as UN secretary general in the mid-'90s, but "you don't need diplomacy if you are so powerful."[1] He was wrong. The victims of terror attacks need diplomacy. Our children need diplomacy. And in any case America is not, nor will ever be, Rome. It is simply not in America's national DNA to impose a pax Romana. We are a nation whose reason for existence is to maximize freedom. We cannot be, in any traditional sense, an empire.

For some countries, such as the states of the European Union, navigating the divide between sovereign and global interests is an easier problem; they have already given up considerable sovereignty. (A senior Bush administration official, with typical self-approbation, described the key difference in sensibility between Europe and America by saying that the nation-state hasn't worked very well for Europe—yielding only war, and necessitating the EU—while for the United States nationhood has worked very well indeed.) For other peoples, such as the Taiwanese and Kosovars, the sovereignty they treasure hasn't even arrived yet, and they still want it. Such struggles mean that history has not ended yet, not by a long shot— there are too many terror groups, too much economic discontent, too many disenfranchised groups, such as the Palestinians and Kurds, who still seek a better deal. But on the positive side history *has* seemed to consolidate its gains, especially when it comes to a consensus of the great powers over the benefits of the international system.

For all the complexities of the Permanent Quagmire, in other words, a new consensus on preserving peace and prosperity may be easier than we think. A consensus both between America and the rest of the world, and between the right and left in America, is possible. Indeed, we Americans have no choice but to create such a consensus if we are not to go the way of previous empires, to hark back to Edmund Burke's words quoted in the epigraph.

For Americans the consensus must run along the following lines: Our military and economic dominance is a decisive factor and must be maintained—as the U.S. right believes—but mainly to be the shadow enforcer of the international system we Americans have done so much to create in the last century, in which the Wilsonian left places its trust. It is this international system and its economic and political norms that, again, must do the on-the-ground scut work of keeping order and peace and the values-driven work of deepening the ties that bind us together, of co-opting failed states such as Afghanistan, potential rogues, and "strategic competitors," and of isolating, if not destroying (that's still mostly up to brute force) the terrorists. As Henry Kissinger has written, echoing Rousseau: "The dominant trend in American foreign-policy thinking must be to transform power into consensus so that the international order is based on agreement rather than reluctant acquiescence."[2]

Given the nature of the open international system we have created, American presidents run, at best, a loose hegemony. The international community cannot have a boss or a Big Brother. We therefore have no choice but to strike a middle course between the soft globalism that the Bush hegemonists despised and the take-it-or-leave-it unilateralism they offered up as an alternative.

As we have seen, Bill Clinton and George W. Bush—two very different men with different outlooks—each initially tried very different and somewhat simplistic approaches to the Permanent Quagmire. Clinton staked his foreign policy largely on negotiation and norms, all in the optimistic hope that other nations would see that their future lies in the munificent rising tide of globalization. Bush, taking a harsher view, sought at first to master what he considered a more hostile foreign-policy landscape with the assertion of hard power and little else. But neither president, especially toward the beginning of his tenure, confronted the full breadth of the international challenge—the Permanent Quagmire—that he was handed as president.

And yet the differences between Clinton and Bush were never as great as they seemed to be, even at the beginning. In truth the Bush hegemonists were as hemmed in as Clinton was, and in some ways just as cautious. Beholden to the Pentagon's aversion to casualties, Rumsfeld failed to put enough troops on the ground to capture hundreds of al-Qaeda fighters who escaped from their stronghold at Tora Bora near the end of the Afghan campaign. "I think we probably screwed that up," says a former Pentagon planner who now serves in a senior command post. "They sought not to have a role for land force. As a result, with a one-time advantage of strategic surprise, when the enemy were consolidated, with all the eggs in one basket, we missed our chance." And Bush in late 2002 took an even more pacifist line toward the threat from North Korea than had Clinton (who threatened to attack in 1994 if Kim Jong Il did not stop breeding plutonium). At the same time the Bush team exaggerated Clinton's interventionist tendencies, which were just as meager as their own—until, like them, he got pulled in. Despite his popular image as a feel-your-pain president, full of empathy for the world's downtrodden, Clinton was as reluctant to intervene as most American presidents. Wary of entanglements, Clinton cravenly ignored the genocide of eight hundred thousand Tutsis in Rwanda in 1994–95—and any reasonable history of his presidency should record that this was a far more shameful moment for him than the Monica Lewinsky scandal. He diplomatically averted his gaze from Chechnya, where the Russians tried to quash an independence movement with every bit as much brutality as Slobodan Milosevic had in Kosovo. Clinton had been dragged only reluctantly into Somalia, Haiti, Bosnia, and Kosovo, where failed states or humanitarian crises also beckoned for Washington's attention. And he grew almost as chary of the UN as Bush. But it is also true that toward the end of his two terms Clinton was beginning to understand the full dimensions of his role as overseer of the international community. From 1999 to 2000, he deftly intervened in East Timor, as discussed in Chapter 6, and put on a display of military ferocity in the Kosovo war.

For a long time the Bush administration's back-and-forth policies continued to be defined by the tension between its powerful hegemonists, including Rumsfeld, Cheney, and Wolfowitz, and its multilateralists, mainly Powell and his small band of loyal deputies. The hegemonists dominated thinking inside the White House—not least because their views continued to earn the president high popularity ratings. Unilateralism, after all, is so much easier to sell and so much conceptually cleaner than multilateralism. The benefits are immediate, including a strong leaderly image for the president, and the costs long-term and diffuse: the distant threat of weapons of mass destruction, the distant notion that Europe or China may tip into opposing U.S. hegemony decades hence, the degree-by-degree warming of the globe, and so on. As for multilateralism, on the other hand, its benefits are long-term and diffuse, and its costs immediate: an image of compromise and indecisiveness.

All that multilateralism has on its side is reality: the reality of sustaining the international system that is today central to securing America's future. And it is only when Americans truly accept that they are part of this system that they will elect a president who recognizes that direct responsibility for this system is written into the job description. That blithe Cold War title "leader of the free world" must be restored and broadened. The "free world" is no longer just the West; today it spans the globe. That doesn't mean the U.S. leader has to become President Pothole, intervening in every civil war or regional dispute. But it does mean that, in practical terms, the president must talk forthrightly about the international system that benefits all; he must systematically support its institutions even if he doesn't always agree with them; and he must dwell somewhat less on what is purely good for "America." The debate we face today is no longer over American engagement versus American withdrawal; isolationism is long dead. The issue is whether what was once heresy will become orthodoxy to Americans in the twenty-first century: the idea that the norms and institutions of this global system are now as critical to securing our freedom as our own domestic laws and institutions. Must the American president always seek a multilateral solution at the WTO, UN, and other forums, and must he bow to their every wish? No, of course not, just as he doesn't bow to every whim of Congress. But he must accept these forums as part of the American system.

Presidents will accept this new orthodoxy only if the American people force them to. And yet—to reiterate a central theme of this book—the American people scarcely seem aware of these issues. Bill Clinton, who had more experience managing the global system than anyone else, was enlightening on this point in the talk he gave in 2002: "If you took a poll among the American people and you asked them what percentage of the budget do we spend on foreign assistance, and what percent should we spend, there's been research on this for ten years, it never changes. The biggest bloc always say we spend between two to fifteen percent of the budget, and that is too much, we should spend between three and five percent. Now, I actually agree with them. Of course we spend less than one percent, and we're dead last among all the advanced economies of the world in what we spend on foreign assistance."[3] In addition, as we have noted, Congress continues to slip free of its responsibility for the UN and other institutions largely because they continue to be "nonvoting" issues. If we are to preserve the global system our children will inherit, these must start to become "voting" issues. We need a national consensus that is at least as solid as the Cold War consensus—one in which "the yahoos of the right and the softies of the left" are once again marginalized. This is not up to our leaders, but to we who elect them.

Some of my views in this book, especially my advocacy of the international community, will no doubt peg me as a liberal in some readers' eyes. I resist political labels—I've spent most of this book trying to shatter them—but so be it. Still, note that I have argued that America's unprecedented hard power must be maintained in order to make this global system work, that collective security administered by UN multinational forces is a wispy dream long gone, and that crusading Wilsonian idealism isn't going to work very well either (largely because of ideological blowback). I also believe that the Clinton administration, while its heart was in the right place on integrating the international system, was hamstrung by its scandal-crippled president's unwillingness to risk American casualties abroad. As I suggested above, even his more bellicose successor, with far less political baggage, was cautious in putting Americans in jeopardy (at least until he invaded Iraq). Yet a volunteer military serving a nation whose national interest is the globe does permit a more aggressive approach, at least when it comes to peacekeeping and military/civilian nation-building corps. As Max Boot has argued, the kind of interventions Clinton attempted were once commonplace in U.S. history, but were often more successful, in places such as the Barbary Coast and the Philippines at the turn of the century, because of U.S. willingness to put "boots on the ground."[4] (Of course, the U.S. troops who brutally put down the Philippines rebellion didn't have to deal with the "CNN effect.") We can argue, as we inevitably will, about where and to what degree this is necessary, as opposed to where we would like others, such regional policemen, to put their own boots on the ground and commit their resources.

Neoconservatives such as William Kristol and Robert Kagan often end up with conclusions similar to mine. "Today's international system is built not around a balance of power but around American hegemony," these two authors write. "The present danger is that the United States, the world's dominant power on whom the maintenance of international peace and the support of liberal democratic principles depends, will shrink from its responsibilities as the world's dominant power and—in a fit of absentmindedness, or parsimony, or indifference—will allow the international order that it sustains to collapse. The present danger is one of declining strength, flagging will, and confusion about our role in the world."[5] I couldn't agree more. Unfortunately Kristol and Kagan's solution is the unilateral assertion of U.S. power and the unilateral promulgation of American values. Much of this book, quite obviously, is an argument that this solution is far too simplistic.

The scholar Walter Russell Mead dissects American foreign policy into four main traditions. To use his terms, we are engaged in a global task that requires Wilsonianism (international-community-building), as well as Hamiltonian (trade-enhancing) and Jacksonian (war-readiness) thinking. But I agree with Mead that as a cure for too much hubris we need a dose of the fourth tradition, the Jeffersonian obsession with fixing our problems at home first. As Mead says, "The Republic needs Jeffersonian caution, Jeffersonian conservation of such precious resources as liberty and lives, and the Jeffersonian passion for limits. . . . Our power can grow so great, and our use of it seem so unpredictable to others, that in self-defense the rest of the world can unite to limit our power and perhaps to undermine our security."[6] In other words, we must measure our commitments, and our rhetoric, in small doses.

But it was Thomas Jefferson, after all, who once called upon America to become an "Empire for Liberty," and who prayed in the last words he ever wrote that America's Revolution would be "to the world, what I believe it will be (to some parts sooner, to others later, but finally to all): the signal arousing men to burst [their] chains."[7]

Jefferson and his latter-day acolytes, like Jesse Helms, will always remain the scolds of our national conscience, warning us against too many overseas entanglements. But we will find that, despite the ever-present fear that we are compromising our sacred American sovereignty—our exceptionalism—using the international system that is so profoundly the creation of this exceptionalism will make things *so* much easier in the end. We live in a world where China, for example, will almost certainly want to throw its weight around in Asia, in accordance with the predictions of realists such as John Mearsheimer. Yet this need not provoke panic and fears of a second Cold War in Washington, as China's belligerence occasionally does. Beijing is unlikely to overdo things as long as the American power is there in the skies above and patrolling the seas, Japan is kept on our side with assiduous diplomacy, and China remains encumbered enough by the thousand pressure points of this global system—WTO rules, UN Security Council norms, international consensus in general. America doesn't want China to become a regional hegemon, but we do want a country that can occasionally supply regional muscle in places such as North Korea. China can help do this as long as it acts within the international system. If China has never in its history been an imperial power, in the world of the twenty-first century, as it seeks to sell its products worldwide, import the best that the international community has to offer, and at the same time retain its status as a major power and permanent Security Council member, there simply will be no reason for it to become one.

Indeed, the evolution of the China problem, from Washington's point of view, illustrates the themes of this book better than any other example. For all its inherent complexities, China was once a relatively simple issue for Washington. First it was an ideological enemy. Then it was a Nixonian strategic chip in the Cold War (Henry Kissinger, who launched the opening in 1972, once admitted that he never actually walked a Chinese street until 1998). Later, in the early '90s, China was a political football in the post-Tiananmen debate between trade and human rights. But today the relationship is a mind-boggling farrago of cooperation and contention on many levels, with no easy agenda. For national security reasons, we are suspicious of China's desire for U.S. technology. Yet we want it to take part in the globalized economy and import more U.S. goods. We face down China over Taiwan in 1996, yet a year later, during the Asian financial crisis, China proves to be the hero by keeping its currency firm, while Japan, our longtime ally, turns out to be the goat by failing to stimulate and open up its economy. We seek to isolate Beijing because of its authoritarian practices, but we watch happily as the Communist Party's mandarins, with less and less success, try to clamp down on the seething openness of their Internet culture, which is being rapidly developed since its accession to the WTO. In such an environment is "constructive engagement" of Beijing appeasement, as many Republicans say, or smart policy? Similarly, it is difficult to imagine China agreeing, as a UN Security Council permanent member, to authorize Australian troops as peacekeepers in East Timor had Beijing not been engaged in the issue along with Clinton at APEC. Participation in that rescue, in turn, made certain that Beijing's "face" was on the line if it disrupted a peaceful settlement.

As long as the many buffers of the international system are in place, we really don't need to fret constantly about which way China will go—ahead toward democracy or stuck back in authoritarianism. Even marginal capitalism and openness integrate and enmesh China into the global system. The goal is not a democratic political system—that may come later rather than sooner, and in a more illiberal way than Westerners would prefer—but to bring China into the Americanized global system, probably beyond a point of no return. We don't need to be there monitoring its progress every step of the way.

The China scholar David Lampton makes the argument that the United States and China have fundamentally different views of the international system: The United States wants it to be unipolar, while China wants it to be multipolar.[8] My point is that there is a meeting in the middle of these two views as long as American unipolarity, the hard backbone of the international system, is well disguised as the multipolarity of the international community. Undoubtedly Jiang Zemin was, while he was in power, a Chinese hegemonist. He and his fellow mandarins wanted to take back Taiwan, and as this book was being written there were new doubts that his putative replacement, Hu Jintao, a technocrat whose main interest is making China more competitive in the global economy, would be given full rein. But the aging Chinese president was not just dishing rhetoric when he summed up the change at a news conference with Bush in 2002. "China and the United States now have more rather than less shared interests."[9]

Will such encumbrances help to avert a U.S.–China clash over Taiwan? Will they prevent China from becoming a twenty-first-century ideological foe, and today's strained engagement from turning into another Cold War? We don't know for sure. What we do know is that the global system and its constraints are probably the only thing standing between some kind of cold war and a safer, if less well defined, relationship.

We live in a world where Russia, too, someday is going to want to resume great power status and throw its weight around Eurasia. Already it is making some trouble in Afghanistan, funneling weapons to the Northern Alliance faction in the new government, playing a latter-day version of the great game. "Their agenda is to ensure that Western powers stay away from central Asia," one Afghan source suggested to me when I was there. Washington will voice its objections to meddling by Moscow, and it should. Russia, like China, will also make trouble for Washington in the UN Security Council, as it did by resisting a U.S. military campaign against Iraq. But these are headaches, not major crises. We must expect them, and we can afford to let them happen as long as Russia remains under the broader tent of globalism. Vladimir Putin knows that there is no alternative to joining the international system; in a speech to the Duma in 2002 he explicitly tied Russia's future to its integration into the global economy.

In other words, while in many areas, such as nation building, we Americans must be far more involved, in a world so dominated by American power and an international system that is for the most part conforming to our interests, we can relax a little about the various actions of different powers within the overall strategic picture. In a world that *is* tending toward democracy and open markets, it is no longer as necessary for the United States to be in the forefront of values promotion. Staying behind the scenes, prodding or remonstrating with countries that resist, will be much more effective in the long run than standing on a soapbox and getting tangled up in our own hypocrisy, as we inevitably will. Regional policing helps that along. So does the Bush administration's idea of building self-reliance—for example, by focusing on the construction of an Afghan national army (as long as it supplies sufficient aid). Economic reform in the Arab world will help as well; it may take many generations, but we need not hurry the process along as long as we can maintain stability and hunt down disaffected groups like al-Qaeda. This can be a virtuous cycle, and it can continue indefinitely—as long as we get the details right.

Simple diplomacy can do wonders to ensure that these countries remain part of the international community. The Bush administration unilateralists could help to make U.S. hegemony much more palatable merely by *talking* more multilaterally, even as they continue to behave unilaterally. Saving face still matters a lot in international relations. Kings, emperors, and autocrats once went to war over snubs by rival monarchs or, in the case of Kaiser Wilhelm, to gratify their egos. Today, in a world largely defined by great-power democracy (with the signal exception of China), that fear of precipitous war has receded. Realist scholars continue to debate a central tenet of the liberal program going back to Kant—that democracies are less likely to wage war—but the global landscape effectively proves the point. "Face" still counts, except now it is popular support, rather than ego, that has become a driving force in how nations behave. And elected leaders in other countries will not want to suffer a loss of face in being forced to bow publicly to the überpower.

Where do we have to work hardest to give other leaders multilateral cover? In addressing the No. 1 threat to Americans for decades to come: stopping the spread of nuclear weapons that might fall into terrorist hands. The Nuclear Non-Proliferation Treaty, one of the few arms controls accords that Bush still had some use for, was built on a bargain that required considerable diplomatic fudging. It still does. In effect since 1970, the NPT permitted the already-declared nuclear states, America, Russia, Britain, France, and China, to keep their nuclear arsenals while forbidding these weapons to everyone else—as long as all parties would strive "in good faith" to achieve nuclear disarmament. That is one reason why a later pact, the Comprehensive Test Ban Treaty, was so important to much of the world: It was seen as a confidence builder that all nations were eventually working toward this goal. The NPT bargain permitted other states to forgo the expense of developing nuclear weapons and gain access to civilian nuclear power. Yet these states would agree to do so only if they felt secure enough in the global system. It was this international consensus that gave the Bush administration the legitimacy to demand that Iraq and North Korea dismantle their programs: Each country was in violation of its pledge to stay nuke-free as an NPT signatory. And it was this international consensus that gave Bush the global support he needed to see the ultimatum through. Here was international law at work.

In truth, none of the "legitimate" nuclear arms states, including the United States, intends to fully dismantle its nuclear arsenal (even under the test-ban treaty, Washington can do "nuclear stockpile maintenance"— upgrade its arsenal—with virtual testing on supercomputers). But the non-nuclear states, to save face, insist that the nuclear states at least continue to *say* they plan to observe the letter of the NPT. This diplomatic solution has worked, for the most part—at least until now. With only three exceptions—Israel, which is in a uniquely hostile situation, surrounded by enemy states, and India and Pakistan, two nations engaged in an unusually tense rivalry—every nation on earth has now signed the NPT, and most continue to show little interest in developing nuclear weapons. (Some NPT signatories, such as Iran, may be trying to flout the treaty secretly, but they are a small minority.) In response to surveillance loopholes, such as those demonstrated by the discovery of Iraq's secret nuclear program after the Gulf War, the UN adopted a new protocol in 1997 that permits more aggressive inspections to assure compliance (though only twenty-eight nations have signed that). The NPT is, for the most part, a wonderful shield for Americans.

Hence, the monumental stupidity of the Bush administration's cavalier approach to arms control, its insistence that it could build and deploy as many nuclear weapons as it pleased, and its many gratuitous floutings of international law. Washington was, in effect, rubbing the world's face in the fact that America had no intention of disarming (though the 2001 Moscow Treaty, in which Bush and Putin agreed to drastically reduce their arsenals, helped somewhat). Bush was busy frittering away a consensus on reducing nuclear weapons that it was clearly in America's interest to maintain.

## A New Global Consensus

By midway in its tenure, ever so slowly, the Bush administration began to move in this direction, toward an acceptance of the international system it once abjured. As we saw in Chapter 1, Powell's State Department began espousing a "doctrine of integration" that sounded very much like the Clinton administration's doctrine of enlargement of democracy. "In the 21st century, the principal aim of American foreign policy is to integrate other countries and organizations into arrangements that will sustain a world consistent with U.S. interests and values, and thereby promote peace, prosperity, and justice as widely as possible," said the author of the new policy, Richard Haass. "We can move from a balance of power to a pooling of power," Haass said, and while this was not quite Strobe Talbott's notion of "pooled sovereignty," it was close. He also said that "a hard-headed multilateralism" with strong U.S. leadership—an idea that sounded suspiciously like Madeleine Albright's "assertive multilateralism" —was necessary to the success of the Bush administration's strategy.[10] And as we have seen, even realists like Haass began to echo the neocons and the Wilsonians in seeing democracy as a long-term solution, especially in the Arab world.

Haass's ideas also fit neatly into the new consensus emerging across the Atlantic, what the British diplomat Robert Cooper, who serves as Prime Minister Tony Blair's personal philosopher, calls the concept of "postmodern imperialism." This idea recognizes that the world consists largely of "postmodern states," like those of Europe, which no longer want to wage war and willingly have given up some of their sovereignty to the international system, and deeply troubled "premodern states," many of which, like Afghanistan, are failed or failing and "provide a base for non-state actors who may represent a danger to the postmodern world." Cooper recommends a form of benign imperialism that relies, in a Wilsonian way, on the constraints of the international system, but which is also realist enough to recognize that, as he says, more robust means are necessary to corral the chaotic tendencies of the substantial part of the world that remains "premodern." And he argues for regional action. Cooper is worth quoting at some length, especially on the European Union's role in this picture:

> The challenge to the postmodern world is to get used to the idea of double standards. Among ourselves, we operate on the basis of laws and open

cooperative security. But when dealing with more old-fashioned kinds of states outside the postmodern continent of Europe, we need to revert to the rougher methods of an earlier era—force, preemptive attack, deception, what is necessary to deal with those who still live in the nineteenth century world of every state for itself. . . .

What form should intervention take? The most logical way to deal with chaos, and the one most employed in the past is colonization. But colonization is unacceptable to postmodern states. . . . It is precisely because of the death of imperialism that we are seeing the emergence of the pre-modern world. Empire and imperialism are words that have become a form of abuse in the postmodern world. Today, there are no colonial powers willing to take on the job, though the opportunities, perhaps even the need for colonization is as great as it ever was in the nineteenth century. . . .

Postmodern imperialism takes two forms. First there is the voluntary imperialism of the global economy. . . . The second form of postmodern imperialism might be called the imperialism of neighbors. Instability in your neighborhood poses threats which no state can ignore. Misgovernment, ethnic violence and crime in the Balkans poses a threat to Europe. The response has been to create something like a voluntary U.N. protectorate in Bosnia and Kosovo. It is no surprise that in both cases the High Representative is European. Europe provides most of the aid that keeps Bosnia and Kosovo running and most of the soldiers (though the U.S. presence is an indispensable stabilizing factor). In a further unprecedented move, the EU has offered unilateral free-market access to all the countries of the former Yugoslavia for all products including most agricultural produce.[11]

The debate in 2003 over Iraq showed how far Europe has to go in embracing "postmodern imperialism." Europeans were sharply divided in supporting the use of force against Saddam, though few questioned the need to confront him. And like most European diplomats, Cooper tends to minimize the U.S. role in these considerations. So intent are the Europeans on becoming postmodern states that they tend to forget it is principally American power that guarantees the freedom enabling them to entertain such a role. But Cooper's overall concept does comport with the "division of labor" that the Bush administration has sought to impose, and with the concept of regionalization under UN and international auspices—all of it overseen by the United States—that I have advanced in this book. It also meshes with Haass's notion that "sovereignty entails obligations." As Haass has said, "One is not to massacre your own people. Another is not to support terrorism in any way. If a government fails to meet these obligations, then it forfeits some of the normal advantages of sovereignty, including the right to be left alone inside your own territory. Other governments, including the U.S., gain the right to intervene. In the case of terrorism this can even lead to a right of preventive, or peremptory, self-defense."[12] We, of course, don't admit to anyone else the right to intervene in America. But if America must adjust its unilateralism, the rest of the world will have to accept some of the oddities of American exceptionalism and cut us some slack. When Cooper says that "the challenge to the postmodern world is to get used to the idea of double standards," he is referring to the difference between postmodern and premodern states. But if America and Europe are to accept the division of labor that already exists—with the United States overseeing world stability and Europe its own backyard—some double standards here are necessary as well. They are achievable as long as they are diplomatically finessed. That means not constantly reminding Europe that it has become a mere regional muscleman, as the Bush team loved to do. Despite the Bush administration's quest for moral clarity, ambiguity—that cardinal virtue of diplomacy—has also never been as necessary as it is today.

So if Washington gets the diplomacy right, there may be a new international consensus emerging after all. As I have suggested, it seems to be a consensus for defining certain obligations entailed by members of the emerging international community, which for the present happens to coincide with the coalition against terror (al-Qaeda, perhaps inadvertently, reinforced this coalition when it began a post-Afghanistan campaign of hitting European targets as well, such as a busload of French technicians in Pakistan and a group of German tourists in Tunisia). As the Yale scholar Charles Hill points out, the long-term campaign against terrorism "provides a natural bonding agent for today's states and the international states system."[13] Postmodern imperialism, the doctrine of integration, the war against terror—the battle lines of these various paradigms are essentially the same. All that is required is enlightened U.S. leadership.

The possibilities for a new international consensus go well beyond the war on terror and other grand strategic considerations among the great powers. There is, indeed, a remarkable consensus of views emerging in the developing world, and in the private sector among multinational corporations and nongovernmental organizations, about what has gone wrong in the engine room of the international community, globalization. Around the world, there is a new sobriety about what works and what doesn't economically.

True, at the IMF, World Bank, and WTO, alternative approaches to globalization remain largely forbidden. The earlier Washington consensus approach to trade, for instance, is now baked into WTO rules, forbidding countries from legislating East Asian–like subsidies to support critical industries even though economic wisdom has moved in that direction. But on the ground, on the implementation level, policy makers are adjusting to the failures of one-size-fits-all free market absolutism. Among World Bank economists, there is an increasing willingness to circumvent WTO rules and condone some types of "industrial policy," in other words, protection and promotion of infant industries. This is especially true in the bank's Latin American division, where economists have had to confront the fact that a host of countries that fully embraced the free-trade agenda of the '90s have not progressed. There is, says economist Dani Rodrik, "much greater engagement by the state in guiding activity."[14] Yet the backlash against the Washington consensus has not led to an epidemic of protectionism anywhere, the bane of the global system between World War I and World War II. Poor nations increasingly have spoken out against the high-handedness of the Washington consensus and have grown more emboldened by its failures. Even so, their agenda has not become the agenda of the antiglobalization protesters. In fact it is the opposite: They want even *freer* markets, a U.S. goal since the founding of the Republic. There is a new consensus that globalization and foreign-aid programs create growth only when governments are properly managed and large-scale corruption is rooted out—which of course fits right in with the emerging consensus on how to do democracy right. As Stanley Fischer, the former number-two official at the IMF, put it, "Citizens of poor countries are not asking to stop globalization; they are asking for better globalization, for better market access for their products, to make the international financial system less crisis-prone and to help the countries lagging behind to catch up."[15]

And the antiglobalization movement itself is splintering, with its most enlightened members trending toward open trade—even as their avowed enemies, multinationals, are moderating their sometimes rapacious international practices under public pressure. Oxfam International, a left-leaning British aid organization, was one of the first apostates, declaring that international trade was in fact a benefit to the world's poor. "The extreme element of the anti-globalization movement is wrong," said Kevin Watkins, a policy analyst for Oxfam. "Trade can deliver much more than aid or debt relief" for poor countries.[16]

On the other side of the fence, even Bill Gates, perhaps the most iconic capitalist of our times, began to see the light in the late '90s. Once Gates had been one of the hard, glittery men of capitalism. When asked what he would do with his billions in the early '90s, the boy wonder of Redmond used to shrug off the question, saying his long work days didn't leave time for charity and that, in any case, all people needed to prosper were the right skills. "Being 'poor,'" he once said, "won't be as much a matter of living in a poor country as it will be a matter of having poor skills." But by 2002 he and his wife, Melinda, were running the world's largest charitable foundation, sending billions of dollars to Africa to provide vaccines in impoverished villages, and Gates was contemptuously dismissing the idea that exporting his beloved computer culture might make a difference in such down-and-out places. Capitalism had its limits.

In a conversation for this book, I asked Gates whether the systemic failures of globalization—the divide between rich and poor countries—that began jutting forth in the late '90s, like rocks from a draining lake, had changed his confidence in the system. First he gave a Churchillian response, saying that he couldn't think of any good alternatives to capitalism. But then he expressed exasperation with his fellow elites. "The thing that's most surprised me is why aren't more people exposed to the gross inequalities that exist," he said. "If they were exposed, they would act politically and financially."[17]

## The Case for the Überpower

Gates is right: exposure is key, the first step to awareness. Americans have now been exposed, catastrophically, to what can happen when they are not paying attention. And if Americans must make themselves more aware of how the international system works and what their role is in it, so must our partners in this international system. Just as it is all too easy for an American president to scapegoat the UN and other institutions, other nations, even our closest allies, have found America to be a too-easy target in a one-überpower world. That, too, may be an inevitable cost of being the hegemon. Given the disparities in power and the nature of global leadership, some American unilateralism is inevitable. Foreign resentment of American power is not going to go away, but it too must be moderated through greater awareness.

Let's concede, if only for the sake of argument, that many of the typical criticisms of Americans we hear voiced around the world are on the mark. We have heard them so many times there must be something to them: Americans are careless. Americans are arrogant ("unilateralist" is a favorite substitute). Americans are crude. American culture is appallingly superficial and materialistic. Americans are ignorant of history. Americans are hypocrites who betray their ideals of freedom and democracy. Guilty on all counts, and these complaints have always been present in America's relations with the world.

Yet these commentaries still miss a more profound truth by a mile. For all our fumbling, the role played by the United States is the greatest gift the world has received in many, many centuries, possibly all of recorded history. And as I said before, the fact is that many of these same allies, while they snipe publicly at our behavior, privately relish U.S. hegemony. The smartest of our foreign interlocutors know that for our faults, we are essentially benign as a national power. We may occasionally go out into the world in force, brandishing all our high-tech weaponry and flaunting our exceptionalism, but we will always go home again (though we may leave a military base or two behind, as in Central Asia most recently, to secure the peace). Indeed, to make the case for the continued dominance of the überpower requires only that we look at the great powers that came before—and at those that would likely follow if the United States were somehow to disappear from the global scene. From ancient Athens and Sparta to Rome, the British empire, the German Third Reich, and Japan's "Co-Prosperity Sphere" in Asia, every dominant power in history has sought to build an imperium on a tide of blood and conquest.

More important, whereas few previous empires ever willingly gave up a colony or a conquest, America has made this a habit, indeed a national mission. There is no precedent for what America did after World War II, handing Germany and Japan back their countries, replenished. There is no precedent for what America did in the Gulf War, restoring Kuwait's rulers to their rule and then going home. Or during the 1990s in Bosnia or Kosovo, where the national interest, as traditionally defined, was next to nil, and yet an American president staked his and NATO's credibility in order to save Muslims (not that al-Qaeda appreciated this). Britain and France gave up their colonies—but only under American and local pressure.

The key point is this: Our exceptional behavior has nothing to do with American munificence or goodness, just as the ravages brought on by previous empires had little to do with rulers who were intrinsically more evil than we. It is simply that this behavior defines who we are. American exceptionalism can be made to work for the world. Every previous empire has been organized around national, ethnic, or tribal chauvinism (the word *barbarian,* after all, originally referred to the strange language of non-Greek speakers); this has inevitably led to brutal behavior toward those peoples who are not members of the same tribe or ethnic or national group and who are often seen as lesser beings, even subhuman. This is a constant in imperial behavior throughout history. America, its WASP origins aside, began as a nation of people escaping imperialism. This has meant, in practice, that we Americans cannot help it but wish freedom on others (granted, for much of our history this once meant freedom only for Caucasians, hence America's brutal treatment of Native Americans and blacks. But that attitude is no longer acceptable). America will almost certainly be engaged abroad more robustly for a long time to come, occasionally with guns blazing. But we will remain a nonimperial hegemon, a stabilizing power. We now have to persuade allies and enemies alike of this. To quote Kissinger again, "An international order which is not considered just will be challenged sooner or later."[18]

Liberals tend to believe that the global system is likely to survive even without American power behind it; the norms of the international system should be made powerful enough so that if, say, Japan or China or Russia were to become the hegemon, the global system would endure. I tend to doubt this could happen; even if these countries are becoming part of the international community, it is for the most part a forced entry. Ethnicity and nationalism will continue to define the self-identity of most other nations (a possible exception to this rule of great powers is the EU, whose transnational embrace of new international structures could potentially make it an able caretaker, if it can ever achieve a common voice and power structure).

On the other hand, we certainly should be preparing for the possibility of American decline. True, America's dominance in the world today is such that we have a lot of geopolitical capital to play with, a lot of room for error. While there will assuredly be terrorist breakouts, and more Americans will die in them, we will remain unthreatened by full-scale war for decades. But if we treasure our heirs, we should recognize that this status quo is a fool's paradise. At some point that will probably take place later in the twenty-first century, no matter how much we pour into defense, our unparalleled power—the power represented by stealth bombers and a world-dominating economy—will likely decline relative to other countries. This is so, ironically, because of the very global system we are creating, one that is, again, marked by open markets and the free flow of information. As I have argued, I believe we *must* build this system—as opposed to an old-fashioned empire—because openness and democracy define who we are and because we Americans feel more secure and at home within such a system. But we must expect that this system will someday lead to more of a global equilibrium in knowledge and power— a spreading of the wealth. For America, this will be the ultimate challenge posed by ideological blowback. The question now is whether we allow this global system to become our undoing, because we are scarcely paying attention to its maintenance while it may be creating future great-power rivals such as China, or whether this system will be sustained, strengthened, and applied by wise American leadership to co-opt such great-power rivals into it, perhaps permanently.

## The Merger of Realism and Idealism

I close this book in the hope that the arguments I delivered effectively fulfill the promise I made earlier on: to close the gap, conceptually and practically, between Wilsonian idealism and conservative realism, the two poles that have defined American foreign policy for much of the last century. The Wilsonian world we live in, troubled as it is, is an outgrowth of America's inexorable if somewhat unwitting construction of a world order during the twentieth century. Wilsonianism was a natural, organic response to the demands of the times and to the requirements of our own American sensibility. What has it left us with? Let's recall the comment in Chapter 2 from that most seasoned American realist, Walter Lippmann: "The effort to abolish war can come to nothing," he wrote, "unless there are created international institutions, international public opinion, an international conscience which will play the part which war has always played in human affairs." Recall, too, the caveat of that other great realist of the twentieth century, Hans Morgenthau, quoted in Chapter 3 to the effect that non-realist solutions to world order "presuppose the existence of an integrated international society."

My argument throughout this book has been that we have fulfilled the realists' conditions for organizing an international order around something other than just raw power. We *have* created, more powerfully than ever before, "an integrated international society"; there *do* exist, more deeply rooted than ever before, international institutions, international public opinion, and, yes, something like an international conscience. And in these unprecedented conditions lie the hope that the advantages of this integrated international community, secured by American power, are more tempting than the advantages of war, anarchy, and withdrawal from that system. I believe they are more tempting. More important, the major nations of the world now also believe they are.

Realist logic will survive in its most basic (and, one could argue, trivial) form: The exercise of power and influence still define what nations are about. But in the face of the unprecedented primacy of the United States and the realities of the global system it has built, realism has been sidelined as a practical approach to international relations. The hard realities of power and order, of focusing on America's "vital national interest," are now about maintaining this U.S.-engendered international system, and this system in turn is about sustaining "soft" values and consensus. George W. Bush, meet Woodrow Wilson. As Condoleezza Rice—the putative realist who had once contemptuously dismissed Wilsonian world building—conceded after nearly two years as Bush's national security advisor, "In real life, power and values are married completely."[19]

It is America's job to keep this marriage intact. Wilson, one of the most misunderstood of American presidents, may offer the best coda to the argument of this book: "We have come out upon a stage of international responsibility from which we cannot retire."[20] He was right, but it has taken us a full century to recognize it, and even now we're not quite there yet. This *can* be made to work, for both America and the rest of the world, but not if we Americans remain at war with ourselves.

# Notes

**INTRODUCTION: THE AGE OF THE ÜBERPOWER**

1   The term is Richard Holbrooke's. Author interview with Holbrooke, March 21, 2002.

2   Keith B. Richburg and William Branigan, "Attacks from Out of the Blue," *The Washington Post*, November 11, 2001, p. A24

3   Donald H. Rumsfeld, "Transforming the Military," *Foreign Affairs*, May-June 2002, p. 21.

4   Author interview, March 9, 1999.

5   From the German *über*, meaning "over" or "above." Felicitous or not, the term *überpower* is intended to convey something of the idea of Nietzsche's *übermensch*—an entity with powers beyond that of ordinary nations and setting its own rules. The term is meant to be both literal and metaphorical. It reflects the fact that America does actually rule the security environment from above, holding the world's military high ground in the skies and space. It also reflects that America has largely set the rules for the world system. But it is meant to convey as well that, as Zarathustra said, "man is something that should be overcome." As this book argues, this means that America has an opportunity to overcome the age-old power struggle among nations through the maintenance of both American hegemony and the institutions of the global system we have built. But this also leads us into a difficult paradox that we must carefully navigate: Even though we are so powerful, we cannot now abjure the rules of the global system we have done so much to create, for that would undercut the system.

6   For a quantitative account of how much more preponderant U.S. power is over the rest of the world than the comparative power distribution during either the Pax Britannica of the nineteenth century or the Cold War, see William C. Wohlforth, "The Stability of a Unipolar World," *International Security*, summer 1999, p. 12.

7   Vernon Loeb, "Brilliant Bombs: How America Became the World's Only Hyperpower—For Better or Worse," *The Washington Post Magazine*, December 16, 2002, p. 26.

8    Mark Bowden, "The Kabul-ki Dance," *The Atlantic*, November 2002, p. 69.

9    Paul Kennedy, "The Eagle Has Landed," *The Financial Times*, February 3, 2002, weekend section. p. 1.

10   G. John Ikenberry, *After Victory* (Princeton, N.J.: Princeton University Press, 2001).

11   Samuel Huntington, "The Clash of Civilizations?" *Foreign Affairs*, summer 1993, p. 22.

12   Robert D. Kaplan, "The Coming Anarchy," *The Atlantic Monthly*, February 1994.

13   Pat Buchanan, *A Republic, Not an Empire* (Washington, D.C.: Regnery, 2001), introduction to the paperback edition.

14   James Richardson, *Contending Liberalisms in World Politics* (Boulder, Colo.: Lynne Rienner, 2001), p. vii.

15   My use of the terms "soft power" and "hard power" and my discussion of the global agenda have been especially influenced by the work of Harvard's Joseph Nye. See his *The Paradox of American Power: Why the World's Only Superpower Can't Go It Alone* (New York: Oxford University Press, 2002); and Nye and Robert Keohane, "Power and Interdependence in the Information Age," *Foreign Affairs*, fall 1998.

16   David Halberstam, *War in a Time of Peace: Bush, Clinton and the Generals* (New York: Scribner, 2001).

17   Speech at West Point. Little noted at the time, this was the president's clearest statement that he had adopted the view of hard-liners such as Rumsfeld and his deputy Paul Wolfowitz, first put forward in 1992 in the latter stages of his father's administration, that America must consciously act to preempt challenges to its hegemony. See Nicholas Lemann, "The New World Order," *The New Yorker*, April 1, 2002, pp. 42–48.

18   Ronald Steel, *Walter Lippmann and the American Century* (Boston: Atlantic Monthly Press, 1980), p. 586.

19   Steel, *Walter Lippmann*, pp. 565–66.

20   Paul Kennedy, *The Rise and Fall of the Great Powers* (New York: Random House, 1987), p. 332. The figures are from 1937.

21   Author interview, October 17, 2002.

22   Niall Ferguson, *The Cash Nexus: Money and Power in the Modern World 1700–2000* (New York: Basic Books, 2001), p. 418.

23   The figures come from data compiled by the Better World Campaign, Washington, D.C.

24   Quoted in Richard Holbrooke, *To End a War* (New York: The Modern Library, 1998), p. 368.

25   *The National Security Strategy of the United States of America*, September 2002, p. 1.

## 1. Navigating the Permanent Quagmire

1    See George Bush and Brent Scowcroft, *A World Transformed* (New York: Alfred A. Knopf, 1998).

2    George W. Bush, news conference, October 11, 2001.

3    Author interview with Biden, December 20, 2001.

4    The following discussion of the Bush administration's views of its predecessor

comes from numerous background interviews as well as on-the-record views expressed in articles and interviews before the Bush team took power.

5  This was vastly overstated, as we will see further on. But it was true that toward the end of his second term Clinton, in his eagerness to leave a legacy other than scandal, sought to accomplish a lot of peacemaking at once. Indeed, on a trip in his final months in office, when I accompanied him, Clinton tried in one week's ride on Air Force One to mediate the Northern Ireland conflict, China-Taiwan relations, the India-Pakistan conflict, and the Mideast. His all-or-nothing bid to impose a final peace settlement between the Israelis and Palestinians at Camp David in July 2000, a few months after this trip, may have had disastrous consequences (though things got worse under Bush's laissez-faire approach).

6  As Albright explained her own view of enlargement of democracy in an interview with the author on July 7, 2000, six months before she left office: "I believe the organizing principle is—and I've said this from the beginning—there are four groups of countries. The first group is the largest, in which there are countries that understand and function in the international system, even though we might not agree with every aspect of their government. The second group are the societies in transition. The third group are those that we used to call rogues, what we now call states of concern. The fourth are those that are totally falling apart and are literally eating their seed grain. My concept is that ultimately what you're trying to do is to get everybody into the first group."

7  Paul Wolfowitz, "Remembering the Future," *The National Interest*, spring 2000, p. 37.

8  Robert Kagan, "The Clinton Legacy Abroad," *The Weekly Standard*, January 15, 2001.

9  Condoleezza Rice, "Campaign 2000—Promoting the National Interest," *Foreign Affairs*, January-February 2000, p. 47.

10  Bill Clinton, first foreign policy address as a candidate, Georgetown University, December 12, 1991.

11  Michael Beschloss and Strobe Talbott, *At the Highest Level: The Inside Story of the End of the Cold War* (Boston: Little, Brown, 1993), p. 434.

12  Rice, "Campaign 2000."

13  Colin L. Powell, Senate Foreign Relations Committee confirmation hearing, January 17, 2001.

14  For a fuller discussion of the differences between these views, and their deeper intellectual underpinnings, see Gideon Rose, "Present Laughter or Utopian Bliss?" *The National Interest*, winter 1999/2000, pp. 41–47. See also Michael C. Desch, "Liberals, Neocons and Realcons," *Orbis*, September 22, 2001.

15  Charles Krauthammer, "Unilateral? Yes, Indeed," *The Washington Post*, December 14, 2001, p. A45.

16  Victor Davis Hanson, "Wishing War Away?" *National Review Online*, April 5, 2002. See also Glenn Kessler and Peter Slevin, "Cheney Is Fulcrum of Foreign Policy," *The Washington Post*, October 13, 2002, p. A16.

17  Bush–Powell news conference, Crawford, Texas, December 16, 2000.

18  Powell confirmation hearing, Senate Foreign Relations Committee, January 17, 2001.

19  Walter Isaacson and Evan Thomas, *The Wise Men: Six Friends and the World They Made* (New York: Simon and Schuster, 1986), p. 29.

20    Colin L. Powell, *My American Journey* (New York: Random House, 1995), p. 149.

21    Michael Gordon and Bernard Trainor, *The Generals' War* (Boston: Little, Brown, 1995), p. 33.

22    Ibid., pp. 436–37. I am indebted to my colleague John Barry, *Newsweek*'s national security correspondent, for this insight.

23    Author interview, July 17, 2002.

24    Author interview, June 20, 2002.

25    Author interview, August 23, 2002.

26    Author interview, July 23, 2002.

27    Rumsfeld confirmation hearing, Senate Armed Services Committee, January 11, 2001.

28    Evan Thomas, "Rumsfeld's War," *Newsweek,* September 16, 2002, p. 23.

29    Gerald R. Ford, *A Time to Heal* (New York: Harper & Row, 1979), pp. 353–59.

30    Author interview, July 26, 2002.

31    For an exhaustive account of these earlier policy battles in Reagan's first term, see Raymond Gartoff, *Détente and Confrontation: American-Soviet Relations from Nixon to Reagan* (Washington: Brookings Institution, 1985).

32    Author interview, July 26, 2002.

33    Robert Kagan and William Kristol, eds., *Present Dangers: Crisis and Opportunity in American Foreign and Defense Policy* (San Francisco: Encounter, 2000).

34    Author interview, August 23, 2002.

35    William Kristol and Robert Kagan, "Toward a Neo-Reaganite Foreign Policy," *Foreign Affairs*, July-August 1996, p. 23.

36    Richard Haass, *The Reluctant Sheriff* (New York: Council on Foreign Relations Press, 1997), p. 53.

37    Wolfowitz, "Remembering the Future," p. 38

38    Thomas, "Rumsfeld's War," p. 22.

39    Bob Woodward and Dan Balz, "'We Will Rally the World,'" *The Washington Post*, January 28, 2002, p. A1.

40    John Miller, interview with Osama bin Laden, *Esquire*, February 1999.

41    See Robert McNamara and James G. Blight, *Wilson's Ghost: Reducing the Risk of Conflict, Killing, and Catastrophe in the Twenty-first Century* (New York: Public Affairs, 2001), pp. 46–47.

42    "Powell Following Moderate Line," The Associated Press, March 31, 2001.

43    Thomas, "Rumsfeld's War," p. 23.

44    Author interview, September 26, 2001.

45    Bob Woodward, *Bush at War* (New York: Simon & Schuster, 2002), pp. 49, 61.

46    Author interview, August 22, 2002.

47    John Bolton, "Should We Take Global Governance Seriously?" *Chicago Journal of International Law*, fall 2000, p. 206.

48    Author interview, September 3, 2002.

49    Author interview with a former senior administration official who prefers to remain anonymous, March 17, 2002.

50    Thomas Ricks and Vernon Loeb, "Rumsfeld and Commanders Exchange Briefings," *The Washington Post*, March 3, 2001, p. A19.

51    Michael Gordon, "U.S. Nuclear Plan Sees New Targets and New Weapons," *The New York Times*, March 10, 2002, p. A1.

52    Speech by George W. Bush, March 11, 2002.

53  Author interview, September 25, 2001.

54  Interview with ITV, April 15, 2002.

55  Richard Haass, 2002 Arthur Ross Lecture, Foreign Policy Association, New York, April 22, 2002.

56  Testimony before the Senate Foreign Relations Committee, June 26, 2002.

57  In a campaign speech in Minnesota on November 3, 2002, Bush described himself this way no fewer than three times.

58  Author interview, August 29, 2002.

59  *The National Security Strategy of the United States of America*, p. i.

60  John Lewis Gaddis, "A Grand Strategy of Transformation," *Foreign Policy*, November-December 2002, p. 56.

61  Author interview, September 20, 2002.

62  Kofi Annan briefing, November 13, 2002.

63  Nicholas Kristof, "The Greatest Threat," *The New York Times*, October 29, 2002, p. A31

64  Author interview, March 20, 2002.

65  Author interview with Andrew F. Krepinevich, director, Center for Strategic and Budgetary Assessments, January 15, 2002.

## 2. The American Temptation

1  John Lewis Gaddis, "And Now This: Lessons from the Old Era for the New One," in Strobe Talbott and Nayan Chanda, eds., *The Age of Terror: America and the World After Sept. 11* (New York: Perseus, 2002), pp. 6–7.

2  Thomas Paine, *The American Crisis*, December 23, 1776.

3  Quoted in *The Civil War*, a documentary film by Ken Burns, 1990.

4  Author interview with Undersecretary of State John Bolton, February 8, 2002. See also Bolton's essay, "Unilateralism Is Not Isolationism," in *Understanding Unilateralism in American Foreign Relations* (London: The Royal Institute of International Affairs, 2000), pp. 50–82. However, this view is a dubious one. Just one example: In 1942, well after Pearl Harbor, Wendell Willkie, the maverick internationalist in the Republican Party, "urged all GOP candidates to sign a postwar pledge to 'set up institutions of international and political coopera-tion. . . .' None came forward to sign the Willkie pledge." Cited in Townsend Hoopes and Douglas Brinkley, *FDR and the Creation of the U.N.* (New Haven: Yale University Press, 1997), p. 62.

5  Michael Hirsh and Karen Breslau, "Closing the Deal," *Newsweek,* March 6, 1995.

6  Historian Walter McDougall has made the argument that American exceptional-ism is unrelated to the nation's conduct of foreign affairs in the sense that it did not prompt Americans to promote a moralistic policy. That was true in the nineteenth century. But it does justify today's moralism, as we shall see. See "Back to Bedrock," *Foreign Affairs*, March-April 1997, pp. 134–46.

7  Joseph Ellis, *Founding Fathers: The Revolutionary Generation* (New York: Knopf, 2000), p. 142.

8  Quoted in Walter A. McDougall, *Promised Land, Crusader State: The American Encounter with the World Since 1776* (Boston: Houghton Mifflin, 1997), p. 36.

9  "Over the course of history, states that have experienced significant growth in their material resources have relatively soon redefined and expanded their politi-

cal interests abroad." Fareed Zakaria, *From Wealth to Power: The Unusual Origins of America's World Role* (Princeton, N.J.: Princeton University Press, 1998), p. 3.

10    Edmund Morris, *Theodore Rex* (New York: Random House, 2001), p. 397.

11    H. W. Brands, "The Idea of the National Interest," in Michael J. Hogan, ed., *The Ambiguous Legacy: U.S. Foreign Relations in the "American Century"* (New York: Cambridge University Press, 1999), p. 124.

12    Some scholars, such as Henry Kissinger, have sought to contrast the two presidents in stark terms, casting Roosevelt as a hard-headed geopolitical realist and Wilson as a high-minded altruist. Roosevelt himself, a man of exuberant passions and a Republican, despised the Democratic Wilson as a hopeless idealist whose ideas consisted of "milk and water" rather than "blood and iron." See Henry Kissinger, *Diplomacy* (New York: Simon & Schuster, 1994).

13    Quoted in Paul Fussell, *The Great War and Modern Memory* (New York: Oxford University Press, 1975), p. 8.

14    Ibid., p. 18.

15    Margaret MacMillan, *Paris 1919: Six Months That Changed the World* (New York: Random House, 2001), p. 68.

16    Frank Ninkovich, *The Wilsonian Century: U.S. Foreign Policy since 1900* (Chicago: The University of Chicago Press, 1999), p. 49.

17    Lloyd E. Ambrosius, *Woodrow Wilson and the American Diplomatic Tradition: The Treaty Fight in Perspective* (New York: Cambridge University Press, 1987), p. 54.

18    Quoted in G. John Ikenberry, *After Victory* (Princeton, N.J.: Princeton University Press, 2001), p. 124.

19    Author interview with Richard Holbrooke, November 30, 1998.

20    Kissinger, *Diplomacy*, p. 54.

21    Quoted in Ninkovich, *The Wilsonian Century*, p. 14.

22    *The National Security Strategy of the United States of America*, p. i.

23    H. W. V. Temperley, *A History of the Peace Conference of Paris* (London: Oxford University Press, 1920), 1:127.

24    Gene Smith, *When the Cheering Stopped* (New York: William Morrow, 1964), p. 169.

25    Ronald Steel, *Walter Lippmann and the American Century* (Boston: Atlantic Monthly Press, 1980), p. 327.

26    Cited in William Kristol and Robert Kagan, eds., *Present Dangers: Crisis and Opportunity in American Foreign and Defense Policy* (San Francisco: Encounter, 2000), p. 22.

27    The speech, delivered before a joint session of Congress on January 6, 1941, declared a hope for "a world founded upon four essential human freedoms"—freedom of speech, freedom of religion, freedom from want, and freedom from fear.

28    For a well-argued "realist" interpretation of FDR's intentions, see Hoopes and Brinkley, *FDR*. See also Robert Dallek, *Franklin D. Roosevelt and American Foreign Policy, 1932–1945* (New York: Oxford University Press, 1979).

29    John Lewis Gaddis, *The United States and the Origins of the Cold War* (New York: Columbia University Press, 1972), p. 11.

30　Michael Beschloss, *The Conquerors: Roosevelt, Truman and the Destruction of Hitler's Germany, 1941–45* (New York: Simon & Schuster, 2002), p. 12.

31　Hoopes and Brinkley, *FDR*, p. 131.

32　Ikenberry, *After Victory*, p. 258.

33　John Mearsheimer, *The Tragedy of Great Power Politics* (New York: Norton, 2001), p. 25.

34　George Bush and Brent Scowcroft, *A World Transformed* (New York: Alfred A. Knopf, 1998), pp. 302–487.

35　Quoted in Hans J. Morgenthau, *Politics Among Nations: The Struggle for Power and Peace* (New York: Alfred A. Knopf, 1978), p. 150.

36　Quoted in Ikenberry, *After Victory*, p. 193.

37　Author interview with Pentagon architect William Schweber, December 31, 2001.

38　Author interview with Paul Nitze, December 1999.

39　Ikenberry, *After Victory*, p. 201.

40　Hoopes and Brinkley, *FDR*, pp. 58, 206.

41　Geir Lundestad, "'Empire by Invitation' in the American Century," in Hogan, ed., *The Ambiguous Legacy*, pp. 52–91.

42　Talk at the Council on Foreign Relations, June 17, 2002.

43　Author interview with pollster Steven Kull, University of Maryland, October 15, 2002.

44　Ikenberry, *After Victory*, p. 260.

## 3. What Is the "International Community"?

1　Daniel McGinn and Michael Hirsh, "Heavier Metal," *Newsweek*, May 18, 1998, p. 28.

2　James Brooke, "Japan's Export Power Drifts Across the China Sea," *The New York Times*, April 7, 2002, p. A3.

3　G. Pascal Zachary, *The Global Me: New Cosmopolitans and the Competitive Edge* (New York: Public Affairs, 2000), p. xix.

4　Lawrence Lessig, *Code, and Other Laws of Cyberspace* (New York: Basic, 1999), p. 226.

5　The phrase is Jacques Derrida's.

6　Author interview, February 12, 2002.

7　Thomas Friedman, *The Lexus and the Olive Tree: Understanding Globalization* (New York: Farrar, Straus, & Giroux, 1999), p. 8.

8　John Micklethwait and Adrian Wooldridge, *A Future Perfect: The Challenge and Hidden Promise of Globalization* (New York: Crown, 2000), p. 5.

9　George Packer, "When Here Sees There," *The New York Times Magazine*, April 21, 2002, p. 14.

10　Author interview, November 1996.

11　Michael Hirsh, "A Small World After All," *Newsweek*, December 2, 1996, p. 55.

12　Harold Hongju Koh, "Preserving American Values: The Challenge at Home and Abroad," in Strobe Talbott and Nayan Chanda, eds., *The Age of Terror: America and the World After September 11* (New York: Perseus, 2002), p. 146.

13　David Halberstam, *War in a Time of Peace: Bush, Clinton, and the Generals* (New York: Scribner, 2001), p. 11.

14  For a well-argued contrary view, see Niall Ferguson, *The Cash Nexus: Money and Power in the Modern World, 1700–2000* (New York: Basic Books, 2001).

15  It was originally conceived by her policy-planning chief, Morton Halperin.

16  Author interview, June 2000.

17  William Safire, "Needed: Freedom's Caucus," *The New York Times*, May 31, 2001, p. 27.

18  Paul Wolfowitz, "Remembering the Future," *The National Interest*, spring 2000, p. 37.

19  William Drozdiak, "Divided Allies? Only at the Top," *The Washington Post Outlook*, September 8, 2002, p. B03.

20  Press briefing with Schroeder, January 31, 2002.

21  George Wehrfritz, "What to Wear?" *Newsweek* (Atlantic edition), May 13, 2002, p. 28.

22  Dmitri Trenin, *The New Eurasia: Russia on the Border Between Global Politics and Globalization* (Washington: Carnegie Endowment, 2002).

23  *The National Security Strategy of the United States of America*, pp. 26–27.

24  Paul Wolfowitz, "Remembering the Future, p. 43. However, Jonathan Pollack, a China strategist at the Naval War College, says he has never found "credible evidence" from Chinese source documentation that Liu actually made this assertion. Author interview, October 23, 2002.

25  John Mearsheimer, *The Tragedy of Great Power Politics* (New York: Norton, 2001).

26  Michael Hirsh and Melinda Liu, "Beijing's Secret Wish List," *Newsweek* (International edition), April 21, 1997, p. 16.

27  Supachai Panitchpakdi and Mark L. Clifford, *China and the WTO: Changing China, Changing World Trade* (Singapore: John Wiley & Sons), p. 2.

28  Adam Watson, *The Evolution of International Society* (London: Routledge, 1992), p. 304.

29  Author interview with Pentagon research analyst Dean Chang, January 15, 2002.

30  Craig S. Smith, "China Reshaping Military to Toughen Muscle in the Region," *The New York Times*, October 16, 2002, p. A12.

31  Dana Priest, "The Proconsuls," *The Washington Post*, September 30, 2000, p. A1.

32  Fareed Zakaria, *From Wealth to Power: The Unusual Origins of America's World Role* (Princeton, N.J.: Princeton University Press, 1998), p. 192.

33  All this was an overwrought expression of American exceptionalism. International law gave the United States largely a free hand to respond in the war on terror, as Harold Koh points out. Article 51 of the UN Charter recognizes each member country's "inherent right . . . of self-defense if an armed attack occurs." "In two broad resolutions—the first passed the day after the attack and the second several weeks later—the Security Council clearly authorized U.N. member states to take action against terrorism, permitting the United States and its allies to use authorized force against both bin Laden and the Taliban who offer him safe haven. . . . What all this means is that the United States government enjoys considerable freedom under international law to pursue a broad-based strategy that marshals a forceful military response, as part of a larger diplomatic, economic, counterintelligence, and law enforcement strategy." Koh, "Preserving American Values," p. 154. Even preemption could be justified under international

law, as then UN secretary-general Boutros Boutros-Ghali managed to do in approving preemptive NATO air strikes against Bosnian Serb air defenses although they weren't specifically provided for in Security Council Resolution 836, which protected UN "safe areas" in Bosnia. See Boutros Boutros-Ghali, *Unvanquished: A U.S.-U.N. Saga* (New York: Random House, 1999), p. 242.

34  Bernard Lewis, *What Went Wrong? Western Impact and Middle Eastern Response* (New York: Oxford University Press, 2002), p. 151.

35  Ian Buruma and Avishai Margalit, "Occidentalism," *The New York Review of Books*, January 17, 2002, pp. 4–7.

36  Lewis, *What Went Wrong*, p. 159.

37  See William Wechsler and Lee Wolosky, "Terrorist Financing: Report of an Independent Task Force Sponsored by the Council on Foreign Relations," October 2002.

38  Author interview, October 12, 2002.

39  William Greider, *One World Ready or Not: The Manic Logic of Global Capitalism* (New York: Simon & Schuster, 1997), pp. 11–12.

40  Louis Henkin, *How Nations Behave: Law and Foreign Policy* (New York: Council on Foreign Relations, 1979), p. 1.

41  Robert Wright, *Nonzero: The Logic of Human Destiny* (New York: Pantheon, 2000), p. 227.

42  Ibid., p. 209.

43  David Landes, *The Wealth and Poverty of Nations* (New York: Norton, 1998), pp. 513–14.

44  Adam Garfinkle, "Strategy and Preventive Diplomacy: United States Foreign Policy and Humanitarian Intervention," *Orbis*, September 22, 2001, p. 503.

45  Owen Harries, "The Collapse of the 'West,'" *Foreign Affairs*, fall 1993.

46  See Jeffrey W. Legro and Andrew Moravcsik, "Is Anybody Still a Realist?" *International Security*, fall 1999, pp. 5–55.

47  Robert Kagan, "Power and Weakness," *Policy Review*, June 1, 2002, pp. 3–28.

48  Victor Davis Hanson, "Remembrance of Things Past," *National Review Online*, October 11, 2002.

49  Hans J. Morgenthau, *Politics Among Nations: The Struggle for Power and Peace*, 5th edition (New York: Knopf, 1978), p. 559.

## 4. The Argument from Hard Power

1  James Bamford, *Body of Secrets: Anatomy of the Ultra-Secret National Security Agency from the Cold War Through the Dawn of a New Century* (New York: Doubleday, 2001), p. 4.

2  Testimony before the Select Committee on Intelligence, October 17, 2002.

3  Hayden testimony at Joint House and Senate Intelligence Committees hearing, October 17, 2002.

4  Author interview, May 23, 2002.

5  Thomas Ricks and Vernon Loeb, *The Washington Post*, February 2, 2002.

6  Greg Jaffe, "Modern Warfare Strains Capacity to Communicate," *The Wall Street Journal*, April 10, 2002, p. A1.

7  Quoted in Thomas K. Adams, "10 GPS Vulnerabilities," *Military Review*, March-April 2001.

8   CBS's *60 Minutes II,* June 19, 2002. For a detailed accounting of the NSA's tech-
    nological deficiencies, see also Bamford, *Body of Secrets.*

9   Author interview, December 15, 1996.

10  Adams, "10 GPS Vulnerabilities."

11  Defense Department briefing, March 22, 2002.

12  Edward Iwata, "Silicon Valley Techies Suit up Army with Sleeker Gear," *USA
    Today,* February 7, 2002, p. 1B.

13  Stanley B. Alterman, "GPS Dependence: A Fragile Vision for US Battlefield
    Dominance," *Journal of Electronic Defense,* September 1995.

14  Testimony before United States–China Security Review Commission, January 17,
    2002.

15  James Brooke, "Japan Braces for a 'Designed in China' World," *The New York
    Times,* April 21, 2002, Sec. 3, p. 1.

16  Author interview, March 12, 1997.

17  Author interview, December 17, 1996.

18  Author interview, January 10, 2002.

19  Vernon Loeb, "Brilliant Bombs: How America Became the World's Only Hyper-
    power—For Better or Worse," *The Washington Post Magazine,* December 15, 2002,
    pp. 6–27.

20  Wesley K. Clark, *Waging Modern War: Bosnia, Kosovo and the Future of Combat*
    (New York: Basic Books, 2001), p. 572.

21  Jeff Gerth with Raymond Bonner, "Companies Are Investigated for Aid to China
    on Rockets," *The New York Times,* April 4, 1998, p. A1.

22  Jeff Gerth, "Democratic Fund-Raiser Said to Detail China Tie," *The New York
    Times,* May 15, 1998, p. A1; Jeff Gerth, "Satellite Maker Gave Report to China
    Before Telling U.S.," *The New York Times,* May 19, 1998, p. A19.

23  Jeff Gerth and John M. Broder, "Paper Shows White House Staff Favored a
    China Satellite Permit," *The New York Times,* May 23, 1998, p. A1.

24  Michael Hirsh and Melinda Liu, "China's Secret Wish List," *Newsweek* (Interna-
    tional edition), April 21, 1997, pp. 10–16.

25  Roberto Suro and John Mintz, "Bungled Report, Bureaucracy Collide in China
    Waiver," *The Washington Post,* May 31, 1998, p. A16.

26  Author interview, March 19, 2002.

27  William C. Rempel and Alan C. Miller, "Internal Justice Memo Excuses Loral,"
    *The Los Angeles Times,* May 23, 2000. "This was a matter which likely did not
    merit any investigation," Charles G. La Bella, the head of the Justice Depart-
    ment's campaign finance unit, concluded in a memorandum to Attorney Gen-
    eral Janet Reno on August 12, 1998. David Johnston, *The New York Times,* "Justice
    Dept. Memo Says Donor Was Cleared," June 9, 2000, p. A24.

28  Hearing of the U.S. Senate Committee on Commerce, Science and Transporta-
    tion, September 17, 1998.

29  William Broad, "Spies vs. Sweat," *The New York Times,* September 7, 1999, p. A1.

30  Former Senator Warren Rudman, a conservative Republican who headed the
    president's Foreign Intelligence Advisory Board, concluded after reviewing the
    espionage claims, "It is my belief that there was no espionage" connected with
    the W-88 data obtained by China. Regarding China's own design of a small,
    W-88-like warhead, "What they did, they did on their own," he said. Vernon
    Loeb and Walter Pincus, "Guilty Plea, Release Leave Unsolved Questions in Lee
    Case," *The Washington Post,* September 17, 2000.

31    Ironically, while the Wen Ho Lee story was still overtaking Washington—before it was shown to be spurious—the *Times* won a Pulitzer Prize for the earlier Loral-Hughes stories. In the words of the citation awarding journalism's highest honor to the paper, the *Times* reporting team had "disclosed the corporate sale of American technology to China, with U.S. government approval despite security risks, prompting investigations and significant changes in policy." In fact, the *Times* had not "disclosed" these corporate sales because they were never secret; the vast majority of experts believed the security risks were minor or nonexistent; the investigations came to be seen as exercises in McCarthyesque hysteria; and the "significant changes in policy" were, for the most part, harmful to U.S. national security.

32    Michael Hirsh, "Left on the Launch Pad," *Newsweek,* February 28, 2000, p. 45.

33    Evelyn Iritani and Peter Pae, "U.S. Satellite Industry Reeling Under New Export Controls," *The Los Angeles Times,* December 11, 2000, p. A1.

34    Author interview with defense expert Andrew Krepinovich, January 22, 2002.

35    "A Review of the Department of Energy Classification Policy and Practice," a 1995 report of the National Academy of Sciences, concluded, "Access to classified information is not necessary for a potential proliferator to construct a nuclear weapon," p. 19. For example, "the considerable progress of Iraq toward becoming a nuclear power was largely independent of U.S. classification policy," according to a "Classification Policy Study" prepared for the Department of Energy by Meridian Corporation, July 4, 1992, p. 35. Much information about nuclear weapons design has been progressively declassified since 1945, a program that was accelerated during the Clinton administration.

36    See, for example, Lars-Erik Nelson, "The Yellow Peril," *New York Review of Books,* June 15, 1999; Eric Boehlert, *How the New York Times Helped Railroad Wen Ho Lee,* Salon.com, September 21, 2000; Lucinda Fleeson, "Rush to Judgment," *American Journalism Review,* November 2000; Bruce Gottlieb, "Stop Making Sense," *Slate,* April 24, 1999; and Robert Schmidt, "Crash Landing," *Brill's Content,* November 1999.

37    "How U.S. Fears Hurt Business," *The Far Eastern Economic Review,* August 29, 2002, p. 15.

38    Author interview, February 21, 1999.

39    Vernon Loeb, "Dark Cloud Hangs Over Los Alamos," *The Washington Post,* August 27, 2000, p. A1.

40    Author interview, April 22, 2002.

41    See Nelson, "The Yellow Peril."

42    Quoted in *Defense Daily International,* February 22, 2002.

43    Testimony before United States–China Security Review Commission, January 17, 2002.

44    William Broad, "Open Arms," *The New York Times,* May 30, 1999, Sec. 4, p.1.

45    Author interview, December 20, 2002.

## 5. WHEN IDEAS BITE BACK

1    Ivo H. Daalder, James Lindsay, and James B. Steinberg, "The Bush National Security Strategy: An Evaluation," *Brookings Institution Policy Brief,* October 4, 2002, p. 6.

2 Walter Russell Mead, *Special Providence: American Foreign Policy and How It Changed the World* (New York: Knopf, 2001), p. 173.

3 *The National Security Strategy of the United States of America*, pp. 1, 2.

4 Author interview with Jose Ramos Horta, February 2, 2002.

5 Author interview with Richard Holbrooke, November 30, 1998.

6 Michael Dobbs, *Madeleine Albright: A Twentieth-Century Odyssey* (New York: Holt, 1999), p. 144.

7 Colin L. Powell, *My American Journey* (New York: Random House, 1995), p. 576.

8 Author interview, February 24, 1999.

9 Albright's true aims were revealed to the author by Clinton administration officials who prefer to remain anonymous.

10 Agence France-Presse, "Washington Ready to Reward Belgrade for 'Good Will,'" February 23, 1999.

11 State Department news briefing, March 2, 1998.

12 Wesley K. Clark, *Waging Modern War: Bosnia, Kosovo and the Future of Combat* (New York: Basic Books, 2001), p. 554.

13 Margaret MacMillan, *Paris 1919: Six Months That Changed the World* (New York: Random House, 2001), p. 12.

14 Stanley Wolpert, *Gandhi's Passion: The Life and Legend of Mahatma Gandhi* (New York: Oxford University Press, 2001), p. 24.

15 Colin L. Powell news conference, December 16, 2000.

16 Author interview with Madeleine Albright, March 24, 1999.

17 Quoted in Niall Ferguson, *The Cash Nexus: Money and Power in the Modern World, 1700–2000* (New York: Basic Books, 2001), p. 376.

18 Ibid., p. 382.

19 Ibid., p. 384.

20 Stanley Hoffman, *World Disorders: Troubled Peace in the Post–Cold War Era* (Lanham, Md.: Rowman & Littlefield, 1998), p. 3.

21 I am indebted to my old friend Tom Easton of *The Economist* for this phrase.

22 Michael Hirsh, "Protesting Plutocracy," *Newsweek Special Edition*, December 2000–February 2001, p. 67.

23 The ultimate "export promotion" policy may have been President Millard Fillmore's mid-nineteenth-century decision to send U.S. gunboats under Commodore Matthew Perry into Tokyo Bay in order to demand that Japan open its ports and trade; it was the first of many U.S. market-opening initiatives in Japan, which continue to this day.

24 A detailed look at this unfolding problem is beyond the scope of this book. But among the most powerful critiques of globalization, see Joseph Stiglitz, *Globalization and Its Discontents* (New York: North, 2002), and Jagdish Bhagwati, *The Wind of the Hundred Days* (Cambridge: MIT Press, 2002).

25 *The National Security Strategy of the United States of America*, p. 18.

26 Author interview, November 12, 1998.

27 Agence France-Presse, "Milosevic Challenges Tribunal's Jurisdiction," August 23, 2001.

28 Interview with James Lilley, March 18, 2000.

29 "Bush Says Does Not Support Independence for Taiwan," Reuters, October 25, 2002.

30 Joseph Stiglitz, *The New Republic*, April 17–24, 2000, p. 56.

31 Author interview, May 10, 2002.

32  Author interview, July 24, 2002.

33  Author interview with Rima Khalaf Hunaidi, assistant administrator, UNDP, July 24, 2002.

34  Joshua Muravchik, "Democracy's Quiet Victory," *The New York Times*, August 19, 2002, p. A17.

## 6. RETHINKING MULTILATERALISM

1  Samantha Power, *"A Problem from Hell": America and the Age of Genocide* (New York: Basic Books, 2002), p. 437.

2  Richard Holbrooke, *To End a War* (New York: Modern Library, 1998) p. 202.

3  I am indebted to my *Newsweek* colleague Zoran Cirjakovic for this comment.

4  Edward C. Luck, *Mixed Messages: American Politics and International Organizations 1919–1999* (Washington, D.C.: Brookings Institution Press, 1999), p. 7.

5  R. Jeffrey Smith and Julia Preston, "U.S. Plans Wider Role in U.N. Peacekeeping," *The Washington Post*, June 18, 1993, p. A1.

6  John Micklethwait and Adrian Wooldridge, *A Future Perfect: The Challenge and Hidden Promise of Globalization* (New York: Crown, 2000), p. 172.

7  Author interview, March 27, 2002.

8  Jesse Helms, *An Empire for Liberty: A Sovereign American and Her Moral Mission* (Washington, D.C.: Regnery, 2001), p. 3.

9  Ibid., p. 189.

10  The figures come from data compiled by the Better World Campaign, Washington, D.C.

11  Stanley Hoffman, *World Disorders: Troubled Peace in the Post–Cold War Era* (Lanham, Md.: Rowman & Littlefield, 1998), p. 182.

12  Author interview, October 25, 2002.

13  Author interview, March 27, 2002.

14  Suzanne Nossel, "Retail Diplomacy: The Edifying Story of UN Dues Reform," *The National Interest*, winter 2001–02, p. 96.

15  Christopher Wren, "Era Waning, Holbrooke Takes Stock," *The New York Times*, January 14, 2001, p. 10.

16  Jesse Helms, address to the UN Security Council, January 20, 2000.

17  Author interview, March 27, 2002.

18  Nossel, "Retail Diplomacy," p. 98.

19  Author interview, November 21, 2002.

20  Jesse Helms, "We Cannot Turn Away," *The Washington Post*, March 24, 2002, p. B7.

21  Brian Urquhart, who largely defined the UN peacekeeping mission, described it as follows: "The use by the United Nations of military personnel and formations not in a fighting or enforcement role but interposed as a mechanism to bring an end to hostilities and as a buffer between hostile forces. In effect, it serves as an internationally constituted pretext for the parties to a conflict to stop fighting and as a mechanism to maintain a cease fire." Brian Urquhart, "International Peace and Security: Thoughts on the Twentieth Anniversary of Dag Hammarskjold's Death," *Foreign Affairs*, fall 1981, p. 6.

22  John Gerard Ruggie, "Wandering in the Void: Charting the UN's New Strategic Role," *Foreign Affairs*, November-December 1993, p.26.

23    Hoffman, *World Disorders*, pp. 184–85.

24    Boutros Boutros-Ghali, *Unvanquished: A U.S.–U.N. Saga* (New York: Random House, 1999), p. 246.

25    Author interview, March 27, 2002.

26    Nossel, "Rebel Diplomacy," p. 97.

27    Ibid., p. 103.

28    The most recent such plan, submitted in the summer of 2000 by a commission chaired by Lakhdar Brahimi, a top aide to Kofi Annan, called for improved peacekeeping that might cost an additional $200 million a year, according to an internal UN estimate. But few countries, especially in the wake of Helms-Biden, were willing to pledge more money.

29    Adam Garfinkle, "Strategy and Preventive Diplomacy: United States Foreign Policy and Humanitarian Intervention," *Orbis*, September 22, 2001, p. 503.

30    Author interview, February 1, 2002.

31    Michael Hirsh, "The Fall Guy," *Foreign Affairs*, November-December 1999, p. 4.

32    Dana Priest, "The Proconsuls," *The Washington Post*, September 30, 2000, p. A1.

33    Author interview, February 16, 2002.

34    Author interview, October 18, 2002.

35    Author interview, February 16, 2002.

36    Samantha Power, *"A Problem from Hell,"* p.368.

37    Condoleezza Rice, "Promoting the National Interest," *Foreign Affairs*, January-February 2000, p. 53.

38    The Associated Press, "Study Recommends Spending Billions More to Modernize U.S. Forces," June 22, 2001.

39    Townsend Hoopes and Douglas Brinkley, *FDR and the Creation of the U.N.* (New Haven: Yale University Press, 1997), p. 68.

40    Ibid., p. 72.

41    Ibid.

42    Author interview, May 2, 2002.

43    Author interview, November 22, 2002.

44    See "Enhancing U.S. Leadership at the United Nations," report of an independent task force sponsored by the Council on Foreign Relations and Freedom House, October 2002.

## 7. THE DIRTY WORK

1    See Paul Kennedy, *The Rise and Fall of the Great Powers: Economic Change and Military Conflict from 1500 to 2000* (New York: Random House, 1987), especially pp. 16–30.

2    David Landes, *The Wealth and Poverty of Nations* (New York: Norton, 1998).

3    Interview with Zbigniew Brzezinski in *Le Nouvel Observateur*, January 1998. Quoted in Isabel Hilton, "The Pashtun Code," *The New Yorker*, December 3, 2001, p. 59.

4    Larry P. Goodson, *Afghanistan's Endless War* (Seattle: University of Washington Press, 2001), p. 37. See also Stephen Tanner, *Afghanistan: A Military History from Alexander the Great to the Fall of the Taliban* (New York: Da Capo Press, 2002).

5    Author interview, February 6, 2002.

6    Bob Woodward, *Bush at War* (New York: Simon & Schuster, 2002), pp. 130–31.
7    David Zucchino, "Afghanistan's Toughest Battle Lies Ahead," *Los Angeles Times*, December 31, 2002, p. A1.
8    Condoleezza Rice, "Promoting the National Interest," *Foreign Affairs*, January–February 2000, p. 53.
9    Author interview, October 17, 2002.
10   Author interview, Kabul, February 18, 2002.
11   Author interview, December 11, 2002.
12   Author interview, July 27, 2002. The Bush administration, under pressure, later allocated more money for roads.
13   Author interview, February 19, 2002. Among the criteria he outlined: "Those who have tortured and oppressed the people will not be elected," which technically would have excluded every Afghan warlord.
14   Omar Zakhilwal, "Stifled in the Loya Jirga," *The Washington Post*, June 16, 2002, p. B7.
15   Author interview, August 21, 2002.
16   Sudarsan Raghavan, "Afghans Struggle for Autonomy," Knight Ridder wire, March 20, 2002.
17   John Cassidy, "Helping Hands," *The New Yorker*, March 18, 2002, p. 63.
18   Gregg Easterbrook, "Safe Deposit: the Case for Foreign Aid," *The New Republic*, July 29, 2002, p. 16.
19   Author interview, December 11, 2002.
20   Sebastian Mallaby, "Our New Defeatist Attitude," *The Washington Post*, January 7, 2002, p. A17.
21   Talk at the Council on Foreign Relations, June 17, 2002.
22   Gay Alcorn, "Powell Puts Australia on Jakarta Watch," *Sydney Morning Herald*, January 19, 2001, p. 1; Hamish McDonald, "An Unwelcome Pat on the Head from Uncle Sam," *Sydney Morning Herald*, January 19, 2001, p. 12. International Monetary Fund chief Michel Camdessus, prodded by the U.S. Treasury, rushed in and imposed a harsh financial fix on then President Suharto that led to the collapse of many banks and businesses. The IMF later admitted its policy was too draconian, but it was too late. The bailout scheme failed, Suharto resigned, and the West exulted at the expected dawning of democracy. Then, for the most part, it stopped paying attention. See Melinda Liu, "The Bloody Birth of a Messy State," *Newsweek*, March 12, 2001, p. 40.

## CONCLUSION: TOWARD A NEW CONSENSUS

1    Quoted in Edward C. Luck, *Mixed Messages: American Politics and International Organizations 1919–1999* (Washington, D.C.: Brookings Institution Press, 1999), p. 29.
2    Henry Kissinger, "Uneasy Allies, Unsettled Alliance," *San Diego Union-Tribune*, March 3, 2002, p. G-6.
3    Talk at the Council on Foreign Relations, June 17, 2002.
4    Max Boot, *The Savage Wars of Peace: Small Wars and the Rise of American Power* (New York: Basic Books, 2002).
5    William Kristol and Robert Kagan, "Introduction: National Interest and Global Responsibility," in Kagan and Kristol, eds., *Present Dangers: Crisis and Opportu-*

*nity in American Foreign and Defense Policy* (San Francisco: Encounter Books, 2000), p. 4.

6    Walter Russell Mead, *Special Providence: American Foreign Policy and How It Changed the World* (New York: Knopf, 2001), pp. 331–34.

7    Cited in Jesse Helms, *Empire for Liberty: A Sovereign America and Her Moral Mission* (Washington, D.C.: Regnery, 2001), p. xix.

8    David Lampton, *Same Bed, Different Dreams: Managing U.S.-China Relations, 1989–2000* (Berkeley: University of California Press, 2000).

9    Robin Wright, "Diplomatic Tour of Asia," *The Los Angeles Times*, February 22, 2002.

10   Richard Haass, "Defining U.S. Foreign Policy in a Post-Post-Cold War World," 2002 Arthur Ross Lecture to the Foreign Policy Association, New York, April 22, 2002.

11   Robert Cooper, "The New Liberal Imperialism," *The Observer*, April 7, 2002.

12   Quoted in Hugo Young, "A New Imperialism Cooked Up Over a Texan Barbecue: Sovereignty Is Being Redefined, So Why Has Nobody Noticed?" *The Guardian*, April 2, 2002, p. 16.

13   Charles Hill, "A Herculean Task," in Strobe Talbott and Nayan Chanda, eds., *The Age of Terror: America and the World After September 11* (New York: Perseus, 2002), p. 107.

14   Author interview, February 28, 2002.

15   Stanley Fischer, "What I Learned at the IMF," *Newsweek* (Davos edition), December 2001–February 2002, p. 76.

16   Paul Blustein, "New Faith in Free Trade," *The Washington Post*, April 11, 2002, p. E1.

17   Author interview, February 3, 2002.

18   Kissinger, *Diplomacy*, p. 79.

19   Condoleezza Rice, Wriston Lecture, Manhattan Institute, October 1, 2002.

20   Quoted in Frank Ninkovich, *The Wilsonian Century: U.S. Foreign Policy Since 1900* (Chicago: University of Chicago Press, 1999), p. 50.

# Acknowledgments

My first debt is to my colleagues at *Newsweek,* especially the magazine's superb foreign correspondent corps, who I believe are the best, pound for pound, in the American media. While the reporting in the book is my own —except where acknowledged—I have benefited immeasurably over the years from conversations, dinners, lunches, and messages exchanged with my fellow correspondents that have helped to shape my ideas. *Newsweek* magazine, my home for the last eight years, creates a savory soup of stories every week, with many cooks adding to the broth. So deftly blended are the ingredients that the reading public knows nothing of the frenzy going on back in the kitchen, and who is responsible for what. I take sole responsibility for the ideas, observations, and thesis of this book. But to have had the privilege of learning about China and Afghanistan from a Melinda Liu, or about the Arab world from a Christopher Dickey, or about the Balkans from a Rod Nordland is to have learned from the best. The same goes for Jeff Bartholet, Christian Caryl, Josh Hammer, Tom Masland, George Wehrfritz, Stryker McGuire, Dan Ephron, Alan Zarembo, Mark Dennis, and the other journalists who make up *Newsweek*'s reporting network around the world. Their collective wisdom is staggering. Scott Johnson, Mark Dean, Joe Cochrane, and *Newsweek*'s wonderful and brave Afghan staff were enormously helpful to me when I was in Afghanistan, as was Pam Constable of the *Washington Post.*

Thanks also go to my colleagues in *Newsweek*'s Washington bureau, who have also helped to shape the ideas in this book through our many gratifying mutual efforts over the years. My understanding of the international economy has been aided by my conversations over the years with two brilliant colleagues, Bob Samuelson and Rich Thomas. John Barry, a walking library, has enlightened me with his unsurpassed knowledge of the Pentagon, the military, and the strategic history of the West. Donatella Lorch quoted Kipling to me and, especially in the early days after 9/11, drew on her vast reporting experience to provide a running hallway tutorial on the mysterious ways of Central Asia. Dan Klaidman, Roy Gutman, Mark Hosenball, Mike Isikoff, Tamara Lipper, and Evan Thomas have also contributed significantly to my understanding of the foreign-policy landscape I describe in this book.

In New York, my friend Fareed Zakaria has given me nothing but encouragement and support since he first graced the *Newsweek* masthead. Our many conversations have been a huge stimulus to me in the conceptualizing of this book. I have also found his own writing to be an inspiration—especially since we agree so often (except on Iraq). I owe a major debt to Fareed, John Ikenberry, and Michael Lind for their careful criticisms of earlier drafts of this book. Any errors of judgment or fact I have made along the way are purely my own.

Similarly, conversations with other fellow editors in New York have sharpened my thinking over the years. My friend Tom Watson, *Newsweek*'s Nation editor, has been a source of endless merriment and occasional wisdom—as when, with one incredulous look, he killed my original title for this book, "The Permanent Quagmire." I would also like to thank Mark Whitaker and Jon Meacham, *Newsweek*'s editor and managing editor, respectively, for their encouragement and for giving me the time to write this book. I am indebted as well to Lynn Staley and to the sparkling memory of Ken Auchincloss and Sarah Pettit.

Much of the substance of this book came from numerous talks, interviews and travels over the years with senior officials in both the Clinton and Bush administrations, and a wide assortment of Wilsonians, realists, conservatives, and neocons. While many of these encounters were on "background," and I cannot therefore name the officials—especially those still in office—I would like to acknowledge them collectively here, with special thanks to Richard Holbrooke, Robert Orr, Marc Thiessen, Jim Steinberg, Jim Warner, and Charlene Barshefsky. I would also like to thank the Council on Foreign Relations, which continues to be a superb forum for an enlightening ongoing conversation about the role of America in the world. Jim Hoge and Gideon Rose, the editor and managing editor, respectively, of *Foreign Affairs,* helped me to sharpen the argument of this book when they assigned me the lead piece in their 9/11 anniversary issue.

At Oxford University Press, my editor, Tim Bartlett, was an early believer in my ideas—in fact, just about the only one in the pre-9/11 publishing world who thought they would make a good book. He continued to be a believer even as he put me through a peer review process that I found tortuous and dispiriting—but which turned out to have a considerable silver lining. Not only did the slings and arrows of the professorial set make this a much better book, but the review process delayed publication, which saved me from certain irrelevance by pushing the book into the post-9/11 era (forcing me to rewrite much of it). I echo many first-time authors in saying that the progress a book makes from a sprawl of ideas and notes to a neat, bound hardcover still seems to me to be something of a miracle—inexplicable, and requiring an act of faith. It would not have been possible without Tim's sure hand and sharp eye. His able assistant, Rob Tempio, was also enormously helpful in providing astute commentary on the final draft and seeing the book through to publication. Joellyn Ausanka worked tirelessly and uncomplainingly to incorporate my endless revisions—and never made a mistake! Thanks also go to Tara Kennedy and Sue Warga.

My friend Tom Easton of *The Economist* has been a wonderful intellectual sparring partner since we had our first loud argument while tubbing together at a crowded Japanese *onsen* in the early '90s—and looked up an hour later to discover that everyone was gone. Seth Sutel was equally enlightening on East Asia. Another friend and neighbor, Tommy Bruce, helped to guide me through the cryptic ways of both Washington and the UN, as did Richard Richardson. At my former employer, *Institutional Investor,* David Cudaback, Ken Klee, Kevin Muehring, Bob Teitelman, and Peter Derow (all since moved on to other places) brought me up to speed on the world of high finance, gave me all too generous support, a virtually unlimited travel budget, and one of the most enjoyable working environments I have ever been in. Another pal, Greg Vistica, educated me in the strange ways of spooks.

A special note of thanks goes to "da boys," my oldest and dearest friends, who never permit me any pretensions, having witnessed the most embarrassing moments of my life. They have supplied me my own "exit strategy" from the bubble world of press people, pundits, and policy wonks that I inhabit in Washington. (One of them, Gary Zarin, even gave me good book advice.) I treasure my time with them, even though I regularly come in last at the annual Manny Rockoff Memorial Golf Tournament. Another one of my best friends, Michael Kosnett, M.D., has given me intellectual sustenance over three decades and has always inspired me with his activist spirit. Jan Zlotnick, who deprived the writing world of his wild creativity by choosing a career in advertising, has long been a muse as well.

And last but really first, I would like to thank my wonderful family. My parents, Barbara and Charlie, have given me the greatest gift a son could have: unconditional love and unstinting emotional support (not to mention material goods) for forty-five years. There is no way to thank them; all I can do is try to emulate their example with my own children. My sisters, Lisa and Kim, and their husbands, Mark I and Mark II, and families, have always been there for me as well, encouraging me where needed and—no small thing—also taking the "great generalizer" down a peg or two when needed. (Kim, a passionate advocate of short sentences, was also an invaluable editor.) My wife, Denise Couture, not only caught many errors with her deft editorial eye but has long endured the trials of living with a husband who even in the best of times could not be described as low-maintenance, and who during the writing of this book gave a new definition to "high-maintenance." My two beautiful sons, Evan and Calder, gave me the greatest inspiration of all simply by threatening to grow up. For two boys who were six and three when I started this book, their intrusions into my middle-floor study were blessedly infrequent and always joyful (for me, anyway). And, yes, Evan, Daddy is now done with "that silly book."

# Index

Abdullah, Abdullah, 229
Acheson, Dean, 24, 37, 44–45
Adams, John Quincy, 77, 82, 84
Adelman, Ken, 44, 46, 63
Afghanistan: al-Qaeda in, 7, 106, 219, 221; "B-52 peace-keeping," 224; Bush administration and, 4, 59, 222–29; effect of war on, 216–17; as failed state, 24, 232–33, 249; food aid, 214, 230; geography, 218; international community and, 229–32, 239; Iraq conflict and, 226; loya jirga, 220–21, 227–28, 230–32; mujahideen, 2, 26–27, 217, 218; nation building, 24, 70, 219, 222, 224, 234–35, 236; Northern Alliance, 3, 246; postwar reconstruction, 26; Russian involvement, 246; separatist movement potential, 173; September 11 attacks, 1–2; Shamali Plains, 216–17; Taliban in, 221; UN's role, 19, 205–6; U.S. military engagement, 4–5, 7, 45; warlords, 4, 223–24, 227–28, 231
Africa, 185–86, 209. See also specific countries
African Crisis Response Initiative, 212
African Union, 185–86, 210
Agenda for Peace, 191
Aidid, Mohammed Farah, 195
AIDS prevention, 200
al-Qaeda: in Afghanistan, 7, 106, 219, 221, 239; failed states and, 201, 232–33; global nature of, 21, 25, 122, 124; in Indonesia, 236; international coalition and, 251; military operations against, 140; motivations for attacks, 49; nuclear declassification and, 157; in Pakistan, 229; Powell on, 51; reforms in Arab world, 247; Saddam Hussein and, 57; state support for, 5; U.S. military operations against, 26, 224
Albanians, 164–65, 167
Albright, Madeleine: assertive multilateralism, 192; Boutros-Ghali and, 194–95; Community of Democracies, 108–9; enlargement of democracy, 261n. 6; export restrictions, 152; Holbrooke compared to, 187; on ideological blowback, 171–72; Kosovo War and, 164–69; Milosevic negotiations, 177, 189; multilateralism, 249; in North Korea, 221; on regional enforcement, 212–13; Wilsonian perspective, 30
Aldridge, Pete, 141, 156
Allende, Salvador, 170
America First movement, 74
"American Century" (Luce), 83
Angell, Norman, 105
Annan, Kofi: Community of Democracies, 184; East Timor crisis, 207; Helms and, 199; on human rights issues, 176–77; representative in

Afghanistan, 230; UN dues battle, 196; on U.S. hegemony, 62
anti-Americanism, 60–61, 162, 170, 236
anti-ballistic-missile treaty, 45, 53–54
anti-globalism, 54, 112, 122, 124, 190, 253
Arab world. See also Islam; specific countries: democratization, 161, 249; free markets in, 23; globalization and, 123; intifada, 32; poverty gap, 194; reforms, 246; UNDP report on, 184–85
Arafat, Yasir, 59
arbitration role of president, 15, 78
ASEAN Regional Forum (ARF), 210–11
Ash, Timothy Garton, 172
Asia-Pacific Economic Cooperation (APEC) summit, 207
Aspin, Les, 38
asymmetric threats, 142, 156, 235. See also terrorism
Atlantic Charter, 85
Augustine, Norman, 143
Aung San Suu Kyi, 110, 221
Australia, 208, 209
automobile industry, 99–100
autonomy and self-determination: former Soviet states, 182–83; independence movements, 160–61, 185; international law and, 175; Kosovo Liberation Army, 164–69; regional policing and, 246; strength of, 163, 172–73; Taiwan issue, 179–81; U.S. promotion of, 160; Wilson on, 169
"axis of evil," 5, 21, 43, 55, 171

B-52 bombers, 3, 4, 224
Balkans. See also Kosovo war: Bush administration and, 54–55; East Timor compared to, 206; Holbrooke and, 188; nation building in, 32–33; Powell on, 36, 38, 50
ballistic missile technology, 154
Baluchistan, 171, 173
Barshefsky, Charlene, 104, 157, 198
Basques, 178
Berger, Samuel R., 207, 208, 236
Berlin Wall, 170
Beschloss, Michael, 84
Bhutto, Benazir, 171
Biden, Joseph, 26–28, 47, 59, 196–97, 198
Bilderburg meeting, 102
bin Laden, Osama. See also al-Qaeda; terrorism: asymmetric warfare, 156; Bush administration and, 17; Clinton administration and, 16–17; escape of U.S. attacks, 5; exploitation of U.S. hypocrisy, 162, 171; global organization, 122; Islamic support,

bin Laden, Osama (*continued*)
xiii; motivations for attacks, 48–49; UN action against, 266–67n. 33; on U.S. troops in Saudi Arabia, 48; use of Afghanistan, 21; war on terror and, 131

biological weapons, 53, 66
*Black Hawk Down* (film), 2
Blair, Dennis, 120, 210
Blair, Tony, 249
Bolsheviks, 79–80
Bolton, John, 53–54, 75, 121, 122, 263n. 4
Boot, Max, 13, 242
borders, 70–71, 177
Bosnia: Albright and, 164; Clinton administration and, 32, 240; Dayton negotiations, 189; ethnic cleansing, 167; Holbrooke's role in, 188; humanitarian intervention, 24; NATO strikes, 266–67n. 33; peacekeeping mission, 192; "postmodern imperialism," 250; Powell and, 36; UN system, 202; U.S. foreign policy, 255
Boutros-Ghali, Boutros, 191–92, 194–96, 201–2, 205, 238, 266–67n. 33
Bowden, Mark, 8
Brahimi, Lakhdar, 230, 272n. 28
Brazil, 66
Bretton Woods institutions, 84–85
Brezhnev, Leonid, 170
Brinkley, Douglas, 213
Britain: Afghanistan and, 218; on China's inclusion on Security Council, 201; colonial values, 102; economic globalization, 12; imperialism, 73, 86, 90; military, 8; U.S. alliance, 18–19
Brookings Institution, 162
Brooks, Mel, 22
Brown, Mark Malloch, 184, 185, 230
Brown, Ron, 76
Brunei, 199
Brzezinski, Zbigniew, 6, 218
Buchanan, Pat, 10, 75
Burke, Edmund, 237, 242
Burma, 221
Burnside, Craig, 233
Buruma, Ian, 122–23
Bush, George H. W. (and administration): Asia-Pacific Economic Cooperation (APEC) summit, 207; dual use technology controls, 144; foreign policy, 31–32; Gulf War, 22, 26–27, 88; Japan bashing, 99; multilateralism, 52; presidential waivers, 148; recognition of international community, 125–26; Taiwan issue, 180; UN speech, 191; on "Vietnam syndrome," 50
Bush, George W. (and administration): Afghan conflict and, 4, 59, 222–29; "axis of evil," 5, 21, 43, 55, 171; background, x; Biden meeting, 26; budget deficits, 158; "Bush Doctrine," 56–57, 126, 131; campaign position, 35; China issue, 117; Clinton compared to, 7, 16, 18, 86, 239; conservatism, 35, 53–63; criticisms of Clinton, 29–30; critique of, 28, 214; defense spending, 125; "division of labor," 251; East Timor, 240; expansionism, 82; foreign policy, xiii–xiv, 13, 29, 40, 60; free market philosophy, 175; global challenge, 17; hard-liners in administration, 92, 260n. 6, 260n. 17; hegemonists, 67–68; human rights, 175–76, 178; ideological blowback, 161; international community, 17, 88, 186, 248–49; Iraq issue,

236; isolationism, 31, 156; on leadership, 159; nation building, 27–28, 59, 62; NATO and, 62; Naval Academy speech, 141; North Korea, 240; nuclear weapon treaties, 58–59, 91, 247–48; "Permanent Quagmire," 239; post-September 11 agenda, 15; Powell's role in, 35–36; preemption, 20; public opinion and, xi; Schroeder and, 113; on Shanghai Communiqué, 180; speech issues, 57; Supreme Court and, 35; UN and, ix–xii, 62, 74, 130, 200–201, 203; unilateralism, 9, 73; U.S. exceptionalism, 73; West Point speech, 64; Wilsonian perspective, 88, 258

"Buy American" campaigns, 100

Cable News Network (CNN), 24, 109, 207–8, 242
Cambodia, 210–11
capitalism, 118–19
Carter, James Earl, Jr. (Jimmy), 6, 187–88
*Casablanca* (film), 74
Castro, Fidel, 185
Center for Strategic and International Studies, 155
Central Asia, 7, 19
Central Intelligence Agency (CIA), 70, 138–39. *See also* intelligence gathering
Chávez, Hugo, 185, 210
Chechnya, 116, 160, 162, 178, 183, 240
chemical weapons, 66
Chen Shui-bian, 179, 181
Cheney, Dick: avoidance of Vietnam service, 52; conflict with Powell, 39; criticism of Clinton, 65; on Gorbachev, 47; hard-liner staff, 43; on inevitability of conflict, 33; pragmatism, 44; tension with multilateralists, 240; U.S. hegemony, 39
Chiang Kai-shek, 201
Chicago Council on Foreign Relations, 91, 113
China: antiterror campaign, 56; ASEAN Regional Forum, 210–11; capitalism in, 118–19; Chinese Communist Party, 181; democratization, 108; as developing nation, 16; as emerging threat, 54; free market philosophy, 174; globalization, 11–12, 244; Kosovo war, 178; mandarins, 119, 179, 245; North Korea issue, 65; nuclear transfers, 124; role in international community, 19, 67, 86, 116, 117–21, 201, 244–45; strategic importance, 20–22; surveillance plane incident, 59, 117, 145–48; Taiwan issue, 179–81, 244–46; technology transfers, 149, 157; Tibet, 160, 162, 178, 180; U.S. export controls, 142, 155; U.S. hegemony and, 39; wage levels, 100; Wen Ho Lee scandal, 147–54, 156, 269n. 31
Chirac, Jacques, 131
Christianity, 98, 122–23, 126
Christopher, Warren, 30, 76, 188
Churchill, Winston, 187, 209, 213
civil wars, 139, 217
Clark, Wesley, 90, 144, 169, 203, 210, 211
clash of civilizations, 112
Clemenceau, Georges, 169
Clifford, Mark, 119
Clinton, Bill (and administration): arms treaties, 55; Bush compared to, 18, 86, 239; Comprehensive Test Ban Treaty, 157; criticisms of, 28–30, 34–35, 46, 65; cruise missile strikes, 7; defense spending, 30; East Timor crisis, 206, 207; election, 32; foreign policy, xiii–xiv, 13–14, 16–17, 29; globalism, 70, 75, 241–42; hegemonists, 62; international community, 104; on

KLA, 168; Kosovo issue, 22, 213; "Monicagate," 28, 147; multilateralism, 52; nation building, 27–28, 62, 234–35; NATO and, 88; North Korea, 240; peace-making efforts, 261n. 5; "Permanent Quagmire," 239; Powell criticism of, 33; presidential decision directive, 124; on regional action, 211–12; Rice criticism of, 31; Rumsfeld on, 65; Stealth program, 144; Taiwan issue, 179–80; UN and, 91, 192, 195–96, 201; U.S. exceptionalism and, 73; "Vietnam syndrome" and, 50; Wen Ho Lee scandal, 147–54

Cohen, William, 198

Cold War: Bush (H. W.) and, 32; China and, 244; "communist threat," 89–90; consensus during, 243; defense industry, 135; imperialism and, 90; isolationism and, 24–25; Kennedy, 82; legacy of, 16, 27, 154; military power, 40, 41; present contrasted with, 169–73; Soviet Union collapse, 39; treaties and, 104; Truman Doctrine, 75; U.S. leadership and, 14, 154–55; Vietnam and, 38

Commerce Department, 146

Committee of Science Technology and Industry for National Defense (Costind), 118

Committee on the Present Danger, 46

communism, 4, 82, 89–90, 170, 245

Community of Democracies, 108–10, 111, 184, 214

Comprehensive Test Ban Treaty, 66, 91–92, 157, 247–48

Confucianism, 102

Connor, Joseph, 195

consensus, 61, 63, 242

conservatism: antiglobalism and, 9, 122; Bush administration, 53–63, 121; China issue and, 118; critique of Clinton, 28, 34–35; Defense Policy Board, 43; foreign policy and, 40, 41, 43; international community, 112; liberalism compared to, 62–63; Powell, 39; realism and, 132; UN and, 184; Wilsonian viewpoint and, 258

containment doctrine, 44, 169–70

Coolidge, Calvin, 83

Cooper, Robert, 249–50

Coordinating Committee on Multilateral Export Control (COCOM), 138, 145

Coughlin, Charles Edward (Father Coughlin), 85

counterintelligence, 142

Cox report, 146–48, 151, 155

Croatia, 116

cruise missiles, 7, 8, 48

Cuban missile crisis, xi, 49, 87–88

cultural influence of U.S., 8–9

Daniels, Mitchell, 228

Davos, Switzerland, 93, 102

Dayton negotiations, 164, 166, 189, 192, 195

Declaration of Independence, 161

declassification, 269n. 35

Defense Department, 138–39, 158

Defense Department Peacekeeping Institute, 222–23

defense industry: brain drain, 155; commercial sector, 139, 156; export controls and, 156–57; globalization of, 154–58; research and development, 158

Defense Policy Board, 43, 51

Defense Science Board, 141

defense spending, 7–8, 23, 30, 111, 125, 139, 158, 234

Defense Technology Security Agency, 151

democracy and democratization: American promotion of, 37, 159–60; democratic peace theory, 111,

247; economic freedom and, 103, 108; enlargement of democracy, 30, 261n. 6; open markets and, 158; Powell on, 37; self-determination, 172–73; UN and, 184, 191–92, 214

Democratic Party, 104

Democratic Republic of the Congo, 209

Deng Xiaoping, 95

détente, 45–53

developing nations, 175

dictatorships, 80

diplomacy: ambiguities of, 251; American force and, 188; Bush administration and, 40; democratic peace and, 247; military strength and, 188–89; nuclear weapons and, 248; Powell and, 50; terrorism and, 238; trend toward, 127

Dobriansky, Paula, 214

Dole, Robert (Bob), 40, 168

Dollar, David, 233

domestic politics, 22, 37

double standards, 176

drug trade, 5

dual use technologies, 138, 142, 144–45, 148–54, 157

Dumbarton Oaks, 85–86

Durand Line, 173

East Timor, 163, 173, 206–9, 212, 240, 273n. 23

economics and commerce: aid to Afghanistan, 226; Asian financial crisis, 244; automobile industry, 99–100; budget deficits, 158; capitalism, 118–19; Clinton campaign and, 32; defense spending, 7–8, 23, 30, 111, 125, 139, 158, 234; democratization, 103, 108; developing nations, 175; drug trade, 5; East Asian financial crisis, 207; export controls, 138–39, 152, 156–57, 270n. 23; Federal Reserve, 19; foreign aid, 194; free markets, 158–60, 204, 234–35; funding the world body, 23–24; globalization of, 11, 12, 100, 102, 122, 252–53; Great Depression, 84; international organizations, 87; Iraqi oil revenues, 226; market economy, 173–75; middle class, 108; military industrial complex, 135–36; multinational corporations, 99–100, 142, 173; national security, 148–54; peacekeeping, 22–23; privatization, 94–96, 98, 161, 182; protectionism, 112, 252; refugees, 210; Soviet collapse, 182; Taiwan, 179; trade sanctions, 99; transplantation of production, 107; unemployment, 95; U.S. economic strength, 77, 238; U.S. policies, 175; wealth inequality, 174, 253–54

Ecuador, 210

education, 185, 235

Egypt, 19, 161

82nd Airborne Division, 225

Eisenhower, Dwight D., 34, 45, 46, 49, 135, 170

Eisenhower, Susan, 41, 46

elections, 35. See also democracy and democratization

elites, 174, 253

encryption, 138–39, 141, 153

Enlightenment, 72

environmental issues, 53

espionage, 146, 147–54, 268n. 30, 269n. 35

ethnic conflicts: Afghanistan, 218; Balkans, 38; imperialism and, 255–56; Kosovo war, 177–78; Milosevic, 167, 188; self-determination and, 169, 172

Europe. See also specific countries: dictatorships, 80; economic vs. military power, 53; European Commission, 153; European Court, 145; European Space

Europe (*continued*)
Agency, 153; European Union (EU), 12, 112, 114, 153, 238; geography, 218; Iraq issue and, 53; isolationism, 11; monetary union, 16; postmodern imperialism and, 250; U.S. military planning and, 66–67

exceptionalism, U.S.: American überpower, 129; expansionism, 81–82; foreign policy and, 40, 255; as founding myth, 70–71; globalism, 76–88; "inclusive exceptionalism," 92; isolationism, 74–75; military power, 41; moralism, 263n. 6; postmodernism, 251; rebuttal of, 126; redefinition of, 92; sovereignty issues, 205, 244; U.S. imperialism, 255; war on terror, 266–67n. 33

expansionism, 81, 82. *See also* imperialism

export controls, 152, 156–57, 270n. 23

failed states, 24, 201, 215, 232–33, 249

*Far East Economic Review*, 155

fascism, 4, 82, 123, 170

Federal Bureau of Investigation (FBI), 70

Federal Reserve, 19

Feith, Douglas, 43

Ferguson, Niall, 23, 172

Fillmore, Millard, 270n. 23

Fischer, Joschka, 114

Fischer, Stanley, 253

Fleischer, Ari, xi, 27

food aid, 214, 230

Ford, Gerald, 34, 41, 43

*Foreign Affairs*, 102

foreign aid. *See also* foreign policy: AIDS prevention, 200; food aid, 230; Helms on, 194; Millennium Challenge Account, 233; nation building and, 234–35; public opinion and, 241–42

Foreign Intelligence Advisory Board, 268n. 30

foreign policy. *See also* foreign aid: Bush (H. W.) administration, 31–32; Bush (W.) administration, 13, 29, 40, 60; Clinton administration, 13–14, 16–17, 29; conservatism and, 40, 41, 43; FDR administration, 13, 37; four traditions of, 13, 243; historical precedents, 13; international community and, 130; Korean War, 45; Kosovo War, 16; "Permanent Quagmire," 29; Powell and, 36, 37, 38; Rumsfeld, 43; Truman administration, 37; U.S. exceptionalism, 40, 255; Wilsonian perspective, and 258

Foreign Relations Committee, 82, 194, 200

Four Freedoms, 176

"Four Policemen" concept, 83–84, 213

Fourteen Points, 85

France, ix, 53, 67, 178

Frederick the Great, 112

Friedman, Milton, 182

Friedman, Thomas, 97, 102–3, 104–5, 219

Fujimori, Alberto, 210

Fukuyama, Francis, 127–28

Fulda Gap, 117, 170

G-7, 102

Gaddis, John Lewis, 60–61, 69

*gaman*, 217

game theory, 128

Gandhi, Mohandas, 171

Garfinkle, Adam, 205

Gates, Bill, 253

Gelbard, Robert, 168

General Agreement of Tariffs and Trade (GATT), 86

General Motors, 144

Genghis Khan, 216

geography, 217–18

Gephardt, Dick, 107

Geremek, Bronislaw, 108–10, 126

German Marshall Fund, 113

Germany: anti-Americanism, 61, 170; export licenses, 155; fascism, 123; globalization and, 12; international community and, 120; Iraq issue and, 53; reaction to September 11 attacks, ix; sovereignty issues, 112; U.S. alliance with, 19; westernization, 128; World War II, 255

Gill, Bates, 118

Gingrich, Newt, 23, 150

Global Hawk aircraft, 140

global positioning systems (GPS), 153

globalism and globalization: American domination of, xii; Arab world and, 123; Bush administration and, 31; China and, 11–12, 244; Clinton administration and, 30–31; domestic politics and, 22; economics of, 11, 12, 100, 102, 104–5, 122, 252–53; eras compared, 106; failures of, 253–54; global economy, 11, 100, 102; "institutionalized order," 9; international community and, 18; Japan and, 11–12, 98–99, 101; national interest and, 237; presidential power and, 14–15; resistance to, 10; sovereignty issues, 126, 172; U.S. influences, 8, 254; war on terror and, 6

Gorbachev, Mikhail, 45, 47, 182

Gore, Al, 28, 32, 35

Great Britain. *See* Britain

Great Depression, 84

Greider, William, 126–27

Gulf War: Bush (H. W.) administration and, 22, 26–27, 88; internationalism and, 88; Japan and, 53; from Kuwaiti perspective, 90; Powell and, 36, 38, 45; UN involvement, 200; U.S. exceptionalism in, 255

Haass, Richard, 47, 48, 58, 249

Hagel, Chuck, 52, 60

Hague, 178

Haiti, 16, 32, 50, 240

Halberstam, David, 16–17, 107–8

Hamiltonian tradition, 243

Hamre, John, 133, 137

Hanson, Victor Davis, 34, 131

"hard power," 7, 242

Harding, Warren G., 83

Harries, Owen, 130

Harvard Institute for International Development, 182

Havel, Vaclav, 108–9

Hayden, Michael V., 133–34, 135, 137–38, 140, 142

health care issues, 14, 200, 221

hegemony, U.S.: Bush administration and, 39–40; hard-liners and, 112; international system and, 67–68; neoconservatism and, 46–48; non-imperial hegemony, 256; UN Security Council and, 203; world order and, 163

Helms, Jesse, 190, 194–201, 215, 230, 243–44

Helms-Biden reform package, 196–97

Henkin, Louis, 127

Herat, Afghanistan, 223, 227

Hicks, Don, 136

Hill, Charles, 251
Hitler, Adolf, 84, 112–13, 170
Hobbes, Thomas, 33, 34, 47, 65
Hoffman, Paul, 89
Hoffman, Stanley, 173, 196, 202
Holbrooke, Richard: background, 187–94; Bosnia conflict and, 202; East Timor crisis, 206, 208; on importance of UN, 213–14; Roosevelt and Wilson compared, 81; on self-determination, 163–64; UN dues battle, 204; on UN General Assembly, x
homeland security and defense, 63, 69–70, 235
Hong Kong, 94, 102
Hoopes, Townsend, 213
Hoover, Herbert, 37, 83
Horta, Jose Ramos, 163, 208
House of Commons, 193
House of Representatives, 193
Hu Jintao, 181, 245
Hughes Electronics, 148, 151, 153
Human Development Report, 184–85
human rights issues, 175–76, 178, 209, 222, 230
Huntington, Samuel, 9
Hussein, Saddam: al-Qaeda and, 57; Bush (H. W.) administration and, 22; Bush (W.) administration and, x, 5, 88, 130; Clinton and, 14; international law and, 186; international opinion on, 61; occupation of Kuwait, 38; preemptive action against, 224–25; September 11 attacks and, 48; U.S. hegemony and, 39; weapons programs, 51, 62
Hutus, 172–73, 212, 240
hypocrisy, 162, 171, 175, 246

ideology and "ideological blowback": collective security and, 242; described, 160; economic component, 181–83; forms of, 173–75; globalism trends and, 256–57; history of, 171; hypocrisy, 162, 171, 175, 246; international law and, 175–78; political component, 181–83; Russia and, 181–83; in UN Security Council, 203; U.S. policy and, 8–9, 183
Ikenberry, G. John, 9, 87, 92
immigration, 72, 106
impeachment, 50
imperialism: British empire, 73, 86, 90; China, 120; empire by invitation, 90; empires compared, 255; imperial overstretch, 23; Monroe Doctrine and, 73–74; in post–Cold War era, 88–91; "postmodern imperialism," 249–50; A Republic, Not an Empire (Buchanan), 10; Roman Empire, 25, 26, 238; Roosevelt (TR) on, 79; U.S. example contrasted with, 238
independence movements, 160–61, 185
India, 209, 248
Indonesia, 173, 206–9, 235–36. See also East Timor
Information Age, 71
information technology, 103, 136
"the Inquiry," 85
intelligence gathering, xi, 134–35, 142, 148–54
international community. See also United Nations (UN): advantages of, 121–26; Afghanistan and, 221; antiterror campaign and, 56–57; Bush and, 17, 33, 60; China and, 244–45; Clinton and Bush contrasted, 7; defining, 111–16; globalization and, 18; Gulf War and, 88; historical trends, 127–28; human rights and, 176–77; ideological blowback and, 183; "inclusive exceptionalism," 92; influence on China,

244; loya jirga and, 220–21; Permanent Quagmire and, 21; realism and, 93–97, 132; Rice on, 106; role of, 239; Russia and, 16, 67, 116; Security Council's role in, 203; stages of development, 97; structure of, 103–4; tensions with U.S., x–xi; U.S. creation of, 160; U.S. military power and, 137; U.S. presidency and, 14–16, 241; value of, 183–84; war on terror and, 131–32; as work in progress, 237
International Criminal Court, 175–76, 186
international institutions and organizations, 71, 229–32. See also specific institutions
international law, 127, 175–78, 183–84, 186, 247–48, 266–67n. 33
International Monetary Fund (IMF): budget, 125; criticisms of, 87; East Timor crisis, 208, 273n. 23; free market philosophy, 174; globalization and, 252; indispensability of, 190; nation building and, 234; origins of, 85; Soviet collapse and, 182
International Trade Organization (ITO), 84, 86
International Trust and Investment Corporation (CITIC), 96
Internet, 134–35, 140, 154, 185
intifada, 32
Iran, 5, 209
Iraq. See also Hussein, Saddam: Afghan conflict and, 226; "axis of evil" comments, 5; espionage, 269n. 35; ethnic divisions, 172; as focus of Bush administration, 64; postwar oil revenues, 122; Rumsfeld's focus on, 51–53; UN Security Council and, 62, 205; U.S. hegemony and, 39; weapons program, 247–48
Iraq issue and, 53
Isaacson, Walter, 37
Islam. See also Arab world: Albanian Muslims, 164–65; dominance of West and, 122–23, 126; fundamentalism, 171; globalization and, 12; Islamist movements, 123, 132, 161–62, 234, 235; madrasas, 235; U.S. foreign policy and, 255
isolationism: Bush administration, 31; "Buy American" campaigns, 100; consequences of, 10–11; declining viability of, 241; Henry Cabot Lodge, 82–83; Korea and, 24–25; missile defense as, 55–56; Republican Party and, 41; sovereignty issues, 232; unilateralism and, 74–75, 194; U.S. exceptionalism and, 74
Israel, 51, 61, 162, 185, 209, 248
It's a Wonderful Life (film), 10–11

Jacksonian tradition, 243
Japan: economic collapse, 16, 244–45; export licenses, 155; free market philosophy, 174; geography, 217–18; globalization and, 11–12, 98–99, 101; international community and, 120; isolationism, 101; Meiji Restoration, 101, 123; military, 53, 78, 123; multinational corporations, 142; North Korea issue and, 65; Russo-Japanese War, 14, 78; sovereignty issues, 112, 114–15; U.S. alliance with, 18–19; westernization, 128; World War II, 255
Jefferson, Thomas, 10, 13, 72, 73, 77, 243–44
Jiang Zemin, 180, 245
Jinnah, Muhammad Ali, 171
Johnson, Lyndon Baines, 40

Kagan, Robert, 30, 46–47, 130, 243
Kaminski, Paul, 139–40, 141, 143–44, 156–57
Kandahar, Afghanistan, 4

Kant, Immanuel, 33, 172
Kantor, Mickey, 76
Kaplan, Lawrence, 118–19
Kaplan, Robert D., 9, 112
Karzai, Hamid, 223, 227
*keiretsu*, 99, 100
Kellogg-Briand Pact, 83
Kelly, James, 64
Kennan, George, 82
Kennedy, John F., 40, 49, 82, 87–88, 170
Kennedy, Paul, 8, 23
Kennedy, Robert F., 49, 97
Keynes, John Maynard, 11, 85, 105
Khan, Ismail, 223
Khobar Towers bombing, 70
Kim Dae Jung, 55, 109
Kim Jong Il, 55, 64–65, 163
Kipling, Rudyard, 2
Kissinger, Henry: China and, 244; "conversion of the adversary," 160; détente, 45; on international consensus, 239; on international order, 256; on Roosevelt and Wilson, 264n. 12; on Shanghai Communiqué, 180; Vietnam and, 51; on Wilson, 81
Koh, Harold Hongju, 107, 266–67n. 33
Koizumi, Junichio, 115
Korea, 2, 20, 24–25, 45, 200. *See also* North Korea; South Korea
Kosovo war: Clinton administration and, 50, 240; foreign policy and, 16; General Wesley Clark, 90; humanitarian intervention, 24; independence movements, 160; international law and, 177–78; Kosovo Liberation Army (KLA), 164–69; national interest and, 255; "postmodern imperialism," 250; Powell on, 36; regional enforcement and, 212; sovereignty issues, 238
Kostunica, Vojislav, 168
Krauthammer, Charles, 34
Krepinevich, Andrew, 67
Kristol, Irving, 47
Kristol, William, 43, 46–47, 48, 243
Kuomintang, 179
Kupchan, Charles, 13, 114
Kurds, 160, 167, 238
Kuwait, 38, 90, 255
*kyosei*, 99
Kyoto Treaty, 53

Lake, Anthony, 30, 192
Lampton, David, 245
Land Warrior sensing system, 141
Landes, David, 128–29, 216, 217
Langer, William, 194
Lansing, Robert, 169
Larkin, Philip, 80
laser-guided bombs, 143–44
Latin America, 19, 54, 170, 210, 252
Law of the Sea Treaty, 43
League of Nations, 79, 82–83, 84–86, 88
Lee, Wen Ho, 147, 148–54, 156, 269n. 31
Lee Kuan Yew, 101–2, 116, 198
Lessig, Lawrence, 103
Lewinsky, Monica, 28, 147, 240
Lewis, Bernard, 122, 123
Lewis, James, 142, 155–56
*The Lexus and the Olive Tree* (Friedman), 104–5

Li, Aubrey, 96, 98, 118, 128
Li Peng, 97
Libby, Lewis "Scooter," 43
liberalism, 9–10, 33–34, 63, 129
Lilley, James, 179
Lincoln, Abraham, 72–73
Lindbergh, Charles, 85
Lippmann, Walter, 20, 83, 85, 257
Liu, Melinda, 149
Liu Chao-ying, 148–49
Lloyd George, David, 88–89
Lodge, Henry Cabot, 54, 82–83, 85
Loral Space Communications, 148–49, 151, 153, 269n. 31
*Los Angeles Times*, 153
Luce, Henry, 83
Luck, Edward, 190

Maastricht Treaty, 114
MacArthur, Douglas, 115
MacLeish, Rod, 216
*madrasas*, 235
Mallaby, Sebastian, 234
*A Man for All Seasons* (Bolt), 186
mandarins, 119, 179, 245
Mandelbaum, Michael, 77
Manifest Destiny, 72, 78
Margalit, Avishai, 122–23
Marshall, Andrew, 117
Marshall, George C., 35–36, 39, 89, 228
Marshall Plan: for Afghanistan, 59–60, 228; compared to current foreign aid, 23; Marshall's concerns about, 89; nation building and, 234
Matthews, Owen, 3
Mazar-i-Sharif, Afghanistan, 217
McCain, John, 167
McCarthy era, 155
McCloy, John, 39
McDonnell Douglas, 142
McDougall, Walter, 12–13, 77, 263n. 6
McGinn, Dan, 100
McKinley, William, 37, 78
McNeill, Dan, 225
Mead, Walter Russell, 13, 163, 243
Mearsheimer, John, 13, 77, 87, 118, 244
media, 106, 109, 115, 207–8, 242
Megawati Sukarnoputri, 236
Meiji Restoration, 101, 123
Mexico, 54
Micklethwait, John, 97, 105, 193
Mideast, 32, 36, 54–55. *See also* Arab world; Islam
military power: arms reduction, 124–25; "Army After Next" program, 137; asymmetric threats, 142, 156, 235; ballistic missile technology, 154; chemical weapons, 66; commercialization of, 139; communications, 134, 136, 138; cruise missiles, 7, 8, 48; Defense Policy Board, 43; defense spending, 7–8, 23, 30, 111, 125, 139, 158, 234; diplomacy and, 188–89; 82nd Airborne Division, 225; globalization and, 12; guided weapons, 143; importance of, 242; Kagan on, 130; militarism, 123; military industrial complex, 135–36; missile defense, 5, 36, 45, 55–56, 63, 125, 181; national missile defense (NMD), 55–56; Naval War College, 120; peacekeeping missions and, 195; People's Liberation Army, 118; Predator

aircraft, 140; preemption, 49, 121–22, 251, 266–67n. 33; protection of Taiwan, 179; realism and, 132; regional commanders, 210; special forces, 3, 38, 225, 235; standoff weapons, 8; Stealth program, 144; surveillance plane incident, 145–48; U.S. dominance, xiii, 7, 12, 26, 41, 45, 224, 238; U.S. presence in Afghanistan, 229; USS *Cole* attack, 48–49, 70; Wolfowitz and, 112

Millennium Challenge Account, 233

Miller, Franklin, 150–51

Milosevic, Slobodan: Clinton and, 14, 213, 240; ethnic cleansing, 165, 177–78, 188–89; peace negotiations, 167–68; withdrawal from Kosovo, 90

Minow, Newton, 42

missile defense: Bush administration and, 125; cost of, 5; hard-liners and, 45; isolationism and, 55–56; Powell on, 36; Taiwan and, 181; terrorism and, 63

missionaries, 98

modernity and modernization, 128–29, 136–37. *See also* postmodernism

Mogadishu, Somalia, 50, 192, 195

Mondale, Walter, 75–76

"Monicagate," 28, 147

Monnet, Jean, 24

Monroe Doctrine, 19–20, 73–74, 78, 170

Morgenthau, Hans, 129, 131, 257

Mori, Yoshiro, 54

mujahideen, 2, 26–27, 217, 218

multilateralism: "assertive multilateralism," 192; Bosnian war and, 189–90; Bush (H. W.) administration and, 52, 62; Iraq issue and, 130; nuclear weapons and, 247–48; Republican Party and, 46; in UN setting, 186, 203; unilateralism contrasted with, 240–41

multinational corporations, 99–100, 142, 173

Musharraf, Pervez, 161, 171

Muslims, 255. *See also* Arab world; Islam

Myers, Richard, 69

Namibia, 198

nation building: Afghanistan, 24, 219, 222, 224–25, 234–36; Bush administration and, 28–29, 59, 62; Clinton and Bush compared, 27–28; defense spending and, 234; NGOs' role in, 233–34; UN Security Council and, 205–6

nation-states, 125, 201

*National Geographic,* 3

*The National Interest,* 47

national missile defense (NMD). *See* missile defense

national security, 148–54. *See also* military power

National Security Agency (NSA), 133–35

nationalism, 255

NATO. *See* North Atlantic Treaty Organization (NATO)

Natsios, Andrew, 226, 230, 233–34

Naval War College, 120

negotiation, 30. *See also* diplomacy

Nehru, Jawaharlal, 171

neoconservatism, 33, 37–38, 46–48, 51–52, 161, 185

"New Covenant," 13–14

*New York Times,* 109, 110, 147, 191, 269n. 31

*Newsweek,* 2, 35

NGOs (nongovernmental organizations), 15, 125, 201, 233–34

Nicholson, James, 150

Nietzsche, Friedrich, 259n. 5

Ninkovich, Frank, 12–13, 80

Nitze, Paul, 89

Niven, David, 74

Nixon, Richard, 21–22, 34, 45, 180, 244

Nixon Doctrine, 211

Nobel Peace Prize, 176–77, 208

*Non-Zero: The Logic of Human Destiny* (Wright), 127–28

nongovernmental organizations (NGOs), 15, 125, 201, 233–34

nonpartisanship, 37

nonproliferation treaties, 58–59, 64–66, 130

North Atlantic Treaty Organization (NATO): Bosnia conflict, 266–67n. 33; Dayton negotiations, 192; decreasing relevance, 52; expansion of, 182–83; Germany, 89; Kosovo war, 90, 165–69, 213; NATO-Russia Council, 116; in post-Cold War era, 86–87; Rumsfeld and, 44; satellite technology and, 152; success of, 85

North Korea: Bush administration and, 5, 240; nuclear program, 54–56, 64–65, 247–48; South Korea compared to, 221; U.S. policy on, 163

Northern Alliance, 3, 246

Northern Ireland, 15

Nossel, Suzanne, 204

Nuclear Non-Proliferation Treaty, 66, 130, 247–48

nuclear weapons. *See also* weapons of mass destruction: Bush administration and, 124; computer technology and, 146–48; Cox report, 147–48; international law and, 247–48; Iraq, 247–48; missile defense, 5, 36, 45, 55, 63, 125, 181; North Korea, 64–65; Nunn-Lugar nuclear materials reduction plan, 125; technology transfers to China, 157; treaties, 66, 91, 125, 130, 247–48

Nunn-Lugar nuclear materials reduction plan, 125

Nye, Joseph, 97, 142–43

occidentalism, 122–23

Ogura, Kazuo, 115

Operation Rolling Thunder, 144

Organization of African Unity, 185–86

Organization of American States, 185, 210, 214

Orr, Robert, 199

Oxfam International, 253

pacifism, 115

Packer, George, 106

Paine, Thomas, 40, 72

Pakistan, 124, 161, 162, 209, 224, 235, 248

Palestine, 160, 163, 238

Panama Canal, 78

Panitchpakdi, Supachai, 119

Parker, Wayland, 223–24, 225

Pashtunistan, 173

Patten, Christopher, 56

Peace of Westphalia, 173

peacekeeping missions: Afghanistan, 223, 224; Clinton, 26in. 5; failures of, 192, 202–3; funding, 272n. 28; nation building and, 205–6; Powell and, 50; Presidential Decision Directive 25, 195–96; Rice on, 225; UN definition, 27in. 21; UN dues fight, 199; U.S. military officers on, 225–26

Pearl Harbor attack, 74, 89

Pentagon, ix, 89

Pentagon Papers, 47
Perle, Richard, 39, 48, 52
"Permanent Quagmire": Bush and Clinton compared, 239; complexities of, 238; described, 19–21; diplomacy and, 188; economic component, 142–43; foreign policy approaches, 29; ideological component, 172; national defense, 158; navigating middle ground, 63; perfect order contrasted, 128; realism and, 126
Perry, William, 144–45
Persian Gulf, 19. See also Mideast
Peru, 210
Philippines, 242
Pickering, Tom, 197, 198
Pinochet, Augusto, 170
Poland, 108–10
Pollack, Jonathan, 120, 124
Pope, Alexander, 127
postmodernism, 127, 249–52
Powell, Colin Luther: battle with Rumsfeld, 41; Community of Democracies meeting, 110; conservative reaction to, 35, 39; criticism of Clinton administration, 33; on détente, 45; "doctrine of integration," 249; on engagement policy, 36–37; hegemonists and, 63; on Indonesia issue, 236; on Iraq issue, 51; Kosovo War and, 164; on leadership of U.S., 159; military intelligence, 134; on missile defense, 36; as moderating influence, 57–58; multilateralism, 46; optimism, 37; policy battles, 50; "Powell Doctrine," 38; quoted, vii; role in Bush administration, 35–36, 59; UN and, xi, 61–62, 134; Wilsonian perspective, 171–72
Power, Samantha, 212
Predator aircraft, 140
preemption, 49, 121–22, 251, 266–67n. 33
presidency, U.S., 14–15, 241. See also specific presidents
Presidential Decision Directive 25, 195–96
privatization, 94–96, 98, 161, 182
Project for a New American Century, 43
protectionism, 112, 252
public opinion, xi, 61, 91, 241–42
Putin, Vladimir, 54, 116, 170, 183, 246, 248

Qadir, Abdul, 223
Qasimyar, Ismail, 220, 227

racial issues, 115. See also ethnic conflicts
Rambouillet, France, 165–69, 177
Reagan, Ronald, 4, 28, 35, 45, 51, 72
realism, 126–32, 257–58
refugees, 210
regional policing, 205–6, 209–13, 246
Republican Party, 27, 41, 46, 52, 230
Republican system, 71–72
research and development, 158
Rice, Condoleezza: Bush speeches, 57; on Clinton administration, 31; on East Timor, 212; on inevitability of conflict, 33; on international community, 60, 93, 106; on open-ended military engagement, 32–33; on peacekeeping efforts, 225; on power and values, 258
Robertson, George, 44
Rodrik, Dani, 252
Roh Moo Hyun, 61, 170
Roman Empire, 25, 26, 238

Roosevelt, Franklin Delano: Atlantic Charter, 85; campaign against fascism, 4; conservative critique of, 40; foreign policy, 13, 37; Monroe Doctrine and, 20; NATO and, 89; UN and, x, xi, 84, 191, 200, 209
Roosevelt, Theodore, 14, 37, 78–79, 81, 83, 264n. 12
Root, Elihu, 37
Rousseau, Jean-Jacques, 33–34
Rubin, Jamie, 168, 189–90
Rudman, Warren, 268n. 30
Ruggie, John Gerard, 97, 202
Rumsfeld, Donald: Afghan conflict, 3, 222–23, 229–30, 239; battle with Powell, 41; on Clinton, 65; confirmation hearings, 42; East Timor crisis, 212; export controls, 156; Ford administration, 42–43; foreign policy, 43; on inevitability of conflict, 33; influence on Bush, 26on. 17; Iraq issue, 51–53; on peacekeeping, 228–29; pragmatism, 44; reaction to terrorist attacks, 1, 48; "Rummygrams," 41; tension with multilateralists, 240; U.S. hegemony, 39
Rusk, Dean, 49
Russia. See also Soviet Union: Afghan conflict, 218, 246; antiterror campaign, 56; arms reduction, 125; Chechen conflict, 240; declining military power, 54; economic collapse, 16; ideological blowback and, 181–83; IMF and, 234; international community and, 19, 67, 116; Iran and, 209; Kosovo war, 178; Russo-Japanese War, 14, 78; strategic importance, 20; UN and, 86, 201; war on terror, 162; World War I, 79–80
Rwanda, 172–73, 192, 203, 240

S. G. Warburg & Co., 95
Safire, William, 110
SALT II arms control treaty, 43
Santayana, George, 13
satellite technology, 134, 148–54
Saudi Arabia, 19, 51, 56, 70, 122, 161
Schroeder, Gerhard, 61, 107, 113–14, 131, 170
Schwartz, Bernard, 148–50, 153
Scowcroft, Brent, 88
Security Council (UN): American hegemony, 203; Bush's dismissal of, xi, 121; China's role, 21, 201, 244, 246; Cold War, 191; democratic peace and, 111; East Timor crisis, 208; Helms's speech at, 197; influence of, 62; international law and, 176; Iraq and, 62, 205; Kosovo war, 213; NATO and, 178; public opinion and, xi; "regional cops" concept, 205–6; regionalizing conflicts, 209; sovereignty issues and, 23; structure of, 103–4
self-determination. See autonomy and self-determination
separatist movements, 172–73, 178, 206–9
September 11 attacks. See terrorism
Serbia, 38, 116, 164–65, 178, 188
Shamali Plains, 216–17
Sharif, Nawaz, 171
Sharon, Ariel, 59
Sierra Leone, 212
signals intelligence (Sigint), 134, 135
Singapore, 101–2, 198, 204
smart bombs, 140
Smith, Adam, 107
Smoot-Hawley Tariff Act, 84
"soft" power, 7
Somalia: al-Qaeda in, 48–50; bin Laden in, 235;

Clinton administration and, 240; humanitarian efforts, 24; peacekeeping failures, 32, 192, 195–96; Powell on, 38; weakness of intervention, 16

South Africa, 66

South Asia, 7, 15, 19

South China Sea, 117, 119

South Korea, 19, 55, 61, 65, 108, 221

South West Africa People's Organization, 198

sovereignty issues: conservatism and, 9; European Union, 238; international community and, 112–14; international law and, 175, 176–77; isolationism and, 232; obligations of sovereignty, 251; "pooled sovereignty," 249; UN and, 22, 200

Soviet Union. *See also* Russia: Afghanistan war, 217; China compared to, 54, 118, 119; collapse of, 27, 39, 107–8, 139; détente, 45–46; legacy of, 16; military deterrence, 41; U.S. military compared to, 2

Spain, 78, 178

Spanish-American War, 78

special forces, 3, 38, 225, 235

Spratley Islands, 120

Srebrenica, Bosnia, 192

Stalin, Josef, 170

standoff weapons, 8

State Department, 144, 152, 155, 156, 187, 211

Stealth program, 144

steel industry, 100

Stevenson, Adlai, xi, 42, 88

Stiglitz, Joseph, 182

Stimson, Henry, 37

Stockholm International Peace Research Institute, 172

Suharto, 173, 273n. 23

Summers, Larry, 198

sunshine policy, 55

supercomputers, 137, 146, 156. *See also* technology

superpowers, 7. *See also specific nations*

Supreme Court, 35

surveillance planes, 59, 117, 134, 145–48

systems integration, 136

Taft, Julia, 227, 230, 231–32

Taft, Robert, 75

Taipei, Taiwan, 180

Taiwan: China and, 179–81, 244–46; independence movements, 160; middle class, 108; sovereignty issues, 179–81, 238; U.S. deterrence power, 225

Tajikistan, 7

Talbott, Strobe, 31, 201, 249

Taliban: "B-52 peacekeeping," 224; effect on Afghanistan, 218–19; escape from U.S. attacks, 5; financial support, 226; remaining in Afghanistan, 221; U.S. defeat of, 26, 131; U.S. preemption and, 266–67n. 33

tariffs, 162

technology: computing industry, 140; defense spending and, 144–45; democratization of, 103; dual use technologies, 138, 142, 144–45, 148–54, 157; economics and, 119; fiber optics, 153; global positioning systems (GPS), 153; Information Age, 71; information technology, 103, 136; intelligence gathering, 148–54; military strength and, 3, 41, 136–37; national security and, 134; research and development, 158; satellite technology, 148–54; supercomputers, 137, 146, 156; telecommunications, 134, 138,

140; television guided bombs, 143; terrorism and, 134; U.S. export restrictions, 155

telecommunications, 134, 138, 140

terrorism. *See also* al-Qaeda; bin Laden, Osama: Afghanistan's connection to, 1; anti-Americanism and, 236; Arab world and, 185; diplomacy and, 238; failed states and, 215, 232–33; global nature of, 106; inevitability of, 256; international reaction to, ix; Khobar Towers bombing, 70; neoconservatism and, 48; nuclear weapons and, 247–48; "postmodern imperialism" and, 252; preemption and, 251; September 11 attacks, ix, 1–2, 33, 56, 112, 156; technology and, 134; U.S. inconsistency and, 171

Texas Instruments, 143–44

Thaci, Hashim, 166, 168

Thailand, 108

Thanh Hoa bridge, 144

Thatcher, Margaret, 43

Thomas, Evan, 37

Thucydides, 33, 50, 111

Tibet, 160, 162, 178, 180

*Times*, 148–49

Tocqueville, Alexis de, 77

Tokugawa, Ieyasu, 101

Tokugawa, Tsunenari, 100–101

Tora Bora, Afghanistan, 223, 239

transnationalism, 201

Treaty of Portsmouth, 78

Trenin, Dmitri, 116

tribalism, 255

Trident II missiles, 147

Trilateral Commission, 102

Truman, Harry: Bretton Woods institutions, 84; conservative critique of, 40; containment policy, 46; foreign policy under, 37; Monroe Doctrine and, 20; NATO and, 89; on preventative war, 49; Truman Doctrine, 44, 75; UN formation, x, 200; World War II, 83

Tsongas, Paul, 16

Turkey, 160

Turner, Ted, 199

Tutsis, 172–73, 212

"überpower": American exceptionalism and, 129; anti-UN attitudes and, 201; argument for, 254–57; compared to superpower, 7; international law and, 176; origin of term, 259n. 5; paradox of, 237; technology and, 136

Ukraine, 66

unemployment, 95

unilateralism: Bolton on, 263n. 4; Bush administration and, 40–41, 73; global resentment of, 9; inevitability of, 254; isolationism and, 74–75, 194; League of Nations, 82–83; multilateralism contrasted with, 240–41; technology trade and, 145; in UN setting, 203; "unilateral overdrive," 56

unions, 100

United Arab Emirates, 199

United Auto Workers, 100

United Nations (UN). *See also* Security Council (UN): Afghanistan and, 220, 229–30; agencies, 213–14; Bosnia conflict, 202; bureaucracy, 193–94; Bush's address at, ix, x, 17, 130; Bush's dismissal of, 54; Conference on Trade and Development, 107; Congressional relationship with, 242; Dayton

United Nations (UN) (*continued*)
negotiations, 189; democratization and, 191–92; Development Programme (UNDP), 86, 184–85, 227, 229–30; division of labor, 250; dues fight, 196, 199, 204, 215; East Timor crisis, 206; failures of, 191–200; "Four Policemen" concept, 83–84, 213; funding, 23, 125, 197–99, 215; General Assembly, x, 93, 193; globalization and, 9, 159; humanitarian crises and, 209; inception of, x; indispensability of, 190, 200–201, 203; inefficiency of, 193; international community and, 104; Iraq inspections, xi; Law of the Sea Treaty, 43; multilateralism, 186; North Korea issue and, 65; in post–Cold War era, 86–87; Presidential Decision Directive 25, 195–96; reform bills, 196–97; regional policing, 205–6, 209–13, 246; restructuring, 196–97; sovereignty issues, 9; UNICEF, 230; U.S. relations with, 19, 195–98, 201–2, 232

United States: anti-Americanism, 61, 162, 170, 236; cultural influence of, 8–9; defense spending, 7–8; democratization, 37, 160; economic strength, 77, 238; exceptionalism (*see main entry*); export controls, 142, 155; foreign policy (*see main entry*); globalism and globalization, 8, 254; hegemony, 18, 39, 40, 46–48, 67–68, 112, 163, 203, 256; hypocrisy in U.S. policies, 175; isolationism, 10–11, 24–25, 31, 41, 55–56, 74–75, 82–83, 100, 194, 232, 241; military dominance, xiii, 7, 12, 26, 45, 224; president's role, 15; realism and, 258; in UN, 232

Urquhart, Brian, 271n. 21
U.S. Agency for International Development (USAID), 200, 226
U.S. Congress, 193, 242
U.S. Constitution, 71
U.S. Department of State, 144, 152, 155, 156, 187, 211
U.S. Senate, 193
U.S. Senate Foreign Relations Committee, 82, 194, 200
U.S. Southern Command, 211
*USA Today*, 141
U.S.–Japan Security Treaty, 87
USS *Cole*, 48–49, 70
utopianism, 127, 193
Uzbekistan, 7

values, 8–9, 98, 159, 246
Vandenberg, Arthur, 75
Védrine, Hubert, 109
Vietnam: Diem coup, 170; intervention criteria and, 45; legacy of, 49–50; military technology used in, 143–44; Monroe Doctrine and, 20; Powell on, 38; Rumsfeld and, 42–43; "Vietmalia" syndrome, 1
Virginia Military Institute (VMI), 228

Walesa, Lech, 108–9
Wallace, Henry, 89
War Department, 89
war on terror: American global role in, 6; Bush administration and, 40–41; "Bush Doctrine," 126; global community and, 122, 123–24, 131–32, 176, 203; Islamic fundamentalism and, 171; military technology, 140; "postmodern imperialism" and, 252; public opinion, 91–92; U.S. exceptionalism and, 266–67n. 33; world order altered by, 56
warlords, 4, 223–24, 227–28, 231
Warsaw Declaration, 109–10

Washington, George, 10, 13, 69, 73, 74–75
*Washington Post*, 109, 113, 136, 155, 191, 210
Wassenaar Arrangement, 145, 155–56
*The Wealth and Poverty of Nations* (Landes), 216
wealth inequality, 174, 253–54
weapons of mass destruction, 49, 51, 62, 63, 124, 162. *See also* nuclear weapons
Webster, Daniel, 103
Welles, Sumner, 213
Wells, H. G., 3, 8
Wilhelm II (Kaiser Wilhelm), 112, 170, 247
Willkie, Wendell, 263n. 4
Wilson, Woodrow: arms reduction, 125; attacks on, 12; Bush compared to, 88; free markets, 160; global institutions, 24; great power cooperation, 40–41; internationalism, 31, 85, 258; League of Nations, 82–83; legacy of, 163, 239; Monroe Doctrine, 20; nation building, 33; paradox of Wilson agenda, 92; quoted, vii, 110, 126; Rice on, 31; Roosevelt contrasted with, 264n. 12; on self-determination, 169; shaping of world order, 174; sovereignty issues and, 177; United Nations formation, x; Wilsonian tradition, 232, 243; World War I and, 79–81, 81–82, 84
Winthrop, John, 72
Wolfowitz, Paul: avoidance of Vietnam service, 52; on Cheney's staff, 43; on Chinese regional hegemony, 117; criticism of moderates, 47; critique of Clinton, 30; export controls, 156; influence on Bush, 260n. 17; on Iraq issue, 51; militarism, 112; reaction to September 11 attacks, 48; tension with multilateralists, 240
Woodward, Bob, 51, 222
Wooldridge, Adrian, 97, 105, 193
World Bank: Afghanistan and, 220, 229–30; budget, 125; criticisms of, 87; free market philosophy and, 174; globalization and, 252; indispensability of, 190; origins of, 85
World Food Program, 214, 230
World Trade Center attacks. *See* al-Qaeda; bin Laden, Osama; terrorism
World Trade Organization (WTO): budget, 125; Bush administration and, 17, 162; China and, 21, 119, 245; criticisms of, 87; democratic peace and, 111; developing nations and, 174–75; export controls and, 157; globalization and, 9, 12, 159, 252; international community and, 104; origins of, 86; sovereignty issues and, 22; U.S. role in, 19
World War I, 79, 90, 139
World War II, 83, 84, 90–91, 139, 255
Wright, Robert, 127–28
Wright-Patterson Air Force Base, 189

Yeltsin, Boris, 182
Yizheng Chemical Fiber Company, 94–97, 117, 128
Yugoslavia (former), 116, 169, 188, 250. *See also* Bosnia; Croatia; Kosovo war; Serbia

Zachary, G. Pascal, 103, 137
Zadran, Padcha Khan, 223
Zahir Shah, 216
Zakaria, Fareed, 77, 120
Zambia, 193
Zimmerman Telegram, 79
Zinni, Anthony, 210–11, 225